The Making of Sikh Scripture

The Making of Sikh Scripture

GURINDER SINGH MANN

OXFORD
UNIVERSITY PRESS
2001

OXFORD
UNIVERSITY PRESS

Oxford New York
Athens Auckland Bangkok Bogotá Bombay Buenos Aires Calcutta
Cape Town Chennai Dar es Salaam Delhi Florence Hong Kong Istanbul
Karachi Kuala Lumpur Madrid Melbourne Mexico City Mumbai
Nairobi Paris São Paulo Shanghai Singapore Taipei Tokyo Toronto Warsaw

and associated companies in
Berlin Ibadan

Published by Oxford University Press, Inc.
198 Madison Avenue, New York, New York 10016

Library of Congress Cataloging-in-Publication Data
Mann, Gurinder Singh.
The making of Sikh scripture / Gurinder Singh Mann.
p. cm.
Includes bibliographical reference and index.
ISBN 0-19-513024-3
1. ầdi-Granth—History. 2. ầdi-Granth—Criticism, Textual.
3. Sikhism—Sacred books—History. I. Title.
BL2017.45.M369 2000
294.6'82—dc21 00-020857

1 3 5 7 9 8 6 4 2

Printed in the United States of America
on acid-free paper

For John Stratton Hawley

Chandan vasu vanaspati afal safal
vich vasu bahale.

Acknowledgments

A close examination of the early manuscripts that are in the private custody of families in the Punjab constitutes the core of the present study. I am indebted to a number of families for permitting me access to their treasures; their names appear alongside discussions of these documents. I am also grateful to the authorities at Sri Takhat Harmandirji, Patna; the Takhat at Damdama; Dehra Baba Miṭha Singh, Damdama; Motibagh Palace, Patiala; Guru Nanak Dev University, Amritsar; Panjab University, Chandigarh; Punjabi University, Patiala; Punjab Language Department, Patiala; Bhai Vir Singh Sahitya Sadan, New Delhi; Balbir Singh Sahitya Kendar, Dehradun; and the archives of Sikh Dharma at Albuquerque and Española, for allowing me access to their manuscript collections.

My sister, Jatinder, and brother-in-law, Manmohan Singh, played a central role in helping me locate and then obtain access to these rare manuscripts. Another sister, Surinder, and brother-in-law, Sukhcharan Singh Bajwa, put me in contact with the families possessing manuscripts in the Damdama area. My uncle Iqbal Singh Dhillon introduced me to the Sodhi family, the custodian of the historic Kartarpur Pothi, and my uncle Bhupinder Singh Mann accompanied me to Sri Takhat Harmandirji, Patna. Rita, Mana, and Raj helped provide the right kind of environment in New York for work on the data I had gathered in the Punjab and other places. I am deeply grateful to them all.

Rabinder Singh Bhamra, Satnam Singh Bhugra, Sulakhan Singh Dhillon, Narinder Singh Kapany, Jagjit Singh Mangat, Avtar Singh Pannu, Amaritjit Singh, Baldev Singh, Kirpal Singh, and Harpreet Singh Toor, along with many others I cannot name here, encouraged the progress of this research project. I am thankful to them and I hope that the book will meet their expectations.

J. S. Ahluwalia, Ainslie T. Embree, J. S. Grewal, Linda Hess, Mark Juergensmeyer, Ruth C. Katz, W. H. McLeod, Christopher Shackle, and Susan VanKoski read the entire manuscript or parts of it at various stages of its development. I am obliged to them for their comments that helped me improve the quality of this study. I am thankful to Cynthia Read of Oxford University Press for her patience in dealing with my continual requests to extend its submission date, and to Cynthia L. Garver and Marta Steele for their editorial help.

Finally, my deepest gratitude goes to John Stratton Hawley. In addition to his unstinted support and encouragement of my work at Columbia University, he invested a tremendous amount of time in helping me construct this study from its very conception to the present form. I dedicate this book to him as my tiny "leaf" offering to a great scholar and a generous friend.

Santa Barbara, California G. S. M.
June 2000

Contents

Note on Transliteration

1 Sikhs and Their Scripture, 3
The Adi Granth, 4
The Early Sikh Community, 6
The Plan of the Book, 16

2 Writings on Sikh Scripture: An Overview, 18
Eighteenth-Century Accounts, 19
Nineteenth-Century Accounts, 23
Twentieth-Century Accounts, 25

3 The Beginning of the Scriptural Tradition, 32
The Guru Harsahai Pothi, 33
The Goindval Pothis, 40

4 The Expansion of the Scriptural Text, 51
MS 1245, 51
The Kartarpur Pothi, 59

5 Toward the Adi Granth, 69
The Seventeenth-Century Manuscripts, 69
The Adi Granth, 82

6 The Emerging Structure of the Adi Granth, 86
Rag as the Organizing Principle of the Adi Granth, 87
Evolution of the Structure of the Adi Granth, 89
The Adi Granth and Other Scriptures, 99

7 The Adi Granth and the Issue of the Bhagat Baṇi, 102
Date of Inclusion of the Bhagat Baṇi, 103
The Purpose of Incorporation of the Bhagat Baṇi, 109
The Selection and Evolution of the Corpus, 111
The Status of the Bhagat Baṇi, 117

8 The Guru Granth Sahib, 121
Three Centuries of Sikh Scriptural History, 121
The Authority of the Adi Granth, 129
Future Prospects, 134

Notes, 137

Glossary of Punjabi Terms, 179

Bibliography, 183

Index, 191

Note on Transliteration

No diacritical marks are used in the text, but the pronunciation of the Punjabi words is recorded in parentheses in the glossary. The Punjabi vowels /a/ /i/ /u/ /e/ /o/ /ai/ /au/ are fairly close to the sounds that appear in the English words *but*, *bit*, *book*, *bait*, *boat*, *bat*, and *bout*. Macron (¯) is used to indicate an increase in the length of /a/ /i/ and /u/, and these sounds correspond to vowel sounds in the English words *balm*, *beat*, *boot*. The Punjabi stops /kh/ /ph/ correspond closely to the aspirated /k/ and /p/ as used in initial syllabic position in words such as *cat* and *pat*. The Punjabi stop /ch/ corresponds to affricate used in the English word *chair*. I have used /chh/ to mark the aspirated /ch/ in Punjabi. The Punjabi /th/ comes close to the dental fricative used in English words *thick* and *myth*. The Punjabi retroflexes /ṭ/ /ṭh/ /ḍ/ /ḍh/ /ṇ/, and the flap /ṛ/, for which there are no corresponding sounds in English, are marked with a subscript dot throughout the text.

The Making of Sikh Scripture

1

Sikhs and Their Scripture

The history of the Sikhs is closely associated with the Punjab, a region in northwest India that has long served to connect South Asia with the Middle East.[1] Nanak (1469–1539), born in an upper-caste Hindu family, founded the Sikh community in central Punjab in the 1520s. A line of gurus (preceptors) guided the early phase of its evolution. By the turn of the seventeenth century, the community expanded its base and came to be perceived as a threat by the Mughal administration at Lahore. The tensions that followed between the Sikhs and the local administration resulted in the execution of Guru Arjan (born 1563, guru 1581–1606), the fifth Sikh guru, at Lahore, and the consequent move of the Sikh center to the Shivalik hills in the 1630s. Guru Gobind Singh (born 1666, guru 1675–1708), the tenth in line, dissolved the office of the personal guru, vesting its authority in the Adi Granth (original book), the primary Sikh scripture, and in the Panth (literally "path," and by extension, "community").[2]

Working within this newly acquired frame of authority, the Sikhs were able to wear down the Mughal and later the Afghan rule in the Punjab, and eventually establish a powerful kingdom under the leadership of Maharaja Ranjit Singh (1780–1839). They were the last and the most difficult political power in the Indian subcontinent to fall to the British. The annexation of the Sikh kingdom in 1849, however, generated interesting opportunities for the Sikhs to immigrate to distant countries as part of the British imperial work force.[3] In the protracted negotiations that preceded the departure of the British from the subcontinent in 1947, the idea of an independent Sikh state figured prominently, but the small size of the Sikh population in relation to other groups in the Punjab made this impossible. In independent India, the Sikhs have been engaged in ongoing conflict with the central government in Delhi. A sustained Sikh effort led to the founding of the present-day state of Punjab in 1966, where Sikhs are in the majority and Punjabi the official language. In the 1980s, a Sikh secessionist movement led by Sant Jarnail Singh Bhindranwale (1947–1984) to create Khalistan (Land of the Khalsa) paralyzed the Punjab. At the beginning of the twenty-first century, there are some 20 million Sikhs, approximately 18 million of whom live in the Punjab; the others are settled overseas with pockets of concentrations in Southeast Asia, East Africa, England, and North America.

The Adi Granth

The Sikhs consider the Adi Granth as the highest authority within the community, and it plays a central role in Sikh devotional and ritual life. Sikh belief in the authority of the Adi Granth is based on two fundamental assumptions: that its text is revealed and hence immutable and unchangeable, and that answers to all religious and moral questions are available in it.[4] Both in its concept and its role in day-to-day living, the Sikh understanding of scripture comes close to the Jewish and Muslim treatment of their respective sacred texts. By according the Adi Granth the status of the manifest guru (Guru Granth Sahib), the Sikhs have in one sense taken their conception of the sacred book farther than that of Jews and Muslims. As a result, Sikh belief in the status of their scripture has strengthened through the years.

The Adi Granth consists of approximately 3,000 hymns of carefully recorded authorship.[5] Over 2,400 of these hymns were written by the six Sikh gurus who lived between 1469 and 1675 in the Punjab. The remaining hymns are attributed to fifteen or so bards associated with the sixteenth-century Sikh court in the Punjab and fifteen non-Sikh saint-poets known in Sikh tradition as the Bhagats (literally, "devotees"), who lived between the twelfth and the sixteenth centuries in the northern and northwestern regions of the Indian subcontinent.[6]

The compositions in the Adi Granth celebrate the unity and uniqueness of God, a primal being (*Adi Purakh*) who is the lord of the universe (*Sahib*).[7] The theology propounded in these hymns is monotheistic, with absolute insistence on the nonincarnate nature (*ajuni*) of the deity. The world came into being in historical times as a result of the divine command (*hukam*), and God maintains the course of human history and individual destinies by means of the twin principles of justice (*nian*) and grace (*karam*).[8]

The hymns in the Adi Granth also state the way human beings should live in this God-created world so as to attain liberation, the ultimate goal of human life. This liberation is achieved through meditating on the divine name (*nam*) and cultivating a relationship of love (*bhau*) and fear (*bhai*) for the creator. In its mystical ascent, the human soul rises through the stages of duty (*dharam*), knowledge (*gian*), humility (*saram*), grace (*karam*), and finally ineffable state of truth (*sach*).[9] Nonetheless, the Adi Granth sets forth a view of spirituality that rejects asceticism of any kind and instead mandates an effective fulfillment of the routine obligations of our lives within society. Liberation is attained by living actively as an individual who is also part of a family and a community and is guided by a strict code of ethical conduct (*achar/rahit*) built on the values of hard work, charity, and service to humanity.[10]

In addition to the praise of God and a statement of the ethical demands that human beings should meet, some hymns appeal for divine help to fulfill personal and collective Sikh aspirations.[11] Still others express gratitude for divine blessings bestowed on the Sikh gurus and for the success of community ventures like the establishment of cities and the construction of *gurdwaras* (Sikh temples).[12] A set of hymns composed by the bards glorify the Sikh gurus and present them as the representatives of God on earth.[13]

The text of the Adi Granth is divided into three parts.[14] The opening section is liturgical and includes three daily prayers. The *Japji* (Meditation) by Guru Nanak consists of thirty-eight stanzas and two couplets. The *Rahiras* (Supplication) contains nine hymns: four composed by Guru Nanak, three by the fourth Sikh guru, Guru Ramdas (born 1534, guru 1574–1581), and two by the fifth Sikh guru, Guru Arjan. The *Sohila* (Praise) consists of five hymns: three by Guru Nanak, and one each by Guru Ramdas and Guru Arjan. The Sikhs recite the *Japji* at sunrise, the *Rahiras* at sunset, and the *Sohila* at the end of the day just before going to sleep.

The hymns in the main body of the Adi Granth are divided into thirty-one separate subsections created according to the musical mode (*rag*) assigned for their singing. Each subsection begins with hymns of four stanzas (*chaupadas*) and goes on to include hymns of eight stanzas (*ashṭpadis*), four stanzas of six verses each (*chhants*), and other longer compositions containing a sequence of couplets and stanzas (*vars*).[15] These smaller units within each subsection open with the hymns of Guru Nanak and include the compositions of his successors and those of the Sikh bards and the Bhagats. The hymns of the Bhagats are treated as distinct units but follow the same principle of organization based on the number of stanzas.

The final section of the text of the Adi Granth is composed of miscellaneous hymns not set in any musical mode. These compositions include couplets authored by Guru Nanak, Guru Arjan, Guru Tegh Bahadur (born 1621, guru 1664–1675), Kabir (d. 1448), Farid (d. 1265), and a set of panegyrics (*savaiye*) by the bards. The text closes with the *Ragmala* (Garland of musical modes), a hymn of twelve stanzas grouping *rags* prevalent in the medieval Indian system of music into six families.[16]

The language of the hymns recorded in the Adi Granth has been called "Sant Bhasha," a kind of lingua franca used by the medieval saint-poets of northern India. But the broad range of contributors to the text produced a complex mix of regional dialects. The Sikh gurus themselves used Punjabi in many of their hymns, but like other contributors they also used elements of Apabhramsha (a later dialect of Sanskrit), Braj Bhasha (the language of the Braj region around Mathura), Hindui (the language spoken around Delhi), and a heavily Persianized Punjabi.[17] All this makes the Adi Granth a rich repository of dialects that were prevalent in medieval northern India.

From the outset, the Sikh manuscripts were recorded in a distinct script, Gurmukhi (literally, "from the mouth of the guru," but in this context "of the Gurmukhs/Sikhs"), which contains thirty-five characters.[18] The script existed in an elementary form before the Sikhs appropriated it to record their writings and in the process modified the shapes of several of its characters and developed a complex system for its usage.[19] The Sikhs assigned to it a high degree of sanctity. For Guru Nanak, the status of Gurmukhi for the Sikhs corresponded with that of Arabic and Devanagari, the sacred scripts of the Muslims and the Hindus, respectively.[20]

Given the centrality of scripture in the tradition, almost all the Sikh chroniclers refer to the compilation of the original text and its eventual expansion into the Adi Granth.

These authors constructed their accounts primarily around oral traditions, using them with varying degrees of ingenuity. By the middle of the nineteenth century, there emerged a common narrative of the history of the Adi Granth, one that holds sway in both popular and scholarly circles within the Sikh community. We trace the evolution of this narrative in detail in Chapter 2. Here, let us begin by reconstructing the doctrinal and historical context in which the Sikh scriptural text originated, expanded, and reached its canonical form.

The Early Sikh Community

We know that in the early 1520s Guru Nanak acquired a piece of agricultural land on the right banks of the river Ravi, founded a town named Kartarpur (City of God), and spent the last fifteen years or so of his life there.[21] There is a scholarly consensus that the families who gathered at Kartarpur formed the original nucleus of the Sikh community; but the beliefs and intentions of Guru Nanak that originated this enterprise remain a subject of debate. Did Guru Nanak intend to found a new community with an independent institutional structure, or was what came to be known as the Sikh community a product of later developments?

W. H. McLeod has systematically presented the view that Guru Nanak was a participant in the medieval *sant* tradition, whose constituency of holy people believed in one nonincarnated God and preached a religion of interiority through meditation on the divine name. In this beatific vision, all external forms of religious life including institutional authority, scriptural texts, communal centers, and so on were emphatically rejected. Simply put, the belief system to which Guru Nanak belongs does not jibe with the founding of an organized community.[22]

With varying degrees of rigor, other scholars have taken the opposite position, locating the origin of a distinct Sikh community during the lifetime of Guru Nanak; they have gone on to interpret the community's later growth as completely harmonious with the vision of its founder.[23] Representing this line of thought is J. S. Grewal's statement that "by the time Guru Nanak breathed his last the nucleus of a new social group had come into existence with an acknowledged Guru to guide its social and religious life according to a pattern set by the founder and in the light of ideas expounded by him."[24] In Grewal's view, the "pattern of social and religious life" set by Guru Nanak at Kartarpur was significant in shaping the responses of the later community to the changing social and historical circumstances.

McLeod is correct to point out the centrality of meditation in the thinking of the medieval *sants*. In Guru Nanak's case, however, meditation is one critical piece in an otherwise larger vision of life that constituted the basis of the community at Kartarpur. For Guru Nanak, three key virtues—meditation on the divine name (*nam*), charity (*dan*), and purity (*ishnan*)—are prerequisite to a successful search for liberation.[25] While "meditation on the divine name" and "purity" mark the personal dimension, the "charity" is a social obligation. Guru Nanak's commitment to hard work and service to humanity as the two enduring assets in pursuit of liberation (*Ghali khae kichhu hathahu deh. Nanak rahu pachhaṇahi sae*, M1, AG, 1245; *Vichi dunia sev kamaiai ta dargah baisaṇu paiai*,

M1, AG, 26) further emphasizes the significance of social context in the attainment of spiritual goals.

In Guru Nanak's view, the community does not simply provide a passive backdrop for an individual's search for liberation; it is very much a part of that agenda. He believes in the individual's obligation to work toward collective liberation (*Api tarai sangati kul tarai*, M1, AG, 353; *Api tarahe sangati kul tarahe tin safal janamu jagi aia*, M1, AG, 1039). A successful individual is one who attains liberation for himself or herself but who in addition assists in the liberation of everyone around. It is not an issue of choice but a moral imperative.

Only against this background does Guru Nanak's experiment with communal living at Kartarpur attain proper meaning. During this final phase of his life, we see him translating the theological and ethical ideas in his hymns into reality. Using families as building blocks, Guru Nanak gathered his followers at Kartarpur, involved them in agricultural activity for sustenance, and attempted to replicate what he thought to be the ideal way of life.

On the basis of the information present in the hymns of the gurus, the compositions of Bhai Gurdas (d. 1637), a Sikh savant of the period and an important poet in his own right who in all likelihood had first-hand contact with the residents of the Kartarpur community, and also on the basis of the janam-sakhi accounts of the life and mission of Guru Nanak, which began to evolve in the late sixteenth century, I assemble a picture of Sikh life during the first phase of its existence.[26] The details that emerge point to the beginnings of the institutional structure at Kartarpur itself.

This structure was simple. It had two components: the guru, the center of the group, and his Sikhs (*So guru so Sikh kathialai*, M1, AG, 503). In the words of Bhai Gurdas, after returning from his extensive travels, Guru Nanak donned worldly garb and revealed himself in a position of authority.[27] In this role Guru Nanak provided direction to the lives of his followers. (See Figure 1 for the genealogy.) For Guru Angad (born 1504, guru 1539–1552), his successor, those who have come to Guru Nanak for guidance need no further instruction (*Tin kau kia updesiai jin Guru Nanak deu*, M2, AG, 150).

In the janam-sakhi accounts, Guru Nanak was the preceptor of the age (Jagat Guru) and an agent of liberation for the Sikhs. In the early phase of his life, he went to the four ends of the earth to achieve his spiritual conquest, but after the founding of Kartarpur, it was the turn of his followers to visit the guru and the town he sanctified with his presence.[28] Guru Nanak himself believed that there is no pilgrimage center like the guru (*Gur samani tirathu nahi koi*, M1, AG, 1328–1329). Kartarpur was thus the center of Sikh sacred geography; Guru Ramdas states that the space associated with the guru automatically attains sacredness for his Sikhs (*Jithai jae bahai mera satiguru so thanu suhava ram raje*, M4, AG, 450). (See Table 1 for the towns associated with the gurus.)

Guru Nanak, through his compositions, his public sermons (*Suṇi Sikhvante Nanaku binavai*, M1, AG, 503), and his personal lifestyle, generated the rules of conduct by which the inhabitants of Kartarpur were to live. In this role as a guide, Guru Nanak must have laid down the daily routine of his life and the lives of others at Kartarpur centered on the values of meditation on the divine name, charity, personal purity, hard work (*ghal khae*), service (*seva*), self-respect (*pati*), and taking one's rightful share (*haq halal*).[29] These values are mentioned repeatedly in his hymns.

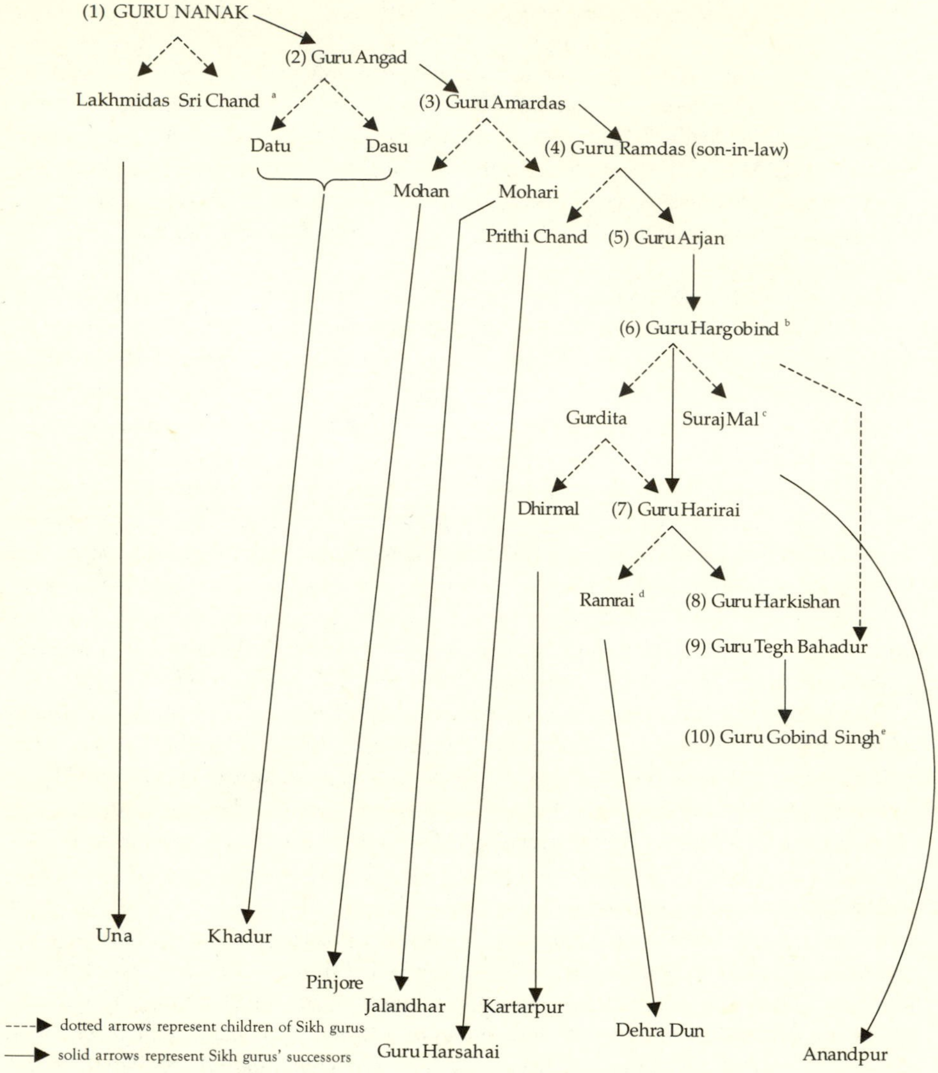

a. Sri Chand was an ascetic and remained unmarried. b. Guru Hargobind had two more sons, who played no role in history. c. Suraj Mal's descendants moved to Anandpur after Guru Gobind Singh left the town in 1704. d. Ramrai did not have children but his seat continues at Dehra Dun. e. Guru Gobind Singh had four sons, who predeceased him.

Figure 1. Current Residence of Sikh Gurus' Descendants

It is hard to accept the idea that Guru Nanak first rejected the institution of religious authority, only to reverse his stance and ensconce himself as the chief authority figure at Kartarpur. Nor is there any substance to the argument that Guru Nanak did not enjoy any power within the community during this period. His careful attempt to maintain the office of the guru in appointing his successor at the time of his death is evidence of the seriousness with which he took the institutional authority associated with

Table 1. Towns Associated with the Sikh Gurus

Guru Nanak	Founded Kartarpur in the 1520s and stayed there until his death in 1539.
Guru Angad	Stayed in his native Khadur throughout the period of his leadership, 1539–1551.
Guru Amardas	Founded Goindval and led the community from there between 1551 and 1574.
Guru Ramdas	Founded Ramdaspur (Amritsar) and helped it expand during the years 1574–1581.
Guru Arjan	Inherited Amritsar and led the community from 1581 to 1606. He also established a new Kartarpur, Hargobindpur, and Tarn Taran.[a]
Guru Hargobind	He had his base in Amritsar (1606–1628) and Kartarpur (1628–1634) and founded Kiratpur in 1634, remaining there until his death in 1644.
Guru Harirai	Led the community from Kiratpur (1644–1661).
Guru Harkishan	Remained at Kiratpur during his brief tenure of leadership from 1661 to 1664.
Guru Tegh Bahadur	Founded Anandpur in 1664 and led the community from there until 1675. He traveled extensively and had close ties with congregations in distant places like Dhaka and Patna.
Guru Gobind Singh	Led the community from Anandpur (1675–1704). He founded Paunta in 1685, and Damdama, Bhatinda, in 1705, and stayed there for two years, before moving to Nanderṛ, southern India, where he died in 1708.

a. The distinction between two Kartarpurs needs to be kept in mind: one was established by Guru Nanak and the other by Guru Arjan. The Kartarpur Pothi, one of the early scriptural manuscripts, gets its name from Guru Arjan's town.

the office.[30] In the following two centuries, a line of his nine sucessors played the central role in Sikh history.

There are other instances of institution building at Kartarpur. During this early phase of the community's institutional development, Bhai Gurdas refers to the tradition of reciting three prayers: the *Japji* in the morning, the *Rahiras* at the time of sunset, and the *Sohila* at the end of the day.[31] These prayers would have provided structure to the daily lives of the people at Kartarpur, as they continue to even today. The times of these prayer seemingly corresponded to the daily routine followed by the Sikhs at Kartarpur and may also have marked the community's autonomy.[32]

The establishment of the community kitchen (*laṇgar*) was another significant development of this early period.[33] This institution established food sharing as a central feature of Sikh piety, an unequivocal emphasis on social and gender equality within the community, and a forum for service. The food was cooked in one place and all participated in its preparation, and then, irrespective of caste or gender, all partook of it together. Guru Nanak's idea of human equality was rooted in his fundamental belief that God is the creator and sustainer of us all, and consequently any hierarchical or gender distinctions within society have to be absolutely meaningless (*Fakaṛ jati fakaṛu nau sabhana jian ika chhau*, M1, AG, 83; *So kiu manda akhiai jitu jamahi rajan*, AG, 473).

There are other instances of early Sikh institutional formation. For example, it seems certain that the Sikhs during this time coined their own greetings *dhan nirankar* (God is great), and *dhan guru* (Guru is great).[34] These details of the life at Kartarpur indicate that as the founder of a new community, Guru Nanak was aware of the social needs of his followers and helped create an institutional structure to fulfill them. In this context I next focus on the issues pertaining to Sikh scripture.

The Origin of the Scriptural Text

The seventeenth-century traditions refer to the existence of a pothi (literally, "book" or "volume") compiled at Kartarpur, which contained the hymns of Guru Nanak and was ceremonially given to Guru Angad at the time of his ascendance to the office of the guru.[35] The compilation of this pothi fits in within the context of Guru Nanak's perception of the nature of his hymns on the one hand, and the institution of scripture on the other.

Guru Nanak believed that he had been assigned by God the vocation of singing his praises (*Hau ḍhaḍhi vekaru karai laia*, M1, AG, 150) and that his hymns were the result of direct communication from God (*Jaisi mai avaai khasam ki baṇi tesṛa kari gianu ve Lalo*, M1, AG, 722, and *Ta ma kahia kahaṇu ja tujhai kahaia*, M1, AG, 566). He urged his followers to regard his writings as truth (*Satigur ki baṇi sati sati kari manahu*, M1, AG, 1028, and *Gurbaṇi nirbaṇu shabadi pachhaṇia*, M1, AG, 752) and follow the word of the guru (*sabad, bachan, sakhi*). Given the organizational concerns of Guru Nanak at Kartarpur, a safe preservation of the hymns "containing the divine message" for the use of the community of his followers seems appropriate.

Indeed, inscribing the word of God appears to be a theme in its own right in the hymns of Guru Nanak. He saw the writing of God's name as an act of devotion and he urged learned people to leave their futile pursuits and devote themselves to God this way (*Suṇi paḍe kia likhahu janajala. Likhu ramnam gurmukhi gopala*, M1, AG, 930). Inscribing the divine word, Guru Nanak said, is no ordinary activity but demands the heart and soul of the scribe (*Jali mohu ghasi masu kari mati kagadu kari saru*, M1, AG, 16). These images of writing within the hymns of Guru Nanak may be taken to support the assumption that the Sikhs, if not the guru himself, became involved in the devotional act of inscribing the divine word and attained blessings that accrued to this act.

Along with this belief in the revelatory nature of his compositions and the devotional dimension of committing to writing the word of God, Guru Nanak's attitude toward existing scriptures and by implication toward the institution of scripture should be carefully examined. In Sikh literature, three key views on this issue emerge.

First, beginning with Gulab Singh (born 1729), the Nirmala scholars, who maintained a special interest in Sanskrit learning and gave a strong Vedantic coloring to Sikh doctrine, assert that Guru Nanak accepted the authority of the Vedas and that the Adi Granth, as an extension of the Indian spiritual tradition, contains the essential Vedic wisdom.[36] For these writers, the Sikh gurus' central purpose in composing their hymns was to make the contents of the Vedas accessible to ordinary people of their age in their own language, and the Sikh writings can only be understood in the context of the Vedic tradition.

Second, an opposing view regarding Guru Nanak's attitude toward the Vedas, and by extension the institution of scripture in general, was first articulated by Bhai Kahn Singh Nabha, a leading Sikh scholar at the turn of the twentieth century.[37] While emphasizing the distinct character of the Sikh tradition, he argued that the Sikh gurus categorically rejected the Vedas and that the Sikhs recognize only the Adi Granth as their sacred text. This view holds currency within current Sikh scholarship.

Both these positions, though opposed, share a fundamental failing: the scholars who proposed them argue not on the basis of the evidence available in the Adi Granth, but instead, that of the doctrinal and social context in which they worked. The thinking of the Nirmala scholars is based on the premise that Sikh doctrine is essentially an outgrowth of the Hindu religious tradition. If this is true, they would argue, then how could anyone, including the Sikh gurus, reject the authority of the Vedas? For Nabha, the situation is precisely the opposite. In his view, the categorical Sikh rejection of the authority of the Vedas was one of the core doctrines that distinguished the Sikhs from various sectarian movements within the larger Hindu fold in the Punjab.

These scholars have not presented a single instance of Guru Nanak's own utterance to suggest his acceptance or rejection of the Vedas. The verses of later gurus cited to support the cases for either acceptance or rejection of the Vedic authority, when read in their appropriate context, lead to a conclusion different from the one proposed by scholars quoting them.[38] The lines of thought presented in these two opposing positions, however, continue to derive support from current Sikh scholarship.[39]

Third, a middle position can be supported with firm evidence. It appeared for the first time in Giani Badan Singh's commentary on the Adi Granth, prepared in the closing decades of the nineteenth century and was developed later in Bhai Jodh Singh's long essay "Guru Sahib ate Ved" (The Sikh gurus and the Vedas) written in 1911.[40] Bhai Jodh Singh points out that there is no evidence to support an argument that Guru Nanak rejected the Vedas or for that matter any other sacred books. Guru Nanak's position seems rather to have been that sacred books are the creation of God (*Chauthi upae chare Beda*, M1, AG, 839, and *Oankari Bed nirmae*, M1, AG, 930) and that reading these divine texts, therefore, helps to save us from evil (*Bed paṭh mati papa khae*, M1, AG, 791).

Simultaneously, this does not imply that Guru Nanak accepted the authority of the Vedas and wanted his Sikhs to follow them. The heart of the matter is that Guru Nanak neither accepted, nor contested the authority of existing scriptural texts; but he perceived himself as having access to a higher and more complete truth, which was directly revealed to him and was manifested in his own hymns. And for Guru Nanak and the community of his followers, these hymns included everything that they needed to know and possess (*Sabhi nad Bed gurbaṇi*, M1, AG, 879). Thus, at this stage of their history, the divine message for the Sikhs was ensconced in the hymns of Guru Nanak; this is their revelation, and their counterpart to the Vedas and to the Kateb (literally, "books," a term used in Punjabi, to describe the holy books of Islam, Christianity, and Judaism).

Nor does Guru Nanak reject the institution of scripture as such; his criticism, if any, centers on the way the sacred texts are used by the followers of the various traditions. He denounces the ritualistic reading of the Vedas by Brahmins, who use it without ever comprehending the underlying truth of the text. Repetitive reading in the case of these people does not generate peace (*Paṛi paṛi dajhahe sati na ai*, M1, AG, 1026); instead, it creates arrogance (*Ved paṛihe tai vad vakhaṇahe*, M1, AG, 638). Guru Nanak does not challenge the reading of scriptures but is unhappy with the way it is done (*Haṭhu ahankaru karai nahi pavai. Paṭh paṛai le lok suṇavai*, M1, AG, 905–906; *Paṭhu paṛai mukhi jhuṭho bolai nigure ki mati ohai*, M1, AG, 1013).

Guru Nanak's compilation of a pothi, a scriptural text for the use of his followers, may have also been related to the immediate religious and political context in which he established his new community. He knew the Qur'an and he could not possibly have missed the emphasis it places on the *ahl-i-kitab* (the possessors of the revealed book). On the basis of this Qur'anic idea, Muslim jurists had classified non-Muslims into three groups: *ahl-i-kitab*; *mushabah ahl-i-kitab* (those who resemble the possessors of the revealed book); and *kafirs* and *mushariks* (infidels and polytheists).[41] It was only the *ahl-i-kitab* who were exonerated from paying the *jizyah* (the religious tax).[42]

Guru Nanak refers to the role of the Qur'an in Muslim devotional life (*Panj vakhat nivaj gujarahe parahe Kateb Qurana*, M1, AG, 24). In the setting of an Indian *khanqah* (Sufi center), with which Guru Nanak must have been familiar, the Qur'an played a significant role, placed out in the open to allow lower-class converts full access to the scripture of their new religion—a kind of access denied to them in their earlier belief system.[43] Whether or not the new converts were literate and able to read Qur'an, they were permitted physical access to it.

In the context I have just reconstructed, the idea that Guru Nanak compiled his hymns in the form of a pothi seems sensible. His perception of himself as the recipient of divine revelation and his hymns as manifesting the divine truth, in combination with his recognition of the significance of the institution of scripture and its importance in the political definition of the community under the law of the times, would have led him to compile a text of his own hymns. Leaving unpreserved what he thought to be the divine message—the compilation of which would carry the political weight of the *ahl-i-kitab* classification for his community, bringing both prestige and economic benefit of acquittal from paying the *jizyah*—would contradict his organizational concerns, which led to the creation of liturgical prayer, the *langar*, and a careful choice of successor to lead the community.

The assumption that a scriptural text was compiled during the lifetime of Guru Nanak is supported by the existence of the Guru Harsahai Pothi discussed in detail in chapter 3. If one accepts the firm tradition of this pothi in terms of its role in the succession ceremony—and we have no evidence to challenge it—we can reasonably argue that both the text of Sikh scripture and the authority accompanying it began to take shape during Guru Nanak's own lifetime. I address these issues in detail in the chapters that follow.

The Expansion of the Scriptural Text

The expansion of the scriptural text also fits well into the context of the overall development of the Sikh community. The expansion, consolidation, and protection of the community of followers of Guru Nanak remained the enduring concern of his successors. To create the optimal environment for community life, the Sikh gurus founded towns in the central Punjab and expanded the institutional structure at Kartarpur.

Guru Nanak died in 1539, but before his death he nominated Angad as his successor. Since Guru Nanak's eldest son, Baba Sri Chand (d. 1592), inherited Kartarpur, his successor Guru Angad had to return to his native village Khadur.[44] Most Sikhs accepted Guru Angad, offered their allegiance to him, and moved to Khadur with him. Guru Angad's tenure was uneventful, but after his death a phase of expansion took place under the leadership of his nominated successor, Guru Amardas (born 1479, guru 1552–1574).

Guru Amardas established a new town on the right bank of the river Beas along the lines of Kartarpur and named it Goindval (the original name seems to have been Govindval).[45] The community at Goindval witnessed major developments in its institutional structures. The guru provided guidance to the Sikhs at Goindval, and the festival days of Vaisakhi and Divali enabled distant congregations to come together and participate in the communal life there. While an audience with the guru on these festival days met the spiritual needs of Sikhs who lived away from Goindval, Sikh social solidarity was strengthened by meetings between community members.

Guru Amardas's period also saw the emergence of the institution of the *manji* (literally, "cot," but here it refers to the position of authority in Sikh congregations away from Goindval). According to this system the guru nominated twenty-two individuals well versed in Sikh doctrine to lead distant congregations and handle the local issues.[46] Their responsibilities included bringing new members to the Sikh fold, and serving as links between their congregation and the central court at Goindval. In all likelihood they regularly visited Goindval and also brought members of their congregations to participate in the biannual gatherings there. This decentralization of authority aided the expansion and efficient running of the congregations away from Goindval.

So began a period of Sikh self-assurance. The Sikhs issued an open invitation to both the Hindu and Muslim religious elites to avail themselves of the shelter offered by the guru if they wanted liberation. The words of Guru Amardas to the Brahmins were clear: "Your faith in God can work only if you listen to the advice of the guru" (*Brahamu bindihe te brahamaṇa je chalahe satigur bhae*, M3, AG, 849–850). Since the guru lived under Islamic rule, his invitation to Sufis to join the Sikh fold and submit to his leadership was strikingly bold: "O Shekh! Leave violence and with the fear of God control the inner confusion. Many have attained liberation by fear of the guru" (*Sekha andarahu joru chhadi tu bhau kari jhali gavae. Gur kai bhai kete nistare bhai vichi nirbhau pae*, M3, AG, 551). He further stated: "O Shekh! Bring your mind to focus on the One. Discard your futile pursuits and realize the word of the guru. If you follow the guru, . . . you will gain respect in the divine court" (*Sekha chauchakia chauvaia ehu manu ikatu ghari aṇi. Ehaṛ tehaṛ chhadi tu gur ka sabadu pachhaṇu. Satigur agai dhai pau, . . . ta dargah pavahe maṇu*, M3, AG, 646).[47]

Under the leadership of Guru Amardas, we see the updating of the Guru Harsahai Pothi, and from this point onward the expansion of the Sikh text seems to become an extraordinarily sensitive indicator of the evolving concerns of the community. As we discuss in chapter 3, the Goindval Pothis were compiled during the time of Guru Amardas and contained the complete corpus of hymns of the first three gurus. The addition of the hymns of the Bhagats from all levels of the social hierarchy to the sacred Sikh text was rooted in Guru Amardas's belief in the continuous nature of revelation and in an emphasis on the comprehensiveness of the Sikh community. By the time of Guru Amardas's death, the Sikh community had grown much larger than it had been at Kartarpur, it had more developed social institutions, and it possessed a four-volume scriptural text.

Guru Ramdas, the nominated successor of Guru Amardas, assumed leadership, and a replay of the earlier struggle for authority between the legal and the nominated leader ensued. Baba Mohan and Baba Mohari, the two sons of Guru Amardas, took control of their father's establishment as his legal heirs, while the nominated successor had to move to Ramdaspur (present-day Amritsar) along with the large following of his predecessor. The name of the newly established town provides an interesting illustration of an evolution in the community's perception of its guru at this particular phase of expansion. It was not Kartar or Govind—epithets for God in Sikh literature—but was the town of Guru Ramdas. Such naming may indicate a strengthening of the authority of the guru, who was believed to be God's representative on earth. For Bhai Gurdas, there was no question that the Sikh guru was the true lord while all other temporal kings held false authority.[48] (See Map 1.)

The distance that the Sikh community had traveled from Kartarpur to Ramdaspur (via Goindval) was not merely geographical but marked an important evolution in its history. According to Guru Arjan, God himself had created a firm foundation of the Sikh community on which it was now thriving (*Abichal niv dhari Gur Nanak nit nit charai savai*, M5, AG, 500–501). Kartarpur, a village whose inhabitants engaged primarily in agriculture for their sustenance, expanded into Ramdaspur, the spiritual and temporal capital of the Sikhs in the closing decades of the sixteenth century. A town built around the central shrine (the Darbar Sahib), dedicated to the sovereign Lord of the universe, represented the divine kingdom (*Ramraj ramdaspuri kine gurdev*, M5, AG, 817), and in this reign of humility everyone was living in comfort (*Sabh sukhali vuṭhia ihu hoa halemi raju jio*, M5, AG, 74) without having to pay any religious tax (*Jejiah ḍanu ko lae na jagati*, M5, AG, 430).

At Ramdaspur the meditation on the divine name, charity, and purity of the Kartarpur era took the concrete form of a pilgrimage to the city of the guru, a bath in the holy pool, an audience with the guru (*darshan*), and the offering of the tithe (*dasvandh*) that the Sikhs had brought with them. The bath in the holy pool, according to Guru Arjan, washed off previously committed sins (*Ramdas sarovari nate. Sabhi utare pap kamate*, M5, AG, 625), and the offering of the tithe marked the continued commitment toward the Sikh communal solidarity.

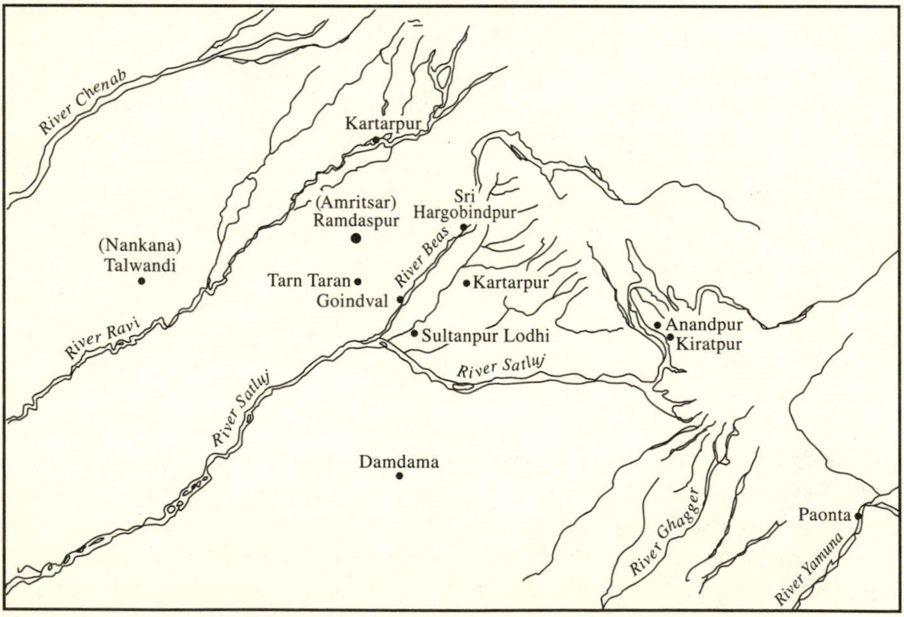

Map 1 Sikh Sacred Geography

This phase of expansion, under Guru Arjan's leadership, corresponded with another updating of the scriptural text. As Sikh traditional sources report and our discussion in chapter 4 fully supports, Guru Arjan borrowed the Goindval Pothis from the Bhallas at Goindval, and to their contents he added his own hymns and those of his father to produce an expanded Sikh text. The manuscript he compiled is at present in the custody of Karamjit Singh Sodhi at Kartarpur, a town founded by Guru Arjan in 1593.

The religious liberalism of the Mughal emperor Akbar (1556–1605) had provided a protective environment for the growth of the Sikh community and the rise of their court at Amritsar. However, the ascent to power of Emperor Jahangir (1605–1627), who enjoyed the support of orthodox Muslims in Delhi, created an atmosphere of hostility that resulted in the execution of Guru Arjan in Lahore in 1606 and initiated a period of instability for the Sikhs. They were forced to leave Amritsar and the central Punjab in the 1630s and move to the Shivalik hills.

In the late 1660s, under the leadership of Guru Tegh Bahadur, the community was, however, able to stabilize itself. Guru Tegh Bahadur, the most widely traveled guru besides Guru Nanak and Guru Amardas, established his court in the newly founded town of Anandpur in the Shivalik hills. During his period of leadership, he revived the distant congregations in eastern and central India, made successful tours of the Malwa, bringing the local landed families of the region into the Sikh fold and expanding the base of the community in the central Punjab as well.[49]

Guru Tegh Bahadur also revived the earlier tradition of writing sacred hymns. His three immediate predecessors, Guru Hargobind (born 1595, guru 1606–1644), Guru Harirai (born 1630, guru 1644–1661), and Guru Harkishan (born 1656, guru 1661–1664), did not compose poetry. The writing of new hymns created the need to update the contents of the existing sacred corpus recorded in the Kartarpur Pothi. MS 1192, compiled in 1674 and presently available at the Panjab University library, Chandigarh, is the first document manifesting the expansion of the sacred text at this point in history. As we discuss in chapter 5, the manuscripts of this period leave no basis to accept the traditional Sikh belief that Guru Tegh Bahadur's hymns were added to the scriptural text only after his death.

This period of relative consolidation led to further persecution and to the second martyrdom in the tradition. Guru Tegh Bahadur was executed in Delhi in 1675. His young son, Guru Gobind Singh, took over the leadership in these difficult circumstances. In the years that followed, he was able to expand the Sikh court at Anandpur considerably. The town became the main Sikh pilgrimage site; a third festival, Holi (at the end of the severe Punjab winter), was added to Vaisakhi and Divali in the Sikh calendar, and by the mid 1690s the Sikhs were able to regain the confidence they once enjoyed at Amritsar. In the late 1690s, the guru declared the Sikhs as the Khalsa (literally, "the pure") and by doing this radically revised the existing structure of authority within the community. The personal authority was to be permanently replaced by the divine authority as manifested in the Sikh scripture (Granth), and the collective community (Panth) was assigned the right to interpret it. The declaration of the community as the Khalsa also involved a new ceremony, an expanded code of conduct that the Sikhs were to follow, and a new understanding that the lives of the Sikhs must be dedicated to the establishment of the kingdom of God (Khalsa Raj).[50]

On the basis of the information available in the seventeenth-century manuscripts, we now know that the Kartarpur Pothi began to be copied soon after its compilation and that these texts proliferated as the times passed by. As we examine in later chapters, the process of copying and arbitrary scribal decisions on complex textual details resulted in variation within the contents of different manuscripts, and a need for standardization of the text seemed to have been felt in the closing decades of the seventeenth century. Data at our disposal suggest that at the initiative of Guru Gobind Singh a new text was compiled, which came to be known in Sikh tradition as the Adi Granth. Although the criteria for the compilation of the Adi Granth are not entirely clear, it is apparent that it was seen as the canonical text. Extant manuscripts, both in the Anandpur and Damdama, Bhatinda areas—the center of Sikh activity in the late seventeenth and early eighteenth centuries—support the contention that an overwhelming number of them contain the Adi Granth.[51]

The Adi Granth seemingly enjoyed the status as the canonical text in central locations, but in distant congregations the earlier versions of the scriptural texts continued to be copied. By the time we reach the nineteenth century, Sikh writers begin to categorically denounce the noncanonical versions and attribute fantastic motives for their creation. These versions eventually died out with the arrival of the printing press in the Punjab and the streamlining of the production process in places like Amritsar and Lahore. The printing presses had to publish the canonical text, and the Adi Granth was the only answer. Simultaneously, a concerted effort in producing a standardized text of the Adi Granth began. The Kartarpur Pothi was declared to be the *textus receptus*, and this process continued over half a century, culminating in the publication of the authoritative text of the Adi Granth by the Shiromani Gurdwara Prabandhak Committee (Supreme Gurdwara management committee, thereafter SGPC), the premier Sikh religious organization of the twentieth century.[52] Yet more work seems to be required toward the finalizing of this text of the Adi Granth.[53] Since its compilation, the Adi Granth has also served as the nucleus of a rich tradition of Sikh scholarship; extensive commentaries, translations, and detailed thematic studies are available in Punjabi and other languages.[54]

The Plan of the Book

In this volume, I argue that traditional reconstruction of the historical formation of the Adi Granth should be extended at both ends from the period of Guru Arjan—back to Guru Nanak and forward almost to the present day—before we have a comprehensive picture of the text's history. My research is constructed on two fundamental assumptions: canon formation in Sikhism was closely related to other developments in the community; and the best source to understand this complex process is the scriptural manuscripts themselves. Because of the community's relatively recent beginnings, a considerable number of early scriptural manuscripts are still extant. In my past ten years of work, I have made a concerted effort to examine these early manuscripts and reconstruct the history of Sikh scripture primarily on the data available in them. The results are remarkable, as I show in later chapters—exciting if you see it one way, but unsettling if you see it another.[55] At almost every critical juncture, my research confronts the received wisdom about how the Sikh scriptural text began, expanded, and became canon.

The book contains eight chapters. In chapter 2, I survey relevant literature, to understand Sikh perceptions of the history of compilation of the Adi Granth and the difference of views among scholars regarding the text's origin and its various stages of expansion. The chapter lays out the important issues constituting scholarly debate and popular Sikh discourse on the compilation of the text of the Adi Granth.

The following three chapters examine in detail the extant manuscripts. In chapter 3 I analyze the information available about the Guru Harsahai Pothi (1530s?) and the Goindval Pothis (1570s?) traditionally associated with Guru Nanak and Guru Amardas, respectively. I draw on the contents of these manuscripts to assess the early formation of the Sikh scriptural corpus. In Chapter 4 I analyze two major manuscripts, MS 1245 (1600?) and the Kartarpur Pothi (1604), to describe the stage of development of the scriptural text at the turn of the seventeenth century. In chapter 5 I begin with an analysis of the seventeenth-century manuscript to reconstruct the history of the text up to the compiling of the Adi Granth (1680s). On the basis of the firm evidence available to us, I propose to modify the traditional characterization of the Kartarpur Pothi as the original attempt at compilation of the Sikh sacred literature, as well as existing understanding of its evolution into the canonical text in later history.

In chapter 6 I focus on a different area and analyze the data available in early manuscripts to understand how scribes organized the sacred corpus at various points in its expansion, all the while drawing in principles from both Hindu and Muslim religious texts of the time. In Chapter 7 I address the presence of the hymns of fifteen Bhagats in the Adi Granth and the community's responses to this portion of Sikh scripture. On the basis of the information available in the early manuscripts, I argue for a radically revised view of Sikh traditional beliefs about the dates of these hymns' entry into the Sikh text, and the possible reasons for their introduction.

In chapter 8 I trace the history of the text of the Adi Granth from its compilation in the closing decades of the seventeenth century to the present; address in detail the origin and evolution of scriptural authority and its manifestation in Sikh life, and future prospects for its role with the Sikh community in a process of transformation from a religious group based in the Punjab to a world community with adherents all across the globe.

I have attempted to enlarge the existing debates by introducing new sources and raising fresh questions. My findings on various key issues differ from the traditional Sikh position as well as those presented by other twentieth-century scholars. I hope that this revised and expanded history of the text and the institutionalization of Sikh scripture will interest not only scholars of the Sikh religion, but also those of comparative canon formation, and will initiate a more concerted examination of the Sikh tradition's relationship with the monotheistic traditions of the Middle East.

2

Writings on Sikh Scripture

An Overview

With the hymns of Guru Nanak at its core, Sikh literature developed in two key ways: the doctrinal and the historical. Exegetical literature emerged from the belief that Sikh sacred hymns manifest the divine revelation, and that the foremost obligation of the members of the community was to understand and follow the theological and social ideas enshrined in them.[1] Historical literature responded to the need to know how the gurus actually lived out the contents of their teaching.[2] These two strands in early literature developed as the Sikh tradition matured.

The exegetical writings began as Guru Nanak's successors reinforced, elaborated, and responded to his ideas while composing their own hymns. Thus, in the Adi Granth itself, we see the emergence of an ongoing dialogue.[3] This engagement paved the way for formal exegesis of gurus' compositions, the written records of which can be traced to the turn of the seventeenth century.[4] Since then, several independent schools of interpretation of the contents of the Adi Granth have emerged.[5]

Sikh historical writings also began in the sixteenth century. Early references to the activities of the gurus appear in their own hymns. In addition, the bards at the Sikh court whose compositions are included in the Adi Granth wrote about the unique status of the gurus within the community, and the magnificence of the Sikh court.[6] These writings developed into the janam-sakhis, stories about the life and mission of Guru Nanak, which then went on to include details about his successors.[7] The elevation of the Adi Granth to the status of the Guru Granth Sahib brought it to the focus of subsequent Sikh chroniclers writing about the community.

This chapter presents a chronological survey of sources dealing with the Adi Granth, highlighting their authors' perceptions of the making and expansion of its text, as well as its status and function within the community. In a brief conclusion, I discuss how these early writers have contributed to the current Sikh understanding of the history of compilation of the Adi Granth.

Eighteenth-Century Accounts

Although extremely important details appear in the colophons recorded in some of the seventeenth-century manuscripts, the *Rahitnama* (Manual of conduct) of Chaupa Singh (d. 1723), a prominent member of the Sikh court at Anandpur, is the earliest document to refer to the history of the Adi Granth.[8] First, Chaupa Singh traces the creation of the Adi Granth to the decision of Guru Arjan and attributes a key role in the compilation of the original text to Bhai Gurdas. Second, he reports that Guru Arjan had to compile the authoritative text to protect the purity of the sacred Sikh writings from the interpolations of the Miṇas (scoundrels), the name given in Sikh tradition to the family and followers of Prithi Chand (d. 1618), the older brother and rival of Guru Arjan. Furthermore, Chaupa Singh points out that the original manuscript compiled by Bhai Gurdas under the supervision of Guru Arjan was in the custody of the descendants of Dhirmal (d. 1677), a great-grandson of Guru Arjan, who posed a major challenge to the leadership of the Sikh gurus at Kiratpur and later Anandpur during the middle decades of the seventeenth century. Finally, he informs us that in the late 1670s, Guru Gobind Singh tried to borrow this manuscript from Dhirmal's descendants, who declined the guru's request and challenged him to prepare his own manuscript of the sacred text without seeking their help.

The two other major sources of the first half of the eighteenth century, Sainapati's *Sri Guru Sobha* (The radiance of the guru) written in 1711, and Koer Singh's *Gurbilas Patishahi 10* (The splendor of the tenth master), completed in 1751, primarily deal with the life story of Guru Gobind Singh.[9] Within this context, they both report that at the time of his death, the guru dissolved the office of the personal guru and vested its authority in the Adi Granth. For Sainapati, sacred hymns (*baṇi*), and the Khalsa Panth were to replace the guru's authority; for Koer Singh, however, Guru Gobind Singh ceremonially declared the Adi Granth to be his sole successor and commanded the Sikhs to consider it as their primary guide in the future.

In the second half of the eighteenth century, we come across a set of sources that refer to the history of the Adi Granth. Kesar Singh Chhibbar's *Bansavlinama Dasan Patishahian ka* (Genealogy of the ten masters), completed in 1769, is the first attempt to write a comprehensive history of the community and includes information about the compilation of the Adi Granth.[10] Chhibbar's account is followed by two others found in Sarupdas Bhalla's *Mahima Prakash* (The rise of glory) written in 1776, and *Sikhan di Bhagatmala* (Garland of Sikh saints), traditionally associated with Bhai Mani Singh (d. 1738), an important Sikh figure of the opening decades of the eighteenth century, but attributed in recent research to Giani Surat Singh, a late-eighteenth-century Sikh writer.[11]

Chhibbar repeatedly mentions that he is reporting what he heard from his ancestors and other community members. The primary source of information for the other two writers must also have been oral tradition, which they all used creatively to construct their understanding of the compilation of Sikh scripture. The backdrop of these traditions deserves our attention. The two centuries between the compilation of the Sikh text and the writing of these accounts were politically tumultuous and resulted in shifts in the center of Sikh power from the town of Amritsar in the central Punjab to Anandpur in the Shivalik hills, and then back to Amritsar.[12]

The core picture of the compilation of Sikh scripture which emerges in all these accounts is centered on Guru Arjan. All three sources attribute the compilation of the original text to him, with an important role in writing and collating the material assigned to Bhai Gurdas.[13] There are, however, variations in the details pertaining to the process of compilation. Guru Arjan's decision to compile the Sikh text is explained in two ways. *Bansavlinama* elaborates on the line referred to in Chaupa Singh. According to this view, the Miṇas produced a text that incorporated the hymns of the first four gurus and the compositions of Prithi Chand's son Miharban (1581–1640). Guru Arjan saw this text as a threat to the purity of Sikh sacred literature and therefore compiled an authentic scripture for posterity. The same reason is given for the making of the Sikh text in *Bhagatmala*.

For the writer of *Mahima Prakash*, however, Guru Arjan's decision to compile the scriptural text was rooted in the institutional needs of the early community. Guru Arjan was aware that the founding of a new community should be complemented by a new holy book.[14] The creation of the scriptural text was thus inevitable to the new community's growth. While in the explanations of Chaupa Singh and then Chhibbar, the preparation of the Sikh text is presented as a reactive strategy to meet the challenges posed by a rival group within the community, Bhalla presents the creation of the sacred text as part and parcel of the organic development of the early community.

These accounts variously describe Guru Arjan's process of compiling the sacred text. According to the brief description in *Bansavlinama*, Guru Arjan dictated the sacred hymns, and Bhai Gurdas recorded and collated them. Chhibbar did not see a need to describe the process involved in Guru Arjan's dictation. The accounts of the compilation process are somewhat more detailed in *Mahima Prakash* and *Bhagatmala*. The preparation of the scriptural text, according to these sources, required the acquisition of the Goindval Pothis, a set of manuscripts that are believed to have been prepared in the town of Goindval during the time of Guru Amardas and remained there in the custody of his son, Baba Mohan, after the guru's death. Guru Arjan is said to have acquired these pothis by personally visiting Goindval and appealing to Baba Mohan for their loan.

In addition to the Goindval Pothis, which served as the written source for Guru Arjan's new pothi, *Mahima Prakash* mentions the existence of another group of the gurus' hymns that needed to be collected.[15] We are not told the size of this corpus, which was collected over and above what was available in the Goindval Pothis, nor do we learn of its location or even whether it was kept in an oral or a written form. The *Praṇ Sangali* (The chain of breath), a long composition attributed to Guru Nanak, is the only example we have of this type of text collected from some independent source. According to *Mahima Prakash*, King Shivnabh of Singhladip (that is, Sri Lanka) kept a written copy of the *Praṇ Sangali*, and happily sent it to Guru Arjan upon request. The narrator of *Mahima Prakash* claims that Guru Arjan did not consider the *Praṇ Sangali* an authentic composition of Guru Nanak and consequently rejected it for entry into the Sikh text under preparation. The same account of the *Praṇ Sangali*'s acquisition and eventual rejection appears in *Bhagatmala*.[16]

The rejection of the *Praṇ Sangali* and the absence of any reference to other hymns collected from distant sources implies that the manuscript prepared by Guru Arjan was based primarily on the Goindval Pothis. Nonetheless, these authors were unable to recognize the Goindval Pothis as a part of the evolution of the Sikh scriptural text; principal credit for the creation of Sikh scripture is assigned to Guru Arjan.

In all three accounts, the original scriptural text compiled at this time was considered to be a single manuscript. They follow the tradition available in Chaupa Singh and refer to its presence at Kartarpur. Dhirmal's part of the family had stayed on at Kartarpur after the center of Sikh activity moved to the Shivalik hills in the 1630s. This manuscript is usually referred to as the Kartarpur Pothi, or the Bhai Gurdas Pothi (since Bhai Gurdas inscribed it).

Chhibbar refers to the compilation of the Adi Granth, which he calls the "big text" (*vaḍa granth*), in the closing decades of the seventeenth century at Anandpur.[17] Guru Gobind Singh is said to have sought the Kartarpur Pothi from Dhirmal's family, but having been denied access to it, the guru used "another manuscript" to prepare the Adi Granth. He thus reports that other scriptural manuscripts in addition to the Kartarpur Pothi were available in the community. Unlike Bhalla, Chhibbar does not convey any awareness of the varied versions of the scriptural text prevalent in the seventeenth-century Sikh community; consequently, he gives us no clue about their relationship to the Adi Granth prepared at Anandpur.

Chhibbar offers three additional observations. First, along with the creation of the Adi Granth, he reports the compilation of another text at Anandpur. Guru Gobind Singh, however, considered the compositions included in this second document to be a record of "our light-hearted activity" (*khel*, literally, "playing") and commanded it to be "kept separated" from the Adi Granth, which in the guru's view was the "real scripture."[18] This text is now known in the Sikh tradition as the Dasam Granth (Book of the tenth master).

Second, Chhibbar reiterates that at the time of his death in 1708, Guru Gobind Singh vested the authority of the personal guru in the Adi Granth, turning it into the Guru Granth Sahib.[19] In his account, the Adi Granth is the central authority within the Sikh community (Guru Panth), and all communal issues need to be resolved in its presence. This tradition of elevating the Adi Granth to the Guru Granth Sahib also appears in *Mahima Prakash*. Bhalla states that Guru Gobind Singh commanded the community to recognize the Adi Granth as the guru, and that the only way Sikhs could ever communicate with the ten gurus was by reading the Adi Granth.[20]

Third, Chhibbar's description implies that the text of the Adi Granth is closed, with no provision for additions to its contents or alterations in its structure. He refers to the compilation of a manuscript by Bhai Mani Singh, a leading figure during the period following the death of Guru Gobind Singh, in which the contents of the Adi Granth were reorganized and the hymns of the Bhagats were appended at the closing of the text. Chhibbar views Bhai Mani Singh's violent execution—his limbs were cut off—as a punishment for tinkering with the text of the Adi Granth.[21]

In addition to these three writings, Sarup Singh Kaushish's *Guru kian Sakhian* (The stories of the guru[s]), written in 1790, is another important source of the period.[22] Kaushish was a descendant of Bhikha Bhaṭ, who had come to the Sikh court in the time of Guru Amardas and had attained the honor of having two of his panegyrics incorporated into the Sikh text (AG, 1395–1396). Unlike the sources discussed earlier, which were based primarily on the oral traditions, Kaushish had access to the record books (*vahis*) of his ancestors, which contained many entries pertaining to events in the

Sikh community beginning with the mid sixteenth century. Many of these documents are still in the custody of Kaushish's descendants.[23] Given the active priestly background of the Bhaṭs, the focus of these writings is on the ritual life of the early community, and we discuss them in detail in chapter 8.[24] He supports the view that both the authority of the Adi Granth and its elaborate use in Sikh devotional life were firmly established by the end of the eighteenth century.

For the purpose of the history of the compilation of the text, Kaushish offers an account slightly different from those of the earlier writers on Guru Gobind Singh's attempt to borrow the Kartarpur Pothi.[25] According to him, Ram Chand, son of Dhirmal, died at Baba Bakala in 1678. Guru Gobind Singh could not leave Anandpur to participate in Ram Chand's death rituals and the succession ceremony of his younger brother, Pahaṛmal. The guru sent Dharam Chand Chhibbar and Maniram (later Bhai Mani Singh) as his representatives. Maniram was also asked to use the opportunity to request that Pahaṛmal lend the Kartarpur Pothi so that some manuscripts at Anandpur could be corrected with it. At that point Pahaṛmal was reportedly moving his family back to Kartarpur from Baba Bakala, and he suggested that the guru should send someone later to Kartarpur to get the pothi, or better still, to send a manuscript that could be compared and collated and corrected with the Kartarpur Pothi. Unfortunately, Kaushish does not return to this episode and never mentions what happened afterward.

To sum up our discussion of these accounts—*Gurbilas Patishahi 10*, *Bansavlinama*, *Mahima Prakash*, *Bhagatmala*, and *Guru kian Sakhian*—we are told in categorical terms that at the time of his death, Guru Gobind Singh declared the Adi Granth to be the guru within the Sikh community, and during the eighteenth century its authority, as well as its multifaceted use in Sikh ritual life, was entrenched. The Sikhs visited the *gurdwara* with the Adi Granth at its center twice a day, used the text of the Adi Granth to name their children, performed readings on special occasions, and offered petitions to the holy text when seeking solace for the living and peace for departed souls.

Chhibbar does refer to the Dasam Granth as an additional Sikh scriptural text but categorically reports that its status was lower than that of the Adi Granth. The fact that none of the other sources discussed above mention the Dasam Granth implies the supreme authority of the Adi Granth within the eighteenth-century Sikh community, unchallenged in any visible way by any other text or institution.

These eighteenth-century accounts refer to several manuscripts, which, if located, could serve as important primary sources for the study of the history of the Sikh text. These include two sixteenth-century manuscripts, references to which appear only in relation to the manuscript compiled by Guru Arjan. The first of these manuscripts supposedly contained the hymns of the first four gurus and the writings of Miharban, Guru Arjan's nephew. This manuscript is claimed to have been instrumental in Guru Arjan's decision to compile the authentic Sikh text. The second manuscript is reported to have been in the custody of Baba Mohan at Goindval; Guru Arjan acquired and used it as the source for his compilation. The manuscript prepared under the supervision of Guru Arjan by Bhai Gurdas is reported to be in the possession of the family of Dhirmal, at Kartarpur. The two sixteenth-century manuscripts are believed to have stayed in the custody of Miharban's and Baba Mohan's descendants, respectively.

The accounts available in *Mahima Prakash* and *Bhagatmala* report the creation of the first copy of the Kartarpur Pothi by Bhai Banno, a resident of the village of Khara Mangat in northwest Punjab and a prominent Sikh of Guru Arjan. (This manuscript is at present in the custody of Bhai Banno's descendants at Kanpur, and we will call it the Kanpur Pothi). Kaushish mentions the existence of a manuscript that Ramrai (d. 1687), the eldest son of Guru Harirai, carried to Delhi. In the closing years of that century, there were a number of scriptural manuscripts present in the community, and Guru Gobind Singh compiled a new manuscript of the Sikh sacred text at Anandpur. In *Bansavlinama*, there is also reference to a manuscript compiled by Bhai Mani Singh, in which the original structure of the sacred text was altered in fundamental ways. Bhalla and the author of *Bhagatmala* register an awareness that there were organizational variations between the Kartarpur and the Kanpur Pothis.[26]

Nineteenth-Century Accounts

The nineteenth-century Sikh sources build on the accounts of the compilation of the Adi Granth discussed earlier and offer an interesting case study of how these traditions expanded in the hands of later writers. Completed in the early 1840s, *Sri Gurbilas Patishahi 6* (The splendor of the sixth master), traditionally attributed to Sohan Kavi, and *Sri Gurpratap Suraj Granth* (The book of the gurus' glory) by Bhai Santokh Singh (1788–1844) present the history of the Kartarpur Pothi's compilation in almost identical terms.[27]

Both writers embellish the core episodes of the accounts discussed earlier. They endorse the view that the creation of the Sikh text by Guru Arjan resulted from his attempt to prevent contamination of the Sikh gurus' compositions by those of the Miṇas. However, given their Nirmala background, these scholars introduce a new dimension to the existing story. Guru Arjan compiled the Sikh scriptural text to liberate the world by providing it with an up-to-date version of the essence of all Hindu sacred texts.[28] The Sikh scriptural text is thus interpreted as a "fifth veda," prepared by Guru Arjan for the purpose of liberating the people of his age; what was characteristiclly a Sikh document for Bhalla is now seen as representing the culmination of the Indian spiritual tradition.

Both authors report the Goindval Pothis as the primary written source Guru Arjan used to compile the scriptural text. To make their narratives rich in dramatic details, they focus on the difficulties Guru Arjan faced when he requested the loan of the Goindval Pothis from Baba Mohan and the honor with which he brought the manuscripts from Goindval to Amritsar. A number of additions are attached to the earlier descriptions of this episode. The preparation undergone by Guru Arjan before appearing in the presence of Baba Mohan now includes a bath at the *bauli* (the large well with stairs leading down to the water) which was constructed during the time of Guru Amardas. Guru Amardas appears to Guru Arjan in a vision, warns him that Mohan will treat him badly, and urges him to remain calm. Guru Arjan follows the advice of his predecessor and finally succeeds in obtaining the Goindval Pothis.[29] Aside from the Goindval Pothis, both these sources hold that text of the *Praṇ Sangali* was brought from some distant congregation in the South.[30] In accordance with earlier accounts, however, the *Praṇ Sangali* is not regarded as an authentic composition of Guru Nanak.

Both *Sri Gurbilas Patishahi 6* and *Sri Gurpratap Suraj Granth* address the closed nature of the text of the Adi Granth. They argue that by putting his signature on the Kartarpur Pothi, Guru Arjan sealed the corpus of Sikh sacred literature. The guru is said to have specifically instructed Hargobind, his son and successor, that his mission was not to create sacred hymns but to guard the community from external attacks; no other hymns could be added to the text with the sole exception of the compositions of Tegh Bahadur, who was to sacrifice his life for the cause of righteousness (*din*).[31] This understanding eventually resulted in the view that Guru Arjan himself had left blank spaces in the text of the Kartarpur Pothi to await and incorporate the hymns of Guru Tegh Bahadur. Within this framework of thinking, no variations within the text are acceptable, and it is claimed that the manuscript prepared by Bhai Banno was categorically rejected by Guru Arjan.

Since Dhirmal refused to part with the Kartarpur Pothi, the expansion of its contents was carried out differently than originally intended. Unlike *Bansavlinama*, which argues for the compilation of the Adi Granth at Anandpur, the *Sri Gurbilas Patishahi 6* claims that it was prepared at Damdama, Bhatinda, where Guru Gobind Singh temporarily resided from 1705 to 1706.[32] By the early nineteenth century, the text of the Adi Granth was popularly known as the Damdami recension, a title that resulted from an effort to contrast this text from those available at Kartarpur and Khara Mangat. For these mid-nineteenth-century writers it seemed logical to explain this name by locating the origin of the Adi Granth in the town of Damdama.

Another major nineteenth-century Sikh scholar who addressed the compilation of the Adi Granth in some detail was Giani Gian Singh (1822–1921). In his *Tvarikh Guru Khalsa* (The history of Guru Khalsa), written in 1894, he presented a revised understanding of the making of the Sikh text by Guru Arjan.[33] He revived the notion that a link existed between the Sikh text and the evolution of the community, an idea we first encountered in *Mahima Prakash*. Characterizing Sikh scripture as part of the organic development of the early community, Giani Gian Singh viewed it as the Sikh counterpart of "the Torah, the Bible, the Avesta, the Qur'an, and the Vedas."[34]

In his understanding of the process of compilation of the original text, Giani Gian Singh nevertheless introduced a radical shift. He believed that the great bulk of hymns by the gurus that went into the text was collected from dispersed congregations. Guru Arjan sent his messengers to far-flung communities and collected the hymns of Guru Nanak, an enterprise that is said to have taken many years. Giani Gian Singh's ideas were apparently rooted in the belief that Guru Nanak developed a major following during a lifetime of extensive travel and that the hymns of the guru were preserved as part of the oral traditions of numerous scattered congregations. To these hymns some addition was made from the Goindval Pothis

The earlier accounts referred to above contain no reference whatsoever to the preservation of the hymns of the gurus in an oral form by the dispersed Sikh congregations. The *Praṇ Sangali*, the only composition thought to have been brought from a distant place, was clearly in a written form. Giani Gian Singh, however, argued that the orally transmitted hymns of Guru Nanak served as the primary source for Guru Arjan's compilation. His account of the making of the Sikh text considerably expanded the ongoing search for the hymns of the gurus and radically diminished the role of the Goindval Pothis in this enterprise.

Giani Gian Singh accepted the *Sri Gurbilas Patishahi 6* version of the creation of Bhai Banno's copy, its rejection by Guru Arjan, and the compilation of the Adi Granth at Damdama, Bhatinda. Expanding on earlier accounts of the creation of the final text, Giani Gian Singh argued that Dhirmal's descendants' refusal to lend the Kartarpur Pothi resulted in Guru Gobind Singh's dictation of the complete text from memory over a period of several months at Damdama, Bhatinda, to Bhai Mani Singh, who served as the amanuensis.[35] In the process, the originally revealed text received further authentication by rising from the memory of the guru.

Two other scholarly initiatives need to be mentioned here. First, Giani Badan Singh, who belonged to the line of Sikh scholarship believed to have been started by Bhai Mani Singh, prepared the first complete commentary on the Adi Granth (*Faridkot vala Ṭika*) in 1883.[36] It was a major effort on the part of Sikh scholars to develop an authoritative interpretation of the Adi Granth. Second, Charan Singh, another traditional scholar writing at this time, prepared a detailed essay on the structure of the Adi Granth, and brought to scholarly attention a branch of seventeenth-century manuscripts, which was distinct from both the Kartarpur and the Kanpur Pothi.[37] Building on oral traditions, he traced the text's origin to a seventeenth-century Sikh congregation in the town of Lahore and as a result named it the Lahore version of the early Sikh manuscripts.

In sum, the nineteenth-century sources expand on earlier motifs and introduce important changes in the understanding of how Sikh scripture was compiled. First, following earlier sources, Giani Gian Singh attributed the conception and compilation of the original text to Guru Arjan, but his elaborated details of the collection of the hymns from distant congregations substantially reduced the importance of the Goindval Pothis. Second, with an emphasis on the authentication of Sikh sacred literature as the primary reason for the creation of the Sikh text, the textual variations were considered a product of the conspiracy of which Bhai Banno was just one participant. Third, the compilation of the final text was widely thought to have taken place at Damdama, Bhatinda, instead of Anandpur, and Guru Gobind Singh was claimed to have dictated the complete text from memory. Finally, a need was felt to understand the structure of the Adi Granth and prepare an authoritative statement on its entire contents.

Twentieth-Century Accounts

Western education made inroads in the Punjab in the last quarter of the nineteenth century, introducing new analytical methods into the studies of history, literature, and religion.[38] Ernest Trumpp, a German philologist who taught Indian languages at Tübingen, published his translation of a large portion of the Adi Granth in 1877, and Max Arthur Macauliffe, a Briton who served in India, published his six-volume *Sikh Religion* in 1909, which raised a new set of issues and challenged Sikh scholarly thinking in interesting ways.[39]

By the opening decades of the twentieth century, we begin to witness a reorientation of Sikh way of looking at their literature. Karam Singh Historian (1884–1930), a product of Khalsa College, Amritsar, was the first scholar to apply the new analytical approach to the janam-sakhis; Sahib Singh (1892–1977), a graduate of Government College, Lahore, and Teja Singh (1894–1958), a graduate of Gordon College, Rawalpindi, pioneered the debate about the evolution of the Sikh scriptural text.[40] Working independently, both Sahib Singh and Teja Singh rejected large parts of the traditional accounts in the sources discussed above and presented a new reconstruction of the early history of Sikh scripture. Basing their arguments on internal evidence taken from the hymns of Guru Nanak and Guru Amardas, they argued that the process of compiling the Sikh scriptural text began with Guru Nanak. Guru Amardas's hymns follow the *rag* scheme found in Guru Nanak's hymns and reverberate with direct linguistic and thematic echoes. They were taken as evidence for the view that the hymns of Guru Nanak were available in written form to his early successors.[41] Contrary to the traditional perception that the original text was prepared by Guru Arjan at one specific time, both scholars viewed Guru Arjan's work as the pinnacle of a process begun by Guru Nanak himself.

Although Sahib Singh and Teja Singh shared a broad understanding of the origin of the scriptural text, they differed fundamentally in their evaluation of the status and role of the earlier manuscripts. Teja Singh, who had the opportunity to examine one of the Goindval Pothis in the custody of the Bhalla descendants of Guru Amardas, viewed them as the main source for the scriptural text prepared by Guru Arjan.[42] Sahib Singh, on the other hand, rejected the Goindval Pothis as a source, along with the traditional story of Guru Arjan's visit to Goindval to borrow them from Baba Mohan. For Sahib Singh, the view that the manuscript containing Sikh writings was kept by Baba Mohan instead of conveyed to Guru Ramdas at the time of his ascendance to the office of the guru was simply not acceptable. Although unable to document his contention, Sahib Singh insisted that Guru Arjan received a manuscript from Guru Ramdas, his father, which included the hymns of the first four gurus.[43]

In his monumental work *Shabadarth Sri Guru Granth Sahib Ji*, a four-volume text and commentary on the Adi Granth, Teja Singh registers his awareness of variants in the seventeenth-century scriptural manuscripts and meticulously records them without feeling the need to defend the *textus receptus*.[44] Sahib Singh, on the other hand, vehemently rejects the textual variants and noncanonical compositions as interpolations resulting from the conspiracy against the Sikhs.[45]

Since both Sahib Singh and Teja Singh, in their different ways, accepted the evolutionary nature of the early Sikh text, it is hard to understand why both remained silent about the final product of this process, namely the Adi Granth itself, compiled during Guru Gobind Singh's period. Sahib Singh's major work *Adi Biṛ bare* (About the original manuscript) essentially traces the origin of the Sikh text up to the making of the Kartarpur Pothi. Teja Singh and Sahib Singh both seem to assume that the Adi Granth was an expansion of the contents of the Kartarpur Pothi, with the addition of the hymns of Guru Tegh Bahadur.

G. B. Singh, educated at Forman Christian College, Lahore, and later a senior official in the British government, contributed significantly to the field of textual studies with his book *Sri Guru Granth Sahib dian Prachin Biṛan* (The old manuscripts of the Adi Granth), published in 1944. In the opening chapter, G. B. Singh offers his reconstruction of the history of the Sikh text. He is squarely within the mainstream tradition when he argues that the key reason Guru Arjan compiled the scriptural text was to keep the gurus' hymns free from interpolations. Nonetheless, his view of the origin of the Sikh sacred text differs from that of his predecessors. He argues that Guru Nanak recorded his own compositions, but that they were not passed on to Guru Angad, his successor. Instead, they stayed with Guru Nanak's son, Baba Sri Chand, after the guru's death. G. B. Singh supports the traditional view that Guru Amardas compiled the Goindval Pothis and that these were borrowed by Guru Arjan and used in his compilation of the Sikh scriptural text. But he argues that the Goindval Pothis did not include all the compositions of the early gurus and that Guru Arjan collected hymns that originated in the oral traditions of local communities. G. B. Singh was the first scholar to argue that the addition of the hymns of Guru Teg Bahadur to the sacred text actually occurred during his lifetime, before 1675.[46]

His outstanding contribution to the Adi Granth studies comprised his detailed description of the contents of about forty scriptural manuscripts prepared in the seventeenth and eighteenth centuries and housed at various locations on the Indian subcontinent. To this day his book remains a key source of information on this subject, and very few additional manuscripts have been detected after this seminal work.[47]

He was the first scholar to register an acute awareness of the importance of the early manuscripts in accurately reconstructing the process of expansion of the Sikh scriptural text. But he made some errors of judgment in dating and describing these manuscripts. Indeed, his assessment of three early manuscripts, the Guru Harsahai Pothi, the Goindval Pothis, and the Kartarpur Pothi—none of which he was able to examine because of the hostile attitude of the custodian families toward scholarly attempts to reconstruct the history of these documents during the period of his research—was completely off the mark.

G. B. Singh's nagative evaluation of the Goindval Pothis, and the Kartarpur Pothi, brought condemnation from Bhai Jodh Singh, a graduate of Gordon College, Rawalpindi, and a leading Sikh scholar.[48] Bhai Jodh Singh accused him of attacking the very foundation of the Sikh community and thus created a context in which later scholars completely misinterpreted G. B. Singh's work. To substantiate his critique of G. B. Singh's work, Bhai Jodh Singh prepared a page-by-page description of the Kartarpur Pothi and, building on these details, argued for its authenticity.[49]

Challenging the traditional view of the making of Sikh scripture, G. B. Singh, Sahib Singh, and Teja Singh all worked toward accepting both the evolutionary model of the Sikh text's compilation, on the one hand, and the importance of studying early Sikh manuscripts, on the other. Their researches revolutionized the field and also paved the way for the work of other Sikh scholars, who did not have Western education themselves but, following the lead of these three, went on to make significant contributions toward a comprehensive understanding of the history of the Adi Granth.

In the mid 1940s, Bawa Prem Singh, himself a Bhalla descendant of Guru Amardas, prepared notes on the contents of the Goindval Pothis published later under the title of *Babe Mohan valian Pothian* (The volumes of Baba Mohan).[50] In the 1950s Giani Gurdit Singh succeeded in photographing a small portion of the Guru Harsahai Pothi and later, in the 1970s, one of the Goindval Pothis. He briefly described these manuscripts in his recent book, *Itihas Sri Guru Granth Sahib, Bhagat Baṇi Bhag* (The history of the Adi Granth, The section on the saints).[51] In the late 1960s, Harnamdas Udasi's *Adi Shri Guru Granth Sahib dian Puratani Biṛan te Vichar* (Reflection on the old manuscripts of the Adi Granth) introduced into this debate a set of scriptural manuscripts that the author examined during his travels in the Punjab and other states of India.[52] Randhir Singh, Kundan Singh, and Gian Singh Nihang published *Sri Guru Granth Sahib Ji dian Santha-Sainchian ate Puratan Hathlikhit Pavan Biṛan de Praspar Paṭh-Bhedan di Suchi* (The list of textual variations present in the early sacred manuscripts and printed versions of the Guru Granth Sahib) in 1977, which includes important textual details in the early scriptural manuscripts.[53]

The historical and interpretive work of Mahan Singh, Harbhajan Singh, and Piara Singh Padam further clarified issues related to the history of the Sikh scriptural text.[54] Harbhajan Singh and Padam presented a strong case supporting the compilation of the Adi Granth at Anandpur in the last decades of the seventeenth century, a view that surfaced for the first time in Chhibbar.[55] It is important to reiterate that the scholars mentioned above had neither a Western education nor any direct links with the universities in the Punjab.

The 1990s have proved to be a fertile period for research in the area of the Adi Granth studies. Pashaura Singh completed his doctoral dissertation, "The Text and Meaning of the Adi Granth," at the University of Toronto in 1991. This is the first full-length study of the compilation of Sikh scripture to appear in English. Pashaura Singh constructed his research around the basic assumption that Guru Arjan was primarily responsible for conceptualizing Sikh scripture. He suggests that the Sikh scriptural text was created at the time of Guru Arjan for two reasons: the text was important in crystallizing the Sikh communal identity, and it was necessary to keep Sikh sacred literature untainted by interpolations that Guru Arjan's competitors wished to introduce. Guru Arjan's compilation of the Sikh text, in Pashaura Singh's view, required both the Goindval Pothis and other resources available in the community.[56]

Pashaura Singh has presented the novel idea that Guru Arjan compiled a number of drafts before creating the final text, which he takes to be the Kartarpur Pothi. Pashaura Singh argues that Guru Arjan's elaborate editorial policy needed the compilation of these drafts. His "draft" theory rests on MS 1245, an undated manuscript recently introduced into scholarly debate and presently housed at Guru Nanak Dev University, Amritsar.[57] Building on his limited comparison of the text in MS 1245 with the printed text of the Adi Granth, which he takes to be identical with that of the Kartarpur Pothi, Pashaura Singh attempts to formulate the "editorial policy of Guru Arjan," which resulted in the finished text recorded in the Kartarpur Pothi. He argues that Guru Arjan's work involved selecting hymns of the earlier gurus and others, and then making editorial changes as necessary.

He rejects the nineteenth-century view of the compilation of the Adi Granth at Damdama, Bhatinda, and argues that it was prepared at Anandpur under the supervision of Guru Gobind Singh. The task, he claims, involved adding the hymns of Guru Tegh Bahadur to the contents of the Kartarpur Pothi. He argues further that various dissenting groups within the Sikh community continued to challenge the Adi Granth, and that only in the nineteenth century did the text attain a canonical form as well as the status it presently enjoys in the Sikh community.[58]

His research evoked angry responses among some Sikh scholars, who saw his attempt to locate changes in the early manuscripts as a direct challenge to the revealed status of the Sikh writings. A prolonged debate followed which culminated in Pashaura Singh's appearance before the Akal Takhat ("Throne of the Timeless," the central place where the decisions of the SGPC are formally announced), on June 25, 1994, and his acceptance of their requirement that he do penance for hurting the feelings of the Sikh community.[59]

Piar Singh's *Gatha Sri Adi Granth* (The story of the Adi Granth), published by Guru Nanak Dev University in 1992, builds on G. B. Singh's work in the 1940s. The opening section of the book includes a survey of Sikh literature addressing the compilation of the Sikh scriptural text. Piar Singh neatly summarizes the information found on this theme in Sikh sources and systematically critiques each one of them.

In the main body of the book, Piar Singh presents a detailed description of forty-four manuscripts, thirty of which were prepared during the seventeenth century. He rejects the dating of the extant Goindval Pothis to the time of Guru Amardas and the notion that these manuscripts were used in the compilation of the scriptural text prepared by Guru Arjan, and supports the claim made by G. B. Singh and other scholars that the present-day Kartarpur Pothi is not the manuscript traditionally said to have been prepared by Bhai Gurdas under Guru Arjan's supervision.[60]

In the concluding section of his book, Piar Singh analyzes the issues involved in constructing a history of the text.[61] He views the compilation of the Sikh text as part of the institutional development of the community. He argues for its slow evolution and introduces some thought-provoking ideas to explain its early phases. He suggests that fragments of the gurus' hymns were circulating among Sikh congregations in the form of independent compilations; in some cases, gatherings (*juzan*) recording only the tables of contents of these texts circulated and became attached to manuscripts to which they did not belong. He also points to anomalies in the text of the Adi Granth and expresses the need to rectify them. Although the book is entitled "The Story of the Adi Granth," Piar Singh does not deal with the compilation of the Adi Granth itself.

Piar Singh's evaluation of the Kartarpur Pothi, along with suggestions to alter the existing text of the Adi Granth, conflicted with the views of other Sikh scholars. As a result of the ensuing debate, the SGPC obliged Guru Nanak Dev University, the publisher of *Gatha Sri Adi Granth*, to withdraw it from circulation, and forced Piar Singh to appear before the Akal Takhat, Amritsar, on April 1, 1993, and perform forty days of religious penance, for offending the religious sentiments of the Sikhs.[62]

In January 1994, Amarjit Singh Grewal, a scholar of Punjabi literature and culture, published a long interpretive essay on the relevance of the Adi Granth in building social and moral order in the twenty-first-century.[63] In a convoluted way, the essay argues that the Sikh community needs to build on the teachings of the Adi Granth in order to meet the challenges of changing times. Some scholars interpreted Grewal's argument as a challenge to the fundamental Sikh belief in the timeless nature of the contents of the Adi Granth. They invoked the Akal Takhat to investigate the issue and punish Grewal for opposing Sikh beliefs in the revealed nature of the Adi Granth.

In the wake of the controversies involving Piar Singh and Pashaura Singh, the SGPC authorities rightly realized the limitations of their role in debates dealing with scholarly issues. The outcome of this controversy was thus different. While Grewal was asked to appear before the Akal Takhat, he was exonerated. It was made clear that the Akal Takhat was no longer available to intervene in scholarly debates. This episode brought to an end an unfortunate detour in the history of the SGPC, which as a body has been very supportive of research on Sikhism and had patronized scholars who made major contributions toward the textual studies of the Adi Granth.[64]

My *Goindval Pothis: The Earliest Extant Source of the Sikh Canon* was published in 1996.[65] This is by far the most detailed study of this sixteenth-century manuscript. In the opening section, I argue for the traditionally accepted dating and positioning of the Goindval Pothis in the expansion of the Sikh sacred corpus. In the second section, I present details of the contents of both the extant pothis and provide the text of the compositions that are present in the Goindval Pothis but do not appear in the later Sikh manuscripts. This basic information about these early pothis will help trace the expansion of Sikh sacred corpus. The contents of the Goindval Pothis confirm that at the time of their compilation the entire corpus of the hymns of the first three gurus was available. If indeed Guru Arjan used the Goindval Pothis to compile the Kartarpur Pothi, my study reveals that there would not have been a need for any additional written or oral sources for the hymns of the early gurus. The text of the Goindval Pothis, when collated with that of the Kartarpur Pothi, indicates that the variations in the two texts are not substantive but resulted primarily from scribal preferences in writing.

Pritam Singh's long-awaited research on the Goindval Pothis was released by Guru Nanak Dev University Press in late 1998.[66] The book opens with a critical survey of existing writings on the Goindval Pothis from Kesar Singh Chhibbar up to Piar Singh. In the main body of the book, Pritam Singh describes the physical features of the pothi, at Jalandhar and presents a comparison of its contents with that of the published edition of the Adi Granth. In the concluding part, a set of appendixes includes a commentary from an international forensic criminologist on the handwriting of the manuscript, and a bibliography.

Pritam Singh rejects the traditional notion that the pothi was a source for Guru Arjan's compilation, which eventually culminated in the text of the Adi Granth. His argument is based on the nature and abundance of textual variants between the pothi and the Adi Granth. He examines a set of thirteen compositions attributed to Gulam Sadasevak—who he thinks are two poets—and identifies Gulam with Baba Mohan, the son of Guru Amardas. The presence of these hymns, supposedly composed by Baba Mohan, is his justification for rejecting the idea that the Bhallas inherited the pothi from Guru Amardas. Instead, he argues that the pothi was compiled by Baba Mohan in order to challenge the authority of Guru Arjan.

It was unfortunate that Pritam Singh did not have access to the pothi he describes in detail in his work, nor did he succeed in examining the Goindval Pothi at Pinjore to be able to compare the two documents. His primary data, as he himself admits, come from Piar Singh and in his analysis, too, he follows Piar Singh's general argument that these pothis resulted from independent efforts at collecting Sikh sacred writings within the early Sikh community. Note that Pritam Singh does not accept the authenticity of either the Kartarpur Pothi or the Kanpur Pothi.[67]

W. H. McLeod, the leading Western scholar of Sikhism, has made an important contribution to Sikh scriptural studies. In three of his articles on Sikh sacred literature, he has sought to locate the compilation of Sikh scripture within a larger historical perspective.[68] He has cogently argued that more research is needed on the early Sikh manuscripts before their mutual relationship or special contribution to the evolution of the Sikh text can be accurately established. He has proposed that more work be done to locate the sources to which Guru Arjan had access at the time he was preparing the Kartarpur Pothi. McLeod has also raised important questions about the emergence of the text of the Adi Granth, its conversion into the authoritative Guru Granth Sahib, and its precise function in the present-day Sikh community. Any serious discussion of Sikh scripture and the reconstruction of the history of its making should address these fundamental issues, as I do in later chapters.

J. S. Grewal, the leading Sikh historian, has made an indirect, yet crucial, contribution to this area of study. His seminal research on early Sikh history, including his analysis of dissidence at that phase, created a context in which the history of the Sikh text and the rise of the institution of Sikh scripture could be effectively understood.[69] More recently, he has focused on current controversies in the area of textual studies and analyzed the issues in great depth. In the process, Grewal called for a more sophisticated conceptualization of studies pertaining to the Adi Granth. He rightly points out that the present scholarship in textual studies represents "a kind of confluence of the Western and Sikh streams of interest" and makes an interesting claim that "the textual criticism does not have the same kind of importance in Sikh studies as in Biblical studies."[70]

To conclude this survey of writings on the Adi Granth, one may safely say that the authority of the Adi Granth within the Sikh community began to be evoked soon after the death of Guru Gobind Singh. The references to the text's authority as well as its key role in Sikh ritual life begin to appear in the early eighteenth-century sources and reach a fairly elaborate level of detail by its end. The role of the Adi Granth in Sikh worship continued to expand during the nineteenth century, and it attained a systematized form in the authoritative Sikh code of conduct (*Sikh Rahit Maryada*) produced in the middle decades of the twentieth century under the auspices of the SGPC.[71]

Varied views on the history of the compilation of the Adi Granth continue within the Sikh community. The story of the making of the Adi Granth heard in the *gurdwaras* is synthetic, selectively appropriating the accounts available in early sources. Our knowledge of the origin of Sikh scripture is based on Chaupa Singh's account, according to which Guru Arjan created the Sikh text, the Kartarpur Pothi, to protect Sikh sacred literature from the Miṇas' effort to meddle with it. The description of how the hymns of the gurus were collected comes from Giani Gian Singh's account, according to which the Sikh hymns were available primarily in oral form and collected with great effort by Guru Arjan over a long period of time. The explanation for the variations in the early scriptural manuscripts derives from the mid-nineteenth-century accounts, which claim that they resulted from continuing attempts to interfere with the purity of the Sikh text. Giani Gian Singh's account explains the compilation of the Adi Granth, understood to have been created by Guru Gobind Singh at Damdama, Bhatinda, in 1705–1706, when he recited the entire text from his memory to Bhai Mani Singh, who wrote it down. This text created at Damdama is believed to have attained the status of the Guru Granth Sahib and is thought to be identical with the printed text at the heart of Sikh worship all over the world.

Although the traditional accounts of the history of Sikh scripture continue to be heard in the *gurdwaras*, scholars working in the twentieth century have succeeded in advancing the discussion to a point where a more accurate understanding of the whole issue is well within reach. Sahib Singh and Teja Singh's studies help us understand the compilation of the Sikh text as an evolutionary process. Their research also provides us with sufficient internal evidence to argue that the preservation of the hymns of the gurus in written form began early in the tradition. Other investigations, beginning with G. B. Singh, supply information about the early manuscripts, which were landmarks in the evolution of Sikh scripture. Within the context of this available information, I analyze the data available in early manuscripts and in the following chapters offer my reconstruction of the history of the Adi Granth.

3

The Beginning of the Scriptural Tradition

The traditional Sikh sources refer repeatedly to two sixteenth-century scriptural manuscripts. One is said to have been in the custody of Prithi Chand, the elder brother of Guru Arjan and a fierce contender for his office; the other was reportedly with Baba Mohan, Guru Amardas's son, who challenged Guru Ramdas's succession to his father's office. Guru Arjan's preparation of the Kartarpur Pothi was believed to be a direct response to the manuscript in the family of Prithi Chand, and the actual preparation of the Kartarpur Pothi was thought to have used the Goindval Pothis, which were borrowed from Baba Mohan for this purpose. These two manuscripts are now known in Sikh tradition as the Guru Harsahai Pothi and the Goindval Pothis, respectively.

Although the existence of the Guru Harsahai and Goindval Pothis is taken for granted, there is no inclination on the part of early writers to refer to their actual contents or to assign these documents any distinct significance as the precursors of the Kartarpur Pothi. Instead, the widely accepted position holds that once the Kartarpur Pothi—an up-to-date version of the Sikh sacred corpus—was compiled, the earlier manuscripts automatically became redundant. The fact that these documents have been in the custody of families in competition with families of the Sikh gurus pushed them farther into oblivion. The Sodhi and the Bhalla families, the custodians of these documents, however, have treated them as objects of great sanctity and have held them through the last four centuries as markers of their illustrious spiritual heritage.

It was only in the early decades of the twentieth century that scholars became increasingly aware of the tremendous significance of these early manuscripts and attempted to examine them. New awareness of the historical value of these pothis resulted in the SGPC's decision in the 1930s to go to the law courts to acquire them. The SGPC authorities claimed that as the Sikh national organization, it had the right to acquire all historical relics to ensure their preservation for posterity. The courts, however, ruled that these documents were the families' private property and dismissed the SGPC's contention to be the rightful owner of these relics.[1] The result of this episode was that the custodian families became excessively protective of the documents and distrustful of any efforts even to view them, no matter how sincere.[2]

In the past several years, I have been extremely fortunate in being able to collect data pertaining to these two early manuscripts. Haresh Singh Sodhi, the current occupant of the Sodhi *gaddi* (seat of authority) at Guru Harsahai, kindly shared with me family traditions regarding the history of the Guru Harsahai Pothi and provided me with the photographic copies in his possession. The Bhalla custodians of the Goindval Pothis presently at Jalandhar and Pinjore were also kind to allow me to extensively examine their invaluable manuscripts.

In this chapter I focus on these two early manuscripts and address questions of their history, dating, and location in the formation of the early Sikh sacred corpus. I attempt to fill a significant gap in the scholarly understanding of these rare documents and describe their role in the beginnings and early development of the Sikh scriptural text.

The Guru Harsahai Pothi

This pothi was in the custody of the Sodhi family in the village of Guru Harsahai until 1970, when it was reported stolen during a train journey from Delhi to Ferozepur. The Sodhis were returning from a family visit to Faridabad. The suitcase from which the pothi was stolen also contained a rosary of brown and white beads (*mala*), a precious stone (*padam*), and substantial cash offerings made to these relics during their public display in the house of the Sodhi host.[3] The pothi, the rosary, and the precious stone are all associated with Guru Nanak, according to the Sodhi family traditions. The robber[s] took with them only the pothi; the other items and the money in the suitcase were left untouched. The first investigation report was filed at the police station in Nirvana, the next railway stop after the theft. The police failed to act with expediency and the whereabouts of the pothi have remained unknown ever since. The circumstances of the pothi's loss strongly suggest that it was not a case of simple train burglary, and consequently there is a fair possibility that the pothi is now in some private collection.[4]

History of the Pothi

The Sodhis of Guru Harsahai, the former custodians of the pothi, are descendants of Prithi Chand. The history of the family and their precious possessions is not difficult to reconstruct. We have definite evidence that Prithi Chand refused to accept Guru Arjan as the lawful successor to his father's office but was unable to pose a viable threat to Guru Arjan's authority at Amritsar. Therefore, he eventually moved to Hehar, a village near Lahore, built a temple with a pool, and formally established his *gaddi* there in the mid 1590s.[5] When the Sikhs under the leadership of Guru Hargobind were forced to evacuate Amritsar in the early 1630s, Miharban, son of Prithi Chand, moved to the Darbar Sahib, Amritsar, the central seat of Sikh authority in previous decades. At the time of the death of Hariji (d. 1696), son of Miharban, there was struggle for succession among his three sons, which resulted in the weakening of the family's following and their virtual ejection from the Darbar Sahib in 1698.[6] Hargopal, the elder son of Hariji, went on to establish his new seat in Muhammadpur, near Chunian, Lahore, and the family spent the next half-century or so in this area.[7] The Sodhis developed problems with the administration of Ahmad Shah Abdali in the middle decades of the eighteenth century, and the sixth in line from Prithi Chand, Jiwanmal, left Chunian and settled in the Malwa region. This area was a wasteland inhabited by the Dogar Muslims and the Braṛ Sikhs. Sultan, the local Dogar chief, encouraged Jiwanmal to base himself there and serve as a buffer between the Muslims and the Sikhs. Jiwanmal founded a new village after the name of his son, Guru Harsahai, in 1752, and successfully mediated between the Sikhs and the Dogars. The Sodhi family was eventually able to rectify its problems with the Abdali administration at Lahore, which in turn brought about the recognition of their lands at Muhammadpur and Hehar as revenue-free grants.[8]

In the last quarter of the eighteenth century, Guru Harsahai's son, Ajit Singh (d. 1813), worked out a close relationship with the Khalsa, which provided him with an opportunity to expand the family influence within the larger Sikh community. The presence of the portraits of the Sikh gurus, from Guru Hargobind to Guru Gobind Singh, in murals of the Sodhi fort at Guru Harsahai (*kilah sahib*) built during this period is evidence that the family at this time publicly recognized the authority of the later Sikh gurus, whom their ancestors regarded as rivals during the seventeenth century.[9]

The recognition of the Sodhis as a chief family of the Malwa region was manifested by the initial treatment of their lands as a "protected Sikh state" by the British.[10] This status was eventually amended and the Sodhis were confirmed as *jagirdars* with revenue-free lands (35,796 acres in Guru Harsahai village), according to the settlement reports of 1851. An illustrious spiritual lineage, the possession of large landholdings in the area, and the assistance the family lent to the British during the 1857 crisis resulted in the preferential treatment the British accorded the Sodhis in the following decades. A protracted family litigation for the succession of Fateh Singh followed his death in 1887. Bishan Singh (d. 1910) finally won the lawsuit and his line continues, but this expensive litigation and related strife impaired the family's prestige.

According to the Sodhi family traditions, the pothi along with the *mala* and the *padam*, resided with their family since the time of Guru Ramdas, the first Sodhi Guru. Hariji, writing in the second half of the seventeenth century, claims that Guru Ramdas gave this pothi to his younger son Guru Arjan, who then gave it to his older brother Prithi Chand. And thus it came to what became the Guru Harsahai branch of the Sodhi family. This explanation corresponds with the Sodhi family's belief about their spiritual lineage, which designates them the rightful successors to the high office of Guru Nanak through Guru Arjan.[11] The fact that they controlled the Darbar Sahib during most of the seventeenth century has further strengthened this perception, in their own eyes as well as in those of their followers.

There is an alternative explanation of the acquisition of the pothi by Prithi Chand, besides the one offered by the family itself. Given the serious dispute over succession, it is reasonable to argue that Prithi Chand would have acquired the rare pothi present in his father's household and thought to have belonged to Guru Nanak, and then used it to buttress his own claim to serve as guru within the community. According to the discussion later in this chapter, the Bhalla descendants of Guru Amardas had already posed a parallel challenge by virtue of their possession of the Goindval Pothis—first against Guru Ramdas and then against Guru Arjan. Following the example set by the Bhallas, then, it is plausible that Prithi Chand acquired the pothi in his attempt to establish his leadership.

Once acquired, the pothi was projected as the symbol of authority within the lineage of Prithi Chand. According to Hariji, the pothi constituted the central component of their ceremony of succession (*dastarbandi*).[12] This ceremony, Hariji reports, included the incumbent guru's placing a mark (*tilak*) on the forehead of his successor, tying a turban on his head, and presenting the pothi to him, the first two steps mere preliminaries to the actual transmission of the pothi. Detailed descriptions in the writings of Hariji emphasize the high degree of reverence in which the pothi was held by the family, and this reverence continued until the pothi's unfortunate disappearance in 1970.

Regardless of how they acquired it, there are no grounds for challenging the claims of Prithi Chand's family to possession of the pothi. Nor is there any problem with the family's assertion that they carried the pothi with them when they departed from Amritsar. Although little is known of the happenings at their seat in Muhammadpur, Chunian, the presence of the pothi at Guru Harsahai has been beyond dispute. Even today the residence of the Sodhi family in Guru Harsahai is known both in popular discourse and in the local revenue papers as the *Pothi Mala Sahib* (abode of the pothi and the rosary).

Sodhi tradition regarding the possession of the pothi of Guru Nanak made its way into non-Sodhi writings as well. Nineteenth-century sources such as Khushvakat Rai's *Tarikhe Sikhan* (History of the Sikhs) and Sohan Lal Suri's *Umda-ut-Tvarikh* (Important History) report the Sodhis' claim to possess an early pothi.[13] The pothi surfaced importantly as the central symbol of Sodhi religious authority during family litigation in the 1880s, and British administrators such as Lepel Griffin, writing at the end of the nineteenth century, mention that the pothi was in the Sodhi family's custody.[14] In *Mahan Kosh*, published in 1930, Bhai Kahn Singh Nabha also refers to the presence of an old pothi said to have once belonged to Guru Nanak and now residing with the Sodhi family.[15]

The firm tradition within the Sodhi family of its possessing the rare Guru Harsahai Pothi, and general acceptance of this fact among outside writers, was at the core of the SGPC's attempt to acquire the document. As mentioned in the preceding discussion, in the 1930s the SGPC authorities filed a lawsuit against the Sodhi family, arguing that the pothi, a Sikh national relic, should be handed over to the central Sikh organization. The efforts of the SGPC failed, however, and the courts affirmed the Sodhis claim that the pothi was their private property.

The fifth centennial celebrations of the birth of Guru Nanak in 1969 produced a unique situation in the history of the Guru Harsahai Pothi. The Punjab government asked the Sodhi family to bring the Guru Harsahai Pothi to Patiala to enhance the solemnity of the state-sponsored festivities. Jaswant Singh Sodhi, the scion of the family at that time, was persuaded to cooperate with the government and the pothi was brought and briefly put up for display at the Central Public Library, Patiala.[16] This was the first trip the pothi had made since its arrival in the Guru Harsahai area in the mid eighteenth century. The success of the Patiala visit, nonetheless, set the precedent for taking the pothi to the homes of influential followers of the Sodhi family. It was during such a trip to a family in Faridabad that the pothi was stolen in 1970.

As I stated in the preceding discussion, there is no basis for challenging the family's claim that the pothi and other relics had remained in its possession since the sixteenth century. There are legitimate reasons to believe that Prithi Chand acquired the pothi to strengthen his case against Guru Arjan, and the importance assigned to it in the seventeenth-century literature generated by the family indicates the centrality of the polthi's role in their ceremonies. The pothi moved with the Sodhis from Amritsar to Guru Harsahai, and from that point on it remained in their custody. The pothi and other relics were used for a public display on Vaisakhi, at the beginning of the summer, when Sodhi family followers from throughout the region gathered at Guru Harsahai. The fair continues to be held to this day.[17] The circumstances of its first departure from Guru Harsahai are perfectly clear and its eventual disappearance is a matter of public record.

The Date of Compilation

There are two conflicting claims about the dates of compilation of the Guru Harsahai Pothi. The Sodhi writings report that the pothi in their possession was the original manuscript prepared during Guru Nanak's lifetime. The claim appears for the first time in the writings of Hariji and persists in the family traditions; it is also referred to in independent sources that emerged in the nineteenth century. As discussed in the chapter 2, Sikh writings on the history of Sikh scripture do refer to the existence of a pothi in the custody of the Sodhi family but attribute its compilation to Miharban.

This assessment, which was first alluded to by Chaupa Singh and enunciated by Kesar Singh Chhibbar, is problematic. If accepted, it would locate the creation of the Guru Harsahai Pothi between the birth of Miharban in 1581 and the writing of the Kartarpur Pothi in 1604. Chhibbar argued that Miharban compiled a pothi containing the hymns of the first four gurus and his own. The argument that Miharban, while barely in his early twenties, compiled a pothi that so threatened the purity of Sikh sacred literature that Guru Arjan was compelled to prepare the Kartarpur Pothi, is not convincing. What is convincing is this: for such a line of thought to develop, there must have been a firm tradition regarding the presence of an old pothi within the family of Prithi Chand. Yet the effort to explain the contents of this pothi and its role in the evolution of the sacred Sikh text seems to have resulted from a later, and inaccurate, interpretation of early Sikh history.

In my view, the original Sikh understanding of "spurious writings" (*kachi baṇi*, AG, 920) underwent a radical change in the later Sikh tradition. Guru Amardas coined this term for compositions that were rejected from incorporation into the Sikh text because of their belief in the divine incarnation of the deity. At some point the motive of safeguarding the sacred Sikh writings and keeping them separate from spurious ones was attributed to the compilation of the Sikh scriptural text and in the subsequent period it completely captivated Sikh scholarly imagination. This leaves us with only one option: to scrutinize closely the Sodhi family's claim about the origin of the Guru Harsahai Pothi. There are early independent Sikh traditions regarding Guru Nanak's life (not the Sikh text per se) which corroborate the Sodhi assertion regarding the origin of a pothi during his time. The belief that Guru Nanak possessed a pothi containing his hymns surfaces in the compositions of Bhai Gurdas and the janam-sakhi accounts, both written in the early seventeenth century.[18]

In addition, a janam-sakhi account reports that the pothi was duly given to Guru Angad as part of the succession ceremony. This description attributes a high degree of importance to the pothi as a symbolic marker of the succession of authority. Within the lineage of Prithi Chand, it is significant that Guru Harsahai Pothi continued to play the central role in the succession ceremony until 1970.[19] Here we must emphasize that although Sikh traditions do refer to a pothi associated with Guru Nanak, eventually given to Guru Angad, they are silent about its later history. In the accounts available in the janam-sakhis and the writings of Bhai Gurdas, no direct physical link is made between Guru Nanak's pothi and the one in the custody of the Sodhis. The Sodhi writings, however, claim that the original manuscript prepared during the lifetime of Guru Nanak was in their possession and that it came to them through the line of the gurus.

Evidence to prove that the Guru Harsahai Pothi originated early enough to have been compiled by Guru Nanak himself could have come from the textual data available in the pothi itself. Its current unavailability makes dating it difficult but not entirely impossible. Thanks to the efforts of Giani Gurdit Singh, we have photographs that can help us assess the Sodhi claim that their pothi was created during the lifetime of Guru Nanak. The photographs of the opening section of the Guru Harsahai Pothi show that its script is of extremely early origin. The symbol for the vowel (*kanna*) is left almost entirely unrecorded, and when it does appear, it is in the form of a dot instead of its later shape of half a line. Several letters have not yet attained their standard Gurmukhi forms: /i/, /chh/, /ṭh/, /d/, /j/, and /l/, and the line on the top of the letters follows the Devanagari traditions. To anyone familiar with early Gurmukhi, these photographs confirm that the Guru Harsahai Pothi was compiled at a very early stage in the evolution of Gurmukhi writing.

The invocation (*mangal*, *mulmantar*, or *sirlekh*) recorded on the opening folio of the Guru Harsahai Pothi reads as follows:

> *Oankar sachnam kartar*
> [One] God, the true name, the creator.[20]

This text corresponds closely with the hymns of Guru Nanak. The opening symbol, "ਓ" (*oam* or *oankar*), appears fourteen times in the hymns of the gurus: seven in Guru Nanak, one in Guru Amardas, one in Guru Ramdas, and five in Guru Arjan. The verbal form of ੴ (*ekoankar*), which replaces ਓ in the Kartarpur Pothi, appears some twenty-one times in Guru Arjan's hymns.[21] This may suggest that the word *oankar* was replaced by *ekoankar* in the hymns of the Guru Arjan, a preference apparently reflected in the canonical text of the invocation.

The same type of situation appears with the remaining two segments, *sachnam* and *kartar*, in the Guru Harsahai Pothi. In the hymns of Guru Nanak, both these words appear together (*Bolahu sachunamu kartar*, M1, AG, 1329), as well as separately. This is not true of the words that replace them in the Kartarpur Pothi. Guru Nanak never uses the word *satinamu*, which replaces *sachnam* in the Kartarpur Pothi. It appears for the first time in Guru Ramdas's hymns and takes on significant conceptual content in the hymns of Guru Arjan. Guru Ramdas writes, "O my mind, meditate on the true name always on the true name" (*Japi man satinamu sada satinamu*, M4, AG, 670), and Guru Arjan claims that *satinamu* is the primal name of God (*Satinamu tera para purbala*, M5,

AG, 1083). The words *karta purakhu* appear only thrice in the hymns of Guru Nanak (AG, 138, 1025, and 1291), in contrast to *kartar,* which is used thirty times. Thus, the verbal elements of the invocation recorded in the Guru Harsahai Pothi are more closely tied to Guru Nanak than the corresponding words that appear in later manuscripts.

Giani Gurdit Singh reports that the opening section, the original text of the Guru Harsahai Pothi, contains only the hymns of Guru Nanak.[22] To date, no comparable manuscript that records the hymns of Guru Nanak, and him alone, has come to light. All other manuscripts we know of contain his hymns followed by those of his successors at different stages in the development of the Sikh text. A plausible explanation for the uniqueness of the Guru Harsahai Pothi is that when this section was compiled, the hymns of Guru Nanak were the only ones available and were duly recorded.

Giani Gurdit Singh confirms that there is no attempt to place the hymns according to their *rag* assignment in this section, which also suggests that it was recorded early. Although the hymns are set to *rags*, which in all likelihood was done by Guru Nanak himself, they are recorded in a loose sequence, and without any consideration for the number of stanzas or for generic divisions as we see them in the later manuscripts.

Furthermore, available data enable us to establish the textual relationship between the Guru Harsahai Pothi and the Goindval Pothis. I believe that the hymns of Guru Nanak quoted in the Sodhi family literature came from the opening section of the Guru Harsahai Pothi. For example, the music-related category of *ghar* assigned along with the *rag* in which the hymns available in the Kartarpur Pothi are to be sung, is completely absent in the citations of the hymns of the gurus in Miharban and Hariji's writings. This in turn suggests that the Guru Harsahai Pothi, the source of the hymns of the early Sikh gurus at the disposal of this family, did not include this classification. As we clarify further on in this discussion, this category is also absent from the text of the Goindval Pothis and appears for the first time in the Kartarpur Pothi and continues thence in the Adi Granth.

Other interesting details can be added. The text of Guru Nanak's *vars* found in the Sodhi writings contains only a string of stanzas, the original version to which couplets were added by Guru Arjan at the time of the compilation of the Kartarpur Pothi.[23] The filler "Ram," which appears at the end of the verse, in a special category of the hymns (*chhant*) of Guru Nanak, quoted in the writings of Miharban, is identical with the "Ram" that appears in the extant Goindval Pothis, but distinct from the one in the Kartarpur Pothi.[24] A hymn recorded in the section on *rag* Suhi appears under the authorship of Guru Angad in the writings of Miharban and in the Goindval Pothis but is attributed to Guru Nanak in the Kartarpur Pothi.[25] The shared authorship of this hymn and the Goindval Pothis, along with other textual details, point to the early origin of the Guru Harsahai Pothi.

This relatively limited but persuasive evidence of early orthography, the presence of a variant text of invocation, inclusion of the hymns of Guru Nanak alone, and lack of any principle of organization all suggest that the date of the opening section of the Guru Harsahai Pothi is the earliest in Sikh tradition. Later manuscripts reveal expansion of the pothi's contents through the addition of the hymns of Guru Nanak's successors and those hymns of the Bhagats, and the tightening of the organization of this poetic corpus.

The Internal Structure

According to Giani Gurdit Singh, the Guru Harsahai Pothi has two sections. One includes only the hymns of Guru Nanak, which begin with the *Japji* and the Sikh liturgical text and close with a hymn in *rag* Tukhari. Significant references to these two compositions appear in other sources as well.[26] The other section of the pothi includes the hymns of Guru Amardas and Guru Ramdas and a large number of hymns by the Bhagats. Giani Gurdit Singh also reports that the handwriting in this section is different from that in the opening section.

Giani Gurdit Singh believes that these two sections were inscribed at different times. According to him, the opening section was created during Guru Nanak's lifetime, as the Sodhi family traditions claim, and the second section was compiled by Miharban and appended to it. Giani Gurdit Singh's explanation incorporates both the Sodhi claim that they possessed the original pothi of Guru Nanak and the traditional Sikh view that Miharban compiled a manuscript in the later years of the sixteenth century.

Supporting evidence for the two-section hypothesis proposed by Giani Gurdit Singh is available. Although the script in both sections provides a glimpse into sixteenth-century Gurmukhi, the photographs confirm that the handwriting in the second section does not simply differ but also approximates the writing present in manuscripts such as the Kartarpur Pothi. As to the time of the second section's inscription, I propose a different explanation.

In my view, the opening section of the pothi containing the hymns of Guru Nanak can be dated in the 1530s as Sodhi traditions claim, and as other early-seventeenth-century writings affirm. As the traditions incorporated in the janam-sakhi literature suggest, this text came to Guru Amardas via Guru Angad as part of the succession ceremony. The document then served as the source for the preparation of the Goindval Pothis, which also utilized other sources containing the hymns of Guru Amardas himself and the hymns of the Bhagats. I believe that after the completion of the Goindval Pothis, the additional sources may have been appended to the original text of the Guru Harsahai Pothi. In the conflict of authority between Guru Ramdas and Baba Mohan, the Goindval Pothis, the up-to-date Sikh scriptural text at the time, were kept by Baba Mohan, but the rough (perhaps original) version found its way to Guru Ramdas. Guru Ramdas's hymns were eventually added to this text, and it came to Prithi Chand in that form.

The second section of the Guru Harsahai Pothi thus seems to have evolved slowly; different segments were appended to the original document at various points in time. A rare photograph of the pothi, which Haresh Singh Sodhi gave to me, indicates visible breaks between different sets of gatherings, which may have been added to the original text. The hypothesis that this section consists of several parts is supported by photographs in the possession of Giani Gurdit Singh showing more than one handwriting, and the presence of different types of folios, some with margins and others without them.

An interesting textual detail supports this argument. The text of Guru Amardas's *Anand* (Ecstasy), recorded in the Goindval Pothis, contains thirty-eight stanzas; the version that appears in the Sodhi writings includes thirty-nine stanzas, and the final version in the Kartarpur Pothi has forty stanzas. According to a tradition that appears for the first time in *Mahima Prakash*, the addition to the *Anand* included one stanza each by Guru Ramdas and Guru Arjan.[27] Understandably, the text of the *Anand* at the disposal of Hariji includes the stanza attributed to Guru Ramdas but does not contain the one appended by Guru Arjan. This places the second section of the Guru Harsahai Pothi squarely between the Goindval Pothis on the one hand, and the Kartarpur Pothi on the other.

The photographs of the opening section of the Guru Harsahai Pothi available with Giani Gurdit Singh do offer basic data to support the argument that this pothi was the earliest manuscript of Sikh tradition. If it was not the original manuscript that early-seventeenth-century sources attribute to Guru Nanak, it may have been a copy of that manuscript. The internal evidence concerning its contents and organization, and supportable and consistently held traditions of the Sodhi family, endorse the claim that the Guru Harsahai Pothi was the original compilation of the Sikh scriptural text. It is almost impossible to imagine a reverse process, for a relatively simple organization of the hymns would virtually have to have been the product of an early phase. The use of the Guru Harsahai Pothi as a symbol of authority by the family of Prithi Chand replicated attempts by other dissenting branches of the gurus' families at that time to boost their own authority over the wider community through possession of a scriptural text.

The Goindval Pothis

There is a set of manuscripts known in Sikh tradition as the Goindval Pothis. They are also called the Mohan Pothis, indicating their close association with Baba Mohan, in whose custody they remained after the death of his father, Guru Amardas. Traditions available in Sikh literature and the Bhalla family memories regarding these pothis claim that these manuscripts were prepared during the time of Guru Amardas and were inscribed by Sahansram, son of Baba Mohan.[28] At present, two of these pothis are extant and are in the custody of Bhalla descendants of Guru Amardas. One of them is at 371 Lajpat Nagar, Jalandhar, and the other is at Sundar Kuṭia, Pinjore.

If the claim that these pothis originated during the lifetime of Guru Amardas is accurate, the two Goindval Pothis hold the unique distinction of being the earliest extant manuscripts of Sikh tradition, given the current unavailability of the Guru Harsahai Pothi. In the following discussion, I attempt to locate these pothis in the evolution of the sacred Sikh text.

History of the Pothis

Tracing the history of the Goindval Pothis over the past four hundred years is surprisingly easy. According to Bhalla tradition, the pothis, from their completion during the time of Guru Amardas's leadership to the beginning of the twentieth century, remained at Goindval. Unlike the Sodhis of Guru Harsahai, who had to move several times during the past centuries, the Bhallas have remained at their base in Goindval.

According to reliable Sikh traditions, Guru Arjan borrowed these pothis from the Bhallas, brought them to Amritsar at the turn of the seventeenth century, and used them in the preparation of the Kartarpur Pothi. It seems natural that after this task was completed, the pothis were sent back; there is even an old palanquin in a Goindval gurdwara which, according to a popular local tradition, was used to transport the pothis to and from Amritsar.[29] In the closing years of the nineteenth century, we come across mention that the Goindval Pothis left Goindval again—this time to be brought to Patiala for viewing by the Sikh royal family in 1895.[30] After a brief visit, the pothis were taken back to Goindval.

We have already referred to the SGPC's effort to acquire the Guru Harsahai Pothi and the resulting lawsuit against the Sodhis there. Unlike the Sodhis, however, the Bhalla family avoided a legal battle with the newly formed Sikh body. Their strategy to prevent the pothis from falling under the SGPC's control was simply to send them away to family members living outside Goindval. The SGPC officials could not go to the court seeking custody of the pothis unless their precise location could be found.

At first, it was impossible to obtain knowledge of the new whereabouts of the pothis, but eventually two of them were located. One pothi had reached Bawa Dalip Chand in Ahiapur, District Hoshiarpur, and the other, Bawa Bhagat Singh, who was a resident of Hoti Mardan in the Peshawar area.[31] In the following decades, as the SGPC's claim to the pothis in the custody of the Sodhi families at Guru Harsahai and Kartarpur was rejected by the courts, the Bhalla fears of losing their pothis were largely allayed. The two families eventually began to display the pothis in their custody to the public once a month.

A few years ago Bawa Dalip Chand's family left Ahiapur and settled in Jalandhar. The pothi they had received is presently in the custody there of his son, Vinod Bhalla. In Ahiapur, it was customary to display the pothi every *sangrand* (the first day of the month according to the local calendar), but in Jalandhar this practice has largely been discontinued because of Vinod Bhalla's busy schedule. In special circumstances, if the Bhalla family is exceptionally kind to some visitor, then the pothi is put up for display on the morning of the *sangrand* and one is permitted briefly to view the text.

The other pothi came to Ludhiana, Patiala, and then to Pinjore, as the Peshawar Bhallas relocated after the partition of the Punjab in 1947. It is now in the custody of Bawa Bhagat Singh's son, Kanwarjit Singh Bhalla, and his family in Sundar Kuṭia, Pinjore. According to family tradition, the pothi is displayed on the morning of *puranmashi* (night of the full moon). At about ten o'clock a congregation begins to gather. After about an hour of singing hymns (*kirtan*), beginning with Guru Arjan's hymn in *rag* Gauṛi, which is in praise of Mohan—a common epithet for God—but believed by the family to be used for Baba Mohan, the pothi is unveiled and the congregation is given permission to view it. Normally, the pothi is open at folio 94; according to the Bhalla family memory, the writing there, *gulam mast taiḍa* Jeṭh Chand (Jeṭh Chand your intoxicated slave), is Guru Ramdas's signature. Jeṭh Chand was Guru Ramdas's name before he received the office of guru. At noon the pothi is put to rest (*sukhasan*) and members of the congregation are treated to a meal (*laṇgar*), with great hospitality by the Bhalla family.[32]

There appears to be no complication in this history of the Goindval Pothis. We have the testimony of Bhai Gurdas that after Guru Amardas passed away, his oldest son, Baba Mohan, established his own seat of authority at Goindval.[33] It is not surprising that Baba Mohan would have taken possession of the sacred manuscripts that were in his home and not given them to Guru Ramdas, the nominated successor to his father,

Guru Amardas. Goindval had been founded by Guru Amardas, and even today it is known as the central site of the Bhallas. There appears to be no doubt that the pothis remained in the care of the Bhalla family there.

But for the early tensions between Baba Mohan and Guru Ramdas, the relationship between the Bhallas and the mainstream Sikh community has remained cordial. The Bhalla genealogical tables indicate that several of them began to accept Singh names toward the last quarter of the eighteenth century, and we have on record the visits of Maharaja Ranjit Singh to Goindval and his large gifts to the family.[34] At the beginning of the twentieth century, the Bhalla family's anxiety, which was instrumental in sending the pothis away from Goindval and thus saving them from falling into the hands of the SGPC, is perfectly understandable. This phase of tensions also explains the Bhalla coldness toward any scholarly attempts to study the manuscripts in their custody. As circumstances have eased in the recent decades, the presence of the two Goindval Pothis has become public knowledge.

The Time of Recording of the Pothis

The two extant Goindval Pothis at Jalandhar and Pinjore contain no colophons to reveal their precise dates, but on the basis of internal and external information, it is possible to establish decisively the time at which they were inscribed. The shapes of both vowels and consonants used in the pothis are extremely old, and their close resemblance to those in the Guru Harsahai Pothi leave little doubt that these documents were prepared at an early stage in the evolution of Gurmukhi writings.[35]

Using some old Bhalla family documents, Bawa Prem Singh has located the inscription of the pothis between 1570 and 1572.[36] Others argue for the date of 1595.[37] In these two opinions regarding the date of origin of the Goindval Pothis, the difference of twenty-five years is extremely important. If 1595 were to be accepted as the correct date, it would be necessary to reject the entire tradition that locates their compilation during the lifetime of Guru Amardas.

The claim of 1595 is primarily based on a brief statement recorded in the opening folio of the pothi at Jalandhar. Building on a close scrutiny of the manner in which this statement begins on folio 1 and continues on folio 9, its attempt to establish the Bhalla family's spiritual superiority vis-à-vis the Sodhis, and the broader context of Bhalla-Sodhi competition during the 1590s, I have argued that 1595 is the date when this statement was inserted; that the presence of this statement is in itself proof that the pothis were prepared at an earlier date; and that when this was added in 1595, the pothis were already in the possession of the Bhalla family at Goindval.[38]

There is substantial evidence, however, to support the dating of the Goindval Pothis in the early 1570s. Fourteen compositions are recorded in the pothis under the name of Gulam Sadasevak (whose identity is addressed in the following discussion). These compositions are clearly part of the original writings of both the extant pothis and are recorded following the hymns of the Gurus and preceeding those of the Bhagats. Each composition ends with a verse including the signature "Nanak." Remarkably, the entire group has been crossed out of both extant pothis, but the text of all the compositions remains perfectly legible.[39]

According to Giani Gurdit Singh, the title Gulam Sadasevak was used for Guru Ramdas before he was elevated to the office of the guru; in other words, these fourteen compositions were written by Guru Ramdas prior to 1574.[40] As we noted earlier here, "*gulam mast taiḍa* Jeṭh Chand" is written on folio 94 of the pothi at Pinjore, and according to Bhalla tradition, this is understood to be Guru Ramdas's holy signature. If this belief is based on historical reality, then the pairing of "Jeṭh Chand" with "Gulam" is evidence that Guru Ramdas used the latter word as a name at the same time he was using Jeṭh Chand. Moreover, it is possible that since Guru Amardas decided to make Jeṭh Chand his heir, he gave him permission to use the authoritative signature of Nanak.[41] When later at Goindval, Baba Mohan found himself in competition with Jeṭh Chand, now Guru Ramdas, it is possible that he would have crossed out Jeṭh Chand/Gulam Sadasevak's writings from the pothis in his possession.

Thus several indications—Bhalla family tradition of Jeṭh Chand using the alternative name of Gulam, the recording of Gulam Sadasevak's compositions in the hand of the original scribe in the pothis, their placement following those of Guru Amardas in the text, and the most likely scenario as to why they were struck from the pothis—suggest that Guru Ramdas, before becoming guru, was the author of the compositions attributed to Gulam Sadasevak.[42] This in turn suggests that the pothis originated prior to 1574.

We may also call upon additional evidence to support the conclusion that the Goindval Pothis were prepared during the time of Guru Amardas. The early text of the invocation and the organization of the poetic corpus in the Goindval Pothis suggest that it was recorded prior to the Kartarpur Pothi.[43] The corpus of Guru Amardas's hymns in the pothis, however, is almost identical with that of his hymns as found in the Kartarpur Pothi. It can thus be stated decisively that all of Guru Amardas's hymns had been composed by the time the Goindval Pothis were prepared and that after this task was complete he did not create any new hymns necessary to include.[44] From this, one can conclude that these pothis were compiled during the final years of Guru Amardas's life and that Bawa Prem Singh was correct to date this around 1570.

The Original Number of the Pothis

In Sikh literature the hymns collected at Goindval were understood to have been placed in more than one pothi, but there is no clear agreement as to just how many pothis existed. The first reference to the number of these pothis comes in Giani Gian Singh's *Tvarikh Guru Khalsa*. He says there were two pothis, which is consistent with the fact that there are indeed two extant Goindval Pothis.[45] The difficulty, however, is that the description of the contents of one of the pothis discussed in *Tvarikh Guru Khalsa* does not accord with what we find in either of the extant pothis. In the Goindval Pothis he examined at Patiala, Giani Gian Singh saw hymns in *rags* Ramkali, Soraṭhi, Malar, and Sarang in one pothi, and hymns in *rags* Asa, Gauṛi, Sri, Vaḍhans, and Kanṛa in the other. In the second pothi the *rag* section on Kanṛa would have included only the hymns of Namdev, since the early gurus did not compose hymns in this *rag*. The first pothi in this description is identical with that presently to be found at Pinjore, but the second is not the same as the pothi at Jalandhar. Instead of the *rag* groupings outlined by Giani

Gian Singh, the pothi at Jalandhar contains hymns in *rags* Suhi, Prabhati, Dhanasri, Basant, Bhairo, Maru, and Tilang. There is no overlap, so it would seem clear that until the beginning of the twentieth century there were at least three Goindval Pothis, two of which were taken to Patiala, and one that is now at Jalandhar.

According to Piara Singh Padam and Giani Gurdit Singh, there were initially four Goindval Pothis, but neither has made an attempt to present any detailed supporting evidence.[46] According to information related to me by Man Singh Nirankari, another respected Sikh thinker, there were actually four pothis at Goindval in the early decades of the twentieth century: he saw them all during a visit there with his grandfather, a Nirankari guru, Sahib Gurdit Singh (1907–1947), in 1924–1925.[47] To my knowledge, Man Singh Nirankari stands alone in his crucial claim that there were four Goindval Pothis and that he had actually seen them all. Yet on the basis of internal and external evidence, a strong argument can be made to confirm that the Goindval Pothis were originally four in number.

The Kartarpur Pothi contains hymns by Guru Nanak and Guru Amardas in nineteen *rags*, and the hymns in each are grouped as a separate section. Of these nineteen *rags*, eleven are available in the two extant Goindval Pothis. The third Goindval Pothi, the one examined by Giani Gian Singh, contained hymns in four additional *rags*. If we accept as likely, on the basis of information earlier advanced, that the Kartarpur Pothi contains, in the appropriate *rag* sections, the hymns of these two gurus that were already present in the extant Goindval Pothis, then it would seem likely that hymns in those sections of the nineteen *rags* that were not present in the first three Goindval Pothis would have comprised the fourth pothi.[48]

As discussed in chapter 6, the combination of *rags* in each of the Goindval Pothis whose contents we know appears to reflect an interest in the equal pairing of male and female *rags*, that is, *rags* and *raginis*, and their association with the various times of the day: mornings, midday, evening, etc.. A hypothesized fourth Goindval Pothi would have fit nicely into such a scheme.

The historical context of the Sikh scriptural text can also inform us about the proper number of the Goindval Pothis. In our discussion above of the Guru Harsahai Pothi, we argued that the compilation of the scriptural text had begun during Guru Nanak's time. The Sikh effort to structure their scripture as four pothis may have resulted from their assumpton that two branches of scriptures (Veda and Kateb) contained four texts each.[49] On the Hindu side, the Veda forms itself into four collections (*samhitas*): Rig, Sama, Yajur, and Atharva; and following the Islamic understanding of sacred texts, the Sikhs believe that Judaism, Christianity, and Islam as a group possessed four divine texts: Toret (the Torah), Jumbur (the Psalms), Injil (the New Testament), and Qur'an. The existence of four pothis belonging to the Nanak Panth—the Goindval Pothis—would have seemed a fitting symbol of the Sikh claim to be a distinct religious tradition, parallel to the Hindu tradition on the one side, and the Semitic on the other.

There are convincing arguments, then, that four is the correct number of the Goindval Pothis. But only two are extant: where are the two missing pothis? One, plainly, is the Goindval Pothi seen by Giani Gian Singh in Patiala in the 1890s. We have seen how neatly his description of it accords with what we would expect to find. That leaves one remaining, and for that we must call to mind one of the memories of the Bhalla family residing at Pinjore. They believe that one pothi was given away as part of the dowry of a Bhalla girl married into a family in Phagwara. Unfortunately, they retain no information about when this marriage took place or where this family is now.[50] Hence it is quite possible that the two missing pothis still exist, but at unknown locations. Before we accept that two pothis are hopelessly lost, a communitywide attempt must be made to find them.

Internal Structure of the Pothis

The information contained in the two extant pothis provides important clues about the structure of early manuscripts and the evolution of the Sikh text. Further information to refine our understanding of the structure of the pothis can be gleaned from a close study of the appearance of the manuscripts themselves. I now turn, therefore, to a minute description of the extant Goindval Pothis, relevant to the question of their structure.

In both the extant pothis, the same light brown paper, which is becoming worn out in certain places, has been used. Each folio is carefully framed, but the custodians have no memory of when this repair was done. The folios are thirteen inches long and ten and one-half inches wide, and on the seam between each folio and its frame, a border of five lines is drawn. The opening folios of both pothis have geometric designs drawn in blue and gold on the upper left corner and include decorations in a wavy pattern in the portions left empty between lines of text. The pothi at Jalandhar has 300 folios, and the pothi at Pinjore has 224. In both pothis there are two separate numberings: one is given in the middle of the top side of the right folio and the other, in the top right corner. In literature on the pothis, the number in the top corner has conventionally been used, therefore, I also use that number here. Although the number is written on the right side of the folio, it is intended to include the left side as well. At the time of the binding of both pothis, some problems of numbering had resulted from the dislocation of folios from their original place.[51]

In my view the present appearance of the extant pothis can be explained as follows: The original sheet of paper would have been folded four times to create a gathering of eight folios. Then, before the actual writing began, each of these folded gatherings was given a number, which was written on the lower right corner of the last folio. At the time of binding, the spines of the gatherings were sewn first; then the gatherings were collected and sewn together. The pothi at Jalandhar now contains thirty-seven gatherings and the pothi at Pinjore, twenty-eight. Both pothis exhibit certain structural peculiarities, but these can be explained by close study and need not detain us here.[52]

Both of the extant Goindval Pothis are primarily in a single handwriting. The writing is very clear, and duplications, alterations in words, mistakes in counting of hymns, and other such discrepancies rarely occur. Where a word or verse has been left out, the scribe has made a "+" symbol and entered the text in the bottom margin. If a word has been accidentally duplicated, it is crossed out or covered in ink with great care. If a mistake has been made in the writing of a verse, it is carefully pasted over with a yellow substance, with the correct version written on top of that.

In addition to the handwriting of the primary scribe, another one appears in both pothis as part of the sections containing hymns of the Bhagats. Among other observable differences, the point of the pen used by this scribe must have been somewhat thicker than that preferred by the primary scribe. There are thirty hymns of the Bhagats in this hand, and they all appear in the last portion of various *rag* sections.

Hymns recorded by the second scribe have two special features. First, these hymns seem to have been inscribed on folios left blank at the end of *rag* sections in the original writing of the pothis. Second, not all hymns written in this hand appear in the Kartarpur Pothi. Additionally, in the pothi at Jalandhar, there are five hymns recorded in a third handwriting, one that makes unusually sparse use of vowels.[53]

A close examination of the pothis thus shows that they are primarily written in the hand of one scribe, whose work indicates excellent professional skills. To this original text of the extant pothis, thirty hymns of the Bhagats were added by another scribe. Since several of the hymns from this group do appear in the Kartarpur Pothi, one could surmise that this addition was made in the pothis soon after their compilation. The insertion of five hymns in a third hand and some odd additions in the titles, made at some point later in time, are not instrumental to our argument.

The Goindval Pothis have a very important bearing on the issue of blank folios in early Sikh manuscripts.[54] The blank pages in both the pothis can be divided into two distinct types. The first includes the pages that the scribe seems to have left blank because ink has seeped through or might seep through from the back of the page. For example, in the section on *rag* Soraṭhi, recorded in the pothi at Pinjore, there are five blank folios, which are left sides of folios numbered 131, 143, 145, 162, and 166. These are actually the back sides of folios 130, 142, 144, 161, 165, on which text is recorded. These blanks are thus connected primarily to the quality of paper. The other large set of blanks appears either at the end of a *rag* section or between the hymns of the gurus and those of the Bhagats. These blank folios resulted from the scribe's effort to keep various *rag* sections, and subsections within *rags*, separate from one another. In the same manner, the scribe has sometimes left blank pages at the end of groups of *chaupadas*, *chhants*, or *ashṭpadis*, within a given subsection of hymns of the gurus.

Here, it is necessary to reiterate that blank folios are found only at the end of *rag* sections and subsections of the hymns of the gurus. This fact leaves no doubt that the scribe knew he had all the hymns available to him prior to writing the Goindval Pothis. Thus, after Guru Nanak's *chhants*, for example, Guru Amardas's *chhants* begin directly; after Guru Nanak's *ashṭpadis*, begin Guru Amardas's *ashṭpadis*; and so forth. Hymns in all these groups are given a separate count.

The traditional explanation for the presence of blank folios in early Sikh manuscripts, pertaining primarily to the need for incorporating Guru Nanak's hymns, which is discussed later, is not supported by the data available in the extant Goindval Pothis.[55] The writing of the Goindval Pothis clearly runs continuously, and the scribe left no provision whatsoever for adding a hymn of Guru Nanak in the text.

Received wisdom on how early Sikh manuscripts were compiled is based on the view Bhai Jodh Singh popularized in his elaborate discussion of the Kartarpur Pothi. He argued that the scribe set aside a given number of gatherings for each *rag* section at the outset and later recorded the various hymns into the sections as their texts became available.[56] The evidence from the extant Goindval Pothis bearing on this issue points to a different method of writing. Instead of each *rag* section beginning on the first folio of a new gathering, it begins in the same gathering of the previous section after a few blank folios.[57] There is no evidence in the Goindval Pothis to suggest that particular gatherings were assigned in advance to particular *rags* and then hymns recorded in them. It is perfectly clear that the text of the Goindval Pothis was written serially. It is therefore untenable to argue that at the time of the preparation of the Kartarpur Pothi separate gatherings were kept for each *rag* section, even when the complete corpus of the text to be copied in it was available to the scribe.

In both of the extant Goindval Pothis, a special notation presents further evidence that the writing was accomplished continuously. In both pothis, after recording nine or ten folios of text, the scribe has drawn three or four lines at the end of a hymn and has entered a number below them, and this number becomes consecutively larger.[58] In my view, it denotes the work accomplished by the scribe in a single sitting and probably represents the method they used to keep records of their work in those days. There are both regular sittings, and exceptional ones. The scribe completed these long compositions in one sitting each. If the sign does denote a sitting of a scribe, then the pothi at Jalandhar was written in thirty sittings and the pothi at Pinjore in twenty.

On the basis of important information found in the extant Goindval Pothis, our understanding of the preparation of the early Sikh manuscripts should be revised in several ways. In the case of the Goindval Pothis, the primary scribe began writing on folio 2, and, leaving some folios blank in the process, wrote consistently until the end. Such an endeavor could only have been possible if the scribe already had at hand all of the text he wanted to copy. This leads us once again—and from a different point of departure—to the important conclusion that we can no longer accept Sikh traditional belief that the work of collecting and organizing the Sikh sacred hymns first occurred during the time of Guru Arjan. It was a much more gradual process, in which all the early gurus participated, and very probably it extends back to Guru Nanak.

The Place of the Goindval Pothis in the Transmission of the Early Sacred Corpus

Yet if this study challenges certain long-held notions, it confirms others. The textual evidence at our disposal enables us to determine insofar as possible the precise place of the Goindval Pothis in the early expansion of Sikh scripture, and it fully supports the traditional claim that these pothis are the primary source for the Kartarpur Pothi. The following discussion is centered on two principal aspects: the actual corpus of sacred hymns and their arrangement in a particular order.

We may begin by calling to mind, in another form, what I already reported about the contents of the two extant Goindval Pothis. Hymns in seven *rags* are available in the pothi at Jalandhar: Suhi [folios 2–62], Prabhati [folios 63–113], Dhanasri [folios 120–163], Basant [folios 169–227], Bhairo [folios 228–273], Maru [folios 277–292], and Tilang [folios 182–184 and 300]. The pothi at Pinjore includes hymns in four other *rags*: Ramkali [folios 2–121], Soraṭhi [folios 122–175], Malar [folios 183–215], and Sarang [folios 216–224]. To approach the issue of the evolving corpus of hymns in the early manuscripts, it is useful to compare this information with what we see in the Kartarpur Pothi.

Let us first consider the hymns of the gurus. In Table 2, column 1 gives the name of the *rag* section; column 2 indicates the number of hymns in a given *rag* in the extant Goindval Pothis; column 3 shows the number of hymns recorded in the corresponding

Table 2. A Comparison of the Number of Hymns of the Gurus in the Extant Goindval Pothis and the Kartarpur Pothi

Rag	G. Pothis	K. Pothi	Differences	
Suhi	31	32	+2	-1
Prabhati	34	33	+1	-2
Dhanasri	25	24	0	+1
Basant	38	38	0	0
Bhairo	32	32	0	0
Tilang	05	06	+2	-1
Ramkali	29	29	0	0
Soraṭhi	31	31	0	0
Malar	29	30	+1	0
Sarang	07	08	+1	0
Total hymns	261	263	+7	-5

section in the Kartarpur Pothi; column 4 gives the differences in terms of hymns added (+) and absent (-) in the Kartarpur Pothi from the corpus in the Goindval Pothis. *Rag* Maru also appears in the Goindval Pothis, but since it presents complications I have excluded it from the table.[59]

This table reveals only a minimal difference between the number of hymns of the gurus included in the extant Goindval Pothis and those that appear in the Kartarpur Pothi. The difference between these texts is further reduced when one considers two of Guru Nanak's hymns that appear in *rag* Prabhati in the Goindval Pothis and also in *rag* Suhi in the Kartarpur Pothi, folio 542, Adi Granth, pp. 730–731. The actual difference is thus limited to three hymns that appear in the Goindval Pothis but not in the Kartarpur Pothi, and five hymns that are present in the Kartarpur Pothi but not in the extant Goindval Pothis.

There are several possible explanations for these variations. The dropping of three hymns from the Kartarpur Pothi can be explained as accidental losses in the process of reorganization of the Goindval Pothis' text as it was copied into the Kartarpur Pothi.[60] The additions may be explained differently. As already noted, two hymns of Guru Nanak recorded in the Goindval Pothis in *rag* Prabhati are shifted in the Kartarpur Pothi to *rag* Suhi. We find other examples of such changes among the hymns of the Bhagats as well.[61] Inasmuch as *rag* changes did occur, it may be suggested that these hymns found in the Kartarpur Pothi were probably recorded originally in the Goindval Pothis in a different *rag* section, no longer extant.

As noted in the preceding discussion, the compilation of the Goindval Pothis took place during Guru Amardas's period. On the basis of a comparison of Guru Nanak and Guru Amardas's hymns in the Goindval Pothis and the Kartarpur Pothi, one can safely say that almost all hymns of these two gurus available in the Kartarpur Pothi are present in the corresponding *rag* sections of the Goindval Pothis. The Kartarpur Pothi thus included the text of the Goindval Pothis and the hymns created after their compilations by Guru Ramdas and Guru Arjan.

Judging from the way in which the corpus of Sikh scripture expanded from the Goindval Pothis to the Kartarpur Pothi, we can note with some satisfaction that the traditional view of the relationship between these pothis appears completely correct. Put simply, the Goindval Pothis became the basis for the further elaboration in the Kartarpur Pothi. Besides, we have no other manuscript comparable to the Goindval Pothis that could have served as the source of the Kartarpur Pothi. If we understand that the Guru Harsahai Pothi was compiled before the Goindval Pothis, then two major phases of the evolution of the Sikh sacred text in the sixteenth century come into clear focus.

This story begins with the Guru Harsahai Pothi. Here, only Guru Nanak's hymns appear—for the simple reason, I believe, that only they were available. The classification of *rags* according to which these hymns were meant to be sung was given in the titles, but in recording this manuscript there appears to have been no effort to organize the hymns on the basis of *rag*. In the Goindval Pothis, the size of the sacred corpus expands. Furthermore, it has been arranged according to *rag* sections, and the internal structure of these sections has become much more elaborate.

In addition to the supporting evidence, which suggests that the Goindval Pothis were the main source for the Kartarpur Pothi, there is also important external evidence from Sikh history. We have already referred to Bhai Gurdas's writings, which report that Baba Mohan rejected Guru Ramdas as his father's successor and established his own separate seat of authority at Goindval.[62] Under the circumstances of this competition, it is not surprising that Baba Mohan did not give the Goindval Pothis, which were kept in his house, to Guru Ramdas. Starting with the Bhallas, the possession of the early manuscripts by families who were in direct competition with the Sikh gurus is a historical fact. Baba Mohan had the Goindval Pothis; Prithi Chand had the Guru Harsahai Pothi; and as evidenced in the following discussion Dhirmal acquired the Kartarpur Pothi. These documents played an important role in claims for authority within the early Sikh community.

The later history of the Bhalla family, however, differs fundamentally from that of the Sodhi family, and this difference may account for the use of the Goindval Pothis at the time of the preparation of the Kartarpur Pothi. After Guru Ramdas passed away, the Bhallas continued to struggle for leadership, now against Guru Arjan. The text of the blessing at the beginning of the pothi at Jalandhar, referred to earlier, is clear evidence of the ongoing tension. In the beginning of the seventeenth century, during the time of the preparation of the Kartarpur Pothi, the family struggle between the Bhallas and Guru Arjan appears to have ended with the Bhallas' lending the Goindval Pothis to Guru Arjan. The question whether this settlement occurred because Guru Arjan himself went to Goindval, as tradition remembers or whether it came about for some other reason, is not relevant to our argument.

The seat of authority of Prithi Chand's family in Guru Harsahai, and Dhirmal's family in Kartarpur, are firmly established realities even today, but in the Bhalla family no such tradition of inheriting the office of guru ever became fixed. This fundamental difference is clearly reflected in Sikh documents related to the *rahit*. Any association with the families of Prithi Chand and Dhirmal, including their devotees, is proscribed, and the ban is still in effect in the Sikh community. Yet the Sikh *rahit* contains absolutely no mention of any such proscription regarding the Bhallas.[63] On the contrary, a tradition recorded in Kesar Singh Chhibbar's *Bansavlinama Dasan Patishahian ka* asserts that there was a relationship of mutual love and admiration between Baba Mohan and Guru Arjan.[64]

I argue that by giving Guru Arjan the Goindval Pothis at the time of the preparation of the Kartarpur Pothi, the Bhalla family not only gave the guru essential assistance at this all-important stage of the compilation of the Sikh scriptural text but also accepted his spiritual leadership. After this new turn in their relationship with Guru Arjan, there would no longer have been any purpose in retaining a seat of authority at Goindval, and the Bhalla family's running struggle with Guru Arjan would have ended permanently. The inclusion of Guru Arjan's hymn in the Bhalla family's ceremonial worship, and their displaying to the congregation the signature held to be that of Guru Ramdas, have long evidenced their alliance.

Thus we find no tension between three important sources for reconstructing the early history of the Sikh scriptural text. These are, namely, the internal evidence available in the early manuscripts, the history of the families that have made the claim of appointment as Sikh guru, and the traditions about the prominent place of the Guru Harsahai and the Goindval Pothis in the evolution of Sikh scripture. The hymns of Guru Nanak alone, as well as the complete absence of organization, are evidence that the Guru Harsahai Pothi was the original manuscript of Sikh tradition. The Goindval Pothis, which followed the Guru Harsahai Pothi, show the expansion of the sacred corpus and the evolution of its arrangement. On the basis of this information, we can form a clear picture of the development of the Sikh sacred text in the sixteenth century. This is cause for celebration. No other major religious tradition possesses manuscripts that illustrate the evolution of its scriptural sources so clearly.

4

The Expansion of the Scriptural Text

Sikh literature reports the compilation of the Kartarpur Pothi (1604) as a monumental event in Sikh scriptural history, to which the earlier pothis served only as an obscure backdrop. The making of the Kartarpur Pothi is presented in four succinct stages: Guru Arjan collected the hymns of the Sikh gurus and of the Bhagats; he carefully scrutinized the hymns of his predecessors to separate the authentic ones from the spurious; he established in detail the principles of organization of the text; and finally he dictated the selected corpus to Bhai Gurdas, thus creating the authoritative text for the Sikh community.[1] The Kartarpur Pothi is traditionally recognized as the locus in the history of the Sikh scriptural text.

This view misconstrues the process by which Sikh scripture evolved. Already in the sixteenth century, as we have seen, the contents and organization of the Sikh text had expanded significantly. So instead of producing the original scriptural text as Sikh tradition would have us believe, Guru Arjan's work in the compilation of the Kartarpur Pothi can be better described as an augmentation and elaboration of the process that began with the Guru Harsahai Pothi. Yet it was also a significant moment in the further definition of Sikh scripture.

In this chapter, I focus on this phase of expansion. I begin with MS 1245, a recently discovered document that suggests that an intermittent stage separated the compilation of the Goindval Pothis from that of the Kartarpur Pothi. In the sections that follow, I discuss the Kartarpur Pothi in detail: its history, dating, authenticity, and place in the transmission of the sacred Sikh corpus.

MS 1245

Pashaura Singh and Piar Singh were the first scholars to focus on the importance of this undated manuscript in the history of Sikh scripture.[2] The manuscript was acquired by the Guru Nanak Dev University library in March 1987 from the Chawla brothers, art and manuscript dealers in Amritsar. A note appended to the manuscript by the dealers at the time of its sale provides no details of its earlier ownership, and the Chawlas have refused to reveal any information about the manuscript's location prior to its purchase by the university.[3]

Without a history of the manuscript to even suggest where it was prepared, who wrote it, or where it resided during the past centuries, and without a reference in Sikh literature to any similar manuscript, our understanding of MS 1245 is restricted to the internal evidence provided by its text. I begin with a brief description of MS 1245 and then analyze its date and position in the evolution of the Sikh scriptural text.

The Internal Structure

MS 1245 opens with a set of twenty-seven unnumbered folios, four of which are extensively decorated with geometric motifs along their periphery; the central part of these illustrated folios is left blank for writing. The text of the manuscript begins on the left side of folio 28 and continues up to folio 1267, with blank folios appearing at the end of *rag* sections and the subsections within them. The margins are drawn vertically and the folio numbers are printed on the right side. In its general layout and penmanship, MS 1245 is extremely neat. It is primarily written in the hand of a single scribe, whose firm, accurate writing required very few corrections or additions in the margins.[4]

The text of MS 1245 is structured in three parts. The opening section contains the liturgical texts of the *Japji* and the *Sodar* (folios 28–37), the morning and evening prayers. The main body consists of thirty *rag* sections.[5] The last part includes the couplets and other miscellaneous hymns of the gurus (folios 1232–1262) and the panegyrics of the Bhaṭs (folios 1264–1267). In terms of its contents, MS 1245 contains the complete corpus of the hymns of the first four gurus. It also includes approximately fourteen hundred of Guru Arjan's hymns, which are twelve short of what appears in the Kartarpur Pothi and the Adi Granth.[6] Let us take, for instance, the case of *rag* Basant, which contains the largest number of the early gurus' hymns recorded in the Goindval Pothis (see table 3).

In addition to the hymns of the first five gurus, MS 1245 contains the three couplets by Mardana (folio 515), the *var* in *rag* Ramkali by Satta and Balvand (folio 819), the *Sadu* (Call) by Sundar (folios 858–859) also in *rag* Ramkali, and a set of panegyrics by the Bhaṭs (folios 1264–1267), all of which later appear in the Kartarpur Pothi and the Adi Granth.[7] With the exception of Kabir's couplets, which appear in the *vars* of Guru Amardas (*Gujri ki Var*, folio 477, and *Ramkali ki Var*, folio 890) and those of Guru Ramdas (*Bihagṛe ki Var*, folio 518), the hymns of the Bhagats are absent from the text. In the discussion that follows, I address in detail this striking feature of MS 1245.

The Time of Recording of MS 1245

MS 1245 does not contain a colophon, but its Gurmukhi orthography and other internal features point to its early origin. Within the early time range, however, scholarly assessments differ widely. Pashaura Singh argues for its origin in 1599 during the period of Guru Arjan; Piar Singh claims a later date, during the period of Guru Hargobind

Table 3. A Comparison of the Number of Hymns of the Gurus in Rag Basant in the Early Manuscripts

Author	G. Pothis	MS 1245	K. Pothi
Guru Nanak	20	18	18[a]
Guru Angad	00	00	00
Guru Amardas	18	20	20[a]
Guru Ramdas	00	08	08
Guru Arjan	00	24	24[b]

a. Two hymns attributed to Guru Nanak in the Goindval Pothis are recorded under Guru Amardas's name in MS 1245 (ff. 1076–1077), the Kartarpur Pothi (f. 843), and the Adi Granth, (pp. 1169–1170).

b. A composition attributed to Guru Arjan in MS 1245 (f. 1087) is absent in the Kartarpur Pothi, and three stanzas of Guru Arjan's *var* in *rag* Basant present in the Kartarpur Pothi (f. 854), and the Adi Granth (p. 1193), are absent in MS 1245.

(1606–1644); Balwant Singh Dhillon advances this dating still farther to the late seventeenth century.[8]

In light of the contents and structural features of MS 1245, there is sufficient data to suggest that it was compiled before the Kartarpur Pothi. Its text of the invocation is still evolving, not yet at the canonical level of the Kartarpur Pothi.

G. Pothis *1 Oankar satiguru parsadu sachunamu kartaru nirbhau nirikaru akalmurati ajuni sabhau*
One God, the true Guru's grace, true name, creator, without fear, without form, a form beyond time, unborn, self-born

MS 1245 *1 Oankar satinamu karta purakhu nirbhau nirvairu akalmurati ajuni saibhang satiguru parasadi*
One God, true name, person who creates, beyond fear and opposition, a form beyond time, unborn, self-born, with the grace of the true Guru

K. Pothi *1 Oankar satinamu karta purakhu nirbhau nirvairu akalmurati ajuni saibhang gurprasadi*
One God, true name, person who creates, beyond fear and opposition, a form beyond time, unborn, self-born, with the grace of the Guru.[9]

The text of the invocation in MS 1245 differs from the one in the Goindval Pothis. The term *nirikaru* (without form) in the Goindval Pothis is dropped in MS 1245. The *satiguru parsadu* (the true guru's grace), at the very opening of the text in the Goindval Pothis, is taken to the end in MS 1245, and its nominative form changed to *satiguru parasadi*, an instrumental form. The words *sachunamu* (the true name), *kartaru* (creator), *sabhau* (self-born) in the Goindval Pothis are replaced by slightly varied verbal forms *satinamu* (the true name), *karta purakhu* (person who creates), and *saibhang* (self-born) in MS 1245.

Although the replacements carry identical semantic content, their usage points to an evolutionary process in the text under discussion. As pointed out earlier with reference to the Guru Harsahai Pothi, the term *satinamu* is absent from the writings of Guru Nanak; its usage begins only in the hymns of Guru Ramdas and continues in the compositions of Guru Arjan. In the same way, the expression *karta purakhu* appears far more frequently in the hymns of the later gurus than Guru Nanak, who uses it only thrice. The word *saibhangh* in MS 1245 stands for the term *sabhau* that is found in the Goindval Pothis.

This analysis suggests links between the Guru Harsahai Pothi and the Goindval Pothis, on the one hand, and the Goindval Pothis and MS 1245 and the Kartarpur Pothi, on the other. All the changes that appear in the text of the invocation in MS 1245 continue in the Kartarpur Pothi. Only one further change is made: *satiguru parasadi* in MS 1245 is replaced with *gurprasadi*. The form of the word remains instrumental but it is abbreviated by dropping *sati* (true) and converting the *r* of the *parasadi* to its conjunct form *prasadi*. As the text of the invocation reached its final form in the Kartarpur Pothi, no further change is seen in the later manuscripts.

In the opening section of MS 1245, the text of the *Japji* does not contain the couplet that appears at its beginning in the Kartarpur Pothi and the Adi Granth.[10] Likewise, the text of the evening prayers is also in its early form in MS 1245. Its structure evolves as follows:

MS 1245	*Sodar* (five hymns)
K. Pothi	*Sodar* + *Sohila* (five hymns)
Adi Granth	*Sodar* + *Sopurakh* (four hymns) + *Sohila*

As mentioned, the main body of MS 1245 is divided into thirty *rag* sections. The overall *rag* sequence here differs considerably from that in the Goindval Pothis and appears only with slight alteration in the Kartarpur Pothi. *Rag* sections on Soraṭhi, Kaliaṇ, and Natnaraiṇ, which are recorded as section numbers 9, 12, and 13 in MS 1245, are positioned differently in the Kartarpur Pothi; here they are the eleventh, twenty-ninth, and nineteenth *rag* sections, respectively. *Rag* Gonḍ, which appears prior to *rags* Suhi and Bilaval in MS 1245, follows both of them in the Kartarpur Pothi.[11] This anomalous sequence of *rag* sections in MS 1245 makes sense only if we see it as part of the formative process that reached its final form in the Kartarpur Pothi and was then continued in the Adi Granth.

This is true for the internal structure of *rag* sections as well. In MS 1245, the tables of contents appear separately before each respective *rag* section. These tables include information about each hymn: its author, generic category, opening verse, and any necessary additional information (such as the tunes to which the *vars* were to be sung). The presence of these tables seems to locate the date of MS 1245 somewhere between those of the Guru Harsahai and the Goindval Pothis, which lack any tables of contents, and the Kartarpur Pothi and all later manuscripts, which contain a single table of contents located at the opening of their texts. (The twenty-seven folios at the opening of MS 1245, which were left blank, may have been included to record a master table of contents, but it was never inscribed and the folios were left unused.)

The sequence of *chaupadas*, *chhants*, and *ashṭpadis* in the Goindval Pothis appears as *chaupadas*, *ashṭpadis*, and *chhants* in MS 1245, and this altered sequence appears in the Kartarpur Pothi as well. There are other indications that the text of MS 1245 is located in the transitional stage between the Goindval Pothis and the Kartarpur Pothi. For example, the *Anand* of Guru Amardas in *rag* Ramkali in the Goindval Pothis (folios

55–80) follows the text of Guru Nanak's *Siddh Gosht* (Debate with the Siddhs). The same sequence appears in MS 1245 (folios 881–886). In the Kartarpur Pothi, however, the *Anand* follows the section on the *ashṭpadis* (folios 697–700), and it appears in this same position in the Adi Granth.

The final section of MS 1245 further attests to its early origin. Within the section on *Shalok Varan te Bahar* (Couplets surplus from the *Vars*), couplets attributed to Guru Amardas (folios 1236–1243) are listed according to their opening lines, in a very preliminary form. Since this section lacks a table of contents, the scribe only attempted to create a sequence with the hope of completing these couplets later. Opening verses followed by blank spaces also appear in other places in the manuscript.

In MS 1245, the scribal practice of recording opening verses and leaving blank spaces to fill in later is found only in connection with the hymns of Guru Arjan. Notably, these single verses followed by blank spaces are counted in the sequence as complete hymns. The likeliest explanation for these is that when MS 1245 was inscribed, Guru Arjan's hymns were still unavailable to the scribe in their final form. In the following thirty-six cases, only the opening verse was recorded in the original writing.

1. *Au hamare ram piare* (*rag* Majh, f. 117)
2. *Sevi satiguru apaṇa* (*rag* Majh, f. 144)
3. *Netr pragasu kia gurdev* (*rag* Gauṛi, f. 207)
4. *Dhan ohu mastaku dhanu tere netr* (*rag* Gauṛi, f. 207)
5. *Tuhai maslati tuhai nali* (*rag* Gauṛi, f. 208)
6. *Satiguru pura bhaiạ kripalu* (*rag* Gauṛi, f. 208)
7. *Dhoti kholi vichhae heṭhi* (*rag* Gauṛi, f. 208)
8. *Hai koi ram piaro gavai* (*rag* Gauṛi, f. 210)
9. *Hari ka namu ridai niti dhiai* (*rag* Asa, f. 386)
10. *Abh hari rakhanharu chitaria* (*rag* Dhanasri, f. 577)
11. *Mera lago ram siau hatu* (*rag* Dhanasri, f. 577)
12. *Aukhadu tero namu daial* (*rag* Dhanasri, f. 577)
13. *Din darad nivari ṭhakur* (*rag* Dhanasri, f. 578)
14. *Trisna bujhai hari kai nami* (*rag* Dhanasri, f. 583) [b]
15. *Kite prakari na tuṭao priti* (*rag* Dhanasri, f. 584)
16. *Hari mani tani vasia soi* (*rag* Soraṭhi, f. 634)
17. *Nali naraian merai* (*rag* Soraṭhi, f. 634)
18. *Karankravan hari antarjami* (*rag* Soraṭhi, f. 634)
19. *Hari hari namu sada sad japi* (*rag* Toḍi, f. 676)
20. *Acharaju katha maha anupu* (*rag* Goṇd, f. 694) [c]
21. *Tisu binu duja avaru na koi* (*rag* Suhi, f. 715)
22. *Sarab kaliaṇ kie gurdev* (*rag* Bialval, f. 770)
23. *Sarabh nidhan puran gurdev* (*rag* Bialval, f. 773)
24. *Hari hari aradhiai hoiai arog* (*rag* Bialval, f. 782)
25. *Parbrahm prabh bhai kirpal* (*rag* Bialval, f. 789)
26. *Sanjogu vijogu dhurahu hua* (*rag* Maru, f. 936
27. *Vaido na vai bhaiṇo na bhai* (*rag* Maru, f. 936)
28. *Bhai kau bhau paṛia simrati hari namu* (*rag* Bhairo, f. 1067)
29. *Dui kar jori karau ardasi* (*rag* Bhairo, f. 1067)
30. *Satiguri apanai suni ardasi* (*rag* Bhairo, f. 1067)
31. *Anik gian anik dhian* (*rag* Bhairo, f. 1067)
32. *Manorath pure satiguri api* (*rag* Sarang, f. 1107)

33. *Hari kai nam ki mati sar* (*rag* Sarang, f. 1123)
34. *Tua charan asarau is* (*rag* Sarang, f. 1123)
35. *Dusat mue bikhu khai ri mai* (*rag* Malar, f. 1163)
36. *Pran man eku namu* (*rag* Malar, f. 1165)

With the exception of verse 1, the completed versions of the remaining thirty-five hymns are present in the Kartarpur Pothi. The text of eight hymns numbered 10 to 14 and 23 to 25 is later inscribed in a different hand in MS 1245. The hymn incorporating verse 20 is recorded earlier in the text and begins with *Na uh buḍha na oh bala*.

Still more evidence supports the positioning of MS 1245 between the Goindval Pothis and the Kartarpur Pothi. Let us again take the example of Guru Amardas's *Anand* to illustrate this relationship. In its original version, in the Goindval Pothis, the *Anand* contains thirty-eight stanzas on folios 80–92. The text of the *Anand* in MS 1245 (folios 881–886) contains forty stanzas, and with some sequential variation, the same text is found in the Kartarpur Pothi (folios 697–700). Sikh tradition is aware of the textual expansion and attributes the thirty-ninth stanza to Guru Ramdas and the fortieth to Guru Arjan.[12] The early manuscripts—the Goindval Pothis, MS 1245, the Kartarpur Pothi, and the *Goshti Guru Amardas ki* (Debate of Guru Amardas), written by Hariji—tell a different tale.[13] In the following layout of the stanzas, S4 stands for the stanza composed by Guru Ramdas and S5 for the stanza by Guru Arjan, which are thought to have been added to the original text of the *Anand*.

Goindval Pothis	1–38
Goshti Guru Amardas ki	1–38, S4
MS 1245	1–37, S5, S4, 38
Kartarpur Pothi	1–33, S5, 34–38, S4

The evolution of the text in the later three manuscripts can be explained as follows: Guru Ramdas composed a stanza and added it to the existing text of the *Anand*, and both Guru Arjan and Prithi Chand had access to this expanded text. This early text, in the possession of the descendants of Prithi Chand and containing thirty-nine stanzas, appears in Hariji's *Goshti Guru Amardas ki*.

In the mainstream Sikh community, however, the text of the *Anand* evolved further. Guru Arjan added a stanza of his own to the text, which raised the number of stanzas to forty. Structurally, he kept the final stanza of the Goindval Pothis in its original position and placed Guru Ramdas's and his own stanzas before it. This sequence appears in MS 1245. In the Kartarpur Pothi, however, the changes are not as easily explained. To have placed Guru Ramdas's stanza at the end is perfectly understandable; it seems to have been written for that position. But the reasons for the shift of Guru Arjan's stanza following stanza number 33 in the original version are not at all clear, particularly because this shift does not fit thematically into the sequence of stanzas 32–37—all of which open by addressing an organ of the human body, with the exhortation that it should not forget its creator.[14] Whatever the reasons for this change, one thing is clear again—that the sequence of the final stanzas of the *Anand* in MS 1245 was still evolving, and the *Anand* attained its canonical form only in the Kartarpur Pothi.

The text of the *vars* in MS 1245 also points to its early origin. Physical evidence here suggests that the scribe lacked a complete text of the *vars* from which he could copy, but that he introduced couplets in the sequence of stanzas while inscribing the manuscript. There are several blank spaces within the text of the *vars*; folios 320, 814, 897, and 898 contain blanks that were filled in later; folios 476, 480, 483, 484, 897, and 1147 contain blanks that were not filled in at all. It appears that the scribe originally copied an existing text containing the stanzas, leaving blanks for the couplets still to be added. As he located appropriate couplets, they were duly recorded, usually in the hand of the primary scribe, but with a different pen in some places.[15]

A close examination of MS 1245 thus points to an origin earlier than that of the Kartarpur Pothi. Over fourteen hundred hymns of Guru Arjan are recorded here, and we know that the total corpus of his hymns in the Kartarpur Pothi contains only twelve or so more, which places the compilation of MS 1245 in the later years of Guru Arjan's life. Furthermore, Guru Arjan wrote a set of hymns that deal directly with events in the life of Guru Hargobind, Guru Arjan's only son.[16] The presence of all these hymns in their complete form in MS 1245 indicates that the manuscript was compiled after 1595, the year of Guru Hargobind's birth. The Kartarpur Pothi was completed in 1604, and if MS 1245 was indeed compiled before this time and after the birth of Guru Hargobind, then 1600 seems a safe date to propose.[17]

Reasons for the Compilation and Incompleteness of MS 1245

The internal evidence in MS 1245 justifies the date of inscription attributed to it reasonably clearly, but the question remains as to why a manuscript of 1,267 folios was compiled with such considerable care and labor and then left incomplete. Over and above this, how does one explain the absolute silence in Sikh literature about its compilation and then its existence through later centuries? Different explanations have been offered to account for its compilation.

Piar Singh believes that MS 1245 resulted from an independent effort to record the sacred Sikh hymns.[18] In his view, during the early period of Sikh history the manuscripts were being prepared in a loose manner. MS 1245 was therefore compiled by someone in a distant congregation with access to small portions of the writings of the gurus that were circulating within the community, and the very nature of this process of compilation explains the presence of all sorts of textual variants and differences in *rag* sequence.

There is no empirical evidence to support Piar Singh's argument that manuscripts were being compiled haphazardly in Sikh congregations at the turn of the seventeenth century.[19] As I argued in a preceding discussion, the Guru Harsahai Pothi in all likelihood was prepared at Kartarpur itself, and it remained in the custody of early gurus. The Goindval Pothis were compiled at Goindval, the center of the community during Guru Amardas's time. We also have the strong tradition claiming that the Kartarpur Pothi was compiled in Amritsar. In my view a manuscript of the size of MS 1245 could have been compiled only at the center of the community, and the presence of variations suggests that its compilation preceded that of the Kartarpur Pothi.

According to Balwant Singh Dhillon, the making of MS 1245 resulted from an independent effort but with a well-defined objective of creating "a new seat of Gurudom."[20] For him, MS 1245 represents a parallel scriptural text developed by the descendants of Prithi Chand. He ties his argument with the tradition that Miharban prepared and sent volumes of sacred writings to distant Sikh congregations. By presenting evidence which, he claims, suggests affinity between MS 1245 and the literature produced by this family, he argues that MS 1245 belonged to them as well.

There are fundamental problems with Dhillon's argument. If one accepts that MS 1245 was conceived as a competing scriptural text created by Miharban, how does one explain the careful recording of Guru Arjan's hymns in it? It is not clear how the place of honor given to the hymns of Guru Arjan would have supported this family's agenda of creating their "new Gurudom." There is a hymn by Guru Arjan in *rag* Asa (folios 398–399), which refers to a conspiracy between some dissident Sikhs and the Mughals and the divine intervention to protect the guru. Given the context, there is little doubt that Miharban's family is the subject of the hymn. Its presence in MS 1245 does not support Dhillon's argument that Miharban created this document. We also know that Miharban himself was an eminent writer, and the fact that he did not record his verses in what was supposed to be his family's authoritative text does not make any sense. Finally, if MS 1245 was prepared to be sent to some distant congregation, how does one explain the incomplete nature of the text?

In my view, the limited affinity of the text of MS 1245 with the writings of this family can be more effectively explained in terms of their both belonging to an early phase of the evolution of the sacred Sikh text. In his enthusiasm for attributing the compilation of MS 1245 to the descendants of Prithi Chand and consequently undermining its importance, Dhillon is unable to explain the origin of this important manuscript.

Pashaura Singh pursues a different line of thought and categorically argues that MS 1245 was prepared under the supervision of Guru Arjan, with the specific goal "to fix the hymns of the Gurus."[21] His explanation of the origin of this manuscript is rooted in traditional Sikh thinking. He firmly believes that the entire corpus of sacred Sikh writings was collected during Guru Arjan's time, and then subjected to detailed editing before it was recorded in what was to become the authoritative Sikh text. For Pashaura Singh, MS 1245 was a drafting attempt in this rather complex process.

I agree with Pashaura Singh that MS 1245 was prepared in the central Sikh community. The facts that have emerged in our earlier discussion, however, challenge his interpretation that it was a draft. There is no doubt that modifications were made to the organization present in the Goindval Pothis before the text was recorded in MS 1245 and that these were carried over with some minor changes into the Kartarpur Pothi. Still, the modifications were not of such magnitude that they required drafts on the way to the finalized text. MS 1245 does not appear to be a draft either. Its exceptional neatness, with few erasures and overwriting, its relatively few blank folios (only 8. 5 percent of its total bulk, as compared with 14. 5 percent in the Goindval Pothis and 22 percent in the Kartarpur Pothi), and the extensive artwork on its opening four folios, indicate that it was put forth as a finished document and not as a draft meant to be discarded after its incorporation into the authoritative Sikh text.[22]

I suggest a different hypothesis to explain the origin of MS 1245. As mentioned earlier, the hymns of the Bhagats are not included in this manuscript. The crucial significance of MS 1245 lies not in its origin as an independent effort nor in its serving as a draft for the Kartarpur Pothi, but rather in its manifesting a conception of Sikh scripture different from the type represented in the Goindval Pothis and the Kartarpur Pothi. MS 1245 seems to have been compiled at a time when the earlier conception of Sikh scripture was being reconsidered.

It is true that Guru Arjan held the Bhagats in high esteem and portrayed them in his hymns as a paradigm of successful devotion.[23] Yet the absence of the hymns of non-Sikhs from MS 1245 may suggest that at one time, around 1600, the guru considered dropping them altogether, or at least separating them from the compositions of the Sikhs and appending them as a distinct unit toward the end of the scriptural text.[24] Emerging from this mode of thinking, MS 1245 seems to attempt to draw a line between the Sikh community—the gurus and their court poets who were part of the Sikh fold—and the others, Hindus and Muslims.

One may argue that when the manuscript was nearing completion, Guru Arjan changed his mind and decided to revive the conception of scripture implicit in the Goindval Pothis: he would reintroduce the hymns of the non-Sikhs into the corpus. This conceptual revision left MS 1245 permanently incomplete, with no effort ever to fill in the incomplete verses. The change of direction that resulted in the Kartarpur Pothi left no provision for MS 1245 to survive with it side by side. In order to fit in with the accepted scheme of organization by *rag*, the hymns of the Bhagats had to be integrated with those of the gurus.

In this context, a couplet inscribed on decorated folio 3, and again later, on folio 515, as part of the text of Guru Ramdas's *var* in *rag* Bihagṛa, evokes considerable interest.[25] The note that the dealers appended to MS 1245 claims that the inscription of the couplet on folio 3 is in the hand of Baba Buḍḍha. Since no source is cited, one can only guess that they obtained this information from the previous owners of the manuscript—Baba Buḍḍha's descendants. The manuscript, deemed irrelevant in the final scheme of things, was most likely placed in the custody of Baba Buḍḍha, the most prominent Sikh of the period. His family would have kept the work as a relic of their illustrious ancestor but would eventually have lost all memory of the conception behind it.

Given the later Sikh belief that, once incorporated, the hymns of the Bhagats became an indivisible part of Sikh literature, and the Sikhs' enthusiasm for establishing a close correspondence between the Adi Granth and the manuscripts representing nascent Sikh scriptural history, it is not difficult to understand how in confronting this received wisdom, MS 1245 would have been allowed to sink into oblivion.[26] Yet the fact is that MS 1245 is a work of great importance, since it predates the Kartarpur Pothi and is one of the earliest Sikh manuscripts in existence. On the one hand, it helps us to explain in greater detail the evolution of the Sikh text at the turn of the seventeenth century, and on the other, it raises some very significant questions. Does MS 1245 mark a forgotten development in Sikh scriptural history? Does it suggest that at some point in early history the distinctiveness of the Sikh community was so emphasized that there was a revision of the conception of Sikh scripture and its inclusiveness as manifested in the Goindval Pothis, the Kartarpur Pothi, and subsequently the Adi Granth. The questions are important and one hopes that convincing answers to them will eventually emerge.

The Kartarpur Pothi

This pothi is currently in the custody of Karamjit Singh Sodhi (b. 1952), a descendent of Dhirmal, at Kartarpur.[27] It is housed at the Sodhi residence and is put up for ceremonial display on the *sangrand* of every month, and at the twice-yearly fairs on Vaisakhi and the birth anniversary of Guru Nanak. During these two fairs, which occur in the early summer and in the late fall, the followers of the Sodhi family from the region gather at Kartarpur.[28]

History of the Kartarpur Pothi

The early history of the Kartarpur Pothi is closely intertwined with important developments within the Sikh community. There is a general consensus in Sikh literature that the Kartarpur Pothi was prepared during Guru Arjan's tenure and that it remained in Amritsar, the center of Sikh activities, in the years following the guru's death in Mughal custody at Lahore in 1606. In the late 1620s, when hostilities between the Sikhs and the Mughal authorities at Lahore flared once again, Guru Hargobind left Amritsar and moved to Kartarpur and attempted to settle there. Mughal pressure did not subside, however; so in 1634 Guru Hargobind decided to move into the Shivalik hills. There he founded Kiratpur, which remained the center of Sikh activities during the following three decades.

According to Sikh tradition, the pothi came to Kartarpur along with Guru Hargobind. It is perfectly plausible to argue that since the pothi was a precious possession of the community, it would have been taken along by the guru. Still, the pothi is believed to have been left behind at Kartarpur when the guru moved to the Shivalik hills, and it is supposed to have remained there ever since, which could be accounted for by the difficult circumstances of Guru Hargobind's departure from Kartarpur, which, one might argue, also prevented the Sikhs from carrying their belongings with them.[29] But it is also possible that the guru assumed he would return to Kartarpur and eventually to Amritsar and so left the pothi behind in his family home.

An alternative tradition, which first surfaces in Bhai Santokh Singh's *Sri Gurpratap Suraj Granth*, presents a slightly different version of the pothi's history during the mid decades of the seventeenth century.[30] Bhai Santokh Singh claims that the pothi remained at Kartarpur when Guru Hargobind left for the Shivalik hills, but that after Guru Tegh Bahadur's ascension to the office of the guru in 1664, some of his followers forcibly took the pothi from Dhirmal and carried it to Baba Bakala, a town near Kartarpur where Guru Tegh Bahadur lived at that time. The guru, however, is said to have been displeased with this act. While crossing the river Beas on his way to the Shivalik hills, he buried the pothi on the riverside and sent a message to Dhirmal to collect it. And as the story goes, Dhirmal with some difficulty found the pothi buried in the sand and then took it to Kartarpur.

This episode, part of the popular lore about the pothi, is reiterated by the Sodhis to this day.[31] Given our knowledge of the period, it is not easy to explain how the followers of Guru Tegh Bahadur at Baba Bakala could have confronted Dhirmal, who must have been at the peak of his political power during those years. Nor is it plausible that Guru Tegh Bahadur would have risked leaving the pothi on the riverbank for Dhirmal to retrieve. It is not entirely clear whether this detour in the history of the pothi was the creation of Bhai Santokh Singh, which was later taken up by the Sodhi family to support their ownership of the pothi, or if the reverse was true. The Sodhis had already propagated this version, in which Guru Tegh Bahadur's return of the pothi to the Sodhi family was cited as his endorsement of their ownership, and it appeared for the first time in writing in Bhai Santokh Singh's work.

Another view of the pothi's history at this juncture was offered by G. B. Singh in the 1940s.[32] He argues that Guru Hargobind took the pothi along with him when he left Kartarpur, that it remained at Kiratpur in the following decades and was brought from Kiratpur to Baba Bakala at the time of Guru Tegh Bahadur's succession (1664). G. B. Singh holds that from the custody of Guru Tegh Bahadur at Baba Bakala Dhirmal captured the pothi and took it to Kartarpur.

This modification in the history of the pothi is based on a set of notes referring to "the book of the fifth Guru" recorded in a scriptural manuscript prepared in 1659 and currently housed at Dehra Dun.[33] This manuscript the tradition remembers as having been prepared to accompany Ramrai during his visit to Delhi to meet Emperor Aurangzeb. G. B. Singh supports the belief that the manuscript was actually prepared at Kiratpur. He then refers to a note in its text which claims that the manuscript was checked against the Kartarpur Pothi. On this basis, G. B. Singh argues that the Kartarpur Pothi must have been present in Kiratpur at that time. There is, however, a flaw in this reasoning. Even if the manuscript at Dehra Dun was compared with the Kartarpur Pothi, the pothi need not have been present in Kiratpur to permit that comparison. One could argue that if the Kartarpur Pothi had been in Kiratpur, then the manuscript would have been copied from it directly, and not compared with it later on. As we discuss in chapter 5, several direct copies of the Kartarpur Pothi still exist.

It seems more likely that the Kartarpur Pothi, whether left by design or by necessity, stayed on at Kartarpur with members of Guru Hargobind's family. Later, a branch of this family under the leadership of Dhirmal turned against the guru. This falling out was rooted in the hereditary claim of Dhirmal, whose father, Baba Gurdita, the oldest son of Guru Hargobind, was to have inherited Guru Hargobind's office, except that he died in 1638. Dhirmal must have staked a claim for the office of guru following his father's death, but apparently he was rejected by Guru Hargobind, who instead selected Harirai, Dhirmal's younger brother, as his successor.

There is evidence that instead of helping to bring the guru back from the Shivalik hills to the Punjab plains, Dhirmal worked out an independent relationship with the Mughal authorities. This cordiality with them earned Dhirmal a large land grant at Kartarpur. The royal decree, issued by the Mughal emperor Shah Jahan in 1643, which declares Dhirmal "the occupant of the seat of Nanak Shah," is still in the possession of his descendants.[34] Denied recognition by Guru Hargobind, Dhirmal, like previous dissidents, declared himself guru and established a new *gaddi* that continues to this day. As in the cases of Baba Mohan at Goindval and Prithi Chand at Amritsar, Dhirmal's aspiration to the honor of guru was aided by his possession of a pothi—the definitive one prepared during the time of his great-grandfather, Guru Arjan.

Views may differ concerning the custody of the pothi in the middle decades of the seventeenth century, but there is general agreement that it was present in Kartarpur in the late 1660s and that it has remained there ever since. Guru Gobind Singh is said to have attempted to borrow the Kartarpur Pothi in the closing decades of the century, but the descendants of Dhirmal did not or could not consider his request.[35]

The seventeenth-century tensions between the Sodhi *gaddi* and the mainstream Sikh community subsided eventually, and in the last quarter of the eighteenth century, the

Sodhis were able to establish a workable relationship with the mainstream Sikh community.[36] The spiritual status of the Sodhis as the descendants of the gurus was augmented by widespread knowledge of their large landholdings in the area, and their acceptance by the Sikhs was manifested in the close relationship they developed with Maharaja Ranjit Singh.[37]

It is commonly believed that Maharaja Ranjit Singh appropriated the Kartarpur Pothi from the Sodhis in the early decades of the nineteenth century.[38] There is no doubt that the Kartarpur Pothi was taken to Lahore, but there is also no evidence that it ever left the Sodhis' custody. The Sodhis were presented with the historic shrine of Bauli Sahib, along with its estate, and the Dabbi Bazaar in Lahore. The pothi may have been displayed occasionally at the Sikh court, but it remained with the Sodhis based at the Bauli Sahib, and they even took it back to Kartarpur for some time in 1837.[39]

At the time of the annexation of the Punjab by the British, it seems that the pothi was taken away from the Bauli Sahib and deposited in the Citadel Establishment under the charge of Major G. H. MacGregor, Deputy Commissioner, Lahore. The Sodhis appealed for the restoration of the pothi to Major H. P. Burn, Deputy Secretary of the Board of Administration, Punjab. The petition was granted and the pothi was returned to the family with the understanding that the Sodhis would make a copy for the British government.[40] A copy of the Kartarpur Pothi was prepared and sent to Queen Victoria in the late 1850s.[41] Surprisingly, however, the text of the so-called copy is actually identical with the text of the Adi Granth.

With the exception of its visit to Patiala (1860–1863) at the invitation of the royal house there, the pothi remained at Kartarpur.[42] During their visit to Patiala, the Sodhis allowed a copy of the Kartarpur Pothi to be made, and it is presently available in the maharaja's private collection at Moti Bagh, Patiala.[43] The text of this supposed copy of the Kartarpur Pothi has the same contents as that of the Adi Granth. The presence of the pothi at Kartarpur is recorded in late-nineteenth-century British writings and appears prominently in Bhai Kahn Singh Nabha's *Mahan Kosh*.[44]

I have already referred to the SGPC's bid to retrieve the early manuscripts from their custodians, and the Kartarpur Pothi was the center of this effort. The courts, however, rejected the assertion that as a Sikh communal relic the Kartarpur Pothi belonged to the entire Sikh community, and allowed the Sodhis to retain it as their private property. With the litigation completed, the Sodhis had the pothi reconstructed in 1956–1957: its folios were framed, laminated, and then bound.[45] The Sodhis revived the tradition of offering the pothi for public display, which continues to this day.

During the prolonged litigation, the court permitted access to select scholars, who studied the pothi closely. Bhai Jodh Singh's *Sri Kartarpuri Biṛ de Darshan*, published in 1968—many years after his notes were taken—is the most notable single work describing the pothi's contents. As an after-effect of the SGPC's litigation, however, the Sodhis have usually refused access to the pothi for scholarly examination. This refusal has led many scholars to suspect that they have something to hide and that the manuscript is not the original one prepared by Guru Arjan.[46] I was very fortunate, however, to be given permission by Amarjit Singh Sodhi (1927–1998), the father of the current custodian, for an extended examination of the pothi on three different occasions during the past few years. The information collected at these times forms the basis of our continuing discussion.

The Time of Recording of the Kartarpur Pothi

The Kartarpur Pothi is a dated manuscript. The relevant entry on folio 2 reads, "Having written the pothi [we] reached [this point] on the first day of the increasing phase of the moon, in the month of Bhadon, year 1661" (*Sambat 1661 miti Bhadon vadi ekam 1 pothi likhi pahuche*). Thus the year of the pothi's compilation is 1604. My close examination of the recorded date confirms that it is in the handwriting of the scribe who prepared the pothi's table of contents and inscribed most of its text. There is no perceptible evidence of tinkering in this entry.

There is additional supporting evidence for the Kartarpur Pothi's early date. Eleven hymns of Guru Arjan were introduced into the pothi after its original inscription, none of which is available in MS 1245.[47] The first hymn appears in *rag* Gujri (folio 392) and is recorded at the end of the sequence of Guru Arjan's *chaupadas*. Four hymns appear in *rag* Devgandhari; they are inscribed on folio 415, which was originally left blank. Two hymns are added to the section on *rag* Suhi; they are inscribed at the end of the sequence of hymns assigned *ghar* 3 (folio 551). One each appears in *rag* Bilaval (folio 617) recorded on another writing that is covered with yellow paste, and *rag* Malar inscribed at the end of hymns assigned *ghar* 1 (folio 891). Finally, an opening couplet of what was supposedly a *chhant* was inscribed at the end of the sequence of Guru Arjan's *chhants* in *rag* Ramkali (folio 703), and the three stanzas of Guru Arjan's *Basant ki Var* appear on folio 854, which was originally left blank because it occurs between the hymns of the gurus and of the Bhagats.

The late introduction of these hymns into the Kartarpur Pothi's text indicates that they were composed after the pothi's original compilation and must have been added to it with the permission of Guru Arjan. In the case of the hymns in *rags* Gujri, Devgandhari and Suhi, the scribe entered them in the table of contents. The hymn in *rag* Bilaval is entered twice in the table of contents; but no reference appears there regarding the hymn in *rag* Malar and two fragments in *rags* Ramkali and Basant.

The date 1604, two years before the death of Guru Arjan, allows time for the composition of a set of new hymns and their introduction into the pothi. The two incomplete hymns may be taken to synchronize with Guru Arjan's sudden death. He did not get to finish these hymns and their incomplete texts appear in the Kartarpur Pothi. In spite of these important data at our disposal, influential scholars have still questioned the accuracy of the date recorded in the Kartarpur Pothi, insisting that the manuscript was prepared during the period of Guru Hargobind.[48] Their questions are related to a set of entries present in the Kartarpur Pothi which, these scholars argue, could not have been made in or before 1604, the professed date of its compilation. Two entries in the table of contents (folio 2) read: "the attestation of the fifth Guru" (*nishaṇ guru jio ke daskhat mahala 5*) and "the attestation of the sixth Guru" (*nishaṇ sri guru jio ke daskhat mahala 6*). These refer to the text of the invocation said to have been inscribed in the hand of Guru Arjan and Guru Hargobind on folio 45 (the opening folio of the text) and folio 540 (the opening folio of the section on *rag* Suhi), respectively.

Scholars who question the date 1604 cite the attestation attributed to Hargobind, who attained the office of the guru only in 1606. The substantive issue here concerns the accuracy of the statement referring to Hargobind as the sixth Sikh guru. From these scholars' point of view, this entry means that the second section of the Kartarpur Pothi was prepared when Guru Hargobind had already become guru, and that the date of the completion of the Kartarpur Pothi in 1604 is incorrect. The answer to this line of questioning lies in the evolution of the institution of guru, which had become hereditary by this time. Even in 1604, two years before the death of Guru Arjan, it was clear to the Sikh community who his successor would be. Most likely, the scribe asked the only son of the living guru to inscribe his attestation at the beginning of the second half of the pothi and recorded this in the table of contents as "the attestation of the sixth guru."

A second problem with the recorded date of the Kartarpur Pothi is more complex. Folio 25 records the death dates of the first six gurus and Baba Gurdita, the eldest son of Guru Hargobind and the father of Dhirmal. According to Bhai Jodh Singh, the death dates of the first five gurus—from Guru Nanak to Guru Arjan—are in the hand of the primary scribe; but the pen that entered Guru Arjan's death date is visibly different and finer. The death dates of Baba Gurdita and Guru Hargobind, which follow that of Guru Arjan, are in yet a different hand.[49]

Bhai Jodh Singh was surely correct in asserting that the death dates for the first five gurus are in a single hand, differing from the one that recorded the dates for Baba Gurdita and Guru Hargobind. There is, however, a problem with his implication that the primary scribe recorded the death dates of the first four gurus when he wrote the pothi in 1604 but then added the date of Guru Arjan after 1606, with a pen finer than the first.

On the basis of the evidence available in the pothi, I agree with Randhir Singh and others who argue that the first five death dates are not only in one hand but were also written at one time.[50] My overall conclusion differs from theirs, however. They argue that the presence of the first five dates in one hand suggests that the pothi was inscribed after the death of Guru Arjan. I hold that the list of death dates in the Kartarpur Pothi was inscribed after 1606 on folio 25, which had been left blank in the original writing. This later addition is confirmed by the insertion of the reference to the death dates in the table of contents on folio 2, as Bhai Jodh Singh noted; it is recorded in different ink and with a different pen from the rest of the table of contents.[51]

A different set of arguments challenge the authenticity of the Kartarpur Pothi. Is it, after all, the actual manuscript that was later known in Sikh tradition as the one inscribed by Bhai Gurdas? Scholars who challenge the pothi's authenticity have argued their case on two grounds. The first is the existence of another early manuscript, associated with the village of Bohot. G. B. Singh reports that this manuscript contained the same text as that of the Kartarpur Pothi and was prepared in 1592.[52] He himself admits, however, that his description of the manuscript was collected in a great hurry and may not be reliable, and the actual manuscript is no longer available for checking. In any case, there is no corroborating evidence for such an early dating of the compilation of a scriptural text associated with Guru Arjan.

The second challenge has been directed at the Kartarpur Pothi by Giani Gurdit Singh and others, on the basis of Kesar Singh Chhibbar's assertion that Guru Arjan's manuscript was compiled in 1601.[53] Although this date is not as early as the one claimed by G. B. Singh, it would still challenge the status of the Kartarpur Pothi, compiled in 1604, as the original manuscript. One may, however, argue that Chhibbar simply referred to some early and inaccurate tradition, according to which the work on the Kartarpur Pothi began in 1601. Giani Mahan Singh, in his response to this line of thought, highlighted numerous inconsistencies in Chhibbar's dates and convincingly argued against accepting the date of 1601.[54] It is true that Chhibbar's dates in general are not accurate, and any argument built on them is inherently weak.

In summary, the invocation in the hand of Guru Hargobind, the listing of the death dates of the five gurus, including Guru Arjan's in the hand of the same scribe, and the later reference of Chhibbar to the compilation of a manuscript in 1601, can all be explained without challenging either the correctness of the recorded date of the Kartarpur Pothi or its authenticity in Sikh tradition as the manuscript compiled under the supervision of Guru Arjan.

Internal Structure and Contents of the Kartarpur Pothi

The text of the Kartarpur Pothi begins on folio 2 and goes on to folio 974, with some blank folios at the end. The opening folio and the one that begins the section on *rag* Suhi are illuminated extensively in blue and gold, and the design is an expansion of that found on the opening folios of both of the extant Goindval Pothis. Within the text of the pothi, there are a large number of blank folios. As in the Goindval Pothis, the blank folios appear most frequently at the ends of the *rag* sections into which the text is divided and also at the ends of subsections within each *rag*.[55] The scribe habitually left folios blank within a subsection; in several instances, blanks appear at the completion of a group of hymns in one *ghar*. This technique may point to a scribal expectation that Guru Arjan would create more hymns, which could then be entered on these folios.

There are problems with the numbering of the folios; at points the same number appears on more than one folio, and at others, a number is simply absent.[56] Unlike the Goindval Pothis, the Kartarpur Pothi is not in its original binding and the lamination of the folios makes it impossible to separate the gatherings from each other and understand their sequence. The pothi also contains some extra folios, which do not have margin lines and differ visibly from the original ones. It is not clear why and when these folios were introduced into the pothi, but it is certain that they were not part of the original text.

The complications within the structure of the Kartarpur Pothi bear directly on the issue of the pothi's original contents. There is the problem of reconciling Bhai Jodh Singh's description, given in his book, with earlier descriptions of the pothi. Writing in 1918, Bhai Kahn Singh Nabha reported that the Kartarpur Pothi contained in its concluding section the *Ratanmala* (The garland of jewels), a brief narrative written in prose called the *Hakikati Rah Mukam Raje Shivnabh ki* (The route to the abode of Raja Shivnabh), as well as such entries as those of the land grant of Kartarpur, a fire in Kartarpur in 1777, and a visit by Maharaja Ranjit Singh to Kartarpur in 1831.[57] Bhai Jodh Singh's account from the late 1940s, however, found none of these items in the pothi. Furthermore, Bhai Jodh Singh did not conceal his disdain for Bhai Kahn Singh Nabha for having given what he thought was false information.[58]

There is no question that Bhai Jodh Singh's description of the Kartarpur Pothi is accurate so far as the manuscript's present state is concerned; but it does not explain how a scholar of Nabha's eminence and stature could have reported the presence of compositions in the pothi that were not actually there. Others also claim to have seen these compositions in the text of the Kartarpur Pothi.[59] Instead of dismissing his description as false, one should turn to internal evidence that something far more substantial is at stake.

The last entry in the table of contents of the Kartarpur Pothi (folio 2), which refers to the titles on folio 974, reads, *Ragmala tatha Singhladip ki Shivnabh Raje ki Bidhi* (literally, "The garland of *rags*" and "The recipe of King Shivnabh of Singhladip"). The entry is in part written vertically along the margin, and its latter part clearly refers to two compositions: the *Hakikati Rah Mukam Raje Shivnabh ki* and *Siahi ki Bidhi* (Recipe of ink). In addition, we need to note that the compositions referred to here are part of the set of five compositions that consistently appear in a seventeenth-century branch of scriptural manuscripts, and that according to Bhai Kahn Singh Nabha were present in the Kartarpur Pothi.

At this point in the Kartarpur Pothi, the table of contents contains one thing but the text shows something else. The pothi as it stands today ends with the *Ragmala*, on folio 974, followed by a number of blank folios that are not identical with the original folios of the manuscript; they differ in texture and color of paper. Although Bhai Jodh Singh did not describe in detail the four folios that follow the *Ragmala* text, he did note that they differed from those that preceded.[60]

Tables of contents of the manuscripts were prepared only after their text had been completely inscribed, and an entry at the head of the table of contents confirms this practice. The scribe of the Kartarpur Pothi claims that, having written the pothi, he began recording the table of contents on Bhadon *vadi* 1, Samat 1661. As referred to earlier, some hymns were introduced into the Kartarpur Pothi after its original inscription, and they were entered in the table of contents. The *Ragmala tatha Singhladip ki Shivnabh Raje ki Bidhi* is a unique instance of texts mentioned in the table of contents but not included in the body of the pothi. The *Ragmala* is recorded at the end of the pothi, but the *Hakikati Rah Mukam Raje Shivnabh ki* and the *Siahi ki Bidhi* are both absent.

Bhai Jodh Singh faithfully reproduced the entry in the table of contents for the *Ragmala tatha Singhladip ki Shivnabh Raje ki Bidhi* without commenting on its absence in the text itself.[61] Pashaura Singh argues that this particular entry was inserted into the table of contents with the intention of eventually introducing the compositions mentioned here into the text of the manuscript.[62] Physical evidence confirms that the entry was made in one hand at one time and was recorded along with the rest of the table of contents, in the same handwriting and ink.

Rather than suggesting the table of contents is out of kilter, it is more sensible to assume that the text of the original pothi was subsequently altered: the original probably conformed to what the table of contents indicates. And indeed, Bhai Kahn Singh Nabha's description of the pothi in the early part of the century affirms that the now-missing compositions were still present at that point. This hypothesis could be contested if one could find manuscripts that were known to be copies of the Kartarpur Pothi but that did not end with these compositions. Yet even if such copies were to appear, one would still have to account for Bhai Kahn Singh Nabha's report.

Despite extensive fieldwork, I have not found a single copy of the Kartarpur Pothi as it stands now among the extant seventeenth-century manuscripts. There are other early manuscripts, discussed in Chapter 5, that claim to be copies of the Kartarpur Pothi. They all include at the closing of their text the set of compositions to which the Kartarpur Pothi's table of contents refers. These are the same compositions that Bhai Kahn Singh Nabha claimed to have seen when he examined the Kartarpur Pothi.

I have referred to two nineteenth-century manuscripts, one presently at India Office Library in London and the other at Moti Bagh in Patiala, both believed to have been copied from the Kartarpur Pothi, which are actually identical to the text of the Adi Granth—and not to the Kartarpur Pothi.[63] The simple explanation for this peculiarity is that the custodians of the Kartarpur Pothi were aware of the textual differences between the pothi in their possession and the Adi Granth and were doing their best to generate copies that conformed to what had become the authoritative version of Sikh scripture.

The Sodhis' awareness of this issue provides the background for understanding the differences between the text of the Kartarpur Pothi as seen by Bhai Kahn Singh Nabha in the 1910s and by Bhai Jodh Singh and others in the 1940s. It is certain that changes were made in the Kartarpur Pothi during the late 1920s. According to some senior scholars, Pandit Kartar Singh Dakha, Master Ishar Singh Tarn Taran, and Pandit Wariam Singh Jabboval were involved in the rebinding of the pothi at that time; but what exactly they did is not known.[64] Probably, though, in a misconceived attempt to prove the authenticity of the Kartarpur Pothi, its custodians permitted some anachronistic alterations to its structure. The changes were made primarily to conform to what later Sikh tradition held to constitute the Kartarpur Pothi: the Adi Granth minus the hymns of Guru Tegh Bahadur.

That some changes were made toward the end of the Kartarpur Pothi is confirmed by examining the flaws in its last three gatherings. Folios 958, 959, and 965 are missing; folio 966 contains several thickly pasted layers with new writing recorded over them; and folios 964 and 973 and the four folios following 975 differ from the original folios of the pothi, both in the texture of the paper and in the design of their margins. Bhai Jodh Singh also noted these anomalies but did not note the possibility that alterations had been made when the Kartarpur Pothi was rebound earlier in the twentieth century.[65] Since all persons involved in the rebinding are now dead, only Karamjit Singh Sodhi, the custodian of the pothi and the scion of the Sodhi family at Kartarpur, might be able to clarify what happened if, indeed, the details of the operation were ever revealed to him by his father, who himself was very young when this happened.

The history of the Kartarpur Pothi and the evidence in support of its origin in 1604 confirm that it was prepared as early as it claims to have been. The pothi is the authentic manuscript associated in Sikh tradition with Guru Arjan and is, therefore, a very significant text in the evolution of Sikh scripture. The issue of the pothi's contents, however, is open to debate. In my view the Kartarpur Pothi originally contained the compositions mentioned in its table of contents. As I explain in chapter 5, this information substantially clarifies our understanding of the history of the Sikh scriptural text during the seventeenth century.

The Place of the Kartatpur Pothi in the Transmission of the Sacred Corpus

Twentieth-century debates about the status of the Kartarpur Pothi have remained inconclusive. On the one hand, the traditional view accepts the Kartarpur Pothi as the manuscripts prepared under the supervision of Guru Arjan. On the other, a group of influential scholars—G. B. Singh, Gurdit Singh, Inder Singh Chakarvarti, Piar Singh, Piara Singh Padam, Pritam Singh, and Randhir Singh—reject this position.[66]

In the preceding discussion, I have challenged this position. But one can understand how such a line of thought must have emerged. First, these scholars' attitude toward the Sodhi family, in light of its past history of fierce competition with the gurus, is very skeptical—unfairly so, as discussed. Second, many of these people conducted their research when the Sodhis did not permit extended access to the pothi. Inability to examine the pothi not only truncated their understanding; it also increased their suspicions about the Sodhis' claims regarding the pothi in their custody.

The questions regarding the date and history of the Kartarpur Pothi can be answered. Bhai Jodh Singh, who emerged in the mid decades of the twentieth century as the leading spokesperson for the traditional view regarding the Kartarpur Pothi, presented substantial internal evidence to support the accuracy of its dating.[67] Importantly, however, Bhai Jodh Singh's work was done in an atmosphere of fierce controversy over the continued existence of the *Ragmala* in the Adi Granth.[68] Bhai Jodh Singh argued that because the *Ragmala* appears in the Kartarpur Pothi it is an authoritative composition. Given this context, he interpreted any question about the authenticity of the Kartarpur Pothi as a challenge to Sikh canon and consequently an attack on the very foundation of the Sikh community. This line of thought resulted in the introduction of a complex religious dimension into a purely academic debate with the assumption that those who do not recognize the Kartarpur Pothi as a genuine document pose a threat to the text of the Adi Granth.

In my view, there is no need for such a defensiveness. Traditional Sikh claims regarding the history of the Kartarpur Pothi can be fully authenticated in light of the information available to us: in the first place, the presence of such comments as "correct" (*shudh*), "correct it" (*shudh kichai*), "this is repetition" (*duhragat hai*); the inscription of some hymns and their later deletion (folio 306, 374, 497); and the large number of blank folios in the pothi, which point to its compilation at an early stage of the scriptural evolution. In addition, the tripartite structure of the text, the sequence of *rag* sections, and that of the hymns within each of these sections finalized in the Kartarpur Pothi are all maintained as features of the Adi Granth. The invocation appears in its canonical form for the first time in the Kartarpur Pothi, and no variation ever surfaces in later manuscripts. Similarly, compositions attributed to the gurus in the Goindval Pothis and MS 1245 which are absent from the Kartarpur Pothi never resurface in later manuscripts.[69] All this firmly suggests that the Kartarpur Pothi is at the fountainhead of the later scriptural tradition.

The fact that the Kartarpur Pothi contains the complete corpus of sacred Sikh literature with the exception of the hymns of Guru Tegh Bahadur positions it as the most significant landmark before the compilation of the Adi Granth itself. Nevertheless, the Kartarpur Pothi, like the Guru Harsahai and the Goindval Pothis, is an earlier version of Sikh scripture and can be assigned only historical importance. The discrepancies between the contents of the Kartarpur Pothi and the Adi Granth do not reject the authenticity of the Kartarpur Pothi. Nor does it pose any challenge to the text of the Adi Granth. The Kartarpur Pothi, like other early manuscripts, is part of the unique heritage of the Sikh community, and the information available in it is crucial, since it can help scholars to reconstruct a precise history of the compilation as well as the accuracy of the text of the Adi Granth. The religious issue of sanctity and the integrity of the contents of the Sikh sacred text applies only to the Adi Granth, not to any of the earlier texts, including the Kartarpur Pothi.[70]

5

Toward the Adi Granth

In traditional Sikh literature, the evolution of the scriptural text from the Kartarpur Pothi to the Adi Granth is understood to have occurred in two distinct stages.[1] In the first stage, Bhai Banno, an influential member of the community during Guru Arjan's time, arranged to prepare the first copy of the Kartarpur Pothi, and this copying process continued throughout the seventeenth century. This second stage consisted of Guru Gobind Singh's compilation of the Adi Granth, which involved the induction of the hymns of his father, Guru Tegh Bahadur, into the contents of the Kartarpur Pothi. When this was accomplished, the guru declared the newly compiled text to be closed, and it is believed to have remained unchanged ever after. At the time of his death in 1708, Guru Gobind Singh replaced the office of the personal guru with the Adi Granth, thus elevating it to the status of "Guru Granth Sahib." The text is almost always referred to this way by Sikhs today.

In this chapter I address in detail the compilation of the Adi Granth. I begin by examining the existing classification of various groups of the seventeenth-century manuscripts. Building on data available in the extant manuscripts, I then propose a modified picture of their mutual relationships. In the second section I turn to the Adi Granth itself. Here I reconstruct its production in a way that radically revises the current understanding of the surrounding time and circumstances, as well as the relationship between its contents and those of its textual antecedents, such as the Kartarpur Pothi and other seventeenth-century manuscripts.

The Seventeenth-Century Manuscripts

Writing in the 1770s, Sarupdas Bhalla was the first author to report the variations between the texts of the Kartarpur Pothi and the manuscript prepared by Bhai Banno. Bhalla narrates that soon after the inscription of the Kartarpur Pothi, Bhai Banno obtained Guru Arjan's permission to take it to his village with the intent to prepare a copy for himself. Guru Arjan, however, sent for the pothi, and it had to be returned quickly. Somehow Bhai Banno managed to have a copy made, but because of its hasty compilation organizational discrepancies crept into the text. The newly compiled manuscript, along with the original, was presented to Guru Arjan, who gladly confirmed its authenticity by putting his attestation/signature on the manuscript.[2] Bhalla calls it the Khara recension (*Khare ki misal*), naming it after Bhai Banno's village Khara Mangat and distinguishing it from the Kartarpur Pothi (*Bhai Gurdas ki misal).* Since the manuscript is now at Kanpur, we called it the Kanpur Pothi in chapter 2.

Bhalla's discernment of the differences between the two early manuscripts was endorsed by later writers, but their description of the circumstances of the origin of the Kanpur Pothi (as well as the nature of its differences from the Kartarpur Pothi) underwent important changes. According to the *Sri Gurbilas Patishahi 6* and *Sri Gurpratap Suraj Granth*, Guru Arjan asked Bhai Banno to take the Kartarpur Pothi to Lahore for binding. During this trip to Lahore, Bhai Banno arranged to have a copy made without the prior permission of the guru. There were differences in contents between the original and the copy, and these had resulted from Bhai Banno's deliberate effort to introduce into the sacred corpus some apocryphal hymns. The accounts assign clearly negative connotations to the Kanpur Pothi. The name Khara, Bhalla's description of this manuscript based on Bhai Banno's village, is reduced to its literal meaning, "alkaline" or "brackish," and hence the phrase was understood to mean a "rejected" text.[3]

Writing in the 1870s, Tara Singh Narotam, an influential Nirmala scholar, declared the Kartarpur Pothi to be the "sweet" (*madhur*) version, in total opposition to the "brackish" Kanpur Pothi. He also argued that Bhai Banno's village was actually named Khara because of the presence of the "*khara*" manuscript there.[4] Later writers did not endorse Narotam's untenable position that the village was named after the manuscript, but the perception regarding its compilation by Bhai Banno and its eventual rejection by Guru Arjan continued.[5]

At the turn of the twentieth century, Charan Singh brought to light a hitherto unknown branch of manuscripts, whose origin he traced to the city of Lahore.[6] Charan Singh coalesced the earlier traditions pertaining to the activities of Bhai Banno to explain the making of the original manuscript of this line. He claimed that Bhai Banno first took the Kartarpur Pothi to his village and during its stay there prepared a copy. Afterward, he brought the Kartarpur Pothi to Lahore to have it bound, and local Sikhs, following Bhai Banno's initiative, made another copy. Charan Singh provided some preliminary information about the variations between the contents of this branch of manuscripts and those of the other two but did not see the need to explain the origins of these differences and the resulting formation of an independent branch.

For complex historical reasons, the manuscripts of this branch did not receive the attention they deserved, and with the exception of G. B. Singh and more recently Piar Singh, no serious attempt has been made to incorporate them into the history of the Sikh text.[7] Twentieth-century discussions pertaining to Sikh scripture continued to focus on the variations between the Kartarpur Pothi and the Kanpur Pothi. Working along the lines established by nineteenth-century writers, scholars accepted the presence of additional compositions in the Kanpur Pothi—and the resulting family of manuscripts from this–and elaborated on the possible reasons as to how they were inducted into the sacred Sikh literature.

Sahib Singh dismissed earlier accounts of the compilation of the Kanpur Pothi as fanciful and offered a new hypothesis: the Kartarpur Pothi and the Kanpur Pothi were initially identical, but in the decades after the death of Guru Tegh Bahadur spurious compositions were inserted into the seventeenth-century manuscripts.[8] Sahib Singh went ahead to construct a full-fledged conspiracy theory involving competing groups within the Sikh community whom he held responsible for meddling with the Sikh text.

Building on the work of Sahib Singh, Pashaura Singh went a step farther. He viewed the rise of both the Kanpur and the Lahore families of manuscripts as part of a conspiracy that included not only the dissenting groups within the early Sikh community but also the Mughal administration at Lahore. Pashaura Singh is fully convinced that all variations in the early manuscripts were "interpolations" that resulted from conscious "tampering" with the original text carried out to confuse the message of the Sikh gurus.[9]

Rejecting the traditional description of the seventeenth-century manuscripts, Piar Singh argued for the presence of seven primary branches, some of them with further internal subdivisions.[10] He presents a list of these families on the basis of stylistic variations. His attitude toward the composition recorded in the early manuscripts but not present in the Adi Granth is more complex than that of his predecessors; he considers some of them to be authentic compositions of the gurus which were somehow dropped from the text of the Adi Granth.[11]

In the past several years, I succeeded in collecting relevant data from the extant seventeenth-century manuscripts, which enable us to reconstruct the history of the Sikh text during this period. We now know that the Kartarpur Pothi was copied early on. References exist to the presence of manuscripts compiled in 1605, 1610, 1637, 1640, and 1641.[12] These documents, unfortunately, are no longer extant, but a good number of manuscripts are available from 1642 onward. I restrict the following discussion to manuscripts prepared between 1642 to 1692, the period whose final years saw the compilation of the Adi Granth (see table 4).

The absence of Guru Tegh Bahadur's hymns in the original inscription of the undated manuscripts (21 to 27 in Table 4) suggests that they were also prepared before the mid-1670s.

The existing understanding of the history of Sikh scripture is constructed around the belief that seventeenth-century manuscripts fell into three groups: the exact copies of the Kartarpur Pothi, representing the authoritative line, and two branches following the Kanpur Pothi and the Lahore Pothi. The first striking aspect of the data available in the manuscripts mentioned below is that they fall not into three but two broad groups: manuscripts 3, 4, 5, 7, 8, 9, 19, 20, 22, 23, and 24 follow what is known in Sikh tradition as the Lahore branch, and manuscripts 1, 2, 6, 10, 11, 12, 13, 15, 16, 17, 18, 25, 26, and 27 represent the Khara Mangat branch. (Manuscripts numbered 14 and 21 do not fit into these two groups and need special attention).[13] I prefer to label these two groups as branch 1 and branch 2, respectively, and address in detail the problems in their traditional identification with Lahore and with Khara Mangat in the discussion that follows.

The traditional belief that the Kartarpur Pothi as it stands today produced a branch of manuscripts which culminated in the text of the Adi Granth confronts the unavail-

Table 4. Extant Manuscripts of the Sikh Sacred Text 1642–1692

1. The Kanpur Pothi. 467 folios; Gurdwara Bhai Banno, G. T. Road, Kanpur; Assun *vadi* 1, Samat 1699 (1642).[a]
2. The Gurdwara Bhai Ramkishan Pothi. 760 folios; Sheran vala Gate, Patiala; Haṛ *sudi* 14, Samat 1710 (1653).
3. The Amritsar Pothi. 591 folios; Arjan Singh Bhalla, Gali 5, House 9, Tehsilpura, Amritsar; Phagan *sudi* 1, Samat 1711 (1654) Known in the tradition as the Buṛa Sandhu Pothi.
4. The Dehra Dun Pothi. 651 folios; Darbar Sahib Sri Guru Ramrai; Vaisakh *vadi* 1, Samat 1716 (1659).
5. The Patiala Pothi. 683 folios; Ajaib Singh Sekhon, Lovely Cottage, Sangrur Road, Patiala; Samat 1718 (1661). Known in the tradition as the Kangaṛ Pothi
6. MS 341. 577 folios; Punjab Archives, Patiala; Haṛ 20, Samat 1723 (1666).
7. MS 1084. 464 folios; Guru Nanak Dev University, Amritsar; Samat 1723 (1666).
8. MS 115338. 688 folios; Punjabi University, Patiala; Magh *vadi* 1, Samat 1724 (1667). Known in the tradition as the Jograj Pothi.
9. MS 1229. 679 folios; Guru Nanak Dev University, Amritsar; Samat 1728 (1671). Known in the tradition as the Saranke Pothi.
10. MS 1192. 605 folios; Panjab University, Chandigarh; Jeṭh 9, Samat 1731 (1674).
11. The Anandpur Pothi. 608 folios; Bibi Narinder Kaur Sodhi, Baṛi Manji, Mahala Baṛi Sarkar, Anandpur; Jeṭh 9, Samat 1731 (1674).
12. The Chandigarh Pothi 1. 554 folios; Man Singh Nirankari, 9 Sector 4, Chandigarh; Jeṭh *vadi* 10, Samat 1733 (1676).
13. The Balbir Singh Sahitya Kendar Pothi 1. 638 folios; 20 Pritam Road, Dehra Dun; Assu *sudi* 3, Samat 1736 (1679).
14. The Lukhnow Pothi. 691 folios; Singha vali Gali, Mahala Yahiyaganj, Lukhnow; Asaṛ *vadi* 9, Samat 1743 (1686).[b]
15. The New Delhi Pothi. 530 folios; Mohan Singh, D 913 New Friends Colony, Delhi; Assu *vadi* 1, Samat 1743 (1686).
16. MS 115152. 706 folios; Punjabi University, Patiala; Magh *vadi* 1, Samat 1744 (1687).
17. The Bhai ki Daroli Pothi. 684 folios; Ratan Singh Sangha, Bhai ki Daroli, District Faridkot; Bhado *sudi* 5, Samat 1745 (1688).
18. MS 1189. 682 folios; Panjab University, Chandigarh; Katak *vadi* 1, Samat 1748 (1691).
19. MS 6. 596 folios; Punjabi University; Patiala; Savan *sudi* 1, Samat 1749 (1692).
20. The Patna Pothi. 1036 folios; Sri Takhat Harmandirji Patna; Samat 1749 (1692). Known in the tradition as the Ramrai Pothi.[b]
21. The Gurdwara Bal Lila Pothi. 840 folios; Maini Sangat, Patna.
22. MS 1. 589 folios; The royal collection at Motibagh, Patiala.
23. MS 2. 860 folios; The royal collection at Motibagh, Patiala.
24. MS 3. 992 folios; The royal collection at Motibagh, Patiala.
25. MS 8. 564 folios; Punjabi University, Patiala.
26. The Balbir Singh Sahitya Kendar Pothi 2. 700 folios; 20 Pritam Road, Dehra Dun.
27. The Chandigarh Pothi 2. 517 folios. Giani Gurdit Singh, 56 Sector 4, Chandigarh.

a. I am grateful to Winand M. Callewaert for giving me the film he made of the Kanpur Pothi some years ago.

b. Joginder Singh Ahluwalia kindly arranged to microfilm these manuscripts for my use.

ability of even a single manuscript that can be considered its exact copy.[14] This inconvenient fact has evoked interesting responses. For instance, Sahib Singh argues that soon after the Kartarpur Pothi was compiled, it was put up for public display at the Darbar Sahib, Amritsar and so could not be made available for copying.[15] Given this situation, the Kanpur Pothi was the only source available to scribes who were preparing new copies.

Sahib Singh's argument is based on the traditional belief that the Kanpur Pothi immediately followed the compilation of the Kartarpur Pothi. The date of 1642 recorded in the manuscript, however, invalidates this argument. Nor do the firm references to the presence of manuscripts prepared before 1642 support his thesis that the ritual role of the Kartarpur Pothi at the Darbar Sahib, if there was one, barred its usage in preparing copies. Furthermore, there is no evidence at all to support the traditional belief that the so-called Khara Mangat branch originated from the Kanpur Pothi, as I discuss later in this chapter.

Another attempt to explain the absence of the copies of the Kartarpur Pothi cites the rivalries within the guru family. Scholars who support this view contend that since the Kartarpur Pothi fell under Dhirmal's control, he did not permit it to be copied, placing the entire burden of production of new copies onto the Kanpur Pothi, the only manuscript available in the community.[16] This view is not without problems, either. The Kartarpur Pothi had existed twenty-four years before Dhirmal was born, and forty years or so before tensions arose between his branch of the family and the community under the leadership of Guru Hargobind at Kiratpur. In other words, one supposes that some copies of the Kartarpur Pothi must have been made before Dhirmal took custody of the manuscript, and there should have been no restriction on these copies to serve as the source for preparing new manuscripts even if the Kartarpur Pothi had become inaccessible.

No contemporary evidence supports the contention that Dhirmal or his descendants ever denied access to the Kartarpur Pothi for those making copies or comparing its text to any other manuscript. Several manuscripts in table 4 claim to be the direct copies of the Kartarpur Pothi, and others seem to have been compared with it.[17] Even if Dhirmal did not permit the members of the community at Kiratpur to reach the Kartarpur Pothi, his own followers must have copied it for their devotional purpose—after all, this was their scriptural text as well.

Another group of scholars explains the absence of exact copies of the Kartarpur Pothi in an even more convoluted way.[18] According to them, the present-day Kartarpur Pothi is actually an early copy of the Kanpur Pothi, which Dhirmal declared to be the original manuscript prepared by Guru Arjan. He is supposed to have made this false claim in order to perpetuate his own authority within the community. As discussed in chapter 4, the evidence available in the manuscript fully supports its authenticity, but even if one believes that the present-day Kartarpur Pothi is fake, this does not explain the immediate issue at hand, which is, what actually happened to the branch that was supposed to have exclusively followed the original Kartarpur Pothi?

The existing discussion on this issue centers on two interrelated assumptions: that the text of the Kartarpur Pothi culminated in the Adi Granth with the additions of the hymns of Guru Tegh Bahadur; and that the Kanpur Pothi, containing a set of apocryphal compositions, gave rise to a distinct branch of seventeenth-century manuscripts. Both of these assumptions, in my view, are erroneous.

In chapter 4, I argued that the text of the Kartarpur Pothi was altered in the late 1920s. The deletions were made in order to conform the text to what later Sikh tradition believed to be its original contents. The restructured text does harmonize with the traditional perception of its contents, but as a result, effective understanding of different branches of seventeenth-century manuscripts has become well nigh impossible. Building on what I believe to be the original contents of the Kartarpur Pothi, I present a revised assessment of its relationship with other seventeenth-century manuscripts and a different reading of the evolution of the Sikh text during this period. (See Map 2.)

Branch 1

It is true that a manuscript of this branch ("1") prepared in 1610 was present at Gurdwara Dehra Sahib, Lahore, at the turn of the twentieth century, but there is no evidence to support Charan Singh's view of its origin in Lahore mentioned earlier in this chapter. No reference to branch 1's connection with Lahore appears in the colophons present in the early manuscripts, nor is there any mention of the Lahore connection in the family traditions of their custodian. At the time these manuscripts were discovered, they were

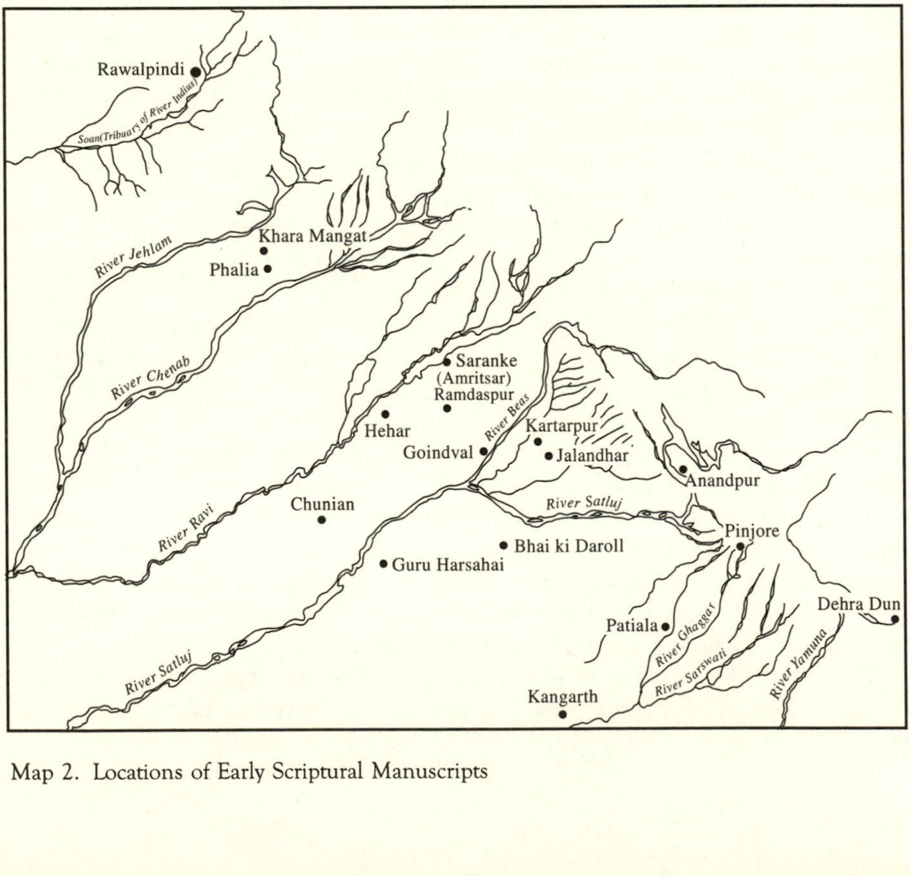

Map 2. Locations of Early Scriptural Manuscripts

scattered: the Amritsar Pothi was in the Rawalpindi area; MS 1084, MS 1229, and MS 11538 were in Majha; the Patiala Pothi was in Malwa; and some had left the Punjab.

The other issues pertaining to the history and development of this branch of manuscripts have remained largely unaddressed. We have no evidence to support Charan Singh's account of the compilation of the original manuscript of this branch. Traditions regarding Bhai Banno are not firm, as discussed later in the chapter; nor does his reconstruction of events that led to the compilation of the original manuscript of this branch account for the textual variations between the Kartarpur Pothi and branch 1 manuscripts.

The Amritsar Pothi is the earliest extant manuscript of this branch. According to the colophon recorded on its last folio, it was prepared in 1654. Its custodians, the Bhallas, trace their family history to Batala, the town they left in the closing decades of the seventeenth century before moving to the Rawalpindi area. There is no family memory available to confirm whether the Bhallas brought this manuscript from Batala or whether they procured it at Rawalpindi. In the 1810s Maharaja Ranjit Singh visited the Bhallas and awarded the manuscript an annual revenue grant of 35,000 rupees.[19] Why were the Bhallas given such a large grant but not invited to visit Lahore along with their possession? Why were they treated differently than the Kanpur Pothi and its custodians, the descendants of Bhai Banno? After the partition of the Punjab in 1947, the Bhalla family settled in Amritsar, and the manuscript is currently housed there. Although the origin of the Amritsar Pothi remains hazy, its later history poses no problem.

There are two views regarding the relationship between the Amritsar Pothi and the Kartarpur Pothi in existing literature. As referred to before, Charan Singh traces the origin of this branch to the Kartarpur Pothi; Piar Singh rejects this relationship and views the line as an independent attempt at compilation of the Sikh text.[20] Neither of them has developed their respective arguments in any detail.

Since the Amritsar Pothi and the Kartarpur Pothi are both available, let us examine their textual relationship. In its broad layout, the Amritsar Pothi follows the Kartarpur Pothi, yet there are variations that we need to identify first and then explain. The differences begin to surface right at the outset of these texts. (See table 5.) Both sequential and substantive variations are also present in the hymns recorded toward the end of the Kartarpur Pothi and the Amritsar Pothi. For instance, the "Couplets Surplus from the *Vars*" appear later in the final section of the Kartarpur Pothi but are recorded at its beginning in the Amritsar Pothi; Guru Arjan's *var* appears in the section on *rag* Basant in the Kartarpur Pothi but is appended at the end in the Amritsar Pothi; and the *Ragmala*

Table 5. Variation between the Kartarpur Pothi and the Amritsar Pothi

Details	Kartarpur Pothi	Amritsar Pothi
Compilation date	At the opening	At the end
Source of copying	At the opening	Absent
Table of rags	2 segments	1 segment
List of death dates	In the opening section	At the end

and the four compositions appearing at the closing of the Kartarpur Pothi were originally absent from the Amritsar Pothi.[21]

The variations within the main body of these two texts constitute a set of eight hymns that are recorded in the Kartarpur Pothi but absent in the Amritsar Pothi, as follows:

Guru Arjan's hymn in *rag* Soraṭhi (folio 481)

The opening verse of Guru Arjan's hymn in *rag* Ramkali (folio 703)

Guru Arjan's *var* in *rag* Basant (folio 854)[22]

Kabir's hymn in *rag* Asa (folio 374)

Kabir's verse in *rag* Soraṭhi (folio 497)

Mirabai's hymn in *rag* Maru (folio 810)

Ravidas's hymn in *rag* Maru (folio 810)

Surdas's verse in *rag* Sarang (folio 885)

In addition, the titles of nine *vars* in the Kartarpur Pothi include references to the tunes to which they are to be sung; in the Amritsar Pothi, however, the titles of only five *vars* include the tunes. Unlike the above-mentioned variations, where the compositions recorded in the Kartarpur Pothi are not available in the Amritsar Pothi, there is a unique case for the liturgical section in the Amritsar Pothi, which contains a set of four hymns (*Sopurakh*) that are not available in the Kartarpur Pothi. These four hymns do appear in the Kartarpur Pothi under their respective *rag* sections but are absent from the liturgical section.

Piar Singh cites these differences as a firm evidence that the Amritsar Pothi represents a line entirely independent of the Kartarpur Pothi.[23] No effort has been made to explain the nature and substance of the above differences and yet relate this manuscript to the Kartarpur Pothi. In the following discussion, I attempt to explain these variations while suggesting that the Kartarpur Pothi is the source of the branch of manuscripts to which the Amritsar Pothi belongs.

In chapter 4 I argued that although the original inscription of the Kartarpur Pothi was completed in 1604, hymns composed by Guru Arjan between 1604 and 1606, along with some other compositions, were subsequently introduced into its text. I propose that the original manuscript that generated the Amritsar Pothi branch was prepared during this period when the Kartarpur Pothi was reaching its finished form.

Let me begin with a discussion of the differences within the main bodies of the Kartarpur Pothi and the Amritsar Pothi. We have definite evidence that four hymns absent from the main body of the Amritsar Pothi—Guru Arjan's couplet in *rag* Ramkali, his *var* in *rag* Basant (recorded toward the end of the Amritsar Pothi), and the hymns of Mirabai and Ravidas in *rag* Maru—were all introduced into the Kartarpur Pothi after its original inscription.[24]

There is firm evidence to argue that this was also true of Guru Arjan's hymn in *rag* Soraṭhi, Kabir hymn in *rag* Asa, and his verse in *rag* Soraṭhi. All of these appear at the end of their respective sequences.[25] This leaves us with the single verse of Surdas in *rag* Sarang; this verse of eight syllables was undoubtedly recorded in the original inscription of the Kartarpur Pothi, but its appearance there without a distinct title may have resulted in its accidental elimination by the scribe. In chapter 6, I address ways in which the texts of the *vars* continued to be worked upon after they were inscribed in the Kartarpur Pothi. In all likelihood the references to the tunes in the titles of some of the *vars* were not originally recorded in the Kartarpur Pothi, and this absence persisted in its early copies.[26]

This explanation—that the original manuscript of the branch to which the Amritsar Pothi belongs was prepared when the Kartarpur Pothi had not reached its final form—accounts for the higher frequency of differences in the opening and closing sections of these manuscripts. We know that the table of contents of the Kartarpur Pothi was prepared after the original inscription, and it is possible that the table of contents as it appears in the Amritsar Pothi represented what was available in the Kartarpur Pothi at that time.[27] In the same way, the sequence of the hymns at the closing of the Kartarpur Pothi seems to have been modified after their original inscription, and the Amritsar Pothi represents the earlier version of this layout. It comes as no surprise that the sequence as it appears in the Amritsar Pothi parallels the hymns present in MS 1245 (folio 1232). The sequence of composition in the closing section of the text appear as follows:

Kartarpur Pothi	Amritsar Pothi
[Recorded later]	*Couplets Surplus . . .
Couplets by Kabir	Couplets by Kabir
Couplets by Farid	Couplets by Farid
Panegyrics by the Bhaṭs	Panegyrics by the Bhaṭs
*Couplets Surplus . . .	[Recorded earlier]
[Recorded later]	The recipe for ink
[At the beginning of the text]	List of death dates
[At the beginning of the text]	The colophon
[Recorded earlier in *rag* Basant]	*Var* in *rag* Basant
The *Ragmala*	[Absent]
Four compositions	Absent
The recipe for ink	[Appears earlier]

This brings us to the expansion of the liturgical section in the Amritsar Pothi, which apparently points to the later origin of this branch. The data at our disposal suggest that the expanded liturgical section is not an essential feature of the manuscripts of this branch. For instance, MS 1084 (recorded in 1666,) and MS 1229 (inscribed in 1671) do not contain them. This in my view implies that these hymns were absent from the original manuscript of this branch. The daily Sikh prayers seem to have undergone expansion in the mid seventeenth century, and the scribe of the Amritsar Pothi, along with some others, incorporated the changes into the manuscripts they prepared. For instance, the Dehra Dun Pothi (1659) also contains the expanded version of the liturgical text.

The relationship of the Amritsar Pothi to the Kartarpur Pothi can be scrutinized in another way. The Kartarpur Pothi contains a set of textual anomalies not present in MS 1245. For instance, Guru Amardas's hymn of four stanzas, which begins *Gurmukhi kripa kare bhagati kije* (When guru is gracious, one can be devoted to God," Kartarpur Pothi, folio 65, AG, 31), also appears in an eight-stanza hymn attributed to Guru Amardas (Kartarpur Pothi, folio 93, AG, 64–65). This duplication duly appears in the Amritsar Pothi and MS 1084 (folios 24 and 35). Furthermore, a set of couplets in the Kartarpur Pothi appears twice in the text with varied attribution and continues in the manuscripts of branch 1.[28] These limited yet significant data point to the close relationship between this branch of manuscripts and the Kartarpur Pothi.

Finally, an entry recorded in the Amritsar Pothi (folio 591) offers critical evidence to support my argument. This has two parts: the first contains the death dates of the first four gurus and the second goes as follows:

> In the presence of the Guru [Arjan], the manuscript was completed. It was inscribed by Bhai Buṛa Sandhu in the presence of the fifth Guru. Bhai Milkhi of Peshawar commissioned its inscription. He who will come to the presence of the manuscript will see the body of Guru Nanak. Forgive [my] flaws and omissions. God! The true guru! [The manuscript] is completed in Samat 1662 (1605 C.E.).

G. B. Singh accepted 1605 as the date of preparation of the Amritsar Pothi and named it after Buṛa Sandhu, its supposed scribe.[29] Piar Singh continues to associate the manuscript with Buṛa Sandhu but argues that the entry is false and was inserted later to increase the significance of the Amritsar Pothi by tracing its origin to the time of Guru Arjan.[30]

I argue that this entry does not record the date of preparation of the Amritsar Pothi as G. B. Singh claims; neither is it a deliberate attempt to falsify its date of compilation as Piar Singh believes, but rather represents a typical instance in which the scribe of the Amritsar Pothi reproduced the colophon recorded in the source from which he copied (a manuscript prepared in 1605 by Buṛa Sandhu). If this line of reasoning is correct, the Amritsar Pothi becomes a copy of the copy of the Kartarpur Pothi compiled in 1605.

The appearance of only the death dates of the first four gurus further supports the idea that Buṛa Sandhu prepared his manuscripts before 1606, the year Guru Arjan was executed by the Mughals. The placement of this entry toward the closing of the text synchronizes with its appearance in MS 1245 (folio 1255). In the Kartarpur Pothi, the entry of death dates appears in the opening part of the text and also includes reference to Guru Arjan in the same handwriting. In chapter 4, I argued that this entry was shifted to the opening section in the Kartarpur Pothi from its original position at the end of the manuscript.

By reporting that the manuscript was prepared for Bhai Milkhi of Peshawar, the colophon provides an interesting clue to the early history of the original manuscript of this branch. It is reasonable to assume that after its completion, Bhai Milkhi took it to his hometown, Peshawar. Once there, the manuscript served as a source for copies generated in the area, and the Bhallas, living in the vicinity, were able to procure one for themselves.

Although this branch of manuscripts continued to multiply, the corpus of hymns recorded in them shows an interesting evolution. There was a visible effort on the part of scribes to incorporate into their texts the hymns recorded in the finished Kartarpur Pothi, as well as to conform to the sequence present in its closing section.[31] Interestingly, while the manuscripts belonging to branch 2 expanded with the hymns of Guru

Tegh Bahadur and continued to appear even after the creation of the Adi Granth, the manuscripts of branch 1 disappeared after the turn of the eighteenth century.[32] The early manuscripts, however, survived, thanks to the judicious care of their custodians. They provide us with details attesting to their one-time primacy.

Branch 2

The Kanpur Pothi, the earliest extant manuscript of this branch, is dated 1642 but contains no information about its place of compilation. Sikh sources and the family traditions of the manuscript's custodians attribute its compilation to Bhai Banno. Whatever the circumstances of its making, the manuscript remained at Khara Mangat with Bhai Banno's descendants. Its reputation as a historical document resulted in an invitation to bring it to the court of Maharaja Ranjit Singh at Lahore.[33] The details concerning the family's stay at the Sikh court are not clear. We have no idea whether the manuscript was deposited in the royal treasury or the family was assigned a *gurdwara* in Lahore where they put it up for public display, as occurred with the Kartarpur Pothi. At the time of the annexation of the Punjab by the British, the manuscript surfaced in the Citadel Establishment and was returned to its custodians, who then took it back to Khara Mangat.[34] The partition of the Punjab led to the family's departure from their village; the manuscript was housed temporarily at Amritsar and at Barauta, District Meerut, before arriving at its present location at Kanpur.[35]

There are serious problems with the traditional explanation of the manuscript's origin. The date of 1642 does not correspond to the time of Guru Arjan. Bhai Banno's name does not appear in the list of the important Sikhs of the period in the writings of Bhai Gurdas, nor is the name of Khara Mangat included in the lists of the seats of regional centers of the community in the sixteenth century.[36] If Bhai Banno was an influential Sikh in the early 1640s, he would have to have been closely tied with Dhirmal's family to borrow the Kartarpur Pothi from them. The manuscripts prepared before the Kanpur Pothi falsify the traditional claim that this was the first copy ever made of the Kartarpur Pothi. If the compilation of the Kanpur Pothi was a key event, Sikh tradition has forgotten its details; and unless an early source of information appears, we will never be able to construe them with any certainty.

Yet these problems have no direct bearing on the claim that the Kanpur Pothi is a direct copy of the Kartarpur Pothi, which can be evaluated in light of information available to us exclusively in these two documents. The Kartarpur Pothi and the Kanpur Pothi have identical structures. They share the same table of contents. The main body of the texts is divided into two parts. The first opens with the *Japji* and ends with the section on *rag* Tilang; the second begins with *rag* Suhi and concludes with miscellaneous hymns lacking any *rag* assignment. The opening folio of the *Japji* and that of the section on *rag* Suhi are illuminated, with the invocation recorded in the hands of the gurus.[37] The compositions at the closing of both the texts are identical and end with the formula for preparing the ink.

Other details also connect the Kanpur Pothi with the Kartarpur Pothi. For instance, the *Japji* recorded in the Kartarpur Pothi is reported in the table of contents to be "a copy of the text of the *Japji* available in the hand of Guru Ramdas" (folio 2). The scribe of the Kanpur Pothi duly reports, in its table of contents, that the text of the *Japji* was a copy of a copy of the text recorded by Guru Ramdas. He thus specifies that his manuscript was a stage farther removed than the Kartarpur Pothi that contained the copy of the original text of the *Japji*. This feature of recording the exact number of stages by which the newly prepared manuscript was removed from the original continued in later manuscripts of this branch.

These data support the traditional claim that the Kanpur Pothi is a direct copy of the Kartarpur Pothi. The traditional understanding of the variations within the contents of the Kartarpur Pothi and the Kanpur Pothi, and the belief that the Kanpur Pothi generated an independent branch of manuscripts, however, are questionable. Sikh literature referred to earlier reports that the Kanpur Pothi includes a set of compositions that are absent from the Kartarpur Pothi. Three of them appear within the main body of the text. These are attributed to Guru Arjan, in *rag* Ramkali; to Mirabai, in *rag* Maru; and to Surdas, in *rag* Sarang. The remaining four appear in the final section and include three (two sets of *shaloks*, and the *Ratanmala*) attributed to Guru Nanak, and the *Hakikati Rah Mukam Raje Shivnabh ki*, which is without attribution.[38]

A close study of the contents of this branch of manuscripts reveals that this description of differences between the Kartarpur Pothi and the Kanpur Pothi is only partially correct. The variations between these two manuscripts in fact form a much more complicated pattern. In table 6, I present a comprehensive chart to show what they are. The manuscripts are recorded in terms of their number in table 4. The third column reports the manuscript's copy number (CN) from the Kartarpur Pothi. The next three columns show the status of Guru Arjan's hymns in *rag* Soraṭhi (Mahala 5 Soraṭhi), *rag* Ramkali (Mahala 5 Ramkali), and *rag* Malar (Mahala 5 Malar). The next columns show, respectively, the status of Mirabai's hymn in *rag* Maru (Mira Maru); Surdas's in *rag* Sarang (Surdas Sarang); and four compositions (4C) that appear at the end of the text along with the *Ragmala*, which appears in all the manuscripts of this branch mentioned in table 6.

The data in the chart clarify the relationship of the Kanpur Pothi to the Kartarpur Pothi, on the one hand, and to the later manuscripts, on the other. First, no one thus far has recorded the fact that two of Guru Arjan's hymns recorded in the Kartarpur Pothi in *rag* Soraṭhi, and *rag* Malar (present in the Amritsar Pothi, folio 525), respectively, do not appear in the Kanpur Pothi. This absence is significant, in that it suggests that later manuscripts that contain these hymns are not likely to be copies of the Kanpur Pothi.

Second, the traditional belief that the Kanpur Pothi contains seven additional compositions absent from the Kartarpur Pothi is not supported by the data at our disposal. The Kanpur Pothi contains only two compositions absent from the Kartarpur Pothi, but even here the situation is more complex than the one envisaged in Sikh literature. Neither of these compositions is entirely new; their opening verses appear in the Kartarpur Pothi—but without the full text. In all, the Kartarpur Pothi contains three cases, attributed respectively to Guru Arjan in *rag* Ramkali, Kabir in *rag* Soraṭhi, and Surdas in *rag* Sarang, where the opening verses are recorded and some space is left blank for anticipated later completion of the hymns.[39]

The scribe of the Kanpur Pothi handles these three verses in three different ways. He records the opening verse of Kabir's hymn in *rag* Soraṭhi (folio 244) as it appears in the Kartarpur Pothi but leaves no blank space following it. In other words, he does not

Table 6. Substantive Variations Between the Kartarpur Pothi and the Early Manuscripts of Branch II

MS	Date	CN	M5S	M5R	M5M	MM	SS	4C
Kartarpur P.	1604	0	P	OV	P	P	OV	P
Kanpur P.	1642	1	A	C	A	P	C	P
2	1653	2	P	C	P	P	OV	P
6	1666	2	P	C	P	P	OV	P
10	1674	A	A	C	A	P	OV	P
11	1674	2	A	C	A	P	OV	P
12	1676	2	A	C	A	P	OV	P
13	1679	1	A	C	A	P	OV	P
15	1686	5	A	C	A	P	OV	P
16	1687	1	A	C	P	P	OV	P
18	1691	3	A	C	A	P	OV	P
20	1692	A	A	C	P	A	OV	P

A = absent; P = present; C = complete hymn; OV = opening verse only.

understand that this hymn is incomplete. In the second case, he records the opening verse of Surdas in *rag* Sarang and leaves some blank space, in which a different hand inscribed the complete composition at some later point in time. In the third instance, he inscribes a complete composition under Guru Arjan's name in *rag* Ramkali (folio 319).

The composition attributed to Guru Arjan is thus the only true addition we have in the original inscription of the Kanpur Pothi. Sikh literature attributes this composition to Bhai Banno and his people. In fact, there is no evidence of Bhai Banno's involvement. The composition was not only available to Bhai Banno, but it appears in all manuscripts that claim to be the direct copies of the Kartarpur Pothi. It is not clear why this composition was not included in the Kartarpur Pothi. It seems to have been available to the scribes preparing copies of the Kartarpur Pothi and they recorded it in the manuscripts they inscribed. Scholarly opinions vary: Sahib Singh and Pashaura Singh propose a complex set of ulterior motives to explain its introduction into the Sikh text, while Giani Badan Singh and Teja Singh do not have any problem in accepting it as Guru Arjan's creation.[40]

The traditional claim that the Kanpur Pothi generated an independent branch of seventeenth-century manuscripts was based on the misconception that all the manuscripts which included the supposedly extra compositions were its copies. A precise understanding of the original contents of the Kartarpur Pothi suggests that the manuscripts supposed to have followed the Kanpur Pothi were in fact the copies of the Kartarpur Pothi itself. The composition attributed to Guru Arjan was, however, available to the scribes and they all added it to their manuscripts.

The Kanpur Pothi is simply one member of this family of manuscripts. There may well be some copies made directly from the Kanpur Pothi, but no evidence is available to place this manuscript at the head of an independent branch of seventeenth-century manuscripts.[41] The geography of the Punjab helps us understand this situation. The

Kartarpur Pothi and its other copies were available in the central Punjab itself, and there was no need for the scribes from Kiratpur or Anandpur, the centers of Sikh activity during the period under discussion, to travel to Khara Mangat, some 200-odd miles away, to prepare copies of the Sikh text.

To sum up the discussion of the pre-Adi Granth manuscripts, the evidence at our disposal upholds the traditional perception that the Kartarpur Pothi was at the fountainhead of the Sikh text in the seventeenth century. Instead of the presence of the traditionally accepted three branches—the Kartarpur, the Khara Mangat, and the Lahore, among the manuscripts of the period—the data support the existence of two branches originating from the Kartarpur Pothi at two points in time, pre-1606 and post-1606. Furthermore, the traditional perception of the nature of variations and the reasons for their emergence among the manuscripts has no basis in historical reality.

In my view the story of evolution of the Sikh text during the seventeenth century that emerges from the extant manuscripts is as follows: the Kartarpur Pothi began to be copied while still in the process of reaching its final form; a copy of it made in 1605 was taken to the Peshawar area where it served as a source for manuscripts that constitute branch 1; the Kartarpur Pothi reached its final form in 1606 and then its copies became the manuscripts of branch 2. It is certain that manuscripts of both these branches proliferated evenly within the community in the middle decades of the seventeenth century. By the mid 1660s, however, the scribes seem to have become aware of the hymns originally absent from the manuscripts belonging to branch 1 and they began to add them into the copies they prepared.

It is not clear if any distinction was made between the scriptural manuscripts of these two branches in terms of their status within the community. There is sufficient evidence to argue that the Kartarpur Pothi was considered to be the authoritative manuscripts during the seventeenth century. But Sikh tradition also recalls a manuscript assigned to accompany Ramrai during his visit to Delhi to meet Emperor Aurangzeb in 1660, and this is presently available at Ramrai's seat at Dehra Dun.[42] Interestingly, this manuscript belongs to branch 1, which implies that at the Sikh court itself it was treated as the authoritative text.

Additional evidence supports the claim that manuscripts that belonged to both these branches enjoyed equal recognition in the seventeenth-century Sikh community. There seems to have been the tradition of preparing a copy of the scriptural text, bringing it to the presence of the guru at the Sikh court, and receiving his attestation in the form of his inscription of the Sikh invocation on the opening folio.[43] The signatures recorded in the hands of different gurus appear on the opening folios of manuscripts of both these branches. The scenario I envision is that the distant congregations prepared copies from the accessible manuscripts, presented them to the gurus to receive their sanctification, and they placed their attestation on these documents irrespective of the details of the contents.

The Adi Granth

A note in the Patna Pothi (1692) confirms that the importance of the Kartarpur Pothi as the original document was fully recognized in the community, and a manuscript that was copied directly from it or was collated and corrected with it enjoyed special status. Chaupa Singh, the first author to refer to the compilation of the Adi Granth, reports that Guru Gobind Singh sought to borrow the Kartarpur Pothi from Dhirmal's family in 1678 but did not succeed.[44] The request understandably emerged from the realization that an authoritative scriptural text should be created directly from the Kartarpur Pothi for the use of the community at Anandpur. Kesar Singh Chhibbar, writing a few decades later, contends that after this denial of access to the Kartarpur Pothi, the guru used another manuscript at Anandpur to create the Adi Granth.[45]

The view that has dominated Sikh thinking since the nineteenth century, however, places the event at Damdama, Bhatinda, in 1705–1706. Giani Gian Singh expanded this tradition to claim that Guru Gobind Singh, unable to access the Kartarpur Pothi, and seemingly with no other written document around, dictated the complete text of the Adi Granth from memory to Bhai Mani Singh, who served as the amanuensis.[46]

The earlier traditions seem more accurate in light of the information available in extant manuscripts. The reports that the Sikhs at Anandpur in the late 1670s felt the need to prepare the authoritative scriptural text with the help of the Kartarpur Pothi are supported by the appearance of the earliest manuscripts of the Adi Granth. The first manuscript was dated 1682 and was followed by the ones inscribed in 1688, 1691, and 1692; references to at least three others are also available.[47] These data fix the time of compilation of the Adi Granth with reasonable certainty.

What went into the making of the Adi Granth is, however, a more complex issue. Sikh sources repeatedly claim that Guru Gobind Singh compiled the Adi Granth by adding Guru Tegh Bahadur's hymns to the contents of the Kartarpur Pothi. This coheres with the fact that Guru Tegh Bahadur was the only guru to have composed hymns after the inscription of the Kartarpur Pothi. The thrust of the traditional accounts is twofold: first, Guru Gobind Singh was responsible for updating the Sikh text at this stage in its evolution; second, this updating involved the addition of Guru Tegh Bahadur's hymns to the corpus recorded in the Kartarpur Pothi. Both these claims are problematical in light of the data available to us.

We have firm evidence that the hymns of Guru Tegh Bahadur were introduced into the Sikh text during his lifetime, that is, before 1675. G. B. Singh located a manuscript extant at Dhaka prepared in 1675 (Samat 1732, *miti* agahan *vadi*), which contained all of Guru Tegh Bahadur's hymns recorded in their appropriate *rag* sections.[48] G. B. Singh maintained that this manuscript completed at Anandpur seventeen days after the death of Guru Tegh Bahadur confirms that the decision of adding his hymns to the Sikh text must have made by the guru when he was still at Anandpur.

Further evidence supports this argument. MS 1192 inscribed in 1674 also contains the complete corpus of Guru Tegh Bahadur's hymns.[49] On its opening folio, the invocation is followed by a note that reads, "This attestation was obtained by presenting [the manuscript] to the ninth master, in the presence of the whole congregation, on Samat 1731, the full moon day of Jeṭh." The invocation is recorded in the hand of Guru Tegh Bahadur as we know his handwriting from other records. This date corresponds with another date, of a week earlier (Samat 1731 Jeṭh 9), recorded at the head of the table of contents in the manuscript. These dates indicate that the work on the table of contents began on Jeṭh 9 and was finished by the full-moon day, when the manuscript was presented to the guru for his ceremonial attestation.

Piar Singh argues that the dates, the invocation, and the note recorded underneath in MS 1192 are all fake.[50] In my view, Piar Singh is unable to unload the weight of the tradition that Guru Tegh Bahadur's hymns were inducted into the Sikh text only after his death and consequently finds it impossible to deal with this important document. All the entries in MS 1192 are authentic and there is no evidence of any tampering. Nor is there anything unusual in Guru Tegh Bahadur's updating the Sikh text by adding his hymns to the existing corpus. In doing this, he followed his predecessors, Guru Amardas and Guru Arjan, who prepared the scriptural texts that included their own hymns. MS 1192 and the manuscript examined by G. B. Singh surely suggest that the hymns of Guru Tegh Bahadur were incorporated into the Sikh text during his lifetime, and the later Sikh tradition's association of this development with Guru Gobind Singh is inaccurate.

Sikh literature claims that addition of the hymns of Guru Tegh Bahadur to the corpus of the Kartarpur Pothi resulted in the creation of the Adi Granth. Instead, the data available to us suggest that the addition of Guru Tegh Bahadur's hymns into the existing corpus and the compilation of the Adi Granth mark two distinct stages in the evolution of Sikh scripture. MS 1192 and the manuscript seen by G. B. Singh represent the first stage of updating of the text of the manuscripts of Branch 2 in the 1670s; the compilation of the Adi Granth in the 1680s marks the final stage of this evolution. In later Sikh tradition these two stages were incorrectly coalesced. Table 7 shows the contents of the Adi Granth in comparison with the Kartarpur Pothi, Amritsar Pothi, and MS 1192. These data clearly present the details of the contents of the Adi Granth in relation to other early manuscripts. The compilation of the Adi Granth did not involve a simple addition of the hymns of Guru Tegh Bahadur to the existing corpus, but some decisions seemed to have been taken and a set of compositions available in the earlier manuscripts of branch 2 were probably dropped from the final text.

Many of the changes can be easily explained. As I referred to earlier, the liturgical section had expanded during this period and manuscripts beginning with the mid sev-

Table 7. Substantive Variations between the *Adi* Granth and Its Antecedents

	K. Pothi	A. Pothi	MS 1192	Adi Granth
Liturgical Section	10 hymns	14 hymns	14 hymns	14 hymns
M5 Soraṭhi	P	A	P	A
M5 Ramakali	OV	A	C	OV
M5Malar	P	P	A	A
KabirAsa	OV	A	A	A
Kabir Soraṭhi	P	A	A	A
Mira Maru	P	A	P	A
Surdas Sarang	OV	A	OV	OV
Kabir Couplet	P	A	A	A
Ragmala	P	A	P	P
Four Compositions	P	A	P	A
Death Dates	P	P	P	A
Mahala 9	A	A	P	P

A = absent; P = present; C = complete hymn; OV = opening verse only.

enteenth century reflect that. This expansion was formalized in the Adi Granth. Second, although all the seventeenth-century manuscripts in Table 6 contain the complete hymns of Guru Arjan in *rag* Ramkali, the single verse in Kartarpur Pothi was accepted in the Adi Granth. As to the dropping of Guru Arjan's hymns in *rag* Soraṭhi and in *rag* Malar, no explanation seems to be forthcoming at this stage of my research. A prose piece about a Sikh's visit to South India which appears in the four compositions at the closing of the text may have been thought irrelevant and deleted. The remaining three may not have been considered authentic compositions of Guru Nanak and let go. The death dates of the gurus must have become a part of the Sikh communal lore, resulting in their deletion from the scriptural text. As I discuss in chapter 7, these particular hymns of Kabir and Mira are misfits within the framework of Sikh doctrine and may have been dropped for this reason.

During my fieldwork in Anandpur and Damdama, almost all the manuscripts I came across were of the Adi Granth. This provides a basis for arguing that the Adi Granth in the closing decades of the seventeenth century was seen as the canonical text in the central community. The two major collections of manuscripts at Takhat Damdama and at Dehra Baba Miṭha Singh include over 60 eighteenth- and nineteenth-century manuscripts, all of which are of the Adi Granth.[51]

To sum up, the history of the Sikh scriptural text since the compilation of the Kartarpur Pothi has been varied and complex. Built primarily on the traditions prevalent within the later Sikh community, many details of the existing understanding of this period cannot be sustained in light of the data available in the extant manuscripts. From our discussion, the time line of the Sikh text works as follows: in the seventeenth century we begin with two branches of manuscripts, one of which contained an additional set of compositions; the larger text is updated to create the MS 1192 version in the mid-1670s; the Adi Granth, which is distinct from the MS 1192 version, is compiled in the early 1680s and acquires the status of the canonical text. We take up the history of the Adi Granth in subsequent centuries in chapter 8.

6

The Emerging Structure of the Adi Granth

The complex organizational structure of the Adi Granth has attracted considerable scholarly attention. Charan Singh's *Sri Guru Granth Baṇi Biaura* (Details of the contents of the Adi Granth), written at the turn of the twentieth century, was the first detailed study of this theme.[1] Mohinder Kaur Gill's *Guru Granth Sahib di Sampadan Kala* (The art of editing the Guru Granth Sahib), written in 1974, and Joginder Singh Talwaṛa's *Baṇi Biaura, Bhag 1*, published in 1992, are the other full-length works on this subject.[2] In addition, there are some brief but helpful discussions of the structure of the Adi Granth.[3] All these studies are primarily descriptive; none addresses the question of how the scriptural text came to be organized the way it is today.

The analysis of the Sikh manuscripts that I present in previous chapters sheds important light on the evolving structure of the Sikh scriptural text. The information at our disposal now refutes the traditional belief that the organization of the contents of the Adi Granth was primarily the work of Guru Arjan, with some assistance from Bhai Gurdas—a task performed in connection with the compilation of the Kartarpur Pothi.[4] The early manuscripts point instead to a slow yet steady development of the arrangement of the contents of the Sikh text, beginning with the Guru Harsahai Pothi in the 1530s, continuing through the Goindval Pothis (1570s) and the Kartarpur Pothi (1604), and arriving climactically at the Adi Granth (1680s). The structure available in the text of the Adi Granth at that date has remained in place ever since.

In this chapter I trace the evolutionary process that resulted in the Adi Granth. I begin by briefly addressing the significance of *rag* in Sikh devotion and its relationship to the organization of Sikh scripture. I then trace the evolution of the structure of the Sikh text in terms of both the sequential arrangement of *rag* sections and their internal constitution. The chapter concludes with a brief comparison of the structure of the Adi Granth with that of Hindu and Islamic scriptures.

Rag as the Organizing Principle of the Adi Granth

Each hymn in the main body of the text of the Adi Granth is assigned a *rag* to which it should be sung, and there are thirty-one different *rag* sections. This feature of Sikh scripture is often interpreted as an indication of the unique significance assigned to *rag* in Sikh devotion. With *kirtan* (singing, with musical accompaniment, the praises of God) at the center of Sikh congregational worship since the very inception of the community, *rag* as the organizing principle of the Adi Granth is deemed perfectly natural.[5]

We begin our discussion with the issue of *kirtan* itself. Although the term *kirtan* is rarely used in the hymns of Guru Nanak and Guru Amardas, it is implied throughout. Guru Nanak called himself a singer (*ḍhaḍhi)* who has been employed by God to sing his praises (*Hau ḍhaḍhi vekaru karai laia . . . ḍhaḍhi kare pasao sabadu vajaia*, M1, AG, 150). Guru Amardas specifically urged his followers to perform *kirtan* of the hymns of the gurus (*Andinu kirtanu sada karahi gur kai sabadi apara*, M3, AG, 593), believing that the performance of *kirtan* cleanses the mind of all impurities (*Andinu kirtanu karahi din rati. Satiguri gavai vichahu juṭhi bharanti*, M3, AG, 1174). The *Sadu* of Sundar recorded in *rag* Ramkali provides us with contemporary testimony that Guru Amardas gave instructions for the performance of *kirtan* after his death (*Ante satiguru bolia mai pichhai kirtanu kariahu nirbaṇu jio*, AG, 923).

Kirtan apparently grew in importance as time went on, emerging as a significant theme in its own right in the hymns of Guru Arjan. For Guru Arjan, *kirtan* takes away disease, sorrow, and discomfort (*Rog sog dukh tisu nahi. Sadh sangi hari kirtanu gahi*, M5, AG, 1085) and generates peace, ecstasy, comfort, and relaxation (*Kari kirtanu man sital bhae*, M5, AG, 178; *Anand sukh bisram nit hari ka kirtanu gae*, M5, AG, 962). The effect of *kirtan* goes beyond life-related issues—it results in eliminating the fear of death and helping one attain liberation (*Michu huṭai jam te chhuṭai hari kirtan paraves*, M5, AG, 297; *Hari dinu raini kirtanu gaiai, bahuṛi na joni paiai*, M5, AG, 624).

Building on Guru Nanak's self-identification as a singer, the janam-sakhis depict him as a powerful performer of *kirtan*.[6] Early Sikh traditions stress Guru Nanak's long and close association with Mardana, a rebec player, and explain how Satta and Balvand led the *kirtan* at the Sikh court in the second half of the sixteenth century.[7] Bhai Gurdas claims that the sounds of *kirtan* emerging from every house symbolized the spiritual victory of Guru Nanak, and he refers to people known for their singing in the early Sikh community.[8] And from then until now, many Sikh writers have stressed the importance of *kirtan* in Sikh worship.

Although the significance of *kirtan* cannot be disputed, it must not be overstated.[9] A Sikh, by definition, is a learner, and his or her professed goal in life, according to Guru Nanak, is to understand God and God's relationship with the world.[10] Sikh devotion, with its musical component, is only part of the search for an understanding of God which, in the words of Guru Nanak, includes talking about God (*Gali gala sirjaṇhar*, M1, AG, 351), reading about God (*Paṛiai namu salah hori budhi mithia*, M1, AG, 1289), and writing about God (*Likhu namu salahu*, M1, AG, 16; *Likhu ramnam gurmukhi gopala*, M1, AG, 930). While *kirtan* is important, it takes on its significance in a larger matrix that includes the reading of scripture (*paṭh*), listening to its exposition (*katha*), and performing service to fellow human beings (*Vichi dunia sev kamaiai. Ta dargah baisaṇu paiai*, M1, AG, 26).

Moreover, the essence of the Sikh experience of *kirtan* is not the *rag*-related component but the genuine spirit of the devotee yearning to know God and develop a relationship of his constant remembrance. Guru Nanak abhorred those who sang *rags* while their hearts were elsewhere (*Gavahi gite chiti anite. Rag suṇae kahavahe bite*, M1, AG, 414) and believed that they would suffer for their hypocrisy (*Ragi nadi manu dujai bhae. Antari kapaṭu maha dukhu pae*, M1, AG, 1342).

Guru Ramdas puts this strongly. He claims that God is beyond *rags* (*Ragai nadai bahara ini hukam na bujhia jae*, M4, AG, 1423), and that liberation can be attained only by serving God, leaving *rags* and other sounds along the way (*Rag nad chhoḍi hari seviai ta dargah paiai manu*, M4, AG, 849). In the Sikh belief system, a *rag* is simply an effective carrier of the message, which is the element of primary significance in devotional singing. There is absolutely no provision to deify *rags*.[11]

The absence of assigned *rags* in the *Japji*, the best-known text in the Sikh community, which appears at the opening of the Adi Granth and in another large set of hymns recorded at its end, shows that *rag* is not an indispensable part of the text of the Adi Granth. Nor is *rag* truly central in most Sikh rituals. For instance, the reading of the Adi Granth without the musical accompaniment is the core ritual performed both at the time of thanksgiving and in emergency situations where divine help is sought; *kirtan* is performed only to mark the successful completion of the reading of the Adi Granth. In the Darbar Sahib, Amritsar, *kirtan* is done when the Adi Granth is open for public display during the day; however, devotion continues in the form of a simple recitation of the *Sukhmani* (Jewel of comfort) once the Adi Granth has been taken to its place of rest (*koṭha sahib*) for the night.[12]

The role of *kirtan* in Sikh devotion and the principle of *rag* in organizing the Sikh scriptural text came to the Sikhs from the religio-cultural context of sixteenth-century India. The Sikh gurus knew enough about music to set their own hymns to thirty-one *rags*, both classical and regional; Guru Amardas's hymns in particular include numerous direct references to *rags*.[13] This level of knowledge of *rags* was not unique to the Sikh gurus. Similar skill in music is demonstrated in the compositions of all other saint-poets of this period.[14] We have testimony as to the importance of *kirtan* in the activity of such holy people as Ravidas, Pipa, and others, both in Anantdas's *Parichai* (Introduction), probably written in the last decades of the sixteenth century, and in Nabhadas's *Bhaktamal* (Garland of saints), probably written in the first quarter of the seventeenth century.[15]

The same can be said of decisions regarding the organization of the Sikh scriptural text. The process evolved slowly. We have evidence from Guru Harsahai Pothi that the distinct association of hymns with specific *rags*, as we now know it, goes back to Guru Nanak. His hymns recorded in this manuscript were assigned *rags*, but were placed in a loose conglomeration with no apparent organizing principle. The arrangement of hymns according to *rag* in the extant Goindval Pothis indicates the next logical step. Each hymn here is assigned a *rag*, and the text as a whole is neatly divided into separate *rag* sections. The principle appeared with some minor modification in Guru Arjan's compilation of the Kartarpur Pothi and then later in the Adi Granth.

The organization of the Sikh scriptural text around the principle of *rag* fits neatly into the religio-literary context in which it was created. The tradition of assigning *rags* to religious poetry had existed since medieval times; early forerunners of this Sikh practice include the Buddhist Siddhacharyas of the Vajrayana and Sahajayana schools of the tenth and eleventh centuries and the work of the twelfth-century Hindu poet Jaidev (that is, Jayadeva).[16] The principle of *rag* division seems to have emerged from the practices of singers, to whom collecting hymns according to *rag* must have come naturally.[17] It seems to have been well entrenched by the late sixteenth century, as evident in *The Padas of Surdas*, a manuscript compiled in 1582, and in the *Panchavaṇi* (Hymns of the five) manuscripts compiled in the early seventeenth century.[18]

The knowledge of *rags* and the organization of sacred literature in *rag* sections was part of the medieval Indian religious milieu. The Sikh use of *rag* and the compilation of their sacred text according to *rag* assignments of the hymns was in no way unique. The structure of the Goindval Pothis and the Kartarpur Pothi, however, indicates a high degree of originality on the part of the Sikh gurus in the way they applied *rag*-related knowledge while compiling these texts, as evidenced in the following discussion.

Evolution of the Structure of the Adi Granth

In the sixteenth century, certain theorists of music assigned each *rag* a gender based on the types of feeling (*ras*) it was thought to evoke in the listener.[19] They also associated *rags* with particular seasons of the year and times of the day. The year was divided into six main seasons: winter, spring, summer, rains, autumn, and early winter. One core *rag* was assigned to each season: Sri, Basant, Bhairo, Megh, Pancham, and Natnarain, respectively. The day was divided into eight *pahirs* (an Indian unit of time equal to three hours), with one *rag* allotted to each one of them. There were variations, however, between different *rag* systems and regions.[20] This elaborate system of *rag* classification sheds light on the arrangement of the *rags* found in the Goindval Pothis.

Sequencing of Rags in the Adi Granth

The conception of gender among *rags* is reflected in the structure of the Goindval Pothis. Although the word *ragini* (female *rag*) is never used in the titles recording the *rag* assignment in the Goindval Pothis, the postpositions that follow the names of *rags* in some cases reveal a clear acceptance of gender distinction. For example, in the title *Suhi Babe di* ("[hymn] by Baba [Guru Nanak] in *rag* Suhi") and *Basant Babe da* ("[hymn] by Baba [Guru Nanak] in *rag* Basant"), the postpositions *di* and *da* indicate that the gender of Suhi is taken to be female and that of Basant, male. These titles offer just one manifestation of a gender distinction that in fact permeates the pothis.[21]

This principle is best displayed in the balance of female and male *rags* in these works. In my view the primary structure of the four Goindval Pothis was as in Table 8.[22] Two broad principles seem to be at work in giving these texts their final shape. The female *rags* precede the male *rags*, and the *rag* groupings include an equal number of male and female *rags* in the Goindval Pothis.[23]

The principle of associating *rag* with time also seems to be at work in the Goindval Pothis. Analysis of the *rag* groupings on the basis of the writings of Pundarika Vitthal, a sixteenth-century south Indian commentator of musical texts, offers some interesting results.[24] Based on the information in Vitthal's book about the relationship of *rag* to

Table 8. *Rag* Sections in the Goindval Pothis

	raginis	*rags*
Jalandhar	Suhi, Prabhati, Dhanasri	Basant, Bhairo,
Maru, Pinjore	Ramkali, Sorathi	Malar, Sarang
Pothi at Patiala	Asa, Gauṛi	Sri, Vaḍhans
Fourth pothi	Gujri, Tukhari	Majh, Bilaval

the time of the day, the following broad scheme emerges: Gujri, Tukhari, and Bilaval *rags* pertain to the early hours of the morning; Suhi, Prabhati, Dhanasri, Basant, and Bhairo are of the morning; Asa, Gauṛi, and Sri belong to the evening; and Ramkali, Malar, and Sarang are *rags* that can be sung at any time of the day. Broadly speaking, the *rags* in the Goindval Pothis are arranged to follow exactly such a scheme.[25]

O. C. Gangoly, a twentieth-century historian of Indian music, refers to a twofold division of *rags*. The first group consists of Purva *rags*, which are sung between 7 A. M. and noon and from 7 P. M. to midnight; the second consists of Uttra *rags*, which are sung from 4 A. M. to 7 A. M. and from 4 P. M. to 7 P. M.[26] Although the distinction is a broad one, it seems to work in connection with the Goindval Pothis. The pothi at Jalandhar and the pothi seen by Giani Gian Singh at Patiala contain the Purva, and the pothi at Pinjore and the fourth pothi include the Uttra *rags*.

Thus, the sequential arrangement of *rags* in the Goindval Pothis is not arbitrary but rather seems to be part of a complex design that can be understood in terms of mutual *rag* affinity, based on gender and the *rag* time relationship. The complexity of the *rag* sequence in the Goindval Pothis does not stop here, however, but seems to go farther, as suggested by the selection of the opening *rag* for each pothi as well as by the arrangement of *rags* in the group of pothis as a whole.

The selection of the opening *rags* of the two extant pothis appears to have been affected by competition between the Sikhs and other religious communities in the early years of Sikh history. The two extant pothis open with *rag* Suhi and *rag* Ramkali. Suhi (literally, the color red) was popularly allied with the Sufis, and the hymns of the gurus referring to Sufi themes often appear in this *rag*.[27] Hymns composed by the Nath Yogis are frequently in *rag* Ramkali, which would explain why the major hymns of the Sikh gurus relating to yogic themes are primarily in this *rag*.[28] The opening *rags* suggest that the Goindval Pothis may have been construed as a Sikh response to the other religious communities of medieval Punjab.

In summary, the Goindval Pothis provide sufficient evidence that the Sikhs, working within contemporary traditions, created a far more complex structure than first meets the eye. The grouping together and sequencing of various *rag* sections, first within each pothi and then within the larger whole made up of four pothis, shows their awareness of the genders and times popularly associated with *rags* in the sixteenth century. The carefully selected opening *rags* refer to the non-Sikh communities about which Guru Amardas may have been most concerned. The organization of the pothis thus represents a conscious attempt to perfect a classificatory system available during the sixteenth century.

The organization reached a level of finality in the Kartarpur Pothi. This expanded text contained the hymns of Guru Ramdas and Guru Arjan set to thirty *rags*, thus adding eleven *rags* to the nineteen employed by Guru Nanak. Along with the additional material, organizational modifications were also introduced here. The Kartarpur Pothi manifests a technical refinement of the structure that was first established in the Goindval Pothis and had developed through MS 1245.

A new major musical category of *ghar* (home), which is assigned seventeen different forms, now appears. According to Charan Singh, the *ghar* indicates the variation of *tal* (rhythm) in singing; Teja Singh, however, relates it to the category of *gah* (place) in Iranian music.[29] Sikh tradition seems to have forgotten *ghar*, and not much information is available about this category among present-day Sikh musicians.

The Kartarpur Pothi also exhibits a few instances of changes in *rag* found in the Goindval Pothis. For example, in the Goindval Pothis *rag* Maru and *rag* Kedara (folios 277–292) are joined under the name *rag* Maru-Kedara. This combination is not permitted in the Kartarpur Pothi, where the hymns are sorted out and recorded under each *rag* separately. The Goindval Pothis permit another combination, *rag* Prabhati-Lalat (folios 83–84, 105, and 113–114), which is changed into *rag* Suhi and *rag* Suhi-Lalat in the Kartarpur Pothi.

The Goindval Pothis frequently employ Dakhaṇi (southern) forms of *rags* as variants of Suhi, Prabhati, Basant, Bhairo, Ramkali, Malar, Soraṭhi, and Sarang, a practice that is trimmed considerably in the Kartarpur Pothi. Some of the changes are truly enigmatic. For example, in the section on *rag* Ramkali, the usage of Ramkali-Dakhaṇi is very prominent in the Goindval Pothi while it is largely eliminated in the Kartarpur Pothi; but there is a reverse instance in which Guru Nanak's long composition, the *Oankar* (One God; folio 35), assigned *rag* Ramkali in the Goindval Pothis, is changed to *rag* Ramkali-Dakhaṇi in the Kartarpur Pothi (folio 707).

The gender distinction between *rags* so clearly manifested in the *rag* titles of the Goindval Pothis was eliminated in the Kartarpur Pothi. Titles were standardized to provide the name of each hymn's *rag* followed by the name of its author. For example, *Rag Ramkali Mahala 1* indicates that the following hymn is in *rag* Ramkali and was composed by Guru Nanak. This standard form does not require the use of the postposition that indicates the gender of the *rag* in the Goindval Pothis. Nor is there any evidence of the grouping together and sequencing of *rags* on the basis of gender.

The most significant change that took place from the Goindval Pothis to the Kartarpur Pothi consisted of the reworking of the sequence of *rags*. The revised sequence appears in the Kartarpur Pothi as Sri, Majh, Gauṛi, Asa, Gujri, Devgandhari, Bihagṛa, Vaḍhans, Soraṭhi, Dhanasri, Jaitsri, Toḍi, Bairaṛi, Tilang, Suhi, Bilaval, Gonḍ, Ramkali, Natnarain, Maligauṛa, Maru, Tukhari, Kedara, Bhairo, Basant, Sarang, Malar, Kanṛa, Kalian, and Prabhati. It is not clear why the existing *rag* sequence in the Goindval Pothis was changed in the later compilation.

Since the Kartarpur Pothi served as the source for later scriptural manuscripts, all additions in contents, new organization, and music-related changes in its text continue in the Adi Granth. The *rag* sequence of the Kartarpur Pothi further expanded with the addition of the hymns of Guru Tegh Bahadur in *rag* Jaijavanti, bringing the total number of *rags* in Sikh scripture to thirty-one.

The placement of *rags* in the given sequence in the Adi Granth did not interest Sikh scholars, but recently there has been some effort to understand the issue. Surinder Singh

Kohli, writing in 1961, was probably the first scholar to touch upon the rationale of the *rag* sequence. He writes:

> The arrangement of the Ragas in the Adi Granth has no special significance. It should not be misconstrued that the Gurus had a special liking for a particular Raga. Some say that Sri Raga is the first Raga, therefore the Gurus have given preference to this Raga, but we have already seen the attitude of the Gurus towards the Ragas. They liked every Raga that created love for the Name of the Lord.[30]

Kohli paid direct attention to an important phenomenon; but since he was unable to account for it, he concluded that the *rag* sequence in the Adi Granth was simply arbitrary.

In the past two decades, three more attempts have been made to address this issue. Pritam Singh, writing in 1976, tried to show that the *rag* sequence of the Adi Granth was affected by a conscious decision by Guru Arjan to reject the religious implication—that is, the Hindu meaning—of the *rags*.[31] He argued that in placing *rag* Sri at the beginning and *rag* Prabhati at the end of the Kartarpur Pothi, Guru Arjan was reversing the commonly held time sequence of Vaishnava worship, according to which *rag* Sri is to be sung in the evening and *rag* Prabhati in the morning.

By contrast, writing in 1991, Pashaura Singh, interprets the positioning of *rag* Sri at the opening of the Adi Granth as a marker of the prominence assigned to it both in the Sikh and the classical Hindu traditions:

> First, it is linked with Guru Amar Das' assertion that "the *siri* raga is chief among the ragas" (*raga vichi siri ragu hai*). Second, Bhai Gurdas describes the understanding of his times when the *siri* rag was acknowledged as "chief" among the ragas (*ragan mai siri rag* . . .). Third, in two other musical traditions the position of *siri* raga was regarded as number one. Finally, the character of *siri* raga is mysterious, gentle, and often depicts the meditation of love and the nostalgic prayerful mood of early evening.[32]

As to the position of *rag* Prabhati at the end of the Adi Granth, it is, according to Pashaura Singh, a sign of the "spirit of optimism."

Jasbir Singh Sabar claims that the placement of *rag* Sri at the beginning and of *rag* Prabhati at the end of the Adi Granth can be interpreted as follows: Prior to singing the praise of God, human consciousness is covered in the mist of ignorance. Through the *rag* of evening time (*rag* Sri), the message of the hymns of the gurus removes the mist of ignorance and transmits the light of knowledge. Beginning with *rag* Sri, human desire for union with God continues to increase until it receives the final light of knowledge in *rag* Prabhati, at the close of the Adi Granth.[33]

Thus, these scholars have attempted to explain the placement of the *rag* sequence of the Adi Granth, insofar as the positions of *rag* Sri and *rag* Prabhati are concerned. None of their explanations takes us beyond the placement of these two *rags*, and the explanations themselves leave some questions unanswered. For example, the text of Guru Amardas quoted by Pashaura Singh in his discussion of the special significance of *rag* Sri is actually part of a longer passage, which reads in full:

> *Raga vichi Sri ragu hai je sachi dhare piaru.*
> *Sada hari sachu mani vasai nihchal mati aparu,* (M3, AG, 83)
> Sri *rag* can only be a distinct *rag* [if by listening to it] one can place one's heart in the truth.
> The Lord inhabits the mind and makes it steady.

These lines do not in fact point to any unique status for *rag* Sri that would justify its prominent position at the head of the scriptural text. The emphasis instead is on keeping the remembrance of God in one's heart. The passage actually supports both Kohli's contention that the Sikh gurus favored no one particular *rag* over any other, and my contention, stated earlier, that Sikhs were little concerned with technical aspects of the *rags*. If anything, only cultural factors seem to have been at work. The importance of *rag* Sri for the Sikh Gurus seems to have been in the professed association of the Vaishnavas with this *rag*, rather than in its preeminent position, according to some *rag*-related system.

Important data in the Kartarpur Pothi itself caution against finding too much significance in the fact that *rag* Sri and *rag* Prabahti are placed at opposite ends of the scriptural text. For while it is true that the contents of the four Goindval Pothis were incorporated into a single manuscript, the Kartarpur Pothi is clearly structured in two distinct parts. The opening section begins with *rag* Sri and ends with *rag* Tilang; the second begins with *rag* Suhi and ends with *rag* Prabhati. We know this from the physical appearance of the manuscript itself. The opening folio of the main text is embellished with artwork and contains an invocation written by Guru Arjan, but the opening folio of *rag* Suhi is also decorated with an invocation—this one written by his son Hargobind. The twofold structure of the Kartarpur Pothi continues in the Kanpur Pothi, with a special position assigned to *rag* Suhi in the middle of the text.[34] Beginning with the mid-seventeenth-century manuscripts, however, the prominence assigned to the *rag* Suhi section in the Kartarpur and the Kanpur pothis is abandoned and the text becomes a single unit.

This division has genuine significance. The Kartarpur Pothi begins with *rag* Sri, a favorite *rag* of the Vaishnavas, and its first section ends with *rag* Tilang, a favorite *rag* of the Sufis. Then in the second part of the text this sequence is exactly reversed. It commences with *rag* Suhi, a favorite among Sufis, and ends with *rag* Prabhati, which was especially associated with Vaishnavas. The placement of these *rags* in key points in the Sikh text seems to indicate Guru Arjan's engagement with the two major religious groups in the Punjab, and to show that he thought of the Adi Granth as superseding the scriptures of both.

A further key to the significance of the overall *rag* sequence in the Adi Granth may possibly be found in the manuscript version of the Kartarpur Pothi, in a notation that was not carried forward to the Adi Granth's printed edition. I refer to the end of the Kartarpur Pothi's table of contents, which divides up the thirty *rag* sections in order of appearance in the text, as follows:

Sri, Majh, Gauṛi

Asa, Gujri, Devgandhari

Bihagṛa, Vaḍhans, Soraṭhi

Dhanasri, Jaitsri, Toḍi, Bairaṛi, Tilang

Suhi, Bilaval, Gonḍ, Ramkali

Nat-[Narain], Maligauṛa, Maru, Tukhari, Kedara

Bhairo, Basant, Sarang, Malar, Kanṛa

Kalian, [Bibhas]-Prabhati.[35]

The main significance of this system may be found in the eight uneven groups into which the thirty *rag* sections are divided. The only possibility could be that this division may have been related to the eight *pahirs* that make up the day, with each set of *rags* intended for one *pahir*. This same principle forms the basis for the eight *artis* (prayers) performed throughout the day in Vaishnava temples.[36] The reason for the inclusion of specific *rags* within each of the eight groups is not, however, clear, and my efforts to determine it have not as yet borne any concrete results.[37]

The fact that the number of *rag* sections in the Kartarpur Pothi was kept to thirty may not be a coincidence either. The Indian system divides eight *pahirs* into sixty *gharis*, and the thirty *rag* sections will thus provide one *rag* section for every two *gharis*. Although the details of Frederic Pincott's argument are not clear to me, he does claim that the thirty *rags* in the Kartarpur Pothi "exactly correspond with the 30 semitones of the Indian *stabaka*, or musical staff, reckoning the minor intervals as single tones."[38]

Guru Tegh Bahadur's addition of *rag* Jaijavanti to the thirty *rags* of the Kartarpur Pothi is difficult to understand. Did he have any special reason for introducing this to the existing scheme, raising the total number of *rags* to thirty-one? Or was the attainment of this number merely a coincidence? These hymns are positioned at the end of the manuscripts of the Adi Granth. But was the placement of the section on *rag* Jaijavanti at the end of the text simply an easy way of incorporating these hymns into the earlier text, or is there some musical significance to the sequence? The answer to this question is not yet known.[39]

As we have seen from the preceding discussion, the *rag* arrangement in the Adi Granth, unlike that in the Goindval Pothis, defies an entirely satisfactory explanation. The structure of the Goindval Pothis is easily understandable in terms of gender and the relationship between *rag* and the time of day, but these principles do not illuminate the sequence of *rags* in the Adi Granth. My suggestions toward interpreting the structure of the Adi Granth may yet yield no perfect answers, but I hope they are sufficient to challenge any argument that the *rag* combinations of the Adi Granth are insignificant.

Internal Arrangement within Rag *Sections of the Adi Granth*

Each *rag* section in the Adi Granth is neatly divided into subsections, and in each of these subsections, hymns are further organized on the basis of authorship: a typical subsection begins with the hymns of Guru Nanak and continues with the hymns of his successors, of the bards at the Sikh court, and of the Bhagats, in chronological order.[40] In the discussion that follows, I trace the evolution of the internal organization of the *rag* sections from the Goindval Pothis to the Adi Granth.

In the Goindval Pothis, each *rag* section opens on a fresh folio, with the invocation neatly inscribed at the top. The first striking division within each section lies between the hymns of the Sikh gurus and those of the Bhagats (the hymns of the bards are not available in the extant pothis); the hymns of the gurus appear in the first part of each section, while those of the Bhagats are placed at the end. The two divisions receive unequal attention. In terms of both genre classification and the attribution of each hymn, the compositions of the Bhagats have not been treated with the same meticulous care that went into organizing the hymns of the gurus. Indeed, the hymns of the Bhagats were viewed as one unit in which internal distinctions did not really matter. Since for these hymns *rag* is the only functional principle of organization, genre classification and authorship have been passed over. For instance, a typical title for the hymns recorded in this section is *Basant Baṇi Kabir Name ki* (Hymns of Kabir and Namdev in *rag* Basant). Under this title, however, we find hymns recorded in a sequence with no attention to their length or authorship. The sequence not only includes hymns attributed to Kabir and Namdev, as the title indicates, but also of other Bhagats all jumbled together.

The basic twofold division of each *rag* section of the Goindval Pothis continues with some modifications in the Kartarpur Pothi. As in the Goindval Pothis, each *rag* section in the Kartarpur Pothi opens with the invocation and is divided into two sections: the hymns of the gurus with those of the bards appended at the end, and the hymns of the Bhagats. The hymns of the Bhagats, unlike those of the gurus and the bards, are not recorded individually in the Kartarpur Pothi's table of contents.[41] Instead, at the end of the entry for each *rag* section, the phrase *Baṇi Bhagatan ki* (Hymns of the Bhagats) appears. Here, too, as in the Goindval Pothis, the compositions of the Bhagats are treated as a group. The standard entry for each hymn of a guru, recording the first line recorded, along with its attribution, has been dispensed with in the case of the Bhagats' hymns. In the body of the Kartarpur Pothi, however, an attempt has been made to group these hymns according to the authorship of each Bhagat and thus apply the same standards to this section that are used with such great care for the hymns of the gurus.[42]

The single entry "*Baṇi Bhagatan ki*" that appears in the Kartarpur Pothi's table of contents was expanded later to include details of authorship and the hymns' first lines.[43] A list of this type became a permanent feature of the scriptural text and is now part of the printed edition of the Adi Granth. No visible distinction between the recording the hymns of the gurus and those of the Bhagats remains.

In the Goindval Pothis, each *rag* section opens with *chaupadas* and goes on to include *chhants*, *ashṭpadis*, and longer hymns. Each of these subsections is further organized according to authorship, beginning with the hymns of Guru Nanak (Mahala 1) and continuing through those of Guru Amardas (Mahala 3). In Guru Nanak's hymns, and these alone, the Mahala reference is often dropped, leaving only the *rag* designation: a composition simply entitled *Suhi* or *Basant* would imply that it belongs to Guru Nanak.

The organization of the Goindval Pothis was carried over to the Kartarpur Pothi with one alteration in the sequence of subsections. In the Kartarpur Pothi, unlike the Goindval Pothis, the *chhants* are placed after the *ashṭpadis*. It is not clear why this was done, since the *ashṭpadis* (eight stanzas of four verses each) are longer than the *chhants* (four stanzas of six verses each), and, given the criterion of increasing length, should have followed them. A possible explanation could be that the standard form of the *chhant* was taken to include six stanzas of six verses each, a form that does appear in the hymns of the gurus, which made the *chhants* longer than the *ashṭpadis*.

The longer compositions in the Kartarpur Pothi are still placed at the end of the *rag* sections. The positioning of some of these compositions in the extant Goindval Pothis is modified slightly in the Kartarpur Pothi. The most noticeable such shift is that of the *Anand* of Guru Amardas, in *rag* Ramkali. This composition is included in the grouping of the longer compositions in the Goindval Pothis (folio 80) and MS 1245 (folio 881) but is recorded at the end of the subsection on the *ashṭpadis* in the Kartarpur Pothi (folio 697). The reason for this alteration is not clear.

Another important feature of the internal structure of each *rag* section in the Goindval Pothis is the numbering of hymns. In the *rag* Suhi section, which opens the Goindval Pothis sequence, each hymn is assigned three numbers. The first one refers to the number of stanza in the hymn—stanza (*pada*), not verse (*tuk*) being taken as the basic unit. The second number refers to the position of the hymn in the subsection. The third indicates the grand total (*jumla*) at that particular point. The number 8/4/31 in *rag* Suhi would therefore indicate that this particular hymn has eight stanzas and is therefore part of the subsection of the *ashṭpadis*; it is the fourth hymn in that subsection and number thirty-one in the overall sequence of *rag* Suhi.[44]

After the completion of the section on *rag* Suhi, however, the scribe of the Goindval Pothis stopped recording the third column. We may well ask why. As we know from the manuscripts, the scribe of the Goindval Pothis left some folios blank at the end of subsections, and these may have been meant to record a fresh hymn that the incumbent guru might compose after the compilation of the pothis. In other words, if Guru Amardas had composed a new *ashṭpadi*, in, say, *rag* Suhi, there would be blank space available for recording it in the Goindval Pothis. With the three-column numbering, however, an addition in the middle of the sequence would disturb the number in the third column of the hymns that followed. In my view, having realized this difficulty, the scribe of the Goindval Pothis discontinued the third column, and it does not appear in any other *rag* section. The scribe of the Kartarpur Pothi simply adopted the numbering system as he found it in the Goindval Pothis. The three-column numbering appears in the *rag* Suhi section, and in all other sections the third column is dropped.

Within the text of the hymns, the refrain (*rahau*) is a prominent feature; in general, the refrain is recorded after the opening *pada*. The singing of the hymn begins with the refrain verse and is repeated after the singing of every subsequent stanza. Growing out of musical recitation, the refrain seems to have been used even before the compilation of the Goindval Pothis: it is marked in the opening section of the Guru Harsahai Pothi.

There are variations in this standard use of the refrain, and instances of more than one refrain per hymn are also found in the Goindval Pothis. For example, in hymns with two refrains, the first appears in its usual position after the opening stanza, and the other appears in the final stanza.[45] In the hymn of Guru Nanak in *rag* Dhanasri which begins *Jiau ḍaratu hai apaṇa kai siao kari pukar* (My heart is sinking, to whom should I appeal?), each of the four stanzas are assigned the status of the refrain (folio 120), and this feature continues in the Adi Granth (p. 660).

The use of the refrain and its normal placement after the first stanza of any given hymn in the Goindval Pothis continues in the Kartarpur Pothi. The practice of using more than one refrain within one hymn, following some examples in the Goindval Pothis, is also found in the Kartarpur Pothi. A hymn of six stanzas by Guru Nanak is assigned three refrains, and another hymn of six stanzas by Guru Ramdas is assigned six refrains (AG, 81–82).[46] The only difference between the usage in the Goindval Pothis and in the Kartarpur Pothi appears in Guru Arjan's placement of a refrain verse at the very opening of the hymn in some cases.[47]

Table 9. Structure of the *vars in* the Kartarpur Pothi

Att.	*Rag*	*Pauṛis*	*Shaloks*	M1	M2	M3	M4	M5	Others
M 1	Majh	27	63	46	12	03	02	–	–
M1	Asa	24	60	44	15	–	–	–	01[a]
M1	Malar	28	58	24	04	28	–	02	–
M3	Gujri	22	44	–	–	43	–	–	01[b]
M3	Suhi	20	47	21	11	15	–	–	–
M3	Ramkali	21	51	18	07	24	–	02	–
M3	Maru	22	47	18	01	23	03	02	–
M4	Sri	21	43	07	02	33	–	01	–
M4	Gauṛi	33	68	–	–	07	53	08	–[c]
M4	Bihagṛa	21	43	02	–	33	02	02	3+1[d]
M4	Vaḍhans	21	43	03	–	40	–	–	–
M4	Soraṭhi	29	58	02	01	48	07	–	–
M4	Bilaval	13	27	01	25	01	–	–	–
M4	Sarang	36	74	32	08	25	06	03	–
M4	Kanṛa	15	30	–	–	–	30	–	–
M5	Gauṛi	21	42	–	–	–	–	42	–
M5	Gujri	21	42	–	–	–	–	42	–
M5	Jaitsri	20	40	–	–	–	–	40	–
M5	Ramkali	22	44	–	–	–	–	44	–
M5	Maru	22	69	–	–	–	–	69	–
M5	Basant	03	–	–	–	–	–	–	–[e]

a. One couplet is without author assignment.
b. This couplet is attributed to Kabir (AG, 509).
c. Five stanzas in this var are attributed to Guru Arjan (AG, 315).
d. Three are attributed to Mardana, and one to Kabir (AG, 553, 555)
e. This var of Guru Arjan is incomplete.

In broad outline, the Kartarpur Pothi thus follows the patterns set in the Goindval Pothis, with minor elaboration and modifications, all of which continue in the Adi Granth.[48] There is, however, a major change and it appears in the *vars*. The original text of the *vars* seems to have contained only the stanzas (*pauṛis*), to which couplets (*shaloks*) were affixed at this stage of expansion. The title recorded at the head of each *var* refers to the author of the stanzas in it; the situation with the couplets is more complex, however. The couplets do not necessarily belong to the original author. The Kartarpur Pothi contains twenty-two *vars*, of which three are attributed to Guru Nanak, four to Guru Amardas, eight to Guru Ramdas, six to Guru Arjan, and one to Satta and Balvand. Except for Guru Arjan's *var* in *rag* Basant and Satta and Balvand's in *rag* Ramkali, the remaining ones appear in their expanded form.

In Table 9, the first column indicates the attribution of the *var*, with M (Mahala) standing for the gurus—that is, M1 is Guru Nanak, M2, Guru Angad, and so on; the second shows the *rag* section in which the *var* appears; the third column gives the number of stanzas recorded; the fourth shows the number of couplets contained in it; and the later columns indicate the breakdown of couplets according to their attribution, M1, M2, etc.

Table 10. Repetitions in the Text of the Adi Granth

Opening verse	First Appearance	Repetition/Repeated Couplet
Gurmukhi kripa kare bhagati	M3, AG, 32,	M3, AG, 64
Manu mare dhatu mari jae	M3, AG, 159,	M3, AG, 665
Jo jan parmiti parmanu jana	Kabir, AG, 325	K, AG, 1161
Sukh sagaru surtaru	Ravidas, AG, 658	R, AG, 1106
Adi sachu jugadi sachu	M 1, AG, 1	M5, AG, 285*
Pavaṇu guru paṇi pita	M 1, AG, 8	M2, AG, 146*
Satgur ki seva gakhṛi	M3, AG, 27	M3, AG, 649
Dati sahib sandia	M1, AG, 83	None, AG, 1384
Guri purai harinam	M3, AG, 86	M4, AG, 1424*
Kia hansu kia bagula	M1, AG, 91	None, AG, 1384
Nihfalam tasi janamasi	M2, AG, 148	M1, AG, 1353*
Hathi kalam agam mastaki	M5, AG, 261	M5, AG, 1361
Man antari haumai rog hai	M4, AG, 301	M4, AG, 1317
Nanak vicharahe sant jan	M4, AG, 306	M5, AG, 316*
Vaḍabhagia sohagaṇi jina	M4, AG, 309	M4, AG, 1421
Manmukh mulahu bhulia	M4, AG, 316	M3, AG, 548*
Sikhahu sabadu piariho	M5, AG, 320	M5, AG, 916
Jog sabadang gian sabadang	M2, AG, 469	M1, AG, 1353*
Ek krisanang sarab deva	M2, AG, 469	M1, AG, 1353*
Paṛi pustak sandhia badang	M1, AG, 470	M1, AG, 1353
Kabir mukati duara	Kabir, AG, 509	Kabir, AG, 1367
Binu satiguru seve	M3, AG, 516	M3, AG, 950
Sajan tere charan ki	M5, AG, 518	M1, AG, 989*
Patit punit asankh	M5, AG, 518	M1, AG, 990*
Kabir marata marata jag	Kabir, AG, 555	Kabir, AG, 1365
Loiṇ loi diṭh pias	None, AG, 577	M5, AG, 1099
Mai jania vaḍhansu	M3, AG, 585	None, AG, 1384
Hansa vekhi tarandia	M3, AG, 585	None, AG, 1384
Hari prabhu sajaṇu	None, AG, 845	M4, AG, 1317
Gurmukhi sansa	M3, AG, 853	M4, AG, 1281*
Kabir mahidi kari kai	Kabir, AG, 947	Kabir, AG, 1367
Kabir kasauṭi ram ki	Kabir, AG, 948	Kabir, AG, 1366
Abhiagat ehi na	M3, AG, 949	M3, AG, 1413
Ehu tanu sabho ratu	M3, AG, 949	M3, AG, 1380
So pakhanḍi ji kia pakhalai	M1, AG, 952	Kabir, AG, 1160*
Kabira hamara ko	M5, AG, 965	M5, AG, 1376
Kabir dharti sadhu	M5, AG, 965	M5, AG, 1375
Kabir chaval karaṇe	M5, AG, 965	M5, AG, 1375
Farida bhum rangavali	M5, AG, 966	M5, AG, 1382
Farida umar suhavaṛi	M5, AG, 966	M5, AG, 1382
Dunia husiar bedar	Kabir, AG, 972	Kabir, AG, 1377
Sasurai peiai kantki	M1, AG, 1088	None, AG, 1379
Hova panditu jotaki	M3, AG, 1090	M3, AG, 1413
Maia manahu na visarai	M5, AG, 1093	M5, AG, 1426
Nanak jisu binu ghaṛi	M5, AG, 1097	M4, AG, 1250*
Manahu ji andhe kup	M1, AG, 1245	M1, AG, 1413
Hari hari namudhiae	M4, AG 1313	M3, AG, 1418*
Hau ḍhunḍhendi sajaṇa	M4, AG, 1318	None, AG, 1384
Tanu na tapaie tanur	None, AG, 1384	M1, AG, 1411

Fourteen couplets marked with an asterisk have varied attribution when they appear a second time, and at other places there is no attribution at all. I have built this list on the basis of notes given in Teja Singh, ed., *Shabadarth Sri Guru Granth Sahib Ji*, and Joginder Singh Talwaṛa, *Baṇi Biaura, Bhag 1* (Amritsai: Singh Brothers, 1992), pp. 103–123.

In my view, the *vars* containing the stanzas and the couplets were treated as two independent groups and recorded in the Goindval Pothi no longer extant. In all likelihood, Guru Arjan at the time of the compilation of the Kartarpur Pothi decided to merge these two sections and create a new form for *vars*; the beginning of this process of merger can be first seen in MS 1245.[49] In this text, all the couplets are not yet recorded in their appropriate places, in many cases only the opening verse of the couplet appears, and the attribution of the couplets is absent. The evolution of the *vars* continued during the compilation of the Kartarpur Pothi. A large number of couplets were framed within the text of various *vars*, and those that could not fit in were recorded at the closing of the text under the title of *Shalok Varan te Vadhik*. In the original inscription of the Kartarpur Pothi, the scribe did not record the attribution of the couplets but introduced it later with a finer pen in between the lines. The process does not seem to have worked out very smoothly. We see instructions like "correct" (*shudh*) or "rectify" (*shudh kichai*) at the end of the text of the several *vars*.[50] The discrepancies include forty-five couplets appearing twice in the text; in some places the scribe has forgotten to record their attribution, and at others has assigned them different authorship.

In the main text of the Adi Granth, there are only four cases of repetition; the rest are instances of repeated couplets (table 10).

To sum up, the preceding discussion indicates that the corpus of sacred Sikh literature and its organization evolved slowly, and that the sixteenth-century manuscripts played an important role in determining the structure of the Kartarpur Pothi and the Adi Granth. The scribe of the opening section of the Guru Harsahai Pothi had only Guru Nanak's hymns available to him, and he recorded them in a loose conglomeration. In the Goindval Pothis, we see the expansion of the sacred corpus to include the hymns of Guru Nanak, his successors, and those of the Bhagats. The scribe of the Goindval Pothis decided on *rag* division as the organizing principle and then created a complex internal structure for each *rag* section to keep the distinctions between hymns of different authors intact. The scribe of the Kartarpur Pothi, the next major phase of expansion of the Sikh scriptural text, elaborated upon the basic principles of organization already present in the Goindval Pothis. He also made similar changes in the sequence of *rags*—the rationale for which has not yet been determined, in the placement of hymns within each *rag* section, and gave a new form to the text of the *vars*.

The final product of the several stages of evolution that began with the Guru Harsahai Pothi and culminated in the Adi Granth amply manifests the care that went into its conception and development; its structural complexity, both in terms of sequencing of *rags* and the placement of hymns of varied length and authorship within each *rag* section, far exceeds that of other religious compilations of the time.

The Adi Granth and Other Scriptures

The Vedas and the Qur'an, the scriptures of the other major religious traditions of the Punjab, provided the context in which the Sikhs compiled their sacred text. References to both the Vedas and Kateb (Scriptures of Islam, Christianity, and Judaism) appear frequently in the hymns of the Sikh Gurus[51] Not much scholarly attention has, however, been paid so far to the issue of structural parallels between the Adi Granth and these other scriptural texts.[52]

Pincott, writing in 1890, was the first scholar to argue for the existence of broad structural parallels between the Adi Granth and the Rig Veda. The three-part arrangement of the Adi Granth (liturgical portion, the main text, and epilogue), he argued, "accords with that of the Rig-Veda; the first Mandala of which is liturgical, followed by various sets of hymns, and ending with long and short hymns, or miscellaneous collection[s]."[53] There is very little likelihood that the gurus had access to the complete written text of the Rig Veda when they compiled their own pothis, and Pincott's comparison of the Adi Granth with the ten Maṇḍalas of the Rig Veda, including hymns ranging in numbers from 43 to 191, is a bit far-fetched.[54]

Instead of being a conscious imitation of the Rig Veda, the structure of the Adi Granth evolved slowly and independently. The hymns for daily prayer were placed at the beginning, and we have seen the evening prayers in this section expand from the five hymns of *Sodar* in MS 1245 to fourteen hymns in the Adi Granth. This was followed by the main text organized around the principle of *rag* division, and we have traced its evolution from the Goindval Pothis to the Kartarpur Pothi. Hymns that could not fit into the *rag* sections were placed at the end. This, it seems, is how this tripartite structure appeared not through any imitation of the internal organization of the Rig Veda.

If one were to look for a scriptural text of another religious community with which the Sikh Gurus were acquainted that could have served as a model for Sikh scripture, the most logical candidate would have to be the Qur'an. An analysis of structural parallels between the Adi Granth and the Qur'an is more useful. To begin with, a close structural affinity exists between the physical makeup of both texts.

Sikh and Islamic manuscripts share basic physiognomical features of three sorts. First, the early Sikh pothis display a beautifully drawn border on all four sides of each page, like Qur'an and other Islamic texts of the period. Second, there is a distinctive style of geometric drawings on the opening folios of these pothis, which seems to reproduce what one finds in Islamic texts. Third, there is the technique of collecting folios in gatherings, sewing them on the spine, and then placing them in exterior leather binding with a free edge-flap.[55] Again, this is a feature directly from Islamic manuscripts.

A number of seventeenth-century manuscripts of the Adi Granth are embellished with ornate artwork around the margins that seems to follow directly the Islamic tradition with its techniques of Qur'an illumination. The very enterprise of embellishment seems to have been a part of the art of Islamic calligraphy.[56] It is possible that the services of Muslim scribes were used in the preparation of Sikh manuscripts. I have seen one very elaborately illustrated mid-eighteenth-century manuscript of the Adi Granth in which a cityscape, with a mosque at the center, is painted on the last folio of the text. It is noteworthy that the characteristics I have mentioned more or less continued in the preparation of Sikh manuscripts until the 1860s, after which time the printing press completely took over the production of Sikh texts.

In addition to all this, there are other structural features that Sikh scripture shares with the Qur'an. These are not just at the "surface" level—in the final presentation of the holy word—but in its structure and content. The Sikh invocation at the opening of each *rag* section and at each subsection in the Adi Granth, in my view, serves a structural purpose. Although this brief text developed through several reworkings, two of its elements never changed: *1 Oankar*, marking the unity of God, and *gurprasadi*, indicating the role of the Guru.[57] In the core text, thus, God is invoked first, and then a claim is made that the inscription begins by his grace, as mediated to the scribe through the human guru. At every juncture of his labor, thus, the scribe remembers God and seeks his help through the guru.

The terms of the invocation, like *1 Oankar*, and *gurprasadi*, have Hindu analogs, but the function of the invocation in the Adi Granth has no parallels in Hindu manuscripts, which tend to have Om or some other mantric text inscribed at the head of the manuscript but never again. Rather, it comes into focus against the background of the Qur'an. It is structurally identical to the Islamic use of the *Bismillah-arrahman-arrahim* (In the name of God, the Merciful, the Compassionate) in the Qur'an. The phrase, like *1 Oankar* and *gurprasadi*, appears at the head of each new section in the text of the Qur'an and serves the purpose of invoking God.

In its internal structure, the Sikh invocation corresponds not to the *bismillah* per se but to the *shahadah*, the Islamic testimony of faith. This *shahadah* is divided into two halves: *La ilaha illa'llah* (there is no god but God) and *Muhammad rasul allah* (Muhammad is the messenger of God). The first half of the *shahadah* is a statement of the uniqueness of God; the second half refers to the prophet Muhammad's relationship with God. The invocation of the Adi Granth is made up of two similar components. The first part states the essential nature of God (this segment is in fact identical in meaning to the first half of the *shahadah*); and the second points to the guru's function as the messenger of God on earth and the transmitter of his grace, corresponding to the second part of the *shahadah*. Moreover, the use of the text of the invocation in Sikh life parallels the use of *shahadah* by Muslims: both are recited at the beginning and the end of ceremonies ranging from birth rituals to funerals.

The emphasis of the preceding discussion on parallels between aspects of the Adi Granth and Islamic counterparts is in no way meant to deny the importance of Hinduism as a major part of the religious and literary context of the early Sikh tradition. The use of *rag* in worship and the organization by *rag* of the Adi Granth are just two illustrations of the Hindu contribution to Sikh practices. Indeed, in their incorporation of structural elements from both the Qur'an and Hindu religious texts, the framers of the Adi Granth epitomize the meeting of sacred texts of the Indic and Semitic religious traditons.

Nevertheless, the result of the work of compilation was intended by the Sikh gurus to be something completely new, the embodiment of a unique revealed message. For Sikhs, the Adi Granth is a repository of God's word that is distinct from both the Vedas and the Kateb (*Ved Katebahu bahara anahad shabadu agam alapai*).[58] And the gurus took great care to clothe this revelation in Gurmukhi, a local script they appropriated and projected as the Sikh counterpart of Devanagari and Arabic, the sacred scripts of the Hindus and Muslims. Guru Nanak, in his long hymn entitled *Paṭi* (wooden slate used to learn the writing of the alphabet), categorically states that those who attempt to understand God through the writings recorded in Gurmukhi will attain liberation (*Ena akhara mahi jo gurmukhi bhujhai tisu siri lekhu na hoi*, M1, AG, 432). Sikh scripture revealed in a new language was seen to be God's newest gift to humanity.

7

The Adi Granth and the Issue of Bhagat Baṇi

Among the Bhagats whose hymns appear in the Adi Granth, Kabir (224 hymns, 237 couplets, and 3 long compositions), Farid (4 hymns and 112 couplets), Namdev (61 hymns), and Ravidas (40 hymns) are the prominent figures. The remaining 11 Bhagats—Beṇi (3 hymns), Bhikhaṇ (2 hymns), Dhanna (2 hymns), Jaidev (2 hymns), Parmanand (one hymn), Pipa (one hymn), Ramanand (one hymn), Sadhna (one hymn), Saiṇ (one hymn), Surdas (one verse), and Trilochaṇ (4 hymns)—enjoy more of a symbolic presence in Sikh scripture. While Bhikhaṇ, Farid, and Kabir came from a Muslim background, all others were from the large Hindu fold.

The Goindval Pothis and the Kartarpur Pothi prepared in the 1570s and 1604, respectively, are among the earliest documents containing the hymns of these Bhagats, and scholars of Indian religious traditions have used the Adi Granth extensively as their primary source in producing detailed studies of Kabir, Namdev, and Ravidas.[1] The saint-poets whose hymns appear in the Adi Granth enjoy a unique status in the eyes of the Sikhs. Early Sikh writers took great delight in creating narratives detailing the circumstances of the entry of bhagat baṇi into sacred Sikh literature. More recently, however, Sikh scholars have focused on analyzing the doctrinal affinity between the Bhagats and the gurus.[2] They present this as the primary basis for the incorporation of their hymns into Sikh scripture.

Four issues have surfaced sporadically in literature dealing with the bhagat baṇi. These are (1) the date of inclusion of these hymns within sacred Sikh literature, (2) the precise purpose for their incorporation, (3) the process of the selection of this corpus and its evolution, and (4) the status of the bhagat baṇi in relation to the hymns of the Sikh gurus (gurbaṇi) in the minds of Sikh scripture compilers, and later in evolving perceptions within the Sikh community. In this chapter I evaluate the available answers to each of these basic questions and then offer what I think is a more accurate understanding of them.

Date of Inclusion of the Bhagat Baṇi

In existing literature there are three views about the time when the bhagat baṇi entered sacred Sikh literature, targeting three different phases in the evolution of the early Sikh community. The issue is yet to be settled conclusively. The first and traditional Sikh view attributes this development to Guru Arjan. This understanding can be traced back to *Mahima Prakash*, the earliest source to refer in detail to the date of the incorporation of the bhagat baṇi into the Sikh scriptural text.[3] Bhalla reports that various Bhagats had heard about Guru Arjan's plan to compile the Sikh scriptural text and had come to request that he record their hymns also. According to Bhalla, Guru Arjan incorporated the hymns of some of the petitioners but rejected the requests of others.

This narrative reappears with minor variations in *Sikhan di Bhagatmala*.[4] Kabir and a number of other holy men are said to have brought their compositions to Bhai Gurdas. Following Guru Arjan's instructions, he rejected all of the writings they had brought with them but invited them to remain at the Sikh court and create fresh ones. The Bhagats accepted the proposal and wrote new hymns that were then reviewed by Bhai Gurdas, who incorporated some of them into the Sikh scriptural text.

These two sources provided the basic materials for the traditional Sikh understanding of how, when, and under what circumstances the bhagat baṇi found its way into the Sikh scriptural text. The nineteenth-century narrators, however, introduced additional dramatic details.[5] In these accounts, Kabir is presented as the spokesperson for the Bhagats during their visit to the Sikh court. He respectfully introduces each of them to Guru Arjan and announces the precise purpose of their visit—to get their hymns recorded in the sacred Sikh text. We are given details of the arrangements for their lodging in Amritsar. We are told that the locality in Amritsar known as *Bhagatan vala Darvaẓa* (Gate of the Bhagats) was named to commemorate the visit of these holy people to Amritsar. These chroniclers also knew that many of the Bhagats whose hymns are recorded in Sikh scripture were dead by the time of Guru Arjan. Still, they easily circumvented the difficulty of accounting for this historical anomaly by describing the saint's arrival at the Sikh court in ethereal forms.[6]

From the perspective of historical factuality, there are obvious problems with motifs such as ethereal journeys, but the difficulties do not stop there. Even basic facts that concern the holy men and women who visited the Sikh court are open to dispute. They simply do not tally with the names and number of Bhagats whose hymns are recorded in the Adi Granth. Even *Mahima Prakash*, the earliest of these sources, claims that in addition to the fifteen Bhagats whose hymns appear in the Adi Granth, hymns by Araf, Kamal, and Mirabai were also admitted into the Sikh scriptural text by Guru Arjan.[7] Later writers added four more names to the list of Bhagats who visited the Sikh court to request the inclusion of their works in the Sikh scriptural text: Jamal, Maskan, Musan, and Saman.[8] Yet no hymns attributed to these four appear in either the Adi Granth or in any other early manuscript known to us.

Thus, before we even get to the question of how and when the bhagat baṇi came to be introduced in the Sikh scriptural text, we must recognize the internal difficulties in narratives such as these and reject the information available here. Sikh scholars trained in the Western system of education at the turn of the twentieth century were acutely aware of these problems and they went on to address this issue entirely on the basis of internal evidence available in the writings of the gurus and the Bhagats. The position they developed challenged the one available in traditional Sikh sources. By presenting a meticulous analysis of close affinities between certain hymns of Guru Nanak and those of the Bhagats, Teja Singh in the 1930s and Sahib Singh in the 1940s argued that the introduction of the bhagat baṇi into sacred Sikh literature occurred in the early sixteenth century, and they attributed this development to Guru Nanak.[9]

Sahib Singh's early work attempted to establish a firm connection between the hymns of Guru Nanak and those of Farid and Beṇi.[10] One hymn by Guru Nanak in *rag* Suhi (AG, 729) and four of his couplets (AG, 1379, and 1384) were interpreted by Sahib Singh as Guru Nanak's direct response to the hymns of Farid (AG, 794, 1379, 1384). Two hymns by Guru Nanak in *rag* Sri and *rag* Prabhati (AG, 74, and 1331) were put forth to exemplify Guru Nanak's borrowings from the hymns of Beṇi, composed in the same *rag* (AG, 93, and 1351). Sahib Singh presented these hymns as proof that Guru Nanak was acquainted with, and even possessed, the hymns of Farid and Beṇi. He then extended his thesis by claiming that the guru also knew of and possessed the hymns of Kabir and the other Bhagats.[11] Guru Nanak is believed to have traveled extensively in his lifetime, and according to Sahib Singh, these travels provided the guru with the opportunity to collect these hymns. The works of Teja Singh and Sahib Singh were pervasively influential, and their explanation of this issue has remained at the heart of most scholarly discussion on the subject ever since.[12]

Yet a third line of thinking, which attributed the incorporation of the hymns of the Bhagats to Guru Amardas, was briefly proposed by Mohan Singh Dewana and by G. B. Singh in the mid decades of the twentieth century.[13] Referring to reliable traditions that Guru Amardas was a staunch Vaishnava who loved devotional songs and visiting the pilgrimage centers in his early life, G. B. Singh argued that he must have collected the bhagat baṇi during this phase of his life and brought it with him when he joined the Sikh fold. Later he had these recorded in the Goindval Pothis prepared under his supervision. Neither of these scholars addressed this issue in any concerted way, however, and their view on this issue remained largely unheard. Nevertheless, they were the first scholars to raise this possibility. Working independently, Balbir Singh Dil and Giani Gurdit Singh have revived the view recently.[14]

My work with the early manuscripts provides us with data that we can use to scrutinize all three of the above-mentioned views concerning the introduction of the bhagat baṇi into the Sikh text. As I explain later in this chapter, the main body of the bhagat baṇi in both the Kartarpur Pothi and the Adi Granth had already appeared in the corresponding *rag* sections in the extant Goindval Pothis. This hard evidence demonstrates the historical inaccuracy of the traditional claim that these hymns were collected for the first time by Guru Arjan. Because we do not have access to all four of the Goindval Pothis, we cannot assert that each and every hymn of the bhagat baṇi recorded in the twenty-two *rag* sections of the Kartarpur Pothi was present in them. We must therefore admit that when he was compiling the Kartarpur Pothi, Guru Arjan may have added some hymns to the existing corpus of the bhagat baṇi available in the Goindval Pothis. But the categorical assertion that Guru Arjan created this feature of Sikh scripture needs to be dismissed as an inaccurate attempt to explain their inclusion.

While confirming that the bhagat baṇi was present in Sikh tradition some decades before the compilation of the Kartarpur Pothi, its presence in the Goindval Pothis does not automatically indicate when these hymns first found their way into sacred Sikh literature. They may have been included for the first time during the compilation of the Goindval Pothis, or as Sahib Singh and Teja Singh argued so emphatically, they may already have been present in existing Sikh sources, from which they were copied along with the hymns of the first and the second gurus. The presence of these hymns in the Goindval Pothis thus permits both possibilities, the former relating their inclusion to a decision by Guru Amardas, and the latter to the still earlier period when Guru Nanak lived.

One crucial source of information that helps clarify this point is found in the Guru Harsahai Pothi—a manuscript that, I have argued, represents the earliest Sikh compilation. From Giani Gurdit Singh we know that the opening section contains only the hymns of Guru Nanak.[15] The absence of the bhagat baṇi from this text weakens the argument that the hymns of the Bhagats entered the sacred Sikh literature during Guru Nanak's time but in itself does not, however, prove that they were unknown to Guru Nanak. Hence we must analyze in detail Sahib Singh's evidence that Guru Nanak was responsible for the inclusion of the bhagat baṇi in sacred Sikh literature.

As we have seen, Sahib Singh bases his argument on Guru Nanak's awareness of the hymns of Farid and Beṇi. In his discussion of Farid, Sahib Singh refers to one hymn by Guru Nanak in *rag* Suhi and three of his couplets, which Sahib Singh argues were created in direct response to Farid's hymns. Now it is a fact that the *rag* Suhi section of the Adi Granth contains two thematically related hymns, one by Farid and another attributed to Guru Nanak. Farid's hymn reads as follows:

> *Beṛa bandhi na sakio bandhan ki vela.*
> *Bhari sarvaru jab uchhalai tab taraṇu duhela. . . .*
> *Kahai Faridu saheliho sahu alaesi.*
> *Hansu chalasi ḍumaṇa ahi tanu dheri thisi.* (AG, 794)
> You could not make the raft, when it was time to do so.
> When the sea is choppy, it is difficult to swim over. . . .
> Farid says: Friends, when the call of the master comes
> The swanlike soul will leave, and this body then turns to dust.

According to Sahib Singh, Guru Nanak responded to Farid with a hymn of his own:

> *Jap tap ka bandhu beṛula jitu langhe vahela*
> *Na sarvaru na uchhalai esa panthu suhela. . . .*
> *Nanaku kahai saheliho sahu khara piara.*
> *Ham sah keria dasia sacha khasamu hamara.* (M1, AG, 729)
> Make a raft of meditation and self-control for a smooth passage.
> There will be no choppy sea, the passage will be comfortable. . . .
> Nanak says, O Friends! The loving master stands [before us].
> We are all his slaves, and he is our true Lord.

Undoubtedly, the two hymns referred to by Sahib Singh have affinities in both content and language: the images of the raft, the unruly see, and the appeal to friends and the helpful master. Moreover it does seem, as Sahib Singh argued, that Farid's gloomy images of lost opportunities for spiritual elevation are countered, in the hymn attributed to Guru Nanak, by a more calm and confident vision of life. Yet we must stop short of Sahib Singh's conclusion that all this amounts to incontrovertible evidence that Guru Nanak possessed the hymn of Farid, and that he created his own as a response to the issues raised by Farid.

The situation is not so simple, for the latter hymn is attributed not to Guru Nanak but to Guru Amardas in all of the early manuscripts: the Goindval Pothis (folio 9), MS 1245 (table of contents, folio 697, and text, folio 701), the Kartarpur Pothi (table of contents, folio 12, and text, folio 541), and the Kanpur Pothi. How then, we may ask, did it come to be attributed to Guru Nanak? The secret seems to be that although this hymn was clearly attributed to Guru Amardas, it was misplaced in the Goindval Pothis. Rather than appearing with the hymns of Guru Amardas in *rag* Suhi, it was included in the subsection devoted to the hymns of Guru Nanak, and it continued to be copied at that location in the manuscripts that followed. Later scribes, unable to understand its anomalous positioning among Guru Nanak's hymns, evidently changed its authorship, substituting the name of Guru Nanak for that of Guru Amardas. We witness this development first in the manuscripts created in the third quarter of the seventeenth century, and this change continued and is now reflected in the printed version of the Adi Granth (p. 729). This was the text that caused scholars like Sahib Singh to argue as they did.

With the elimination of this hymn, we are left with just four of Guru Nanak's couplets to establish the literary kinship between him and Farid. The proof here is also very tenuous. These couplets (AG, 1377–1384) appear under the title of *Shalok Shaikh Farid ke*. This text contains 130 couplets, 112 of which are actually attributed to Farid. The remaining eighteen are attributed to the Sikh gurus and are understood to provide specific commentaries on the themes Farid enunciated in his verses. It was in part this belief that Guru Nanak expressed specifically to Farid that produced Teja Singh and Sahib Singh's hypothesis. Of these eighteen couplets, thirteen have their authorship firmly attributed—five to Guru Amardas and eight to Guru Arjan. The remaining five, numbered 32, 113, 120, 121, and 124, appear without attribution, but evidence from elsewhere in the Adi Granth has produced clear Sikh convictions as to who their authors actually were. Couplet numbered 121 is attributed to Guru Ramdas on the basis of its appearance in his *Kanṛe ki Var* (AG, 1318), and the other four are thought to belong to Guru Nanak, since they appear elsewhere in the Adi Granth under his name. These four couplets are recorded in *Maru ki Var Mahala 3* (AG, 1088), *Sri Rag ki Var Mahala 4* (AG, 83), the section on *Shalok Varan te Vadhik* (AG, 1411), and *Sri Rag ki Var Mahala 4* (AG, 91), respectively.

In earlier discussion here, I argued that the text of the *vars* in its present form was created by Guru Arjan. The attribution of the couplets does not appear in the original writing of the Kartarpur Pothi and was entered later. This insertion of the authors' names after their couplets were actually recorded in the text of the Kartarpur Pothi created numerous discrepancies, and there are as many as fourteen instances of identical couplets attributed to different authors in the Adi Granth.[16]

In view of this complexity, it is problematic to attribute the four couplets under consideration to Guru Nanak, and then use them as evidence to argue that he composed them as a rejoinder to Farid. Guru Nanak may indeed have been familiar with Farid's hymns, since they were part of the religious and cultural milieu in which he lived, but there is no convincing evidence to support Sahib Singh's contention that Guru Nanak actually possessed the compositions of Farid, responded to them in his own hymns, and made them part of the sacred Sikh text.

Sahib Singh's argument went farther. He also holds that Guru Nanak collected the hymns of Beṇi, basing this on a comparison between three of Beṇi's hymns recorded in the Adi Granth and two that were composed by Guru Nanak. Sahib Singh attempted to show how Guru Nanak repeated sets of words that Beṇi has used, and even two complete verses. These are as follows, and as their comparison shows, they do indeed appear verbatim at two separate locations in the Adi Granth—once in a hymn attributed to Beṇi, and the other time in a hymn attributed to Guru Nanak:

> *Uradh dhiani liv laga.* (AG, 74, and 93)
> Lying upside down [in the womb], he meditates [on God].
> *Binu satigur baṭ na pavai.* (AG, 1351, and 1353)
> Without the true Guru no one finds the right path.

The repetition by Guru Nanak of these verses and other words of Beṇi is Sahib Singh's basic evidence that Guru Nanak was responsible for the inclusion of Beṇi's hymns in the Adi Granth, but he then points out other thematic affinities among the five hymns under discussion. Each of them, he notes, explores the idea that human beings remain in constant remembrance of God while in their mother's womb but tend to forget him and become involved in worldly affairs once they are born. These similarities, textual and thematic, led Sahib Singh to believe that Guru Nanak possessed a collection of hymns by Beṇi and, as we earlier saw, Farid. From this, Sahib Singh concluded that Guru Nanak must have possessed the hymns of all of the Bhagats which appear in the Adi Granth. How is one to deal with such a claim? The evidence in early Sikh manuscripts falsifies the claim about Farid, but that leaves the rest intact.

I would suggest that we widen our lens. The recurrence of the words, verses, and themes found in the compositions of Guru Nanak and Beṇi, and in several cases, those of other Bhagats, needs to be explained in relation to the larger literary and spiritual context in which the medieval saint-poets worked. Commenting on the linguistic richness of the Adi Granth and the language of the gurus and their contemporaries, Ernest Trumpp observed that it is "almost certain that Nanak and his successors employed in their writings purposely the Hindui idiom, following the example of Kabir and the other saint-poets, who had raised Hindui to a kind of standard for religious writings, and by employing which [Hindui] they could make themselves understood to nearly all the devotees of India, while Punjabi was only intelligible to the people of the Punjab."[17]

We may not accept the argument that the Sikh gurus consciously utilized a particular linguistic idiom to widen the intelligibility of their hymns, but Trumpp is surely right about the use of Sant Bhasha, which he calls Hindui, as a kind of standard for religious compositions in the fifteenth and sixteenth centuries. A religious lingua franca seems to have prevailed then in northern India, and poets drew upon this shared reservoir of vocabulary and phraseology to describe spiritual experiences.

In this broad framework, it is not surprising that ideas, phrases, and even whole verses appeared both in the hymns of Guru Nanak and in those of the Bhagats. W. H.

McLeod interprets the recurrence of words and half-verses as examples of "the kind of epigrams which could easily have gained common currency within the circle of the *sants* (believers in a supreme, non-incarnated God)."[18] Thus echoes of the verses of the Bhagats in those of Guru Nanak does not seem to have resulted from conscious imitation on the guru's part, as Sahib Singh argued to the great dismay of some Sikh scholars, but rather from an outgrowth of a broad sharing of ideas and idiom which was the norm at the time.[19]

Sahib Singh and Teja Singh relied primarily on evidence within the hymns of Guru Nanak and the Bhagats to support the argument that Guru Nanak collected the bhagat baṇi; no documentary evidence was ever presented. Their position on the extent of Guru Nanak's knowledge of such hymns is far from clear. They did not see the need to question whether Guru Nanak knew only those hymns that later became part of Sikh scripture, or whether he knew additional hymns from which a selection was made for the Sikh text, or, indeed, whether later gurus might have added hymns to his core selection.[20]

Their view of the incorporation of the bhagat baṇi in sacred Sikh literature during Guru Nanak's time has dominated Sikh scholarship throughout the twentieth century. Nevertheless, in light of the information found in the early manuscripts and our general understanding of the way the poets of this period fashioned their hymns, it is no longer tenable to accept this view. If Guru Nanak had access to the works of fellow saint-poets and accorded them the same status as that of his own hymns, the evidence so far is nonexistent.

I now shift my attention to Guru Amardas, who was proposed by Mohan Singh and G. B. Singh as responsible for this important addition to sacred Sikh literature. Guru Amardas played a crucial role in the early growth of the Sikh community, and, as we know, it was during his leadership that the Goindval Pothis were compiled. Hence it may come as little surprise that Guru Amardas is most likely the one who introduced the bhagat baṇi into the Sikh scriptural text.

The hymns of Guru Amardas offer conclusive evidence of his familiarity with these saints. He claims that Namdev the dyer and Kabir the weaver attained liberation through the perfect guru (*Nama chhiba Kabiru jolaha pure gur te gati pai*, M3, AG, 67). I have referred in the preceding discussion to Farid's hymn in the *rag* Suhi section and Guru Amardas's response to it (attributed, however, to Guru Nanak in the Adi Granth) in the same *rag*. But there are other, even clearer, instances of such dialogue.[21] His responses are quite pointed and addressed directly to Farid and Kabir; no parallel case is available in the hymns of Guru Nanak. The very practice of engaging in dialogue began with Guru Amardas and was expanded by his successors.[22]

In fact, there is a much closer resemblance—and startlingly so—between the vocabulary and phraseology in the bhagat baṇi and some of the hymns of Guru Amardas, than there is between Guru Nanak's hymns and Beṇi, discussed earlier. For example, Guru Amardas's two hymns about Prihalad (a paradigmatic devotee in Hindu literature), in *rag* Bhairo (AG, 1133, and 1154), follow images that appear in the hymns of Namdev in the same *rag* (AG, 1165), and Kabir in *rag* Basant (AG, 1194). The repetition of both ideas and phrases indicates that Guru Amardas had in mind the hymns of Namdev and Kabir when he composed his own; no evidence of such a close correspondence exists between the hymns of Guru Nanak and those of the Bhagats.[23]

Internal evidence thus points to an intimate and specific relationship between the hymns of Guru Amardas and those of the Bhagats as recorded in Sikh scripture. Hagiographical sources indicate that Guru Amardas was deeply fascinated by religious poetry even before he joined the Sikh fold, and that the beauty of Guru Nanak's hymns brought him to the Sikh court.[24] Whether he collected these hymns in the central Punjab (the bulk of them having already been popularized by traveling singers) or brought them back from his travels to Hindu pilgrimage centers, Guru Amardas is probably responsible for incorporating these hymns into the Sikh scriptural text.[25]

The Purpose of Incorporation of the Bhagat Baṇi

In Sikh literature, the purpose for introducing the bhagat baṇi into the Sikh scriptural text receives little focused attention. From *Mahima Prakash* to *Tvarikh Guru Khalsa*, Sikh sources simply attribute this development to Guru Arjan, and there is no inclination on the part of their writers to explain the reasons behind this inclusion. Stray references in these writings do, however, suggest two interesting explanations.

Beginning with *Mahima Prakash*, one view assigns a distinct character to the early Sikh community and presents the compilation of Sikh scripture as part of its institutional development. In this context, the presence of the bhagat baṇi in the Sikh text indicates humble submission on the part of the Bhagats—both Hindu and Muslim—to the superiority of the nascent Sikh tradition. According to this view, the Bhagats came to Guru Arjan seeking to place their compositions in the sacred Sikh text, and the guru in his grace accepted the hymns of those deserving the honor of becoming part of it.[26]

Then there is the second view, beginning with the author of *Gurbilas Patishahi 6*, for whom the presence of the bhagat baṇi in the Adi Granth seems perfectly natural. Nirmala scholars argued that Sikhism was distinct from Hinduism, but only because it was a purified expression of Indian spirituality. For them, the Adi Granth contained the gist of the spiritual wisdom of all ages.[27] As such, it naturally—almost necessarily—included the hymns of the Bhagats, who were, except for the Sikh gurus themselves, the most valued voices of the age.

Both these lines of thinking still enjoy currency among twentieth-century scholars, although they have been phrased in a somewhat different form and in a new idiom. Writing in the middle decades of the twentieth century, Bhai Vir Singh explained the inclusion of these hymns in the Sikh scriptural text in a way that echoed the former line of thinking. For him, the Adi Granth was created by Guru Arjan as the sacred text of a distinct community; the incorporation of the bhagat baṇi, however, resulted from the Sikh gurus' attempts to break narrow religious boundaries in search of the truth in all religions:

> Sri Guru Nanak Dev gave a good direction to the world, urging that people from different religious traditions should not oppose each other. How could envy go hand in hand with religion? . . . The Sikh Gurus gave concrete shape to this idea by incorporating in Sikh scripture, the writings of the Bhagats from different religions, castes, and views.[28]

This view explains the presence of the bhagat baṇi in Sikh scripture as an exercise in religious pluralism which furthered the Hindu understanding that different paths lead to the same truth. Operating within the same framework, Teja Singh presents the inclusion of the bhagat baṇi in Sikh scripture as a marker of the "cosmopolitan nature of Sikhism."[29]

Other scholars have interpreted the presence of these hymns in Sikh scripture as evidence of the nonsectarian character of the early community. Harnamdas, an Udasi writer, proposes—mistakenly, as the early manuscripts show—that the original text of the Adi Granth contained hymns by non-Sikhs at its beginning, and the hymns of the Sikh gurus followed them.[30] This layout manifested the spiritual continuity of the Sikh message. Harnamdas charges the later Sikh scribes with having reversed the order of the hymns in the Adi Granth by placing the hymns of the gurus before those of the Bhagats, and thereby upsetting the whole sequence. Believing that the Sikh gurus were part of the larger religious Hindu context and that the Adi Granth is a representative text of Indian spiritual thinking, he finds it impossible to imagine that the Bhagats did not come first in the Adi Granth. In a more general way, Dharmpal Maini, a scholar trained at Banaras Hindu University, argues that the Adi Granth "is a firm milestone of Indian spiritual literature" and cannot be considered a "sectarian document."[31]

For a student of the history of religion, the incorporation of the hymns by prestigious non-Sikhs into the Sikh text may have resulted from an attempt to legitimize the newly created text, and it seems logical that a nascent community would associate itself with the spiritual stalwarts of the time to gain requisite prestige and a closer identification with their followers. Scholars have alluded to this alignment as a possible reason for the introduction of the bhagat baṇi into the Sikh text.[32]

Yet such explanations—which attempt to account for the hymns of the Bhagats in Sikh scripture by citing the liberal theological outlook of the early Sikh community, or its relatively indistinct character within the larger Hindu context, or its attempt to attain spiritual prestige through this association—are all problematical. The process of the selection of the hymns, which I address in the following section, and my earlier discussion of these hymns' placement in the Sikh text, challenge these views.

I argued earlier here that these hymns became part of Sikh literature during Guru Amardas's tenure, and it is only in the context of his thinking that we can understand this development. Guru Amardas's inclusion of the bhagat baṇi in the Sikh text is rooted in his perception of divine revelation as a constant process. The primary revelation took place when God created the universe and having done that, God speaks to humanity from time to time through the hymns of the saintly people, the recitation of which is a sure means to liberation. Guru Amardas writes:

> *Bhagat jana ki utam baṇi jugi jugi rahi samai.*
> *Baṇi lagai so gati pae sabade sachi samai.* M3, AG, 909–910
> The exalted hymns of the Bhagats appear in all ages.
> One who devotes himself to these hymns and [thereby] immerses himself
> in the word of God will attain liberation.

This passage recognizes the bhagat baṇi as a manifestation of the revealed word. This fundamental belief in the revelatory and liberating nature of the bhagat baṇi motivated Guru Amardas to incorporate these hymns into the Goindval Pothis.

In my view, the criterion for ascertaining the identity of those who brought the divine message to humanity, however, was restrictive. For Guru Amardas, these had to be people who shared the Sikh monotheistic vision and an understanding of human life with its social and ethical obligations. Because the Sikh revelation is authentic, only hymns conforming to the Sikh belief in the unity of God could be accepted as embodying the truth.

The incorporation of the bhagat baṇi into the Sikh text also provided Guru Amardas with the unique opportunity to assert the "Sikh belief in social equality."[33] By selecting the hymns of monotheists from all castes, Guru Amardas brought the social comprehensiveness of the Sikh religious vision to the forefront. The institution of *laṇgar* which rejected Hindu caste taboos about the sharing of food, had already been an indivisible part of the early Sikh community; the hymns of low-caste Bhagats in the sacred text confirmed the Sikh position in the most emphatic terms possible. What better way to manifest Sikh social and spiritual egalitarianism?[34]

The Selection and Evolution of the Corpus

A striking feature of the bhagat baṇi as it appears in the Goindval Pothis is the omission of hymns by saint-poets like Surdas, a Vaishnava composing in Braj Bhasha; Mirabai, another Vaishnava poet; Lala, an important Shaivite of nearby Kashmir; and Kahna, a famous Vaishnava saint living in Lahore.[35] Since we cannot reasonably argue that the hymns of these saints were unknown in the Punjab and were inaccessible to Guru Amardas, their absence from the Goindval Pothis could represent an unambiguous rejection of the conception of God at the heart of the hymns of these holy people.

The first stage in the selection of hymns from the bhagat baṇi thought to be divinely revealed, and fit to be inducted in sacred Sikh literature, was to separate those Bhagats whose theology conformed to the monotheistic vision from other Bhagats with other beliefs. Though these latter may have been deemed holy by others, or even held themselves to be so, from the Sikh point of view they were lost souls. In the Sikh understanding, their compositions were the result of "unripe revelation" and could never lead anyone to liberation. Guru Amardas writes:

> *Kahide kache suṇde kache kachi akhi vakhaṇi.*
> *Hari hari nit karaih rasana kahia kachhu na jaṇi.*
> *Chitu jin ka hiri laia maia bolani pae ravaṇi.* M3, AG, 920
> The people who sing [these hymns] are unripe, the people who hear them are unripe, unripe people have composed them.
> [The singers of these hymns] may repeat "hari" daily, but this [recitation] does not have any effect on them.
> Their minds are stolen by illusion, yet they recite these [hymns] with great speed.

Compositions by holy men and women whose revelations were declared "unripe," because they did not conform to Sikh theology, were summarily rejected from the Sikh text.

Authors who shared Sikh theology were subjected to yet a further stage in the selection process. Their hymns were apparently scrutinized to reject compositions that did not reflect the Sikh emphasis on a strict ethical code for communal living. Karine Schomer rightly points out that "the Guru Granth corpus of Kabir utterances cannot possibly represent the sum total of what was accessible to the Sikh gurus at the time of compilation. A selection must have been made, on the basis of conformity to the 'moods and motivations' of the Sikh community at that particular stage in its development."[36] Schomer argues by contrasting the hymns of Kabir incorporated in the Adi Granth with those in *Kabir Granthavali.* Linda Hess also argues that the hymns of Kabir in the Adi Granth possess distinct nuances that distinguish them from compilations of his verse in other volumes.[37]

Having accomplished this task of selecting hymns, the gurus asserted further the supremacy of the content of the Sikh revelation. Whenever the hymns of the Bhagats seemed to convey a message even slightly different from Sikh thinking, attempts were made to correct them. We have referred to Guru Amardas's response to Farid's pessimistic ideas about the immanence of death—his assertion of a more positive outlook on life. The practice of appending comments by Guru Amardas to the hymns of the Bhagats seems to have resulted from this editorial need to create a scriptural text with a unified theological and social perspective. Evidently the effort succeeded, for despite the presence of hymns by authors of varied religious backgrounds, Sikh scripture presents a relatively coherent theology.

Having laid out the criterion of selection, I now attempt to trace the expansion of the text of bhagat baṇi between the Goindval Pothis and the Kartarpur Pothi, and then between the Kartarpur Pothi and the Adi Granth. I begin with a simple comparison of the number of hymns by the Bhagats, in the Goindval Pothis and in the Kartarpur Pothi. In Table 11, column 1 gives the name of the *rag* section; column 2 reports the number of hymns in a given *rag* in the extant Goindval Pothis; column 3 shows the number of hymns recorded in the corresponding section in the Kartarpur Pothi; and column 4 gives the difference in terms of hymns added (+) and absent (–) in the Kartarpur Pothi. The section on *rag* Maru, because of special complications, is excluded from the table.[38]

These data make it clear that of 133 hymns recorded in the Goindval Pothis, 120 appear in the Kartarpur Pothi. Of these, 113 appear in the same *rag* sections in both

Table 11. A Comparison of Hymns of the Bhagats in the Extant Goindval Pothis and the Kartarpur Pothi

Rag	G. Pothis	K. Pothi	Differences	
Suhi	12	10	+2	-4
Prabhati	11	9	+0	-2
Dhanasri	16	17	+2	-1
Basant	11	13	+3	-1
Bhairo	28	33	+6	-1
Tilang	1	3	+2	-0
Ramkali	23	18	+1	-6
Sorathi	23	23	+4	-4
Malar	5	5	+1	-1
Sarang	3	9	+6	-0
Total	133	140	+27	-20

texts, while seven are recorded in different *rag* sections. The changes in *rags* seemingly resulted from musical considerations; for example, the two hymns added in the section on *rag* Suhi in the Table 11 appear under *rag* Prabhati-Lalat in the Goindval Pothis, a combination of *rags* not included in the Kartarpur Pothi. The remaining five hymns may also have been transferred to new *rag* sections; there is also a possibility that they appeared in the Goindval Pothis in *rags* Asa, Gauṛi, and Gonḍ, as well, and were dropped to rectify the duplication. Because the Goindval Pothis containing these *rag* sections are no longer extant, there is no way we can know definitely if this was the case.[39]

The table confirms that almost 90 percent of the hymns present in the extant Goindval Pothis were included in the Kartarpur Pothi and, subsequently, the Adi Granth. These data indicate that the overwhelming bulk of the writings of the Bhagats had become part of the Sikh sacred literature during the period of Guru Amardas. The omission of the remaining thirteen hymns could not have been an accident, and a close examination of the text of the Goindval Pothis helps us understand the situation.

As we have said in the preceding discussions, there are three different handwritings present in the Goindval Pothis. Two of these thirteen hymns are in the hand of the primary scribe, and the remaining eleven are all in the hand of the second scribe. The two hymns in the hand of the primary scribe of the Goindval Pothis appear in *rag* Suhi (folio 56), and in *rag* Basant (folio 227). Why were these two hymns omitted from the Kartarpur Pothi? They may have been lost accidentally during copying. The disappearance of the hymn in *rag* Suhi may be explained as follows: In the Goindval Pothis, the sequence of nine hymns by the Bhagats in the section on *rag* Suhi written in the hand of the primary scribe is: 1 (Kabir), 2 (Farid), 3–5 (Ravidas), 6–8 (Kabir), and 9 (Farid). In the Kartarpur Pothi, the sequence is expanded and rearranged according to authorship and begins with the three hymns of Kabir numbered six through eight in the Goindval Pothis. These are followed by two hymns of Kabir transferred from the section on *rag* Prabahti in the Goindval Pothis, three hymns of Ravidas (3–5 in the Goindval Pothis), and two hymns of Farid (2 and 9 in the Goindval Pothis). In my view, the scribe of the Kartarpur Pothi copied the cluster of the three hymns by Kabir first, intending to copy the opening hymn later. Having inscribed the three hymns, however, he proceeded to transfer Kabir's two hymns from *rag* Prabhati, and then, while copying the hymns of Ravidas and Farid, forgot to record the opening hymn in the Goindval Pothis.

The same appears to have been the case with the hymn missing from the Kartarpur Pothi that appears in *rag* Basant in the Goindval Pothis. The missing hymn is number nine in the set of eleven hymns recorded in the Goindval Pothis. The sequence of hymns is as follows: Kabir, Kabir, Kabir, Namdev, Namdev, Ravidas, Kabir, Kabir, Namdev, Ramanand, and Kabir (the last two hymns are added later in folios originally left blank between the hymns of the gurus and those of the Bhagats). This sequence with the addition of three hymns (two by Kabir and one by Namdev) appears as follows in the Kartarpur Pothi: 1, 2, 7, 8, 11, K, 3, 10, 4, 5, N, 6, K. Hymn number nine seems to have been dropped in the process of copying.

The remaining eleven hymns that do not appear in the Adi Granth are in the hand of the second scribe. They are as follows: three hymns in *rag* Suhi (folios 61–63), five in *rag* Ramkali (folios 101–106), and three in *rag* Sorathi (folios 174–175). These belong to the group of thirty such hymns that appear in this hand in the two extant Goindval

Pothis. This handwriting appears only toward the end of the various *rag* sections, and these hymns were added after the original writing of the Goindval Pothis was completed. The presence of nineteen hymns from this group in the Kartarpur Pothi confirms that these hymns were present in the Goindval Pothis when they were used for the preparation of the Kartarpur Pothi. The criterion for selection of these hymns in the hand of the second scribe is not clear to me.

An interesting illustration of the selection process can be seen in the *rag* Bhairo section of the Goindval Pothis. This section contains twenty-eight hymns by the Bhagats: the first twenty-two are inscribed by the primary scribe (folios 257–269); the next six hymns are in the hand of the second scribe. These twenty-eight hymns are reproduced in the Kartarpur Pothi as follows:

G. Pothis	1–22, 23, 24, 25, 26, 27, and 28.
K. Pothi	1–22, 23 (shifted to *rag* Gauṛi), 24 (dropped), 25 (25+26+nine additional stanzas), 27, and 28.[40]

The sequence of six hymns in the hand of the second scribe in the Goindval Pothis appears in the Kartarpur Pothi in such a way as to transfer the first, drop the second, expand the third partly through the addition of the fourth and additional stanzas, and retain the fifth and the sixth hymns.

This analysis leads to two important inferences. First, the texts of the bhagat baṇi in the Goindval Pothis and the Kartarpur Pothi are closely related. Second, the data prove that the selection of the bhagat baṇi recorded in the Adi Granth was done largely at the stage of the compilation of the Goindval Pothis. The hymns recorded in the hand of the primary scribe in the Goindval Pothis are all retained, unless missed accidentally. The hymns recorded by the second scribe, however, were subjected to further scrutiny at the time of the compilation of the Kartarpur Pothi. Why was this done? One likely explanation is that when the Kartarpur Pothi was being compiled, the hymns in the handwriting of the second scribe were viewed as later additions to the Goindval Pothis and were thought not to have been authenticated by Guru Amardas. Consequently, eleven of these were considered unfit for inclusion in the Kartarpur Pothi.

As we move on to the next stage of our analysis, problems of this nature persist. Four hymns and two couplets of the Bhagats were originally intended for inclusion in the Kartarpur Pothi; they include two by Kabir, one each in *rag* Asa (folio 374) and *rag* Soraṭhi (folio 497); one by Mirabai, in *rag* Maru (folio 810); and one verse by Surdas, in *rag* Sarang (folio 885). Of the two couplets by Kabir, one appears in his *Var* 7 (a hymn about the seven days of the week) in *rag* Gauṛi (folio 275), and the other at the end of the section of his couplets (folio 943). All these six compositions were either not completed or later deleted from the Kartarpur Pothi.

Let us begin with Kabir. His hymn in *rag* Asa, which opens with *Dekhahu loga hari ki sagai. Ma ghari put dhia sang jai* (See O people! God's betrothal. The mother has married her son and lives with her daughter) was apparently crossed out immediately, since it is not included in the sequential counting of hymns in the Kartarpur Pothi.[41] Of the hymn in *rag* Soraṭhi, only the opening verse, *Audhu so jogi guru mera. Is pad ka kare nibera* (That ascetic is my Guru. Who explains this word to me.), was recorded in the original handwriting; it was crossed out later. Based on the evidence present in MS

1245, the recording of the opening verses of hymns with the intent of completing them later seems a common scribal practice.

It is not difficult to explain the problem that resulted from the deletion of these hymns. The biting satire of the first hymn uses explicit language and images of incest. In family-oriented Sikh thinking, there is no place for this satire no matter what content it carries. For reasons unknown, the hymn recorded in the Kartarpur Pothi, but after it was copied scribes realized that although it might be a genuine hymn of Kabir, it could have no place in the sacred Sikh text. In the case of the hymn in *rag* Soraṭhi, it is likely that the *tantrik* imagery was deemed similarly inappropriate. After the opening verse was copied down, the idea of recording the rest of this hymn was dropped.[42] The same kinds of problems appear regarding the two couplets of Kabir mentioned above which were originally recorded but later deleted.

The hymn of Mirabai in the Kartarpur Pothi appears at the end of the *rag* Maru section. Sahib Singh argued at length that this hymn was not present in the manuscripts compiled before 1675 but was inserted in some manuscripts after the death of Guru Tegh Bahadur.[43] Pashaura Singh notes the hymn's presence in the Kartarpur Pothi but claims that "the decision to exclude Mirabai's hymn must have been made by Guru Arjan himself."[44] In his view, the hymn was crossed out immediately after it was recorded.

To evaluate the conflicting claims, we must look closely at the Kartarpur Pothi text. The *rag* Maru section contains sixteen hymns. It opens with a set of nine hymns by Kabir, which is followed by those of Namdev, Kabir, Jaidev, Kabir, Ravidas, Ravidas, and Mirabai. Only the first eight in this sequence of sixteen hymns are recorded in the hand of the primary scribe, and it is up to this point that the sequential counting proceeds. The ninth hymn, by Kabir, and the hymns that followed, were recorded in various other hands, apparently at different times. With the exception of the hymns of Namdev and Jaidev, which appear in the corresponding section of the Goindval Pothis (folios 283 and 292), none of the other hymns recorded here is to be found in the Goindval Pothis.

It seems that the hymn of Mirabai was recorded in the *rag* Maru section along with the preceding hymn of Ravidas, which begins, *Sukh sagar suritaru chintamani kamdhain basi ja ke re* (God is the ocean of bliss, the tree under which all wishes are fulfilled, the wish-fulfilling stone, and it is under his control that the wish-fulfilling cow stands," folio 810). This hymn appears in the Goindval Pothis in the *rag* Soraṭhi (folio 167) section and was copied in the Kartarpur Pothi in the *rag* Soraṭhi section (folio 498)—in addition, that is, to the *rag* Maru inscription of the hymn. Apparently this hymn, located in a source that recorded it under *rag* Maru, came to the attention of a scribe some time after the original compilation of the Kartarpur Pothi. The scribe failed to recognize that Ravidas's hymn had already been recorded in *rag* Soraṭhi, so he inscribed the hymn again.

The situation in the Kartarpur Pothi, in which Mirabai's hymn entered along with one by Ravidas, substantiates John S. Hawley's observation that "Mira's putative initiation at the hands of Ravidas might have provided a justification for her inclusion within the *sant parampara*."[45] The tradition expounding Mirabai's association with Ravidas was strong in the Punjab, surfacing, for example, in a late-seventeenth-century source entitled *Prem Ambodh Pothi: Parchian Prem Bhakata kian* (The book of love: Introductions to the saints of loving devotion).[46] It seems likely, then, that Mirabai was viewed as a worshiper of the "one God" when her hymn was introduced into the Kartarpur Pothi.

Mirabai's hymn, however, refers to her love for Krishna, whom she regarded as God. The obvious conflict between this notion and the Sikh belief in God's formlessness probably accounts for the subsequent deletion of the hymn. The hymn appears in all mid-seventeenth-century manuscripts (see chapter 5, table 6) but was not incorporated into Adi Granth. Its text was eventually struck out from the Kartarpur Pothi.

In the *rag* Sarang section of the Kartarpur Pothi (folio 885) appears a single verse: *Chhadi man hari bimukhan ko sangu* (O mind, leave the company of those who have turned away from the Lord). The verse is traditionally attributed to Surdas, and there is firm evidence for accepting this belief as true. This single verse is followed by a blank space, which is in turn followed by a hymn under the heading *Sarang Mahala 5 Surdas*. The hymn closes with the signature of Surdas in its last line: *Surdas manu prabhi hathi lino dino ihu parlok* (Surdas! The Lord has taken control of my mind, and given me [access to] the other world). Taken in context, the appearance of Guru Arjan's name alongside that of Surdas indicates that this hymn is composed by Guru Arjan and is in direct response to Surdas's verse that precedes it.[47]

Surdas's hymn, of which we only have one verse in the Kartarpur Pothi, appears in complete form in the Kanpur Pothi.[48] This hymn addresses those who have turned away from God and are, therefore, beyond spiritual redemption. They are like blankets dyed black with no hope for change of colors (*Surdas oi kari kamri chaṛat na duje rang*). Although the hymn's emphasis on the rejection of fallen people may be excessive, little else in it controverts Sikh thinking. Guru Arjan composed and appended a hymn of his own to follow and balance Surdas's rejection of those who had turned away from God. Not that he registers any difference with Surdas regarding these people—they are like leeches sucking lepers' blood (*jiau kusṭi tani jok*)—but the emphasis in Guru Arjan's hymn shifts from people who are dyed black to those who are dyed in the color of the Lord (*hari lok*).

I hypothesize that the opening verse of Surdas's hymn was recorded by itself here because the definitive text of the hymn was not yet available at that time. The blank space that follows the recording of the single verse confirms that the original intention was to introduce the complete hymn into the text of the Kartarpur Pothi at a later date. Subsequent reservations about Surdas's reputation as a prominent Vaishnava poet may have accounted for the incompleteness of the hymn. While Mirabai's Vaishnava credentials had been watered down because of her association with Ravidas, Surdas's presence could not be justified on such grounds. The opening verse continues in the Adi Granth; it could not be deleted without rendering Guru Arjan's response to it in the following hymn irrelevant.

The early manuscripts present data that help us understand the way the hymns of the Bhagats reached their final form in the Adi Granth. As manifested in the extant Goindval Pothis, the main work of selecting the bhagat baṇi incorporated into sacred Sikh literature was done during the period of Guru Amardas. When the Kartarpur Pothi was compiled, some of the hymns of the Bhagats present in the Goindval Pothis were left out, and some additions may have been made. We have instances of two hymns and two couplets (attributed to Kabir and Mirabai) that were fully recorded, and instances of two hymns (of Kabir and Surdas) that were intended to be recorded in the Kartarpur Pothi. All these were subsequently dropped because of their heterodox content (Kabir and Mirabai), or the reputation of their author (Surdas), or both factors at once. This information shows the painstaking nature of the process of selection of the bhagat baṇi, on the one hand, and the complexities inherent in such an enterprise, on the other.

The Status of the Bhagat Baṇi

Although the presence of the bhagat baṇi in the Sikh scriptural text well served the Sikh belief in spiritual egalitarianism, these hymns did call attention to the issue of their status in relation to the hymns of the Sikh gurus. At present, the most common Sikh belief is that once incorporated into the Sikh scriptural text, the bhagat baṇi enjoyed equality with the rest of its contents. The information at our disposal, however, tells a complex story, and as evident throughout Sikh history, a constant need has been felt to explain the presence of the bhagat baṇi in the Adi Granth.

There is no doubt that the hymns of the Bhagats selected for the Sikh text were thought to communicate a divine message, but the explanation of their relation to the hymns of the Sikh gurus began with Guru Amardas himself. He perceived the gurbaṇi (he seems to have been thinking of Guru Nanak as a paradigm for the guru) as the medium of God's word (*Satigur baṇi sabadu suṇae*, M3, AG, 1177); its echo, he said, is present in all four corners of the world (*Gurbaṇi chahu kuṇḍi suṇiai sachai nami samaida*, M3, AG, 1065, and *Gurbaṇi varati jag antari isu baṇi te harinamu paida*, M3, AG, 1066). The hymns of the gurus are the very light of this world, which can be recognized only as a result of divine grace (*Gurbaṇi isu jag mahi chanaṇu karami vasai mani ae*, M3, AG, 67). Guru Amardas's total identification of the gurbaṇi with the word of God places it at the very apex of all revelations (*Baṇi ta gavahu guru keri baṇia siri baṇi*, M3, AG, 920).

Such statements suggest that Guru Amardas considered the hymns of the gurus to have a unique significance, and one far greater than the hymns of the bhagat, which had to be carefully selected before being inducted into the Sikh text. This implied ranking is rooted in Guru Amardas's distinction between guru and Bhagat:

> *Bhagatu bhagatu kahai sabhu koi.*
> *Binu satigur seve bhagati na paiai pure bhagi milai prabhu soi,* (M3, AG, 1131)
> Everyone may call [himself] a Bhagat.
> Without serving the true guru saintliness cannot be attained; it is with good luck that we reach God [and attain this stage].

The Bhagat is one who is devoted to God; "bhagathood" is therefore open to all and can be attained by serving the guru who, in contradistinction, possesses a special status by virtue of the divine gift bestowed upon him with which he can help ordinary human beings progress toward holiness.

This fundamental distinction between guru and Bhagat defined the basic structure of the Goindval Pothis, a structure later adhered to in the Kartarpur Pothi and the Adi Granth. The hymns of Guru Nanak result directly from the original revelation and are taken to constitute the pinnacle of sacred Sikh literature; the next stage belongs to hymns created by the Sikh gurus who carried the light of Guru Nanak; at the third stage came the hymns by the Sikhs who were initiated into sainthood by the gurus themselves; and the hymns of Bhagats, who had no connection with the gurus, are at the lower end of this hierarchy of sanctity.

In his *var* in *rag* Soraṭhi, Guru Ramdas writes about the greatness of God, the liberating power of the guru, and human beings who are blessed with divine grace. In the last group, he refers to the four categories of holy people (Bhagats, Sants, Sadhs, and Sikhs of the guru) and categorically states that the Sikhs are the most fortunate ones among them (*Sabhdu vaḍe bhag gursikha ke jo gurcharaṇi sikh paṛatia*, M4, AG, 649). He has no doubt that the Sikhs belong to a higher level of blessedness than the one enjoyed by the Bhagats.

Bhai Gurdas is not modest in explicating the hierarchical relationship between the Bhagats and the Sikhs (Gurmukhs/Gursikhs").[49] He writes about the Bhagats (*Var* 10), the early prominent Sikhs (*Var* 11), and the Sikh code of conduct centered on their devotion to the guru (*Var* 12). He believes that the Sikhs attained the same bliss received by Beṇi, Dhanna, Kabir, Namdev, Ravidas, and Saiṇ. In other words, only the most prominent saints of the other traditions were on an equal level with the Sikhs of the guru.

This narrative seems to emerge from the need to establish that the status of the Bhagats was lower or at best equal to that of prominent Sikhs in the community and that they all occupied a rung much beneath the place assigned to the gurus. This concern also suggests that the early Sikhs apparently recognized a sacred hierarchy among the contributors to their sacred text, reiterating and expanding Guru Amardas's basic position on the issue.

This decidedly complex response to the presence of the bhagat baṇi in the scriptural text manifests itself in other, more radical forms as well. In MS 1245 the hymns of the Bhagats are absent; and there may be no convincing way to deal with their absence other than to propose that they were dropped from the Sikh text. The fact that MS 1245 does include the hymns of the bards associated with the Sikh court further strengthens the argument referred to in chapter 4 that this text consciously excluded the bhagat baṇi from the emerging Sikh canon in an attempt to draw the line between insiders and outsiders.

MS 1245 is not the only manuscript that excludes the hymns of the Bhagats. The hymns of the Bhagats along with those of Guru Tegh Bahadur were later appended to the text of the manuscript at the Gurdwara Bal Lila Pothi, Maiṇi Sangat, Patna. The additions are recorded on folios that are recognizably distinct from the original text. The existence of these two major early manuscripts represents the presence of an alternative conception of Sikh scripture, that, it should contain only the compositions of the gurus and the Sikh bards. The tensions over this issue have continued—well into contemporary Sikh history.

It is no surprise that the years following the death of Guru Gobind Singh, which saw the dissolution of the office of the personal guru and the elevation of the sacred Sikh text to the unique status of the Guru Granth Sahib, should have brought this issue to the forefront. Debates on the subject reflected the newly acquired status of the scriptural text as the embodiment of the living guru and the resulting need to come to terms with its material structure. The self-proclaimed followers of the book needed to understand the authoritativeness of their text more than ever before, and they needed to know it in the most precise terms. This quest required an explanation of the presence of hymns by non-Sikhs in Sikh scripture. The Sikh thinking of the period dealt with this issue in two ways.

Kesar Singh Chhibbar reports that Bhai Mani Singh prepared a scriptural text in which the hymns of the Bhagats were separated from those of the gurus and then claims that Bhai Mani Singh's painful execution under orders from the Mughal administration at Lahore was a punishment for severing the hymns of the Bhagats from those of the gurus.[50] In Chhibbar's view, if the master decides to lift the servant to his lap, who can separate them? The metaphor reflects the traditional acceptance of a hierarchy within the scriptural text, on the one hand, and the absence of any provision to make changes in the text, on the other.

There is a manuscript with a colophon dated 1713—which was during the lifetime of Bhai Mani Singh—organized just as Bhai Mani Singh's manuscript is thought to have been.[51] In his reorganization of the text, Bhai Mani Singh was not, in fact, introducing a radically new understanding of the status of the hymns of the Bhagats in relation to those of the gurus; his thinking actually goes back to Bhai Gurdas. He was merely attempting to draw a clearer line between the hymns of the gurus and those of the others.

The view of Bhai Mani Singh and those who agreed with him regarding the status of the hymns of the Bhagats was not, however, the only opinion on this subject. Sevadas, a contemporary of Bhai Mani Singh, in his *Parchi Patishahi Dasvin ki*, offers another interesting, if ultimately untenable, new interpretation.[52] Sevadas narrates that Guru Arjan wrote six hymns and dedicated them to the Bhagats—which is to say, he included the signatures of these Bhagats in the final verse, instead of his signature of Nanak. Specific examples of three hymns by Kabir in *rag* Gauṛi and *rag* Bhairo, of one each by Farid and Dhanna in *rag* Asa, and one of Surdas in *rag* Sarang are then given. No claim is made that all hymns attributed to the Bhagats were actually composed by Guru Arjan, but this seems to be implied. Sevadas's contention that the hymns of these Bhagats were the creation of Guru Arjan seems to originate from a need to explain their presence in the Adi Granth, as well as from a desire to entrench them permanently in Sikh scripture and grant them a status equal to that of the other compositions.

Writing in the last decades of the eighteenth century, the chronicler of *Sikhan di Bhagatmala* presented yet another position on this issue, which was emphatically repeated in *Sri Gurpratap Suraj Granth* in the middle of the nineteenth century.[53] According to this view, hymns composed by the Bhagats at an earlier time were rejected for incorporation into the Sikh scriptural text, and only fresh compositions prepared during their stay at the Sikh court were recorded in the Kartarpur Pothi. The implication is clear: the hymns of the Bhagats that find a place in Sikh scripture are composed under the direct spiritual guidance of Guru Arjan.

The attribution of the hymns of the Bhagats to Guru Arjan, as suggested by Sevadas, and their consequent spiritual authority remained current. Tara Singh Narotam endorsed Sevadas's position at the end of the nineteenth century.[54] It was only with the growing awareness that some of the hymns of the Bhagats were also to be found in other sources unrelated to the Sikh gurus that this view gradually lost currency among twentieth-century scholars.

These explanations about the presence of the compositions of the non-Sikhs in Sikh scripture have reverberated throughout later Sikh thinking. In the opening decades of the twentieth century, Teja Singh Bhasoṛ published an edition of the Adi Granth in which the *Ragmala* was omitted.[55] This work represented an initial step toward eventually removing all hymns not composed by the Sikh gurus. In doing this, Bhasoṛ was attempting to dramatically redraw the boundary between the hymns of the Sikh gurus and all others that in his view did not belong in Sikh scripture. The Sikh revelation, according to Bhasoṛ, should include only the hymns of the Sikh gurus. This position, in a way, extended the thinking that went into the making of MS 1245 and the Gurdwara Bal Lila Pothi, and the one created by Bhai Mani Singh. The compiler of the MS 1245 dropped the hymns of the Bhagats but kept those of the Sikh bards; Bhai Mani Singh separated the hymns of the bards and the Bhagats and appended them at the end of the text; and Teja Singh Bhasoṛ's plan was to drop hymns by both these groups altogether.

The explanation offered by the writer of *Sikhan di Bhagatmala* has recently resurfaced in an interesting way in Giani Gurdit Singh's *Itihas Sri Adi Granth*. In this book, Giani Gurdit Singh has painstakingly argued that all of the Bhagats whose hymns are included in Sikh scripture were actually disciples of Guru Nanak.[56] From our point of view, the importance of the book lies not in the historical validity of the claims made in it by Giani Gurdit Singh, but in its concerted effort to explain reasons why hymns by non-Sikhs were included in the Sikh scriptural text.

The data pertaining to this facet of the scriptural history do show that the presence of the bhagat baṇi in Sikh scripture has been a source of ongoing tension within Sikh thinking, and hence a recurrent need has been felt to address this issue. Attempts at explanation have included upgrading the status of the bhagat baṇi by granting it the same standing as the gurbaṇi (Sevadas); arguing that the spirituality of the Bhagats essentially depended on the gurus (*Sikhan di Bhagatmala*); downgrading them by placing them at the closing of the text (Bhai Mani Singh); and even removing them altogether from the text (MS 1245). Such continued attempts are rooted in the genuine tension caused by the presence of hymns by non-Sikhs in a canon that asserts the primacy of the gurus alone yet also espouses the equality of all the works within it.

To sum up then, data obtained from an examination of the early manuscripts help us understand more accurately the ways the bhagat baṇi was incorporated into the Sikh scriptural text. In all likelihood, Guru Amardas was responsible for the decision to introduce the bhagat baṇi as well to select the large corpus that became part of Sikh scripture. This decision, rooted in his belief in the continuity of divine revelation, provided him with the opportunity to emphasize the Sikh vision of social equality. The hymns of the Bhagats were thoroughly scrutinized, however, and only those that were thought to conform to Sikh theological and ethical outlooks were incorporated within the scriptural text. In an extremely selective way, this process continued through the compilation of the Kartarpur Pothi and the Adi Granth itself.

8

The Guru Granth Sahib

I began this study by situating the origin, expansion, and canonization of the text of the Adi Granth within the larger context of Sikh doctrine and in relation to the evolution of early Sikh institutions. I then examined in detail both traditional and scholarly understandings of the compilation of Sikh scripture, and in subsequent chapters considered these views in light of the information available in the early manuscripts, some of which were not accessible for extended scrutiny in the past. In doing so, I suggested revisions and modifications that are needed to accurately represent the process of canon formation in the Sikh tradition.

In this chapter I attempt to bring the story of the making of Sikh scripture to the present and situate its development within a broader historical context. I do this in three steps. First, I trace the history of the Adi Granth from its inception in the late seventeenth century to the present time. The primary data for this discussion are provided by the extant Sikh scriptural manuscripts compiled between 1700 and the middle of the nineteenth century, when creation of new manuscripts virtually ceased, and the printed editions of the Adi Granth proliferated from 1865 on.[1] I then shift my focus to the issue of the development of scriptural authority within the Sikh community and examine in detail its evolution. I also consider the roles the text has played and continues to play in the Sikh religious and community life today. I conclude with a brief assessment of future prospects for the role and status of the Adi Granth as the Sikh community—spread from New Zealand to California—enters the twenty-first century.

Three Centuries of Sikh Scriptural History

As we have seen, Sikh tradition holds that the Adi Granth was compiled by Guru Gobind Singh at Damdama, Bhatinda in 1705–1706, and that its contents included the sacred

Sikh writings recorded in the Kartarpur Pothi with the addition of the compositions of Guru Tegh Bahadur. According to this view, the Adi Granth was at this time created as the canonical text of the community, superseding and rendering redundant other versions, and eliminating the possibility for any variant sacred text to emerge. In the light of the evidence available, we now know that the Adi Granth was compiled in the 1680s at Anandpur, and the precise relationship of its contents with those of the earlier seventeenth-century manuscripts was more complex than we have traditionally understood (see chapter 5, table 7). What remains to be investigated is the extent to which the Adi Granth, once compiled, became the primary Sikh scripture, removing all other texts from the scene, as it has been claimed.

The Adi Granth Manuscripts 1700–1850

Sikhs firmly believe that once the Adi Granth was created—and more particularly, once it acquired its elevated status as the Guru Granth Sahib—there was no reason and no provision for the existence of a variant text. In consequence, the history of Sikh scripture during the past three centuries has remained completely unexplored. Only recently has this process begun with the work of Pashaura Singh, who has examined the period closely. Pashaura Singh comes to two main conclusions: (1) During the eighteenth century and early nineteenth century, the Sikhs used "more than four different versions of the Adi Granth; (2) "Maharaja Ranjit Singh using his political influence" had "a sole authorized canon prepared," at the beginning of the nineteenth century.[2] Pashaura Singh accounts for the continued existence of four different versions after Guru Gobind Singh's time by noting the rivalries between various Sikh groups that also persisted. That, in turn, provides the reason that three branches of the earlier seventeenth-century manuscript traditions continued to flourish alongside the Adi Granth—the fourth scriptural tradition. Maharaja Ranjit Singh, a powerful political figure, could impose upon these fighting groups an authoritative version of Sikh scripture, but even he could not enforce strict uniformity in the Sikh scriptural tradition.

The empirical evidence I have gathered supports Pashaura Singh's claim that more than one version of the Sikh scriptural text proliferated during this period, but other aspects of his argument are harder to maintain. There is no evidence that Maharaja Ranjit Singh played a role in the formation of Sikh canon. He did indeed invite the custodians of the Kartarpur and the Kanpur pothis to Lahore and offered them royal patronage as a way of venerating their relationship with the Sikh gurus. But if this enterprise was focused toward the creation of a "standard text" of the Adi Granth, we have no evidence.

More significantly, Pashaura Singh's description of eighteenth- and nineteenth-century scriptural manuscripts as "four different versions of the Adi Granth" is problematical. In chapter 5, I argue in detail that the seventeenth-century manuscripts fall into two, not three branches and that the manuscripts of branch 1 slowly disappeared from the scene in the later decades of the seventeenth century itself. Pashaura Singh's argument that the manuscripts of this period can be grouped into four branches does not square with the data available. Furthermore, his characterization of these manuscripts as variants of the Adi Granth is incorrect. As he himself says, they are largely copies of early-seventeenth-century manuscripts and hence cannot be seen as variations on the Adi Granth, which came into being later.

On the basis of the data I have collected, the extant manuscripts compiled during the eighteenth and early nineteenth century fall into not one (as Sikh sources contend), not four (as Pashaura Singh claims), but two groups: copies of the Adi Granth, and a version of seventeenth-century manuscripts of branch 2 that adds to their contents the compositions of Guru Tegh Bahadur. I strictly follow traditional usage of the term "Adi Granth" for the text created at Anandpur in the 1680s with Guru Gobind Singh's sanction. If one does this, the very existence of the non-Adi Granth manuscripts raises a fundamental issue: if the Adi Granth came to be regarded as the canonical text within the Sikh community at the turn of eighteenth century, how and why did other versions continue to be compiled?

As mentioned in chapter 5, my extensive fieldwork in the Punjab suggests that in central places like Anandpur, and Damdama, Bhatinda, the extant scriptural manuscripts are almost always the Adi Granth. Once it originated in the 1680s, the scribes copied it as time passed, and this text became available for use in the community. Because these manuscripts grew out of a single source, there are no substantive variations within their contents. Most versions are completely identical with the text of the Adi Granth presently used in the Sikh community.

The Adi Granth manuscripts are distinct in one important respect from others that continued to circulate. They do not contain the date on which they were copied or compiled, while the manuscripts outside this group duly record this information. This scribal practice is the basis for the hypothesis among revisionist scholars that the Adi Granth began to be generated largely in the early nineteenth century, and that the scribes in question tried to ignore or hide its late origin.[3] I take the opposite view. For me, the absence of date and colophon in the Adi Granth manuscripts allows for the exalted status of the text. As the Guru Granth Sahib, it was understood to be the eternal guru—beyond time, and therefore rendering inappropriate the normal requirements connected with identifying a scribe. This also attests to the scribal conviction that they were adding absolutely nothing that was new and that the canon was truly fixed. Where the tradition of the Adi Granth becoming the Guru Granth Sahib was unknown or rejected, scribes continued in their practice of recording the date of compilation as it appeared in antecedents to the manuscripts they created.

Let us consider this second group of manuscripts. Their first striking feature is the substantive variations among them, which suggests that they did not originate from a single source, as was the case for manuscripts in the line that followed the Adi Granth. We now know that the compositions of Guru Tegh Bahadur were incorporated into the existing scriptural text beginning at Anandpur (MS 1192) in 1674, and we know that manuscripts of this type compiled in 1675 and 1677 eventually reached as far as Dhaka and Banaras.[4] Once these were established in congregations distant from the Punjab, scribes in these areas apparently copied them without being aware that their contents differed from those of the Adi Granth.

While some manuscripts of this group closely replicate the Anandpur original, others reveal a different pattern. As the compositions of Guru Tegh Bahadur became available within the community in the 1670s, they were apparently appended to existing manuscripts. The scribes copying from these updated documents sorted out the additions in their own ways. They recorded them in appropriate *rag* sections, while copying the rest of the contents as they existed in their source. In the process, new manuscripts that emerged developed differences of content as well as of organization. Consider a single instance. Guru Tegh Bahadur wrote four hymns in *rag* Jaijavanti, which was not used by the earlier gurus and hence did not appear in the sequence of *rags* that existed in the earlier texts. Faced with this problem, some scribes, it appears, recorded this group of hymns at the end of the text as it is in the Adi Granth, while others placed it in the middle, following *rag* Soraṭhi. Still others associated *rag* Jaijavanti with *rag* Jaitsri and appended these hymns there.

In my view, the data at our disposal do not permit the conclusion that these two groups of manuscripts—the Adi Granth manuscripts and those that escaped its authoritative pull—were competing with each other. Nor is there evidence that the Adi Granth triumphed later in the game, whether due to the intervention of Maharaja Ranjit Singh or any other circumstance. The firm tradition that Guru Gobind Singh created the canonical text and the exclusive presence of the manuscripts of the Adi Granth family in the central areas where the Sikhs lived suggest that in the Punjab it was early and widely recognized as the canonical text. Nonetheless, earlier manuscripts did on occasion continue to be copied, and thus texts were created that were not identical with that of the Adi Granth. It seems plausible that the scribes who produced such manuscripts were simply unaware of the textual differences between the Adi Granth and the earlier texts from which they were copying.

On the whole, thus, there is no indication of any concerted attempt to redefine the emerging Sikh canon. Yet an exception does prove the rule, a manuscript dated 1713, presently in the custody of Manjit Singh Sethi of New Delhi. It is structured in three sections: the first includes the hymns of the gurus recorded in the Adi Granth arranged not according to *rag* but by author (folios 1–536); the second comprises the hymns recorded in the Dasam Granth and traditionally attributed to Guru Gobind Singh (folios 537–1028); and the third, appended at the end, contains the hymns of the Bhaṭs and the Bhagats (folios 1029–1096). The hymns of the gurus include all the additional compositions available in non-Adi Granth manuscripts. As we saw in chapter 2, Kesar Singh Chhibbar attributes the creation of this version of the Sikh text to Bhai Mani Singh and portrays his cruel execution at the hands of the Mughals as the result of his tinkering with the body of the guru.[5] In spite of its rejection, however, this manuscript did generate some copies later in the century.[6] But more significant is the fact that despite its association with a widely respected stalwart like Bhai Mani Singh, this self-conscious modification of the canon could not challenge the status of the Adi Granth in any significant way within the larger Sikh community.

We see, therefore, that the Adi Granth achieved relative hegemony in the Sikh scriptural tradition at the beginning of the eighteenth century, and that this hegemony has remained unchallenged to the present day. Yet historical circumstances continued to impinge upon the physical appearance of the text. The period of severe persecution in the first half of the eighteenth century, which forced the Sikhs to move constantly, resulted in the compilation of small-sized texts called travel manuscripts (*safari biṛ*). These could be easily tied to one's back and carried into battle. Thus Khalsa warriors marched onto the battlefield bearing the guru on their backs. A number of such manuscripts are extant: each can be easily packed into a small briefcase.[7]

Beginning with the last quarter of the eighteenth century, Sikh political supremacy in the Punjab resulted in the opposite effect: large-sized manuscripts were created, along with extensively illuminated ones. The largest manuscript I have examined was created in 1849 and is presently in the custody of the Baghṛias, a leading family in the Patiala area. Working with another reasonably strong person, I could barely take it out of the cupboard and put it up for display to examine its contents.[8] As for illuminated manuscripts, several of the most elaborate are nineteenth-century creations presently at Moti Bagh, in the private collection of the Maharaja of Patiala.

From the Mid Nineteenth Century to the Present

When the British annexed the Sikh kingdom in 1849, profound changes occurred in the lives of the Sikhs and their scripture. The printing press arrived in Lahore in the 1850s, and the first lithograph edition of the Adi Granth was published by Lala Harsukh Rai at Kohinoor Press in 1864–1865. By 1893 eleven different editions and reprints existed.[9] By the end of the nineteenth century, the major work of publication had moved to Amritsar; the first Amritsar edition of the Adi Granth was produced at Wazir Hind Press in 1902. The publication effort of the Sikh community eventually became centered there, and a publishing house called Chatar Singh Jiwan Singh became the major producer of the Adi Granth. In early editions, the Adi Granth was produced with a pagination that varied from 1,168 to 2,202 pages, but its size was eventually standardized to 1,430 pages. Emulating the eighteenth-century innovation of the *safari biṛ*, the British sponsored a limited edition of a remarkably small printed text (2 by 2 inches) and distributed it to boost the morale of Sikh soldiers who participated in World War I.

As early as 1928, three years from its inception, the SGPC resolved to produce a standard edition of the Adi Granth and make it available to the community at a subsidized price.[10] The project started with a four-volume annotated text entitled *Shabadarth Sri Guru Granth Sahib Ji*, in the late 1930s. The SGPC established its own press in 1949 and produced its first one-volume edition of the Adi Granth in 1952.[11] Prominent scholars participated in the production of this text; they used the Kartarpur Pothi and an undated manuscript at Damdama, Bhatinda, as two key sources for this edition of the Adi Granth.[12]

Intended to eliminate any possible controversy about the authoritative text of the Adi Granth, the publication of the SGPC edition actually succeeded in inflaming it, as evident in the response of several commercial publishing houses who had the support of the Chief Khalsa Diwan, a Sikh claimant that rivaled the authority displayed by the SGPC. Although the interests of the publishers were purely business-oriented (they did not want the SGPC to steal away a significant part of the market for the Adi Granth), they presented their arguments in religious terms. They said they were fighting to protect the integrity of the text of the Adi Granth by alleging that the SGPC edition did not always follow the invocation as it was recorded in the Kartarpur Pothi. Hence the SGPC version should not be accepted.

This criticism regarding the precise placement of the text of the invocation in the SGPC edition was valid. Scholars involved in producing the SGPC edition had determined that as a matter of general policy the scribe of the Kartarpur Pothi had placed the invocation on the left side of the folio before beginning each new section of the text. On the basis of this observation, they re-placed the invocation in the SGPC edition to appear consistently before the title of each new subsection of text, which was not always done in the Kartarpur Pothi. Playing on the Sikh religious sensibility, the publishing lobby challenged the SGPC's right to make even positional changes in the text of the Adi Granth.

The SGPC eventually withdrew this edition and replaced it with a revised edition in the mid 1960s. The new text was claimed to strictly follow the invocation as it appeared in the Kartarpur Pothi. Not all scholars accepted the accuracy of the claim, however, and the issue is still not resolved to the satisfaction of all. The SGPC continued with its publication of the revised edition, and with the passage of time the criticism lost its thrust.

In this debate, which lasted for over a decade, the issue of the status of the early manuscripts also came to focus. The SGPC supported the centrality of the Kartarpur Pothi in the history of Sikh canon formation. The Chief Khalsa Diwan authorities, however, argued that the status of the Guru Granth Sahib had been assigned to the Adi Granth, and not the Kartarpur Pothi. Consequently, the original manuscript of the Adi Granth created by Guru Gobind Singh should be located and the authoritative printed text should be based on it, not the Kartarpur Pothi, the basis of the SGPC version.

There was validity to the argument to the extent that the Kartarpur Pothi is incomplete, and one must justify the presence of some compositions in it that were not placed in the Adi Granth. But in the absence of a manuscript of the Adi Granth with comparable history, no scholarly consensus on this fundamental issue has emerged. In the early 1990s, the debate about the status of the Kartarpur Pothi was at the center of the controversy around Piar Singh's work on the early manuscripts.[13]

In the early 1970s, the SGPC released another single-volume edition of the Adi Granth in which the words were separated from each other (*pad chhed*) in the print. Until this time the single-volume printed text had continued the manuscript tradition of connecting words without breaks, the reader had to recognize the words in order to make the appropriate breaks himself. The idea at the basis of the new edition was that separating words would facilitate reading for those who were not trained to read the continuous text. Not surprisingly, this edition also came under vehement attack. Its critics argued that splitting the connected words in the printed edition was tantamount to tearing asunder the limbs of the guru. The text was the body of the guru, and it could not be segmented without threatening its proper life.

Others, however, argued that the connected words were not an essential feature of the text of the Adi Granth, but represented the way scribes wrote in the past. Their point was that separating the words would help make the reading of the text not just easier but more accurate, which aligned the issue with the philosophical position that understanding the text of the Adi Granth is the essence of the Sikh devotional experience, a view we discuss later in this chapter. The SGPC leadership successfully withstood the criticism leveled against this edition and continued to publish it. The text has gained popularity over the years and is now used in homes as well the *gurdwaras*. The commercial publishers finally ended their initial opposition to this edition and began to publish it independently.

In the meantime the SGPC developed yet another edition of the Adi Granth, this one available in two volumes, bringing their tally of various editions to four: the two one-volume editions for ceremonial use (one with words connected to each other and the other in which they are separated), the four-volume annotated edition, and the two-volume edition. All four comprise 1,430 pages. The ceremonial editions are available in three standard sizes: 14 by 17 inches, 11 by 14 inches, and 7 by 11 inches, using type size of 40 points, 32 points, and 24 points, respectively. The largest size is commonly used in the *gurdwaras*, and the others in homes.

The eventual acceptance by the commercial publishing lobby of the SGPC edition has left the impression that a single authoritative text of the Adi Granth is now available. In the mid 1990s, however, the realization dawned that the four editions produced by the SGPC themselves display numerous variants. On March 26, 1996, the SGPC resolved to create a committee to look into this issue and ensure that all four texts published by the SGPC are identical.[14]

Thus the overall picture is of ever greater standardization in printed form. Yet a few detours in the more recent phases of the Adi Granth's textual history still deserve our attention. First we must mention a unique case in which a non-Adi Granth, print version of the Sikh scripture was published in 1881.[15] Notably this was the only printed text published outside of Lahore in the nineteenth century; it emerged instead from Gujranwala, a small district headquarters. The modest press that produced it in all likelihood took the manuscript available in the local *gurdwara* and published it without knowing its precise contents. It is not clear to me what happened to the printed copies after the anomalies in their contents were detected.

Another crucial episode in the history of printing Sikh scripture occured in the mid 1910s. Teja Singh Bhasoṛ, an important Sikh leader of the period, felt uncomfortable with the presence of the writings of the Bhagats, the Bhaṭs, and the *Ragmala* in the Adi Granth. He published an edition of the Adi Granth in which the *Ragmala* was deleted. The circulation of this publication, however, was restricted to a small circle of people directly under his influence and did not reach the larger Sikh community.

There is an interesting parallel between the efforts of Bhasoṛ and the attempted revision of canon attributed to Bhai Mani Singh in the 1710s. Both were major figures in Sikh history and both felt strongly that the contents of the Adi Granth needed revision. But the difference of period is significant. Quite unlike the situation that prevailed in early eighteenth century, Sikhs of the 1920s had a central authority in the SGPC. The SGPC judged that Bhasoṛ's publication was a serious infringement on Sikh belief and expelled him from the community in 1928.[16] An appeal was made to all those who possessed these printed volumes to send them to the SGPC, with the idea that they would be ceremonially cremated. Owing largely to the absence of printing, nothing comparable could have happened a century before.

Other unexpected developments came with the twentieth century. For the first time, whole communities of Sikhs are largely unable to read Gurmukhi. For example, the Sindhi and the Afghani Sikhs understand the language of the Adi Granth but cannot read it, and many Sikhs growing up in Southeast Asia or Europe or North America can understand only a bit of its language in either written or oral from. Several options have been explored to meet this challenge. The problem was first addressed by producing editions of the Adi Granth in Devanagari, in Indo-Persian script, and also in Roman transliteration for people with purely scholarly interests. Both the SGPC and commercial publishers pioneered this effort.[17] A new edition of the Adi Granth in which the original text, a Roman transliteration, and an English translation appear side by side has been recently released.[18]

In the 1990s the text of the Adi Granth also became available in a digital format, produced by a variety of individuals and organizations. The developers of these texts are professionals in fields unrelated to the study of the Adi Granth and generally live and work outside the Punjab. A sample of such versions follows:

1. *Ik Oankar Baṇi System* (1994), a package of four floppy disks developed by Balwant Singh Uppal, an electrical engineer based in Australia. It includes the complete text of the Adi Granth in Gurmukhi and can access the meaning of every word in Punjabi.
2. *Scriptures and the Heritage of the Sikhs* (1995), a CD-ROM developed by Preet Mohan Singh Kapoor and Bhupinder Singh, both computer engineers working in Silicon Valley, California. It includes the English translation of the Adi Granth by Gurbachan Singh Talib, a scholar of scriptural literature.
3. *Gurbaṇi CD* (1995), a CD-ROM developed by Kulbir Singh Thind, a physician working in California. It contains the text of the Adi Granth in Gurmukhi, Devanagari, and Roman, along with English translation by Sant Singh Khalsa, a pediatrician working in Phoenix, Arizona.
4. *Gurbaṇi Informant* (1995), a package of four floppy disks developed by CadCON of New Delhi. It contains the Adi Granth in Gurmukhi and Roman and provides access to every verse in the text with a simultaneous display of author and title.
5. *Gurbaṇi Researcher* (1998), a CD-ROM developed by two Californians—Joginder Singh Ahluwalia, petroleum research engineer, and Gurjot Singh, a computer engineer. It contains the text of the Adi Granth in Gurmukhi along with a verse-by-verse translation in English by Sant Singh Khalsa. A search engine locates a word or a verse by both normal (with correct spellings) and "fuzzy" (without the vocalic markers) modes and reports the number of times it occurs in the complete text.
6. *Encyclopedia of Sikhism* (1998), a CD-ROM developed by Raghbir Singh Bains, a former civil servant working in Vancouver, British Columbia, Canada. It contains Sant Singh Khalsa's English translation of the Adi Granth.[19]

The variant word spellings used in the SGPC text become problematic in a computer environment, where regularization and consistency are required for search and other functions. In many cases it is difficult to locate the same word in its several different forms and usage. It is as yet unclear how, if at all, such difficulties will affect the most easily available forms of the text of the Adi Granth in the years ahead.

Sikh tradition is largely correct in its belief that once compiled, the text of the Adi Granth has remained unchanged over the past three centuries—nothing substantive has been added to it or taken away from it. This narrative, however, needs to encompass the fact that other versions of the scripture than the Adi Granth itself continued to be compiled until the middle of the nineteenth century. In my view, the proliferation of such versions largely resulted from the scribes' ignorance of the precise contents of the canonical text. When the printing press made it possible to reproduce a single widely accessible version of the text, the incumbent hegemony of the Adi Granth further increased. In the past three centuries, the canon was openly challenged on two occasions:

first in 1713 in the form of the manuscript attributed to Bhai Mani Singh, and then in the 1910s in the edition of the Adi Granth published by Teja Singh Bhasoṛ. Although originated by two leading figures of their times, both attempts failed.

Simultaneously, however, the text as a living scripture has been evolving steadily, taking shape as small-sized travel manuscripts, a majestic megatext, a beautifully adorned manuscript, a printed text, and now as a CD-ROM-based interactive program. Meanwhile the SGPC's resolution of 1928 to publish the authoritative text of the Adi Granth has slowly been producing results. A group of earnest Sikh scholars meet daily in the library of the Darbar Sahib, Amritsar, to go verse by verse over the four published texts of the Adi Granth and try to collate them and arrive at a definitive reading. Yet we need to remember that this activity takes place against the backdrop of one major issue—whether the main source for this authoritative edition of the Adi Granth should actually be the Kartarpur Pothi or instead the earliest extant manuscript of the Adi Granth. On this question, no reasoned resolution has yet been achieved.

The Authority of the Adi Granth

As I discussed at the chapter opening, the Sikhs firmly believe that Guru Gobind Singh declared the Adi Granth to be the guru, and the text has played the role of central authority within the community since then. The traditional Sikh sources discussed in detail in chapter 2 primarily attribute this development to the decision of Guru Gobind Singh.[20] Some scholars have felt a degree of discomfort with this position and have argued that more research is needed before the traditional position can be fully affirmed.[21] In order to clearly understand the authority of the Adi Granth, let us locate it in the larger context of the history of the community.

Establishing Scriptural Authority

Authority within the early Sikh community functioned at two levels: personal and symbolic. The guru enjoyed the central authority within the Sikh community, and this belief in his authority grew stronger with the emergence of the idea that he was the representative of God on earth. By the turn of the seventeenth century, Bhai Gurdas claimed categorically that the only authority Sikhs recognized was that of the guru, and that the Mughal emperor was no match.[22]

Yet another tier of personal authority, developed with the *manji* system established during Guru Amardas's time. The holders of this authority were later called the Masands (from Persian *masnad*: a seat of authority). They were appointed by the gurus and their responsibilities included bringing new initiates into the community, sending tithes to the Sikh court, and serving as liaisons between their congregations and the central community under the guru's leadership.[23] This position and role gave the Masands considerable influence over the congregations under their care, as well as with the central Sikh administration.

We have evidence that by the middle of the seventeenth century the Sikh community was experiencing serious problems in the exercise of personal authority. Several competing seats of power, all claiming to follow Guru Nanak, were entrenched in different places. The followers of Prithi Chand controlled the Darbar Sahib, Amritsar; the followers of Dhirmal had their area of influence around Kartarpur; and the followers of Ramrai, the eldest son of Guru Harirai, were based in Dehra Dun. These opposing seats of authority caused deep dissension within the community. Their differences were not doctrinal but rather centered on rivalry among the descendants of the gurus over personal authority. In this politicized atmosphere, the role of the Masands was divisive and the system of authority they represented had become largely dysfunctional or autonomous, or both.

Emerging from this context of fierce rivalries, Guru Gobind Singh's declaration of the Sikhs as the Khalsa in the late 1690s profoundly affected the existing structure of personal authority within the community. First, the creation of the Khalsa formally dissolved the position of the Masands, who were given the option of either participating in the community at equal footing with others, or leaving it. The Sikhs/Khalsa were barred from any social dealings with those who attempted to maintain their earlier positions as Masands.[24] Second, the strong tradition maintaining that Guru Gobind Singh himself partook in a newly created ceremony of *Khande ki pahul* (nectar of the double-edged sword) before administering it to the Sikhs can be interpreted as a symbolic abdication of his own authority as the guru.[25] The very fact that he underwent the ceremony, placed him on a par with others in the community, a reversal of what had existed ever since the first and second gurus elevated their disciples to the guru's position of authority. Guru Gobind Singh, by stepping down, became part of the community, and once and for all dissolved the hierarchy that existed between the guru and his Sikhs. It may be argued that dissension within the community over the extent of the guru's authority, and the vulnerability of the office exposed after Guru Arjan and Guru Tegh Bahadur's executions at the hands of the Mughal administration may have influenced Guru Gobind Singh's thinking. Quite likely, he concluded that the office of the guru had served its purpose and needed to be replaced by a more enduring source of authority than that of a charismatic but vulnerable individual.

All along, the symbolic authority of the divine word as revealed in the hymns incorporated in the Sikh scriptural text coexisted with the personal authority of the guru and later on, the Masands. Guru Nanak's fundamental belief in the revealed nature of his compositions evolved along with the office of the guru. The increased significance of these hymns is already reflected in the position of Guru Amardas, who declared that the hymns of the gurus were God himself (*Vahu vahu baṇi nirankar hai tisu jevaḍu avaru na koi* [M3, AG, 515]) and the light of the world (*Gurbaṇi isu jag mahi chananu karami vasai mani ae* [M3, AG, 67]). Guru Ramdas further emphasized the liberating nature of the compositions of the guru (*Baṇi guru guru hai baṇi vichi baṇi amritu sare. Gurubaṇi kahai sevaku janu manai partakhi guru nistare* [M4, AG, 982]). Guru Arjan believed that the revealed Sikh literature has the purpose of removing suffering from the world (*Dhur ki baṇi ai. Tini sagali chint mitai* [M5, AG, 628]).

The idea of inscribing the word of God as an exercise in devotion, referred to by Guru Nanak, later appears as a key theme in the Miharban Janam-Sakhi.[26] It is against this background that we should understand the recognition granted to the scribes in early Sikh community, and especially the unique honor bestowed on Bhai Gurdas and Bhai Mani Singh, who carried out scribal work of exceptional importance during the crucial phases of scriptural development.[27]

This line of thinking contributed to a vigorous sense of the authority of scriptural manuscripts. As we have discussed in the preceding chapters, in the closing decades of the sixteenth century the Guru Harsahai and the Goindval Pothis formed the basis of the claim for the office of the guru by Prithi Chand at Amritsar and the Bhallas at Goindval. One of the major accomplishments of Guru Arjan's tenure was the compilation of the Kartarpur Pothi, an expanded version of the Sikh texts possessed by families competing with him. He also affirmed that the sacred text was the abode of God (*Pothi parmesar ka thanu* [M5, AG, 1226]).

Writing in 1605, the Sikh scribe Buṛa Sandhu, claimed that the text he prepared manifests the body (*deh*) of Guru Nanak; presenting oneself before it would be equivalent to having an audience with him (the Amritsar Pothi, folio 591). The significant role of the early manuscripts in the claims for central authority within the community continued throughout the seventeenth century. Dhirmal captured the Kartarpur Pothi, and among other things, based his claim as the successor of Guru Nanak on his possession of it. Ramrai, another dissident, who challenged his brother Guru Harkishan and established a separate seat of power at Dehra Dun, possessed a manuscript prepared in 1659.

Thus, from early on in Sikh history, the scriptural text complemented the authority of the gurus, who were at the center of the community. Their role was twofold: They served as the medium for the revealed message and then guided the community accordingly. By the end of the seventeenth century, this divine message to the Sikhs was felt to have reached fruition with the compilation of the Adi Granth, and the community felt ready to assume the burden of representing it, by following out a new understanding of itself as the Khalsa.[28] At the time of Guru Gobind Singh's death, then, we see the two strands of religious authority within the community coming together in a unique form. The symbolic role of the Adi Granth expands to encompass the authority of the personal guru, as manifested in the new title, Guru Granth Sahib, and the community as a whole (Guru Panth) takes up the authority to interpret the text.

The Role of the Adi Granth

The Adi Granth, as the repository of the divine revelation in the Sikh belief system, has long served as the principal source defining Sikh theology and creating the ethical code by which Sikhs live. Sikhs have attempted to read, hear, and practice the message of the Adi Granth, and the text has made a deep impact on all dimensions of Sikh life—devotional, ceremonial, ritual, intellectual, and artistic. The Sikh *gurdwara* is literally the house of the Adi Granth.

Writing in the opening decades of the eighteenth century, Chaupa Singh leaves little doubt that the Adi Granth enjoyed the status of a living embodiment of divine presence in the community.[29] The text was to be given the respect due to the personal guru in earlier Sikh history. Nothing was ever to be put in it as a marker, and it was always to be accompanied by symbols of royalty. The Adi Granth itself constituted the court of the guru. It was an honor to present oneself before it: one had to bow with one's forehead fully touching the ground in front of the text. While in audience one needed to be clean, to sit alert, and always to look toward the text. If one happened to scratch one's nose or body, the hands were to be washed quickly. At the close of every service, *kaṛah prashad* (flour deep-fried in clarified butter) was always to be distributed, as always at the conclusion of a royal audience.[30]

From Chaupa Singh, we also learn that the Adi Granth played an important role in Sikh ceremonies ranging from naming children to death rites. The latter centered around a ceremonial reading of the text, to be completed on the seventeenth day after the death, when a prayer for the peace of the soul was to be offered. Compositions such as Guru Nanak's *Japji* and Guru Amardas's *Anand* had attained a central role in services of worship, and the study, memorization, and inscription of the text were considered important markers of Sikh devotional activity.[31]

Sarup Singh Kaushish, writing in the 1790s, offers further details of the Adi Granth's role in Sikh ceremonial life.[32] If we bring together his several references to the role of the scriptural text in early Sikh congregational prayers, it becomes possible to reconstruct a sequence of events centering on the physical presence of the sacred text. To begin with, the Adi Granth is always covered with a canopy, placed high on a platform, and accorded constant attendance by a Sikh. The ceremony typically starts with a reading from the text (*paṭh*), sometimes followed by an exposition (*katha*) of the passage in question, and is completed by a formal supplication (*ardas*) pertaining to the occasion at hand. The text is then arbitrarily opened and the first hymn on the page, which is considered to be the divine command (*hukam*) in reply to the petition just posed, is recited. The ceremony ends with the distribution of the *kaṛah prashad*.

Kaushish also refers to the role of the text on special occasions. He describes the naming ceremony of a newborn infant. After a formal supplication to the Adi Granth, the text is opened, and the first letter at the top left corner of the page is adopted as the first letter in the name of the child. As indicated by Chaupa Singh, Sikh death rites center around a complete ceremonial reading of the text. Kaushish reports that an unbroken reading (*akhanḍ paṭh*) of the text also took place at Damdama, Bhatinda, when Guru Gobind Singh prepared to leave for Delhi to meet Emperor Aurangzeb, and adds that Guru Gobind Singh's formal declaration of the Adi Granth as his successor was followed by a complete reading of the text.

From elsewhere in Kaushish's writings, we learn that Guru Nanak's *Japji* and his *var* in *rag* Asa, along with Guru Amardas's *Anand*, enjoyed a special role in ceremonies, and we have references to the importance of the exposition of the sacred text in devotional life. For example, when Ramrai was sent to Delhi to present himself before Emperor Aurangzeb, the guru instructed Ramrai and his retinue to read the sacred text and reflect on its contents whenever they stopped to rest during their journey; a scriptural manuscript was prepared to accompany them. The accuracy of Kaushish's claims about the role of the sacred text in seventeenth-century Sikh ritual life may be open to question, but what he says about the subject leaves little doubt that both the authority of the Adi Granth and its elaborate use in Sikh devotional life were firmly established by the time he himself wrote, at the end of the eighteenth century.

With the establishment of Sikh political supremacy in the Punjab at the turn of the nineteenth century, and the need to centralize the decision-making authority in the hands of Maharaja Ranjit Singh, the idea of a self-regulating Guru Panth receded. The Adi Granth itself emerged as the sole symbolic center of authority, which opened the possibility that the maharaja could be understood as its chief executor. The text's role in Sikh ritual life also evolved. We have no contemporary reference as to how Sikh marriage was performed in the eighteenth century, but beginning with 1850s, the Adi Granth moved in to preside over this ceremony as well.[33] The Adi Granth has maintained all elements of its unique position since then; any infringement of its authority meets with great hostility within the community.[34]

In present-day Sikh congregational worship (*divan*), the text of the Adi Granth continues to be physically located at the head of the assembly. All visitors undergo ritual cleansing before presenting themselves to the sacred text. They then make monetary and spiritual offerings and sit down to listen to the *paṭh*, *kirtan*, or *katha*—"reading, singing, or interpretation," the three basic components of Sikh worship. This is followed by the *ardas*, which is enunciated by a representative of the congregation and is addressed to the text of the Adi Granth, and through it to God. The *ardas* traces Sikh history, registers gratitude for divine help at all stages, seeks help for the Sikh community's future aspirations, and appeals for blessings for all humanity. The worship closes with the taking of the Adi Granth's command (*hukam*), which is done by reading the first hymn on the left top corner of the page after the text is opened at random. The message of this hymn is interpreted as the divine answer to the *ardas* made by the congregation.

The Adi Granth plays the same role in family and personal devotion. In many Sikh homes, the text is kept in a separate room and is ceremonially opened in the morning and closed in the evening. Brief readings are performed at both times, the *ardas* offered, and the *hukam* taken. The theme of the hymn of the *hukam* in the morning is considered to be the guiding light of the day, and in many cases Sikhs recite it during their routine activities throughout the day. In case the text of the Adi Granth cannot be kept in the house for lack of proper space, a printed version of liturgical hymns is available. The tradition of keeping these small volumes (*guṭkas*) harkens back to the seventeenth century, and we hear about them as lesser versions of Sikh scripture.[35] Members of Sikh households perform their morning and evening prayers on the basis of these texts.

The role of the Adi Granth in other aspects of Sikh ritual and ceremonial life is equally central. At the beginning and end of all Sikh ceremonies, the *ardas* is addressed to the Adi Granth. The first petition is intended to seek divine help for the performance of the ceremony, whatever it may be, and the second offers thanks for its successful completion. Making an *ardas*, followed by taking the *hukam* from the Adi Granth, should occur at the beginning of every day, at the new month and the new year, in the event of a birth and at the naming ceremony, at an initiation of the double-edged sword, at marriage and death ceremonies, and at other significant events in peoples' lives.

On these occasions, as always, the Adi Granth is treated in such a way as to manifest its royal status within the community. It is always robed in silk or expensive brocade and is displayed on a canopied throne, in a well-lit setting. It is ceremonially opened and closed and carried from one place to another with a proper retinue, who protect it with the fly whisk. If one ever meets a Sikh man or woman in an airport carrying a suitcase on his or her head, rest assured that the contents of the suitcase include the text of the Adi Granth. In Punjabi culture baggage is typically carried on the head, but that position doubtless is one of honor where the Adi Granth is present.

The purpose of Sikh devotion is not merely to present oneself in front of the Adi Granth, but as Chaupa Singh puts it, to listen to and put into practice the divine message enshrined in it.[36] The understanding of its message and its translation into one's day-to-day activity is at the core of a Sikh's experience of the Adi Granth. In the words of Guru Nanak, meritorious action cannot be understood without the guru and reflection on the divine word (*Viṇu satgur guṇ na japani jicharu sabadi na kare bicharu*, M1, AG, 936). Liberation, according to Guru Amardas, does not come through eye contact with the guru, as might be typical in Hindu practice, but through reflection on the divine word communicated to Sikhs through the guru (*Satigur no sabhu ko vekhada jeta jagatu sansaru. Ḍiṭhai mukati na hovai jicharu sabadi na kare vicharu*, M3, AG, 594).

Notably, however, this veneration of the divine word does not result in a conviction that sound is efficacious per se. Any argument that the words of the Adi Granth have to be articulated only in a certain way or are beneficial on the basis of simple repetition has no support in the Adi Granth itself. Its emphasis—and that of the Sikh community—is on understanding the theological and ethical message of the text.[37]

To sum up, the significance of scripture in Sikh communal experience is revealed in at least three ways. First, manuscripts containing the sacred Sikh writings were prepared early in Sikh history, a process that expanded substantially with the arrival of the printing press in the Punjab in the second half of the nineteenth century. Second, the reading and recitation of scripture have apparently always served as the key elements of Sikh worship. Early on, Chaupa Singh asserts that a Sikh who keeps the Adi Granth at home but does not read it himself or has it read by someone else deserves to be punished.[38] And we know that public ceremonial readings of the complete text began early and have evolved over time into a number of distinct forms: *akhanḍ paṭh*, *saptah paṭh* (reading completed in a week), and *khula paṭh* (reading completed over an open-ended stretch of time).

Finally, we know that a tradition of formal reflection on the text began early in the history of the community. It took the form of oral discourses and commentaries that were first committed to writing early in the seventeenth century, and this tradition has continued ever since. These commentaries, including both the interpretation of the text and the history of its compilation in written and oral forms, have kept the text of the Adi Granth at the center of traditional Sikh learning. As discussed in chapter 2, the first complete written commentary on the Adi Granth was completed in 1883; since then several others have followed.

The influence of Sikh scripture on Sikh life has been all-pervasive, ranging all the way from art to weaponry. While the Sikh scribes spared no pains in creating illuminated and calligraphically elegant manuscripts of Sikh scripture, eighteenth-century Sikh blacksmiths inscribed its hymns on swords and shields.[39] The artwork visible on the opening folios of the Goindval Pothis expanded in time to include a full lineage of elaborately illuminated and calligraphed manuscripts. Some of these manuscripts include beautiful landscapes on their closing folios, and in rare instances the portraits of the gurus are painted on the opening folios. Nineteenth-century scribes explored a range of new styles in Gurmukhi calligraphy—all to apply to the Adi Granth. If ever there was a religion of the book, this is it.

Future Prospects

Two important historical developments in the twentieth century may have a lasting impact on the role of the Adi Granth in Sikh life. First, the twentieth century has witnessed a movement of some two million Sikhs to places other than the Punjab, their historic and sacred homeland. Second, for the first time in Sikh history, a small but extremely visible group of people of non-Punjabi ethnic background have joined the Sikh community.[40]

Sikh migration during the twentieth century has turned a regional group into something of a world community. Birth pangs have attended this process. Typically, the children of the Sikh immigrants, born and raised in the lands adopted by their parents, do not have sufficient access to the language and the script of the Adi Granth. Although the teaching of Punjabi written in Gurmukhi script has been placed very high on the agendas of *gurdwaras* overseas, the community leadership is acutely aware that the success achieved has been far from satisfactory.

In addition, under the leadership of Harbhajan Singh Yogi, a Punjabi Sikh who moved to North America in the late 1960s, a small group of Euro-Americans have joined the Sikh fold. Until very recently, the Sikhs have remained essentially a Punjabi ethnic community, even though many left the Punjab as early as seventeenth century. Yogi's persistent efforts to maintain close ties with the Sikh establishment in Amritsar, and his dispatching of youngsters from his community to the Punjab for schooling, have resulted in a deep awareness in Punjabi forums such as the SGPC of their dedication as well as their problems. Typically, these newly converted Sikhs work hard to learn Gurmukhi and Punjabi and achieve a degree of proficiency in the reading of the Adi Granth, but for understandable reasons they cannot do without the use of the translated text as a supporting device.

These two groups—children born into Punjabi Sikh families abroad and the followers of Harbhajan Singh Yogi—have introduced a strikingly new element into Sikh history, which relates directly to the role of scripture within the Sikh community. Neither can read the Gurmukhi script easily nor understand the language it conveys. And since both groups, especially the first, contribute to the future generation, their situation appears critical in the eyes of current Sikh leaders. Many ask, if the children do not inherit the tradition, then how it will survive in foreign lands?

The association of sacred Sikh literature and the Gurmukhi script goes back to the very origin of Sikh scripture. If the adoption of Gurmukhi was rooted in the Sikh gurus' effort to establish a distinct identity of the community of their followers, it served the purpose well. In this important role, Gurmukhi understandably attained a sacred status in early Sikh history. Writing in the early decades of the eighteenth century, Chaupa Singh argued that the folios on which Gurmukhi is written should be treated with respect (*adab*) and should not be trampled upon or used to wrap things.[41] Later sources declared that the learning of Punjabi in Gurmukhi is part of the religious obligation of the Sikhs, and this close relationship between faith and language has been growing ever since.[42]

The present situation questions all this affirming an inevitable need for a non-Gurmukhi text for performative and ceremonial purposes—and in some places sooner rather than later.[43] Then the question of whether a translated text of the Adi Granth can be placed at the center of congregational worship will have to be addressed. To date, there exists among Sikhs a great affection for the use of Gurmukhi and Punjabi and unwillingness to abandon them. The place of *kirtan* in the tradition further complicates the situation, and it is important to maintain this dimension of Sikh scripture. As we have seen, there are those who would go so far as to assert that the text of the Adi Granth is the body of the guru. For them, however, the use of a translated text for devotional purposes is simply beyond imagining. Yet the issue is likely to persist as Sikhs continue to disperse from the Punjab. In this process, what always was the first and foremost sign of communal integration can scarcely avoid becoming a major flash point for communal conflict.

As we consider this dilemma, we must remember that the situation Sikhs face today is hardly unique in the history of scripture. Jews and Muslims perhaps come closest to the Sikhs in their notions of sacred language and script, and both being world communities, they have been through comparable historical experiences. Muslims have leaned toward the strict maintenance of Arabic, keeping the text of the Qur'an in the original for all devotional purposes, and only with considerable reluctance permitting its translation for scholarly work. Jews, by contrast, have reaffirmed the sacredness of Hebrew while simultaneously, in some quarters, permitting the use of translation of the Torah in congregational worship and individual study.[44] Tensions exist as both communities face these issues.

As the twenty-first century dawns, the historic role and authority of the Adi Granth and the linguistic proficiency of Sikh congregations in the overseas context may not be in accord. The fundamental need of Sikhs to understand and bring into their daily lives the word of God as enshrined in the Adi Granth will, in all likelihood, define the future role of the text in the Sikh devotional life. There may eventually be a compelling need to begin using translated texts for ceremonial purposes, while at the same time keeping the sanctity of Gurmukhi and the original text completely intact.

Hints of this already exist. As mentioned earlier, an edition of the text of the Adi Granth with standard pagination and a three-column format has recently been published. The first column includes the original Gurmukhi text, the second a Roman transliteration, and the third an English translation. I myself have already had the opportunity to participate in a ceremony using that text as the center of worship.[45] The same text has already been adopted in the traditional practice of *akhanḍ paṭh* in the Euro-American Sikh community. The reading is performed both in the original Gurmukhi Punjabi as well as in English translation, depending upon who reads.[46] As the Adi Granth enters the twenty-first century, scholars in the field will need to reflect on diglossia such as this, and Sikh religious authorities in Amritsar will need to display a new openness to the changing circumstances of Sikhs who live far from the Punjab.

It is fascinating to trace how Sikh scripture, the eternal word of God revealed to the Sikhs, has adapted to changing historical circumstances. Crucial developments are in the offing. In the coming decades Sikhs living in places far from the Punjab could continue the tradition by insisting that the text of the Adi Granth be presented in Gurmukhi, or could suggest incorporating supplementary ways to help those who do not read the script or understand the language. They could go the way of some branches of Reform Judaism and place the translations of the Adi Granth in congregational worship, or they could blend Punjabi with other languages spoken locally. If this happens, will the original language of the Adi Granth seem even more "scriptural" than it does in the Punjab—even more exalted and elevated above ordinary speech? What would this mean for recitation and interpretation? Whatever course Sikhs take, they will be giving further shape to the ongoing history of their community's relationship with its sacred text. Because the process of creating Sikh scripture continues in all its richness and complexity, my story must necessarily remain incomplete.

Notes

Chapter 1

1. For a general introduction to the history and belief system of the Sikhs, see J. S. Grewal, *The Sikhs of the Punjab* (New York: Cambridge University Press, 1990), and W. H. McLeod, *Sikhism* (New York: Penguin, 1997).

2. One needs to point out that although the title Adi Granth literally means the "original book," there is no connotation in Sikh thought of its being the "primal book." The title differentiates this text from the Dasam Granth ("the book of the tenth guru," Guru Gobind Singh). Throughout the present study I use the terms "Adi Granth," "Guru Granth Sahib," and "Sikh scripture" synonymously, while preferring the term "scriptural text," for noncanonical versions that are either incomplete in their contents or contain apocryphal compositions.

3. For Sikh migration overseas, see N. Gerald Barrier and Verne A. Dusenbery, eds., *The Sikh Diaspora: Migration and Experience beyond Punjab* (Columbia, Mo.: South Asia Books, 1989), and Darshan Singh Tatla, *The Sikh Diaspora: The Search for Statehood* (London: University College London Press, 1999).

4. For a discussion of these issues, see Miriam Levering, ed., *Rethinking Scripture: Essays from a Comparative Perspective* (Albany: State University of New York Press, 1989), pp. 8–9.

5. Scholars count the hymns recorded in the Adi Granth in two ways. Sahib Singh considers a complete hymn as a unit irrespective of the number of stanzas included in it; see his *Sri Guru Granth Sahib Darpaṇ* (Jalandhar: Raj Publishers, 1972), vol. 1, pp. 17–19. According to his figures, the Adi Granth contain 2,497 hymns attributed to the gurus, 150 to the Sikhs, 710 to the Bhagats, and one anonymous composition. Surinder Singh Kohli counts a stanza as an independent unit and comes up with the total figure at 6,003 hymns in the Adi Granth. According to him, 4,956 of these are attributed to the gurus, 137 to the Sikhs, 798 to the Bhagats, and 12 are anonymous; see his *Critical Study of Adi Granth* (Delhi: Motilal Banarsidass, 1976), pp. 2–9.

The hymns of the gurus are recorded under the title of Mahala (Arabic *mahal*, "palace"), which refers to the guru as the palace where God resides, and hence Mahala 1, Mahala 2, and so on. Some scholars associate this with Sanskrit *mahila* (woman) and argue that the title manifests the gurus' understanding of their relationship with God in terms of wife and husband. This is, incorrect, however. The original form used in the Goindval Pothis is *mahalu*, which indicates its masculine gender. For a discussion of this issue, see Sahib Singh, *Sri Guru Granth Sahib Darpaṇ*, vol. 1, pp. 24–27, and Bhai Vir Singh, *Santhaya Sri Guru Granth Sahib* (Amritsar: Khalsa Samachar, 1972 [1958]), vol. 1, p. 180.

6. A large number of these bards were upper-caste Hindus, known in the region as the Bhaṭs. They came to the Sikh court in the sixteenth century and composed hymns in praise of the gurus and their court. Opinions differ about the precise number of Bhaṭs whose hymns are present in the Adi Granth; Sahib Singh gives their number as eleven (see his *Sri Guru Granth Sahib Darpaṇ*, vol. 1, p. 19), and Surinder Singh Kohli counts them as seventeen (see his *Critical Study of Adi Granth*, pp. 8–9). For basic information about the Bhaṭs, see Giani Gurdit Singh, *Bhaṭ ate unahan di Rachna* (Ludhiana: Punjabi Sahitt Academy, 1961), and Raijasbir Singh, ed., *Guru Amardas: Srot Pustak* (Amritsar: Guru Nanak Dev University, 1986), pp. 9–25.

The other bards whose compositions are available in the Adi Granth include Mardana (three couplets framed in Guru Ramdas's *var* in *rag* Bihagṛa, AG, 553), Satta and Balvand (one *var* recorded under their joint authorship in the section on *rag* Ramkali, AG, 966), and Sunder (one hymn in *rag* Ramkali, AG, 923). The janam-sakhi literature presents Mardana as Guru Nanak's companion during his extensive travels; see Kirpal Singh, ed., *Janam-Sakhi Prampra* (Patiala: Punjabi University, 1969), pp. 15, 24. Satta and Balvand sang at the Sikh court in Guru Angad's time, see Bhai Kahn Singh Nabha, *Gurushabad Ratanakar Mahan Kosh* (hereafter, *Mahan Kosh*) (Patiala: Punjab Language Department, 1981 [1930]), p. 150, and W. H. McLeod, *Historical Dictionary of Sikhism* (Lanham, Md.: Scarecrow Press, 1995), p. 48.

Sikh tradition views Sundar as a grandson of Guru Amardas, but there are problems with this identification; see Raijasbir Singh, ed., *Guru Amardas: Srot Pustak*, pp. 34–37. In MS 1245 (folio 819), presently at the Guru Nanak Dev University library, the entry at the head of the hymn attributed to Sundar reads, *Sadu Sundar Nai di* (The call by Sundar, the barber). The implication that Sundar was a barber blends well with the theme of the hymn, which describes the rituals performed at the death of Guru Amardas. The Punjabi barbers handled these rituals as part of their social responsibilities. This identification places Sundar firmly alongside Mardana, Satta, and Balvand, who also came from the lower rungs of the social hierarchy but were elevated to a special status when their hymns were incorporated into the Sikh scriptural text.

The fifteen Bhagats whose hymns appear in the Adi Granth are Beṇi, Bhikhaṇ, Dhanna, Farid, Jaidev, Kabir, Namdev, Pipa, Parmanand, Ramanand, Ravidas, Sadhna, Saiṇ, Surdas, and Trilochaṇ.

7. In the present study, I continue to use the English term *God* to designate the Sikh conception of the Divine. It would have been preferable to use an indigenous Sikh alternative, but the complexity of the context does not allow a satisfactory solution. In the present-day Sikh tradition, the most frequently used name for the Divine is *Vahiguru*. The term seems to have been introduced into the Sikh religious vocabulary in the mid seventeenth century and it gathered increasing popularity in the following decades and centuries. Yet its conspicuous absence in the Adi Granth makes its use somewhat unsatisfactory in a study devoted to that subject.

In the twentieth century, an effort has been made to propose *Akal Purakh* as the formal Sikh name for the Divine; see *Sikh Rahit Maryada: The Code of Sikh Conduct and Conventions* (Amritsar: Dharam Prachar Committee [Shiromani Gurdwara Prabandhak Committee, 1997]), p. 1. The name does appear in the Adi Granth but there is hardly any basis to justify its newly proposed status. In Guru Nanak's compositions, the epithets used for God include *Adi Purakh* (12 times), *Karta Purakh* (3 times), and *Akal Purakh* (once), but more frequent ones relate to the divine sovereignty and come from Arabic and Persian: *Sahib* (137 times), *Khasam* (78 times), *Patishah* (23 times). Yet none of the latter names are appropriate in that they continue to be used in both Sikh and Islamic secular contexts.

Guru Nanak's use of these Arabic and Persian words, however, is not accidental but points to a close affinity between the Sikh conception of the Divine and that of the Middle Eastern religious traditions, see Guru Nanak's hymn 27, AG, p. 6. This long composition, which enjoys the unique distinction of appearing three times in the Adi Granth, presents the magnificence of God and the majesty of his court. For its English translation, see W. H. McLeod,

The Textual Sources for the Study of Sikhism (Chicago: University of Chicago Press, 1990), pp. 96–99.

8. See the Adi Granth, pp. 360, 417, 722–723, and 1035–1037. See also W. H. McLeod, *Guru Nanak and the Sikh Religion* (Oxford: Clarendon Press, 1968), pp. 148–226, and J. S. Grewal, *Guru Nanak in History* (Chandigarh: Panjab University, 1979), pp. 234-286.

9. AG, 7–8, and Ram Singh, *Japji de Panj Khanḍ* (Patiala: Punjabi University, 1989).

10. The Adi Granth is not a formal treatise on ethics, but with some effort a reasonably clear picture of the ethical code can be assembled from the text; see Avtar Singh, *Ethics of the Sikhs* (Patiala: Punjabi University, 1983), and Nripinder Singh, *The Sikh Moral Tradition* (Columbia, MO: South Asia Publications, 1990). In my view, the teachings of the gurus as manifested in their hymns should be considered alongside their lives to reconstruct a comprehensive picture of Sikh ethical beliefs. For references to the daily routine of Guru Nanak at Kartarpur, see Kirpal Singh, ed., *Janam-Sakhi Prampra*, p. 161.

11. AG, 10, 103, 499, 532, 676, 737, 749, 1152, and 1340.

12. AG, 199, 371, 618–624, and 781–782. There is an interesting hymn by Guru Arjan that refers to the destruction of enemies of the Sikh people, AG, 825.

13. AG, 966–968, and 1389–1409.

14. For a description of the structure of the Adi Granth, see W. H. McLeod, *The Evolution of the Sikh Community* (Oxford: Clarendon Press, 1996), pp. 70–73, and W. Owen Cole and Piara Singh Sambhi, *The Sikhs: Their Religious Beliefs and Practices*, rev. ed. (Brighton: Sussex Academic Press, 1995), pp. 212–217.

15. These are broad divisions. For instance, the hymns containing two, three, or five stanzas are recorded in the sections on the *chaupadas*. For metrical structure of these different types of hymns in the Adi Granth, see Surinder Singh Kohli, *A Critical Study of Adi Granth*, pp. 66–91.

16. For a discussion of the *Ragmala* and its relationship with the *rags* in the Adi Granth, see Surinder Singh Kohli, *A Critical Study of Adi Granth*, pp. 8–9, Balbir Singh, *Ragmala da Saval te Jodh Kavi ate Alam* (1945; rpt. Amritsar: Khalsa Samachar, 1969), and *Ragmala bare Vichar* (Amritsar: Sura Masak Patar, 1986).

17. For a discussion of the language of the Adi Granth, see Piara Singh Padam, *Sri Guru Granth Prakash* (Patiala: Kalam Mandir, 1990), pp. 307–322.

18. Piara Singh Padam, *Gurmukhi Lippi da Itihas* (Patiala: Kalam Mandir, 1988), pp. 55–56.

19. G. B. Singh, *Gurmukhi Lippi da Janam te Vikas* (Chandigarh: Panjab University, 1981). For the grammar developed by the Sikhs, see Sahib Singh, *Gurbaṇi Viakaraṇ* (Amritsar: Rabbi Pustakavali, 1939), and Christopher Shackle, *An Introduction to the Sacred Language of the Sikhs* (London: School of Oriental and African Studies, 1983).

20. Guru Nanak's hymn entitled the *Paṭi*, AG, 432–434, contains thirty-five stanzas, each of which begins with a separate character of the Gurmukhi orthography. The text strictly follows the established literary form of *Siharfi* and *Bavan-akhari*, in which poetic stanzas are constructed around the characters in Arabic and Devanagari scripts, respectively. Guru Amardas also composed a *Paṭi*; see AG, 434–435.

21. The river Ravi presently serves as the boundary between India and Pakistan; situated on the right bank of the river, Kartarpur is now in Pakistan. Guru Nanak's selection of this location is quite significant, since it lay on the pilgrimage routes from the Gangetic and Indus plains to the ancient Hindu temples of Amarnath in Kashmir and Jawalamukhi in the Shivalik hills. It was also close to Achal Batala, a center for the Nath Yogis and the site of an ancient temple of the god Shiva, and to Lahore and Sialkot, two centers of Islamic learning. The location of Kartarpur suggests that Guru Nanak wanted his community to keep in constant touch with the world of religious pilgrims—a world in which he had taken part in the previous decades. Until very recently, Nath Yogis from all over India traveling to Kashmir crossed this area before the

start of the summer and returned in early fall to attend their annual gathering at Achal Batala. The area contains rich agricultural land and Guru Nanak is said to have grown rice at Kartarpur; see "Valayat vali Janam-sakhi," in Kirpal Singh, ed., *Janam-Sakhi Prampra*, p. 54.

22. W. H. McLeod, *The Evolution of the Sikh Community*, p. 8, and *The Sikhs: History, Religion and Society* (New York: Columbia University Press, 1989), pp. 41–42.

23. Teja Singh and Ganda Singh, *A Short History of the Sikhs* (Patiala: Punjabi University, 1989 [1950]); Harbans Singh, *The Heritage of the Sikhs* (New Delhi: Manohar, 1983); and J. S. Grewal, *The Sikhs of the Punjab*.

24. J. S. Grewal, *The Sikhs of the Punjab*, p. 41.

25. Guru Nanak writes:

Namu danu ishnanu driṛu hari bhagati sujage. (M1, AG, 419)
Namu danu ishnanu na manmukhi titu tani . . . (M1, AG, 596)
Gurmukhi namu danu ishnanu. (M1, AG, 942)

26. I consider the writings of Bhai Gurdas and the traditions at the base of the janam-sakhi literature as important sources for the belief system of the early Sikh community; see Bhai Gurdas, *Varan*, ed. Gursharan Kaur Jaggi (Patiala: Punjabi University, 1987) and *Kabbitt Savaiye*, ed. Onkar Singh (Patiala: Punjabi University, 1993); also Kirpal Singh, *Janam-Sakhi Prampra*.

27. *Pahir sansari kapaṛe manji beṭh kia avatara* (Bhai Gurdas, *Varan*, 1: 38, p. 73). It seems that Guru Nanak followed the Sufi model. The Sufis normally traveled in the earlier part of their lives and eventually settled down to establish a *khanqah*, where they served the people nearby; see Simon Digby, "Sufis and Travelers in the Early Delhi Sultanate: The Evidence of the Fawa'id al-Fw'ad," in Attar Singh, ed., *Socio-Cultural Impact of Islam on India* (Chandigarh: Panjab University, 1976), pp. 171–177.

28. Shamsher Singh Ashok, ed., *Puratan Janam-Sakhi Sri Guru Nanak Dev Ji ki* (Amritsar: Dharam Prachar Committee [Shiromani Gurdwara Prabandhak Committee], 1969), pp. 129–131.

29. In addition, Guru Nanak urges human beings to avoid lust (*kam*), anger (*krodh*), greed (*lobh*), attachment (*moh*), and arrogance (*hankar*). These are called the "five thieves" (*panj chor*), and the need to control them is a repeated theme in Guru Nanak's hymns; see the Adi Granth, 155, 503, 1018, 1021, 1030, 1039, and 1329.

30. Guru Nanak established the institution of a single successor, a practice distinct from that of the multiple succession popularly followed by the Nath Yogis and the Sufis of the time.

31. *Sodaru Arti gavie amrit vele Japu uchara* (Bhai Gurdas, *Varan*, 1: 38, p. 73); *Amrit vele uṭhi ke . . . Ik mani hoi gur Jap japande. . . . Sanjhe Sodaur gavaṇa . . . Rati Kirati-Sohila kari arati parasadu vaḍande (Varan*, 6: 3, p. 101).

32. We know that it was a farming community. In all likelihood, the members of the community gathered for the morning prayer before leaving for work in the fields. They returned home in the late afternoon to gather for the sunset prayer. The last prayer before sleep seems to be a family affair. The three Sikh prayers are in contradistinction to the five prayers of Muslims, and the eight *artis* of the Vaishnavas. The Sikh prayers structured around the praise of God have closer affinity to their Islamic and Middle Eastern counterparts than to the Hindu prayers centered on mantric recitation and meditation.

33. In their *var* in *rag* Ramkali (AG, 966–967), Satta and Balvand refer to the flourishing *laṇgar* at Khadur during the leadership of Guru Angad. With the general absence of innovations during this relatively quiet period, it is almost certain that Guru Angad inherited this practice from the Kartarpur days and established at Khadur.

The *laṇgar* was also an important part of the Sufi *khanqahs*. The Nath Yogis had their counterpart of *laṇgar* in what they called the *bhandaras*. The difference, however, is that Sikh *laṇgar* was and continues to be maintained through voluntary contributions and never depended on the grants of local rulers or the charity of local people as in the case of the *khanqahs* and the *bhandaras*.

34. "Miharban vali Janam-Sakhi," in Kirpal Singh, *Janam-Sakhi Prampra*. As a standard technique the episodes in this Janam-Sakhi conclude with the Sikh greetings.

35. "Valayat vali Janam-Sakhi," in Kirpal Singh, *Janam-Sakhi Prampra*, p. 57.

36. Pritam Singh, ed., *Nirmal Sampradae* (Amritsar: Guru Nanak Dev University, 1981), pp. 159–178 and 335–361. For a general survey of this literature, see Taran Singh, *Gurbaṇi dian Viakhia Praṇalian* (Patiala: Punjabi University 1980), pp. 119–190.

37. Bhai Kahn Singh Nabha, *Ham Hindu Nahin* (Amritsar: Singh Brothers, 1995 [1898]), pp. 42–50. For an introduction to his life and activities, see Pritam Singh, *Bhai Kahn Singh Nabha* (Amritsar: Guru Nanak Dev University, 1989).

38. The references often quoted in support of this view are:

Veda mahi namu utamu so suṇahe nahi phirahe jiu betalia (M3, AG, 919)
Chare Ved Brahame kau die paṛi paṛi kare vichari. (M3, AG, 423)
Chare Bed Brahame no furmaia. (M3, AG, 1066)

The opening citation claims that the Vedas contain the *nam*, but that does not automatically deem them authoritative texts for the Sikhs unless their relevance is specified. There is no mention to that effect in the Adi Granth. In the same way, the second and third verses mentioned above, claiming that the Vedas were given to Brahma by God, may thus speak of their divine origin but do not support their authority, as far as the Sikhs are concerned. The last verse actually goes on to claim that Brahma, having received the Vedas, made a complete mess of this gift: the foolish Brahma did not really understand the command of God and went through heaven and hell (*Ta ka hukamu na bujhai bapuṛa naraki suragi avatari* [M3, AG, 423]). More important for us, these verses belong not to Guru Nanak but to Guru Amardas. On the basis of Guru Amardas's hymns, one can easily argue that for him more than for any other guru, the Vedas were not a worthwhile medium of liberation as compared to the wisdom of the gurus, and the issue of the Vedic authority for him is inconsequential, as clear in the verses quoted by Bhai Kahn Singh Nabha:

Brahama mulu Ved abhiasa.
Tis te upje dev moh piasa. (M3, AG, 230)
Trai guṇ baṇi Bed bicharu.
Bikhia mailu bikhia vapar. (M3, AG, 1262)
Bed baṇi jagu varatada trai guṇ kare bicharu. (M3, AG, 1276)
Paṛi paṛi pandit moni thake Bedan ka abhiasu. (M3, AG, 1277)

The key issue in these verses is not the rejection of the Vedas as authoritative texts, but their essential limitation. The Vedas are thought to deal only with the three *guṇas* and cannot offer guidance beyond this world—something that the gurus are equipped to do, in Guru Amardas's understanding.

39. While Nirmala commentators continue to perpetuate their line of thought, others have expanded on the views of Bhai Kahn Singh Nabha and have argued that Guru Nanak in fact rejected both the Vedas and the Kateb as belief systems that are "fundamentally wrong." This perception is based on Guru Nanak's verse: Neither the Vedas nor the Kateb know the mystery (*Bed Katebi bhedu na jata*, M1, AG, 1021). The actual focus of this verse in its original context, however, is not on the rejection of the Vedas and the Semitic scriptural texts, but on the nature of the divine mystery, which by definition transcends the comprehension of anyone in creation. There are other instances of this type: *Astdasi chahu bhedu na paia* (M1, AG, 355), *Kete kahahe vakhaṇ kahi kahi javaṇa. Ved kahahe vakhiaṇ antu na pavaṇa* (M1, AG, 148). These verses point to the essential mystery of God. Guru Arjan later put this view even more succinctly: God is immanent in the world and the scriptural texts but is simultaneously far beyond them all (*Bed Kateb sansar habha hun bahara, Nanak ka patisahu disai jahra*, M5, AG, 397).

40. Piar Singh, ed., *Bhai Jodh Singh Gadd Saurabh* (Patiala: Punjabi University, 1986), p. 345.

See also W. Owen Cole, *Sikhism and Its Indian Context, 1469–1708* (New Delhi: D.K. Agencies, 1984), pp. 160–162. See note 54.

41. K. A. Nizami, *Some Aspects of Religion and Politics in India during the Thirteenth Century* (Delhi: Idarah-i-Adabiyat Delhi, 1974), pp. 308–309.

42. Guru Nanak was aware that the *jizyah* was imposed on Hindus (*Deval devatia karu laga aisi kirati chali*, M1, AG, 1191); they were labeled as the *mushabah ahl-i-kitab* and were thus obliged to pay this tax. For details of this issue, see Satish Chandar, "Jizayah and the State in India during the 17th Century," *Journal of the Economic and Social History of the Orient* 12: 3 (1969), pp. 322–340.

43. K. A. Nizami, "Some Aspects of Khanqah Life in Medieval India," *Studia Islamica* 8 (1957), p. 64.

44. J. S. Grewal, *The Sikhs of the Punjab*, pp. 47–48.

45. In the words of the Bhaṭs, Goindval was a heavenly city established on the banks of the river Beas (*Gobindvalu gobindpuri sam jalan tiri Bipas banayo*, AG, 1400).

46. For a detailed discussion of this issue, see Fauja Singh, *Guru Amardas: Life and Teachings* (New Delhi: Sterling, 1979), pp. 116–129 and 143–164.

47. Surjit, Hans, *A Reconstruction of Sikh History from Sikh Literature* (Jalandhar: ABS Publications, 1988), pp. 61–64.

48. Bhai Gurdas, *Varan*, 15: 1, p. 161.

49. Fauja Singh and Gurbachan Singh Talib, *Guru Tegh Bahadur: Martyr and Teacher* (Patiala: Punjabi University, 1975), pp. 41–89.

50. J. S. Grewal and S. S. Bal, *Guru Gobind Singh* (Chandigarh: Panjab University, 1987), pp. 103–126.

51. For detailed discussion, see chapter 5.

52. For a brief history of the Shiromani Gurdwara Prabandhak Committee, see Surjit Singh Gandhi, *Perspectives on Sikh Gurdwara Legislation* (New Delhi: Atlantic, 1993).

53. A committee including Jathedar Joginder Singh Vedanti, Bhai Joginder Singh Talwaṛa, Giani Harbans Singh Patiala, Bhai Bikram Singh Patiala, Principal Parkash Singh, and Bhai Avtar Singh Badhanikalan was formed by a resolution of the SGPC passed on March 26, 1996, to look into the variations between four different editions of the Adi Granth published by the SGPC itself. I am grateful to Jathedar Joginder Singh Vedanti for giving me a copy of the SGPC resolution, and sharing with me the progress of this committee from time to time.

54. For the first complete commentary on the Adi Granth, see Giani Badan Singh, ed., *Adi Sri Guru Granth Sahib Ji Saṭik (Faridkot vala Ṭika)*, 4 vols. (Patiala: Punjab Language Department, 1970). The work was completed in 1883 but published later in the 1900s. The commentaries of Giani Narain Singh Mujangwale in 1932 and Giani Bishan Singh Lakhuwal in 1936 followed. Several commentaries on the complete text of the Adi Granth have appeared since then; for details, see Taran Singh, *Gurbaṇi dian Viakhia Praṇalian*, p. 295. An incomplete translation of the Adi Granth into English appeared in 1877; see Ernest Trumpp, *The Adi Granth or the Holy Scripture of the Sikhs* (Delhi: Munshiram Manoharlal, 1978). The other translations include Gopal Singh, *Sri Guru Granth Sahib*, 4 vols. (Delhi: Gurdas Kapur, 1960–1962); Manmohan Singh, *Sri Guru Granth Sahib*, 8 vols. (Amritsar: Shiromani Gurdwara Prabandhak Committee, 1962); Gurbachan Singh Talib, *Sri Guru Granth Sahib*, 4 vols. (Patiala: Punjabi University, 1985); and Pritam Singh Chahil, *Sri Guru Granth Sahib* (New Delhi: Crescent Printing, n. d. [1995?]). For an interesting translation of compositions used in Sikh prayers, see Nikki-Guninder Kaur Singh, *The Name of My Beloved* (San Francisco: HarperSanFrancisco, 1995). Jarnail Singh of Toronto has published a French translation: *Sri Gourou Granth Sahib*, 4 vols. (Providenciales, West Indies: Intellectual Services International, 1998). Translating sacred writings is never easy and when one is confronted with an original of immense poetic complexity,

the task becomes infinitely difficult. For those interested in the serious study of the Adi Granth, these translations cannot substitute for the original text.

55. The Sikh community, like other scripture-oriented communities, has had its share of acrimonious debates in which belief in the revealed nature of scripture clashed with scholarly attempts to understand its history. The study presented here was part and parcel of these debates in the mid 1990s and progressed in an environment of considerable tension. It may be useful for the reader to keep this specific context of the book in mind while plodding through its contents. For the details of this confrontation, see Bachittar Singh Giani, ed., *Planned Attack on Aad Sri Guru Granth Sahib* (Chandigarh: International Centre of Sikh Studies, 1994); Piar Singh, *Gatha Sri Adi Granth and the Controversy* (Grandledge, Mich.: Anant Education and Rural Development Foundation, 1996); Mohinderjit Singh, *Arthan di Rajniti* (Ludhiana: Simran Publications, n. d. [1997?]); and J. S. Grewal, *Contesting Interpretations of the Sikh Tradition* (New Delhi: Manohar, 1998), pp. 238-267.

Chapter 2

1. Guru Amardas believed that liberation can be attained only by understanding the divine revelation as enshrined in the Sikh text (*Ḍiṭhai mukati na hovai jicharu shabadi na kare vicharu*, M3, AG, 594).

2. Taran Singh, *Gurbaṇi dian Viakhia Praṇalian*, p. 47.

3. A hymn by Guru Nanak opens with the question as to how to meditate on the divine name, and Guru Amardas appended a hymn answering the question (AG, 661). For more instances, see Taran Singh, *Gurbaṇi dian Viakhia Praṇalian*, pp. 28–34.

4. This literature began with the writings of Bhai Gurdas and Miharban; see Bhai Gurdas, *Varan*, and Miharban, *Janam-Sakhi Sri Guru Nanak Dev Ji*, ed. Kirpal Singh (Amritsar: Sikh History Research Department, Khalsa College, 1962).

5. Taran Singh records as many as seven different schools; see his *Gurbaṇi dian Viakhia Praṇalian*, pp. 37–393.

6. AG, 1389–1409.

7. See Kirpal Singh, ed., *Janam-Sakhi Prampra*. For a critical discussion of the janam-sakhi literature, see W. H. McLeod, *Early Sikh Tradition: A Study of the Janam-sakhis* (Oxford: Clarendon Press, 1980), pp. 250–256, and Surjit Hans, *A Reconstruction of Sikh History from Sikh Literature* , pp. 185–220. For other examples of this genre, see *Sri Satiguru ji de Muhai dian Sakhian*, in Piara Singh Padam, ed., *Prachin Punjabi Gadd* (Patiala: Kalam Mandir, 1978), pp. 66–85, created in the middle decades of the seventeenth century; Hariji, "Goshati Guru Amardas Ji," in Raijasbir Singh, *Guru Amardas: Srot Pustak*, pp. 43–207, written in the third quarter of the century; The *Bachittar Natak*, a poetic rendering of the life story of Guru Gobind Singh written in the 1690s and recorded in the Dasam Granth; and Sevadas, *Parchi Patishahi Dasvin ki*, ed. Piara Singh Padam (Patiala: Kalam Mandir, 1988), written in the opening decades of the eighteenth century.

8. Notes recorded in manuscripts numbered 4, 20, and 27 referred to in chapter 5, table 4, mention details of the text's contents and the degree of authenticity of its various copies, and also inform us that the text in hand has been corrected with the Kartarpur Pothi. Chaupa Singh, *Rahit-nama*, ed. W. H. McLeod (Otago: University of Otago Press, 1987), pp. 82, and 92.

9. Sainapati, *Sri Gur Sobha*, ed. Ganda Singh (1967; rpt. Patiala: Punjabi University, 1988), p. 170, and Koer Singh Kalal, *Gurbilas Patishahi 10*, ed. Shamsher Singh Ashok (Patiala: Punjabi University, 1986 [1969]), p. 284.

10. Kesar Singh Chhibbar, *Bansavlinama Dasan Patishahian ka*, ed. Rattan Singh Jaggi (Chandigarh: Panjab University, 1972), pp. 50–51, 126, 163–164, and 202.

11. Sarupdas Bhalla, *Mahima Prakash: Bhag Duja*, ed. Gobind Singh Lamba and Khazan Singh (Patiala: Punjab Language Department, 1971), pp. 358–374, and *Sikhan di Bhagatmala*, ed. Tarlochan Singh Bedi (Patiala: Punjabi University, 1994), pp. 122–123 and 128–129. Piar Singh argues that this text was written in the mid 1780s; see his *Gatha Sri Adi Granth* (Amritsar: Guru Nanak Dev University, 1992), pp. 13–14.

12. For a history of this period, see J. S. Grewal, *The Sikhs of the Punjab* , pp. 62–81. The lineage of these authors is also noteworthy. Bhalla was a direct descendant of Guru Amardas, the third Sikh guru. Since the middle of the sixteenth century, Bhalla's family lived in Goindval, and his ancestors must have been immersed in the traditions regarding the early history of the community.

Chhibbar belonged to the family of Chaupa Singh. Their ancestors joined the Sikh community in the mid seventeenth century and became influential members of the Sikh court in subsequent years. After the Sikh evacuation of Anandpur in 1704, the family lived in Delhi and Amritsar, eventually returning to their original home in Jammu in the middle of the eighteenth century. Thus, Chhibbars had first-hand knowledge of events in Anandpur, and their stay in Amritsar must have exposed them to the traditions regarding the early Sikh history in central Punjab.

If one accepts that Giani Surat Singh wrote *Sikhan di Bhagatmala*, then the author's family entered the Sikh fold at Anandpur at the turn of the eighteenth century, shifting later to Amritsar in the middle decades. Unlike the other two, this family joined the Sikh community only toward the end of the guru period and had less extended first-hand contact with the early phases of Sikh history. For more information on Giani Surat Singh, see Jasbir Singh Sabar, *Gian Ratanavali* (Amritsar: Guru Nanak Dev University, 1993), pp. 45–57.

13. Kesar Singh Chhibbar, *Bansavlinama Dasan Patishahian ka*, pp. 50–51; Sarupdas Bhalla, *Mahima Prakash*, pp. 358–364; and *Sikhan di Bhagatmala*, pp. 122–123.

14. *Yeh man upaji pragtio jag panth. Tih karan kije ab granth* (Sarupdas Bhalla, *Mahima Prakash*, p. 358).

15. Ibid., pp. 365–368. See also Rattan Singh Jaggi, "Praṇ Sangali da Karatritava," in M. S. *Randhawa, Abhinandan Granth* (Delhi: Navyug, 1969), pp. 131–147, and W. H. McLeod, "Hakikat Rah Mukam Raje Sivanabh ki," *Proceedings of the Punjab History Conference* (Patiala: Punjabi University, 1969), pp. 96–105.

16. *Sikhan di Bhagatmala*, pp. 128–129.

17. Kesar Singh Chhibbar, *Bansavlinama Dasan Patishahian ka*, pp. 126 and 135.

18. Ibid., pp. 135–136. For a detailed discussion of this text, see Randhir Singh, *Sri Guru Gobind Singh Ji di Shabad-Murati* (Amritsar: Shiromani Gurdwara Prabandhak Committee, 1962), and Piara Singh Padam, *Dasam Granth Darshan* (Patiala: Kalam Mandir, 1990).

19. Kesar Singh Chhibbar, *Bansavlinama Dasan Patishahian ka*, pp. 163, 198, and 215.

20. Sarupdas Bhalla, *Mahima Prakash*, p. 892.

21. Kesar Singh Chhibbar, *Bansavlinama Dasan Patishahian ka*, p. 136.

22. Sarup Singh Kaushish, *Guru kian Sakhian*, ed. Piara Singh Padam and Giani Garja Singh (Patiala: Kalam Mandir, 1986). For another major document from this corpus, see Seva Singh, *Shahid Bilas*, ed. Giani Garja Singh (Ludhiana: Punjabi Sahitt Academy, 1961).

23. Sarup Singh Kaushish, *Guru kian Sakhian*, pp. 10–11.

24. *Guru kian Sakhian* sheds important light on two interesting aspects of Sikh life in the early period. First, it focuses on the role of Sikh women at this time. Mata Basi, the mother of Guru Harirai, is a case in point. She is presented as an important figure in her own right who runs her clan, arranges marriages, and plays a central role in the succession ceremony of Guru Tegh Bahadur. There are other women, such as Bibi Sulakhani, Bibi Rup Kaur, Bibi Gomadei (wife of Dhirmal), etc., who to my knowledge are not mentioned in any other early source. Second, this text captures a very realistic picture of the dissent within the gurus' families and de-

scribes how fierce competition and differences did not stop them from keeping up ceremonial relationships and visiting each other on occasions of both happiness and sorrow.

25. Sarup Singh Kaushish, *Guru kian Sakhian*, p. 83.

26. Kesar Singh Chhibbar, *Bansavlinama Dasan Patishahian ka*, p. 136; Sarupdas Bhalla, *Mahima Prakash*, pp. 372–374; and Sarup Singh Kaushish, *Guru kian Sakhian*, pp. 41–42.

27. *Sri Gurbilas Patishahi* 6, ed. Giani Inder Singh Gill (Amritsar: Vazir Hind Press, 1977), pp. 52–91, Bhai Santokh Singh, *Sri Gurpratap Suraj Granth*, ed. Bhai Vir Singh (Amritsar: Khalsa Samachar, 1963), vol. 6, pp. 2044–2145. The identification of the author of *Sri Gurbilas Patishahi* 6 is problematical. Bhai Kahn Singh Nabha attributed this text to Gurmukh Singh and Darbara Singh of the Akali Bunga, Amritsar; see his *Mahan Kosh*, p. 421, and *Gurmat Sudhakar* (Patiala: Punjab Language Department, 1970), p. 216. Scholars have noticed close parallels in the story of the compilation of the Kartarpur Pothi as it appears in these two sources; see Piar Singh, *Gatha Sri Adi Granth*, p. 22. In my view, the authors of both these sources were probably students of Giani Sant Singh, son of Giani Surat Singh, the likely author of *Sikhan di Bhagatmala*; and the history of the Adi Granth may have come to them from their common teacher.

28. See chapter 1, n. 36. Their position is: *Bed puraṇ ab sabh math line. Sabh ka sar granth ji kine*, *Sri Gurbilas Patishahi* 6, p. 90; Bhai Santokh Singh, *Sri Gurpratap Suraj Granth*, vol. 6, p. 2083.

29. *Sri Gurbilas Patishahi* 6, pp. 52–54; Bhai Santokh Singh, *Sri Gurpratap Suraj Granth*, vol. 6, pp. 2049–2059.

30. Bhai Santokh Singh, *Sri Gurpratap Suraj Granth*, vol. 6, pp. 2038–2043.

31. *Sri Gurbilas Patishahi* 6, p. 90; Bhai Santokh Singh, *Sri Gurpratap Suraj Granth*, vol. 6, p. 2140.

32. *Sri Gurbilas Patishahi* 6, p. 170.

33. Giani Gian Singh, *Tvarikh Guru Khalsa* (Patiala: Punjab Language Department, 1993), pp. 417–420.

34. Ibid., p. 417.

35. Ibid., pp. 1084–1085.

36. See chapter 1, n. 54.

37. Charan Singh, *Sri Guru Granth Baṇi Biaura* (Amritsar: Khalsa Tract Society, 1945 [1902]), pp. 4–6.

38. For developments in the field of education, see G. W. Leitner, *Indigenous Education in the Punjab Since Annexation* (Patiala: Punjab Language Department, 1970 [1882]).

39. Ernest Trumpp, *The Adi Granth*; Max Arthur Macauliffe, *The Sikh Religion, Its Gurus, Sacred Writings and Authors* (Delhi: S. Chand, 1985). For an overview of their contribution, see J. S. Grewal, "A Brief History of Sikh Studies," in John Stratton Hawley and Gurinder Singh Mann, eds., *Studying the Sikhs: Issues for North America* (Albany: State University of New York Press, 1993), pp. 164–165.

40. Hira Singh Dard, ed., *Sardar Karam Singh Historian di Itihasak Khoj* (Amritsar: Sikh Itihas Research Board, 1960); S. S. Amol, *Professor Teja Singh* (Patiala: Punjabi University, 1977); and Abnash Kaur, *Professor Sahib Singh: Jivan te Rachna* (Patiala: Punjabi University, 1983).

41. This position was at the basis of commentaries of the Adi Granth produced by these two scholars; see Teja Singh, ed., *Shabadarth Sri Guru Granth Sahib Ji, 4 vols.* (Amritsar: Shiromani Gurdwara Prabandhak Committee, 1936–41); and Sahib Singh, *Sri Guru Granth Sahib Darpaṇ*. See also Teja Singh, "Sri Guru Granth Sahib da Sampadan," in *Guru Arjan Dev: Jivan te Rachna*, ed. Giani Lal Singh (Patiala: Punjab Language Department, 1988); Sahib Singh, *Gurbaṇi te Itihas bare* (Amritsar: Singh Brothers, 1986 [1946]), pp. 9–39; and *Adi Biṛ bare* (Amritsar: Singh Brothers, 1970), pp. 9–146. Teja Singh and Sahib Singh conducted most of their research in the 1930s and 1940s.

42. Teja Singh, "Sri Guru Granth Sahib da Sampadan," pp. 135-136.

43. Sahib Singh, *Gurbaṇi te Itihas bare*, pp. 34–39, *Adi Biṛ bare*, pp. 82–84.

44. See notes in Teja Singh, ed., *Shabadarth Sri Guru Granth Sahib Ji*, pp. 661, 927, 1169, 1170, and 1253.

45. Sahib Singh, *Adi Biṛ bare*, pp. 119–147 and 169–183.

46. G. B. Singh, *Sri Guru Granth Sahib dian Prachin Biṛan* (Lahore: Modern Publications, 1944), pp. 9-12, 26–30, and 291-292.

47. For instance, Piar Singh simply repeats information given by G. B. Singh about three major seventeenth-century manuscripts associated with Bhai Painda (before 1640), Dehra Dun (1659), and Piṇḍi Lala (1675). See his *Gatha Sri Adi Granth*, pp. 130, 258, and 309.

48. G. B. Singh, *Sri Guru Granth Sahib dian Prachin Biṛan*, pp. 91-107; for Bhai Jodh Singh's critique of G. B. Singh's position on the Kartarpur Pothi, see Piar Singh, ed., *Bhai Jodh Singh Gadd Saurabh* pp. 416–486. The suspicion lingers on; see Pashaura Singh, "The Text and Meaning of the Adi Granth" (Ph.D. dissertation, University of Toronto, 1991), p. 20, and Daljeet Singh, *Essay on the Authenticity of Kartarpuri Biṛ* (Patiala: Punjabi University, 1987), pp. 30-37.

49. Bhai Jodh Singh, *Sri Kartarpuri Biṛ de Darshan* (Patiala: Punjabi University, 1968). Giani Mahan Singh of the Chief Khalsa Diwan, who had accompanied Bhai Jodh Singh during his examination of the Kartarpur Pothi, actually took these detailed notes. His original file is available in Bhai Jodh Singh's papers in the Punjabi University Library, Patiala; see Piar Singh, *Gatha Sri Adi Granth*, pp. 52–53.

50. Gursharan Kaur Jaggi, ed., *Babe Mohan valian Pothian* (Delhi: Arsi, 1987).

51. Giani Gurdit Singh, *Itihas Sri Guru Granth Sahib, Bhagat Baṇi Bhag* (Chandigarh: Sikh Sahitt Sansathan, 1990), pp. 550-586.

52. Harnamdas Udasi, *Adi Shri Guru Granth Sahib dian Puratani Biṛan te Vichar*, 2 vols. (Kapurthala: Kantesh Pharmacy, n. d. [1969–1972?]).

53. Randhir Singh, et al., eds., *Sri Guru Granth Sahib Ji dian Santha-Sanchian ate Puratan Haṭhlikhit Pavan Biṛan de Praspar Paṭh-Bhedan di Suchi* (Amritsar: Shiromani Gurdwara Prabandhak Committee, 1977). The work is laid out in several columns, which include a page-by-page comparison of the text of the Adi Granth. The three key columns include "incorrect verses as they appear in some manuscripts and printed editions," "their correct forms," and "reference to the manuscripts on which the correct forms are based." This significant work was based on early manuscripts available at that time in Sikh Reference Library, Amritsar. This rare collection was destroyed during the Operation Bluestar in 1984.

54. Giani Mahan Singh, *Param Pavitar Adi Biṛ da Sankalna Kal* (Amritsar: Khalsa Samachar, 1952); Harbhajan Singh, *Gurbaṇi Sampadan Nirṇai* (Chandigarh: Satnam Prakashan, 1989), and Piara Singh Padam, *Sri Guru Granth Prakash*.

55. Harbhajan Singh, *Gurbaṇi Sampadan Nirṇai*, pp. 106–119; Piara Singh Padam, *Sri Guru Granth Prakash*, pp. 57–58.

56. Pashaura Singh, "The Text and Meaning of the Adi Granth," pp. 12–18.

57. Ibid., pp. 24-28.

58. Ibid., pp. 81-84.

59. For a report on Pashaura Singh's appearance before the Akal Takhat, see *Abstract of Sikh Studies* (July 1994), pp. 132–144, see also Bachittar Singh Giani, ed., *Planned Attack on Aad Sri Guru Granth Sahib*. The entire book is devoted to critiquing Pashaura Singh's doctoral dissertation.

60. Piar Singh, *Gatha Sri Adi Granth*, p. 112, and 450–454.

61. Ibid., pp. 411, 432-433, and 148–149, 172, 451, and 456.

62. For details, see *India Today* (April 30, 1993), p. 19, *Abstract of Sikh Studies* (January, 1993), pp. 1-46, and Piar Singh, *Gatha Sri Adi Granth and the Controversy*, pp. 55–74.

63. Amarjit Singh Grewal, "Ikkivin Sadi de Manav ate Samaj di Sirjiṇa lai Guru Granth Sahib di Prasangikta," *Vismad Nad* 3: 1 (Ludhiana: International Institute of Gurmat Studies, 1994), pp. 1–100. For debate on this issue, see Mohinderjit Singh, *Arthan di Rajniti.*

64. For instance, Giani Gurdit Singh, Piara Singh Padam, and Randhir Singh worked under the auspices of the SGPC in the middle decades of the century.

65. Gurinder Singh Mann, *The Goindval Pothis: The Earliest Extant Source of the Sikh Canon,* Harvard Oriental Series (Cambridge: Harvard University Press, 1996). For reviews, see W. H. McLeod, *Indo-Iranian Journal* 40:2 (1997) pp. 406–408; J. S. Grewal, *International Journal of Punjab Studies* 4:2 (1997) pp. 253–258; Christopher Shackle, *Bulletin of the School of Oriental and African Studies* 61:2 (1998) p. 361; and Gurharpal Singh, *Asian Affairs* (June 1998) pp. 220–221. The book was originally prepared in Punjabi and submitted for publication to Guru Nanak Dev University Press, Amritsar. The university authorities were, however, subjected to such pressure that they withdrew their decision to publish it; see "'Controversial' book in offing," *The Tribune* (May 26, 1995), p. 10.

66. Pritam Singh, ed., *Ahiapur vali Pothi* (Amritsar: Guru Nanak Dev University, 1998).

67. Pritam Singh, "Bhai Banno's Copy of the Sikh Scripture," *Journal of Sikh Studies* 11: 2 (1984), pp. 98–115.

68. W. H. McLeod, "The Sikh Scripture," in his *Evolution of the Sikh Community*, pp. 59–82; "The Sikh Scripture: Some Issues," in Mark Juergensmeyer and N. Gerald Barrier, eds., *Sikh Studies: Comparative Perspectives on a Changing Tradition* (Berkeley: Berkeley Religious Studies Series, 1979), pp. 97–111; "The Study of Sikh Literature," in John Stratton Hawley and Gurinder Singh Mann, eds., *Studying the Sikhs: Issues for North America*, pp. 47–68.

69. J. S. Grewal, "A Perspective on Early Sikh History," in Juergensmeyer and Barrier, eds., *Sikh Studies,* pp. 33–39; "Legacies of the Sikh Past for the Twentieth Century," in Joseph T. O'Connell et al., eds., *Sikh History and Religion in the Twentieth Century* (Toronto:University of Toronto, 1988), pp. 18–25; see also J. S. Grewal, *Sikh Ideology Polity and Social Order* (New Delhi: Manohar, 1996), pp. 39–46.

70. J. S. Grewal, *Contesting Interpretations of the Sikh Tradition*, p. 260. Even if one agrees with Grewal that the textual criticism does not have the same relevance for Sikh scripture which it commanded in biblical studies, a historically accurate account of the compilation of the Adi Granth would be of great value for scholars interested in the comparative study of canon formation. The Sikhs constitute the only major religious tradition that still has access to precanonical manuscripts and are in a unique position to present a model of canonization which is fully supported by documentary evidence.

71. *Sikh Rahit Maryada: The Code of Sikh Conduct and Conventions.*

Chapter 3

1. The information about this litigation was given to me by the custodians of the Guru Harsahai Pothi, the Goindval Pothis, and the Kartarpur Pothi. Haresh Singh Sodhi told me that after the SGPC failed in its bid to legally acquire their pothi, his family thought it necessary to appease Sikh leadership and as a result donated fifty acres of their land in Guru Harsahai village to the SGPC, which is presently in the SGPC's possession.

2. For references to G. B. Singh's unsuccessful efforts to reach these pothis, see his *Sri Guru Granth Sahib dian Prachin Biṛan*, pp. 12 and 26.

3. This account was narrated to me by Haresh Singh Sodhi himself during my visit to Guru Harsahai in January 1995. The family was very kind to show me the rosary, the precious stone, and the suitcase from which the pothi was stolen; see also Giani Gurdit Singh, *Itihas Sri Guru Granth Sahib*, p. 560. Piar Singh's claim that the pothi was lost during the return journey from

Delhi, where it was taken to be displayed in some exhibition, is incorrect. See his *Gatha Sri Adi Granth*, p. 113.

4. In my conversations with other scholars in the field, I detected a general feeling that the pothi was stolen and sent overseas. One speculated that it might be in the United States, the others thought it was probably in a European collection.

5. AG, 1200, contains a very touching hymn by Guru Ramdas which is traditionally associated with Prithi Chand's refusal to accept Guru Ramdas's decision regarding succession. See also Bhai Gurdas, *Varan*, 26: 1, p. 285. For Prithi Chand's establishment at Hehar, see Bhai Santokh Singh, *Sri Gurupratap Suraj Granth*, vol. 6, p. 1999, and Bhai Kahn Singh Nabha, *Mahan Kosh*, p. 280.

6. Sarup Singh Kaushish, *Guru kian Sakhian*, p. 117, and Seva Singh, *Shahid Bilas*, pp. 69–71, report that Bhai Mani Singh took charge of the affairs of the Darbar Sahib, Amritsar, in 1698. This date coincides perfectly with the death of Hariji and seems to be more tenable than that of late 1710s accepted in Sikh tradition; see J. S. Grewal, *The Sikhs of the Punjab*, p. 88.

7. The villages around Chunian were probably under Sikh influence since the time of Guru Amardas. Miharban mentions Guru Nanak's visit to this area; see *Janam-Sakhi Sri Guru Nanak Dev Ji*, vol. 1, p. 511. Bhai Gurdas refers to three important Arora Sikhs based in Chunian—Seth Subhaga, Bhag, and Ugvanda (see Bhai Gurdas, *Varan*, 11: 23, p. 140). Beṇi Pandit, who is said to have been an influential follower of Guru Amardas, is also associated with Chunian; see Sarupdas Bhalla, *Mahima Prakash, Bhag Duja*, p. 227. The village also appears as one of the *manjis* in the list given by Bhai Kahn Singh Nabha; see Fauja Singh, *Guru Amardas:Life and Teachings*, p. 126. The earliest extant manuscripts of the literature produced by this branch of the guru family were actually prepared in this area; see *Janam-Sakhi Sri Guru Nanak Dev Ji*, vol. 1, p. 37, and vol. 2, p. 19.

8. For a history of the family, see Lepel H. Griffin and Charles Francis Massy, *Chiefs and Families of Note in the Punjab* (Lahore: Punjab Government, 1939), pp. 234–236; *District and States Gazetteers of the Undivided Punjab* (Delhi: B. R. Publishing, 1985), vol. 3, pp. 626-627; and Bhai Kahn Singh Nabha, *Mahan Kosh*, pp. 421–422. The Sodhi family tree can be reconstructed on the basis of the "Genealogical Table of the Gurus," available in Joseph Davey Cunningham, *A History of the Sikhs* (1849; rpt. Delhi: S. Chand, 1985), pp. 348–349; and Piara Singh Padam, "Sodhian di Gurpraṇali," *Khoj Patrika* (1968–1969), p. 89. Although I could not find the dates of all family scions, their line appears as follows: Prithi Chand (d. 1618), Miharban (d. 1640), Hariji (d. 1696), Hargopal, Gurandita, Jiwanamal, Guru Harsahai, Ajit Singh (d. 1813), Hamir Singh (d. 1834), Gulab Singh (d. 1867), Fateh Singh (d. 1878), Bishan Singh (d. 1910), Jaswant Singh (d. 1971), Haresh Singh (born 1946), Tikka Yuvraj Singh (born 1994).

9. The Sodhi fort, built in the second half of the eighteenth century, has extensive murals, including portraits of the later Sikh gurus and scenes from their lives. The structure and the art work of the fort are becoming steadily damaged by the ravages of weather. I am very grateful to Haresh Singh Sodhi for giving me a large set of photographs of these murals.

10. Haresh Singh Sodhi shared with me a file containing the papers related to the family litigation in the last quarter of the nineteenth century. These details are culled from the letters and judgments that British officials generated while sorting out the family tangle.

11. Hariji, *Gosaṭi Guru Mihirvanu*, ed. Govindnath Rajguru (Chandigarh: Panjab University, 1974), pp. 175–177.

12. Ibid., pp. 178–179.

13. Quoted by Kirpal Singh in the *Janam-Sakhi Sri Guru Nanak Dev Ji*, vol. 2, p. 80.

14. Griffin and Massey, *Chiefs and Families of Note in the Punjab*, p. 236. The case filed by Bishan Singh in the Chief Court of the Punjab on May 2, 1881, was entitled "Claim for the Book and the Lands of the Shrine of Guru Harsahai."

15. Bhai Kahn Singh Nabha, *Mahan Kosh*, p. 422.

16. Using the influence of the Deputy Commissioner, Ferozepur, Trilochan Singh, district public relations officer at Patiala, was able to convince the Sodhis to bring the pothi to Patiala. It was displayed at the library during the day and was taken to the official residence of Inderjit Kaur Sandhu, principal, Government College, Patiala, and the wife of Giani Gurdit Singh, in the evening. Some of the photographs of the pothi now in the possession of Giani Gurdit Singh were taken at this time. One must point out that Giani Gurdit Singh already possessed some photographs that he had acquired with the help of Giani Kartar Singh, the state revenue minister, in the 1950s. With sprawling landholdings in Guru Harsahai and unsettled claims for lands left in the west Punjab, the Sodhis were understandably keen to oblige Giani Kartar Singh during those years.

17. All through the 1980s, with severe political turmoil going on in the Punjab, the tradition of the Vaisakhi fair at Guru Harsahai continued. For a report of the annual fair in 1996, see *Akali Patrika* (March 9, 1996); p. 1, *Navan Zamana* (March 9, 1996), p. 7; *Jag Baṇi* (March 19, 1996), p. 2.

18. Bhai Gurdas, *Varan*, 1: 31, p. 71, "Valayat vali Janam-Sakhi," p. 57, and "Miharban vali Janam-Sakhi," pp. 184–185, in Kirpal Singh, ed., *Janam-Sakhi Prampra*.

19. Since the loss of the Guru Harsahai Pothi, the emphasis has shifted to the *mala* and the *padam*, which are now at the center of public display during the annual fair.

20. For a facsimile of this folio, see Giani Gurdit Singh, *Itihas Sri Guru Granth Sahib*, p. 8. It should, however, be pointed out that Giani Gurdit Singh's transcription of the invocation in the pothi is not accurate. He could not decipher *kartar* and has transcribed the word *sachunam* as *satinam*. The invocation in the Adi Granth has been the key issue of the recent controversy over the works of Pashaura Singh and Piar Singh; see Piar Singh, *Gatha Sri Adi Granth and the Controversy*, p. 132.

In existing Sikh literature, there are two views regarding the authorship of the invocation. Traditionally, the text is attributed to Guru Nanak; see Bhai Vir Singh, *Santhaya Sri Guru Granth Sahib*, vol. 1, p. 2, and Pritam Singh, ed., *Sikh Concept of the Divine* (Amritsar: Guru Nanak Dev University, 1985), p. 1. Others however, have argued that the invocation was authored by Guru Arjan. Giani Narain Singh Mujangwale, writing in 1932, claimed that the text of the invocation evolved over time and reached its final form in the hands of Guru Arjan (cited in Taran Singh, *Gurbaṇi dian Viakhia Praṇalian*, p. 278), Giani Mahan Singh in his "Piau Dade da Khol Ḍiṭha Khazana," *Nirguṇiara* 57: 7 (July, 1959), and Piar Singh in his recent *Gatha Sri Adi Granth and the Controversy*, pp. 139–142, elaborated this view further. Three major commentators of the Adi Granth, Giani Badan Singh, Sahib Singh, and Teja Singh are interestingly silent on this issue, and their position is not clear.

The recent debate over the invocation centered around two issues. First, Pashaura Singh and Piar Singh's attributions of the invocation to Guru Arjan were received with a great degree of hostility by scholars who believe that this text was composed by Guru Nanak. They do not offer any evidence in support of their assertion for the authorship of Guru Nanak, nor do they show any awareness that this issue has been debated since the 1930s; see Bachittar Singh Giani, ed., *Planned Attack on Aad Sri Guru Granth Sahib*, pp. vii-viii, and 350–356.

Second, the argument that while giving the invocation its final form Guru Arjan made theological changes in the existing text is found disturbing by many. Pashaura Singh and Piar Singh's finding of doctrinal variations between the different versions of the invocation is problematical, and I for one disagree. I think the changes made in the text are minor and cannot be assigned any philosophical import. Nor do I see any weight in their critics' argument that these interpretations constitute a premeditated effort to challenge the revealed nature of the contents of Sikh scripture.

In my view, the debate about the invocation has yet to achieve the clarity it needs. Recent emphasis on the invocation seems to emerge from a strange blend of two elements. First, the scholars responsible for generating this controversy have attempted to argue that the textual approach is not pertinent to Sikh scripture, as it was recorded by "the prophet" (Guru Arjan) himself; see "Blasphemous Attacks," *Abstracts of Sikh Studies* (January 1993), p. 8. Within this broad context, any attempt to trace textual evolution in the corpus of sacred Sikh literature is a challenge to the revealed nature of the contents. This response to textual scholarship is not unique to the Sikhs, and I do not need to go into it here.

Second, there is a more specific reason that the invocation is so impartant in the debate on textual issues. Sikh commentators have normally used three Punjabi terms: *sirlekh* (Charan Singh, *Sri Guru Granth Baṇi Biaura*, p. 9), *mulmantar* (Teja Singh, ed., *Shabadarth Sri Guru Granth Sahib Ji*, vol. 1, p. 1), and *mangal* (Harbhajan Singh, *Gurbaṇi Sampadan Nirṇai*, pp. 66–67). Scholars condemning the work of Pashaura Singh and Piar Singh exclusively use the term *mulmantar* and thereby tie this debate with the Hindu understanding of the *mantra*; see Gurmail Singh Sidhu, "Adi Sri Guru Granth Sahib te Yojanabadh Hamla," p. 350; for its usage in Hindu literature, see Harold Coward and David Goa, *Mantra: Hearing the Divine in India* (Chambersburg, Pa.: Anima Books, 1991), pp. 27–29 and 55, and J. Gonda, *Mantra Interpretation in the Satpatha-Brahmana* (Leiden: E. J. Brill, 1988).

The placement of the Sikh invocation in the Hindu *mantric* context is not new. The text of invocation as a group of potent words was first alluded to in the *vars* of Bhai Gurdas (see Bhai Gurdas, *Varan*, 1: 23, p. 69; 1: 49, p. 76, and 6: 19, p 106). These allusions, however, need to be understood in the broader context of Bhai Gurdas's writings. He refers to the invocation thrice in his *vars* but does not even once mention the complete text as it appears in the Adi Granth. In other words, there is no evidence that Bhai Gurdas took the invocation to be a set of sounds that must be quoted in its entirety. Nor is there any emphasis on the mantric power of these sounds; for him, the hymns of the gurus are the core revelation for the Sikhs (Bhai Gurdas, *Varan*, 40: 22, p. 316).

Beginning with the nineteenth century, Nirmala scholars established the tradition of interpretation of the invocation according to the full Hindu meaning of the term; see Pritam Singh, ed., *Sikh Concept of the Divine*, pp. 1–25. The invocation was declared to be the substantive essence of the Adi Granth—an interpretation underpinning the scholarly view that the research findings of Pashaura Singh and Piar Singh are disturbing. According to this line of thought, any attempt to trace the evolution in the text of the invocation constitutes tinkering with the very essence of the Sikh revelatory writings.

This view of invocation has more to do with the Hindu context from which it emerges than anything available in Sikh doctrine. If this text was thought to be the original revelation, as these scholars assert, it would be natural to keep the original form intact as well. But it is not considered original, and there are numerous variations of this text available in sacred Sikh literature. In the Kartarpur Pothi/Adi Granth, there are five distinct versions of the invocation; see Harbhajan Singh, *Gurbaṇi Sampadan Nirṇai*, pp. 66–67. The letters of the command written by the gurus to the Sikh congregations contain yet more variations; see Ganda Singh, ed., *Hukamname* (Patiala: Punjabi University, 1985 [1967]), pp. 75, 77, 127, 139, 159. An altogether different text (*Vahiguru ji ki fateh*) appears in the Dasam Granth, another Sikh scriptural text.

Nor is there any provision in Sikh doctrine for interpreting the invocation as a set of potent sounds to be recited over and over for producing special results, and there is no basis for the claim that this text represents the thematic core of Sikh scripture as a whole. The term *mulmantar* appears once in the hymns of Guru Nanak and its usage implies that the name of God is at the root of all mantras (*Mulmantr hari namu rasaiaṇu kahu Nanak pura paia*, M1, AG, 1040)—the meaning being that all mantras are superseded by the name of God revealed to the Sikhs in the hymns of the gurus. Along similar lines, Guru Arjan wrote that knowledge [of God] has been given to all as the seed mantra (*Bij mantr sarab ko gianu*, M5, AG, 274). The mantras are no longer valid for the Sikhs, since the hymns of the gurus are far superior to them.

In Sikh doctrine, communication between human beings and the divine is, as in other monotheistic traditions, primarily by way of prayer to the personal God; for the distinction between the use of mantra and prayer, see P. Alper Harvey, ed., *Understanding Mantras* (Albany: State University of New York Press, 1989), pp. 2–3. For an interesting interpretation of this issue, see Jaswant Singh Neki, *Ardas: Darshan, Rup, Abhias* (Amritsar: Singh Brothers, 1989).

In my view, the text of the invocation developed as a literary device to seeking divine help before each section of the scriptural text was inscribed, and instead of relating to the Hindu mantra, it may be seen to follow the Qur'anic tradition of the *Bismillah*. For further discussion of this, see Chapter 6.

21. I am grateful to Joginder Singh Ahluwalia for providing me with figures regarding the frequency of these terms.

22. The description of the pothi appears in Giani Gurdit Singh, *Itihas Sri Guru Granth Sahib*, pp. 557-561, and 579-586. Through my meetings with him in New York and Chandigarh in recent years, I have clarified some obscurities in his written account here, and I render his views to the best of my knowledge.

23. *Janam-Sakhi Sri Guru Nanak Dev Ji*, vol. 2, pp. 486–507.

24. For the text of these hymns, see *Janam-Sakhi Sri Guru Nanak Dev Ji*, vol. 1, pp. 33–36; the Goindval Pothi, folios 16–18; and the Adi Granth, pp. 764–65.

25. The opening is, *Jin kau bhanḍai bhau tina savarsi*, M1, AG, 729; see *Janam-Sakhi Sri Guru Nanak Dev Ji* , vol. 2, pp. 67–68, and the Goindval Pothi at Jalandhar, folio 10.

26. Giani Gurdit Singh, *Itihas Sri Guru Granth Sahib*, p. 558. This claim of Giani Gurdit Singh corroborates the seventeenth-century tradition present in the janam-sakhi literature. According to Hariji, the text of *Japji* was culled from a written version of the hymns of Guru Nanak by Lahiṇa, later Guru Angad, at Kartarpur, and these thirty-eight stanzas and two couplets were presented as the core of Guru Nanak's praise of God. Its placement at the head of the pothi fits in well with this thinking, and may be evidence that the pothi itself was prepared at Kartarpur at this time. A second possibility exists that the *Japji*'s placement at the head of the pothi may have contributed to the tradition described by Hariji; see *Janam-Sakhi Sri Guru Nanak Dev Ji*, vol. 2, pp. 248–250.

According to Giani Gurdit Singh, the first section of the pothi closes with a hymn attributed to Guru Nanak, in *rag* Tukhari, which begins: *Tu suṇi kirat karamma purabi kamaia. Siri siri sukh sahamma dehi su tu bhala*, AG, 1107 ([O Lord] listen! Everyone [pays for] his earlier works, and will have to receive comfort or punishment. Whatever you give is best for us). The same hymn in *rag* Tukhari is reported in the *Puratan Janam-Sakhi* to have been Guru Nanak's last composition; see "Valayat vali Janam-Sakhi," in Kirpal Singh, ed., *Janam-Sakhi Prampara*, p. 57. The tradition of this hymn as Guru Nanak's last, in combination with its purported presence at the end of the Guru Harsahai Pothi, is open to various interpretations.

One might argue that the presence of the *rag* Tukhari hymn at the end of the original text of the Guru Harsahai Pothi, and the reference to this hymn as the final one composed by Guru Nanak in the *Puratan Janam-Sakhi*, occurred independently of each other and therefore corroborate each other. Since there is no visible organization in this first section of the pothi, one could argue that it simply records the writings of Guru Nanak in the sequence in which they were composed. In that case the hymn in *rag* Tukhari would have come at the end of the text simply because Guru Nanak composed it last. Certainly the *Puratan Janam-Sakhi* takes such a position.

On the other hand, one might propose that the position of the *rag* Tukhari hymn at the end of the Guru Harsahai Pothi was precisely the evidence that led the *Puratan Janam-Sakhi* to refer to it as Guru Nanak's last hymn, regardless of biographical considerations. Such a reading would imply that the *Puratan Janam-Sakhi*, a source independent of the custodians of the Guru Harsahai Pothi, considered it to have been compiled during Guru Nanak's lifetime; thus it would have been taken for granted that the final hymn in the Guru Harsahai Pothi was the last that Guru Nanak had composed.

Of course, one could also take the opposite position and argue that the placement of the last hymn in the opening section of the Guru Harsahai Pothi was rooted in the *Puratan Janam-Sakhi* tradition. Yet such a chronology, placing the Guru Harsahai Pothi after the *Puratan Janam-Sakhi*, does not seem defensible, because once the organization of the hymns according to *rag* had been developed, there was no reversing it. One is left with two options: Whether the presence of the *rag* Tukhari hymn at the end of the collection of Guru Nanak's hymns in the Guru Harsahai Pothi was the basis for the janam-sakhi tradition or the janam-sakhi represented an independent early tradition that corresponded to the extant text in the Guru Harsahai Pothi, these references suggest a relatively early origin of the opening section of the pothi.

27. Sarupdas Bhalla, *Mahima Prakash*, p. 204. For the text of the *Anand* at the disposal of this family, see Raijasbir Singh, ed., *Guru Amardas: Srot Pustak*, pp. 198–201.

28. Sarupdas Bhalla, *Mahima Prakash*, pp. 208 and 358–359.

29. The palanquin at Goindval is extremely old and it resembles other relics from this early period. See Madanjit Kaur, "Goindval," in Krishaṇ Lal Sharma, ed., *Guru Amar Das: Jivan ate Chintan* (Amritsar: Guru Nanak Dev University, 1986), pp. 41–42, and Bhai Vir Singh, *Santhaya Sri Guru Granth Sahib*, vol. 4, pp. 1585–1586.

30. See Giani Gian Singh, *Tvarikh Guru Khalsa*, vol. 1, p. 418.

31. G. B. Singh, *Sri Guru Granth Sahib dian Prachin Biṛan*, pp. 27–29, and Bhai Vir Singh, *Santhaya Sri Guru Granth Sahib*, vol. 4, p. 1586.

32. In the past several years, the Bhalla family has been extremely kind in making arrangements for me to examine the pothis on *sangrand* and *puranmashi* days. Over the years, they have become increasingly comfortable with my interest in the pothis. In 1999 the family warmly welcomed participants of Columbia-UCSB Summer Program at Chandigarh to their home in Pinjore, and it was a delightful experience for me to be able to show the structure and other substantive details of the pothi to my colleagues in the program.

33. Bhai Gurdas, *Varan*, 26: 33, p. 232. Bhai Gurdas is very critical of the behavior of the sons of the early gurus, beginning with Sri Chand.

34. The Bhalla family at Pinjore records their lineage as follows: Mohan, Sahansram, Ramji, Pashaurimal, Kripa Chand, Pratap Chand, Arurmal, Vastiram, Jawahar Singh, Gurbaksh Singh, Kahn Singh, Amir Singh, Chet Singh, Sundar Singh, Bhagat Singh, and Kanwarjit Singh. I have constructed the Jalandhar line on the basis of information available in Raijasbir Singh, ed., *Guru Amardas: Srot Pustak*, p. 491. With two gaps the line is as follows: Mohari, Arjani, Biharidas, Sultan Singh, Meghraj, Ratan Singh, Baharhmal, Tola Singh, Gulab Singh, Bishan Singh, Sahib Singh, ?, ?, Dalip Chand, and Vinod Bhalla.

For references to Maharaja Ranjit Singh's visits to Goindval, see Sohan Lal Suri, *Umdat-ut-Tvarikh*, daftar III, trans. V. S. Suri (Delhi: S. Chand, 1961), pp. 187, 316, 397, and 398. For other visits of Sikh chiefs, see Ram Sukh Rao, *Sri Fateh Singh Partap Prabhakar*, ed. Joginder Kaur (Patiala: editor, 1980), pp. 116, 343, 479, and 538.

35. For the actual shape of the Gurmukhi letters, see my *Goindval Pothis: The Earliest Extant Source of the Sikh Canon*, p. 17.

36. For references to this particular dating, see Gursharan Kaur Jaggi, *Babe Mohan valian Pothian*, p. 2; Piar Singh, *Gatha Sri Adi Granth*, pp. 109–112; Teja Singh, "Sri Guru Granth Sahib da Sampadan," pp. 135–136; Piara Singh Padam, *Sri Guru Amardas ji di Baṇi* (Patiala: Punjabi University, 1979), pp. 23–24 (Padam appears to place the date for the writing of the

pothi at Jalandhar later than that of the one at Pinjore); and Giani Gurdit Singh, *Itihas Sri Guru Granth Sahib*, p. 565. See also Pritam Singh, "Punjabi Boli," in Mohinder Singh Randhawa, ed., *Punjab* (Patiala: Punjab Language Department, 1960), p. 387, and *Khoj Patrika* 36 (September 1992), pp. 110–133.

37. Gursharan Kaur Jaggi, *Babe Mohan valian Pothian*, p. 2; Piar Singh, *Gatha Sri Adi Granth*, p. 71; Pritam Singh, ed., *Ahiapur vali Pothi*, pp. 228–233. Piar Singh also argues that the pothis began to be written during the time of Guru Amardas but were completed in 1595; see his *Gatha Sri Adi Granth*, p. 112.

38. For a detailed discussion of this issue, see my *Goindval Pothis: The Earliest Extant Source of the Sikh Canon*, pp. 18–25.

39. For the text of these hymns, see ibid., pp. 103–116.

40. Giani Gurdit Singh, *Itihas Sri Guru Granth Sahib*, p. 563. See also Gursharan Kaur Jaggi, *Babe Mohan valian Pothian*, p. 30.

41. Sikh tradition refers to instances of hymns included in the Adi Granth which were written by the gurus prior to taking up the honor of guru. Guru Ramdas's hymn in *rag* Gujri, which opens with the verse *Hari ke jan satigur satpurakha binau karau gur pasi*, is associated with the period before he became guru; see Teja Singh, ed., *Shabadarth Sri Guru Granth Sahib Ji*, vol. 1, p. 10 and vol. 2, p. 492, Giani Badan Singh, *Adi Sri Guru Granth Sahib Ji Saṭik*, vol. 1, p. 32; and Sahib Singh, *Sri Guru Granth Sahib Darpaṇ*, vol. 1, p. 146. Guru Arjan's hymn in *rag* Majh, which opens with *Mera manu lochai gurdarsan tai*, is thought to have been composed before he took the office of guru, see Giani Badan Singh, *Adi Sri Guru Granth Sahib Ji Saṭik*, vol. 1, p. 255, and Teja Singh, ed., *Shabadarth Sri Guru Granth Sahib Ji*, vol. 1, p. 96.

42. Among the group of known Sikhs in this approximate period, other candidates for authorship of these hymns may be ruled out. Baba Mohan, in whose custody the pothis remained, can be taken to be the foremost candidate, but there is little basis for an argument that might identify him with Gulam Sadasevak. Neither in Sikh tradition nor in Bhalla family memory is there any reference to his creation of poetic compositions. Furthermore, if the writings attributed to Gulam Sadasevak were actually Baba Mohan's, then, since the pothis were in the care of the Bhalla family both before and after Baba Mohan's time, there would have been no sense in crossing them out.

Of the gurus' other living children, Baba Sri Chand could have been a candidate; but in the context of numerous traditions about the special respect accorded to him, the recording of his compositions after those of the gurus does not appear likely. Also, as found in his extant writings, instead of the signature of "Nanak," he used the signature "Nanak *puta*"; See Piar Singh, "Solvhin Sadi de Hor Kavi," in Surinder Singh Kohli, ed., *Punjabi Sahitt da Itihas, Bhag Pahila* (Chandigarh: Panjab University, 1973), vol. 1, pp. 273–282. Asides from the hymns of the gurus, the signature "Nanak" appears only in three couplets attributed to Mardana, a disciple of Guru Nanak who had long since died; see AG, 553.

Among leading Sikhs of the time, the name of Baba Buḍḍha is preeminent, but there is no tradition about his having written any hymns. At the time the pothis were written, Bhai Gurdas must yet have been very young: in the absence of strong proof, his birth can only be placed in the second half of the sixteenth century. In his writings there is no effort to use the authoritative signature of Nanak.

43. See chapter 2 in my *Goindval Pothis: The Earliest Extant Source of the Sikh Canon*.

44. This principle is not applicable to the Kartarpur Pothi. After the original inscription of the Kartarpur Pothi, additional hymns of Guru Arjan were added to it; see chapter 4, n. 47.

45. Giani Gian Singh, *Tvarikh Guru Khalsa*, vol. 1, p. 418.

46. In fact, neither has actually written on this specific subject, but it has arisen quite a few times in my conversations with them.

47. This issue surfaced accidentally during my stay with Dr. and Mrs. Nirankari in December 1994. I am obliged to them for both their affection and encouragement. Dr. Nirankari has several early Sikh scriptural manuscripts in his custody and he graciously permitted me to photograph the oldest one, which was prepared in 1676.

48. Keeping in mind the close affinity of the text of the Goindval Pothis with that of the Adi Granth, I have attempted to count the number of pages in the standard edition of the Adi Granth which correspond with the hymns in the four pothis. The following estimate emerges: Pothi at Jalandhar, 104; Pothi at Pinjore, 86; Pothi referred to by Giani Gian Singh, 180; and remaining text of the gurus' and Bhagats' hymns, 125. As expected, the 125-page count is too small to necessitate recording its contents in two pothis, it is instead just the right size to constitute one additional pothi.

49. The common phrase used to refer to the Hindu and Semitic scriptural texts in Sikh literature is *Ved-Kateb*, and for Bhai Gurdas the Sikh revelation is distinct from the earlier ones enshrined in Hindu and Semitic texts; Bhai Gurdas, *Varan*, 23: 19, p. 209, and 33: 2, p. 268. The background to the Sikhs' belief in the existence of four sacred books in Judaism, Christianity, and Islam is manifestly Islamic. The Punjabi word *Jambur* is the local version of the Arabic *Zabur* used for the Psalms in the Qur'an (*sura* 4, 161; 17, 57; and 21, 105). The origin of the word goes back to Hebrew *Zimrah*.

50. This information was given to me by Bibi Agya Kaur, head of the Bhalla family at Pinjore, but she was unable to assist me in my attempts to discover more about the whereabouts of the Bhallas in Phagwara. Mohan Singh Dewana claims to have seen pothis of this set in 1933, at Goindval, and in 1960 at Amritsar, see G. B. Singh, *Sri Guru Granth Sahib dian Prachin Biṛan*, pp. 456–457. Giani Gurdit Singh dismisses this information; see his *Itihas Sri Guru Granth Sahib*, p. 567. The information provided by Dewana about the text of the invocation used in the documents he viewed seems to be significant; unlike Giani Gurdit Singh, I am unwilling to dismiss lightly Dewana's claim to have seen the pothis that belonged to the Goindval set.

51. The folio numbers recorded in the following six gatherings include discrepancies resulting from incorrect folding of the folios at the time of their framing. Pothi at Jalandhar: 14 (folios 105–113); 19 (folios 147–155); 30 (folios 235–243); 36 (folios 283–291). Pothi at Pinjore: 10 (folios 73–81).

In the pothi at Jalandhar, the confusion in the folios resulted from their dislocation. In the pothi at Pinjore, the closing verses of the *Siddh Goshṭ* and the opening stanzas of the *Anand*, which appear on these folios, run smoothly, but the folio number is entered incorrectly. The number of the ninth gathering appears on the bottom corner of the left side of folio 76 (actually folio 73), and this is followed by a gathering containing six folios. Folios numbering 78 and 77 are turned in the reverse direction and have become part of the following gathering.

52. The pothi at Jalandhar is constructed of thirty-seven gatherings of eight folios each. There are, however, ten folios in gathering 18, and two loose folios, which were left over originally from the last gathering in the pothi, attached at the end. In my assessment, at the time of the framing of the folios and the rebinding of the pothi, the last gathering was misplaced; two folios remain at their initial position at the end, three were attached in the *rag* Basant section, and the other three were perhaps lost. In any case, with thirty-seven gatherings and four extra folios, the total number of folios of this pothi comes to three hundred. The pothi at Pinjore has twenty-eight gatherings and a total of 224 folios. There are discrepancies: in gatherings 10 and 14, there are six folios, but the loss of four folios is covered by gatherings 11 and 26, which contain ten folios each. The gathering's numbers have been written with extreme care in the lower right corner of the last folio of each gathering. In the pothi at Jalandhar, these numbers appear on the left-side page of the following folios: 9, 17, 25, 33, 41, 49, 57, 65, 73, 81, 89, 97, 105, 113, 121, 129, 137, 147, 155, 163, 171, 179 (some extra folios with hymns in *rag* Tilang from the last gathering have been shifted and attached here, and the number of the twenty-fifth gathering is

printed on folio 203). After this the series' numbering runs correctly: 211, 219, 227, 235, 243, 251, 259, 267, 275, 283, 291, 298. In the pothi at Pinjore, the gatherings' number appear on the following folios: 9, 17, 25, 33, 41, 49, 57, 65, 76, 79, 89, 97, 105, 111, 119, 127, 135, 143, 151, 159, 167, 175, 183, 191, 199, 209, 217, 225 (the last half-page). The number entered on folio 76 is a mistake: this is actually folio 73.

For paper making in this period, see Dard Hunter, *Paper Making: The History and Technique of an Ancient Craft* (1943; rpt. New York: Dover Publications, 1974), pp. 103–109, 178–179, and 191–197.

53. For a discussion of this issue, see my *Goindval Pothis: The Earliest Extant Source of the Sikh Canon*, pp. 31–32, and 196–197.

54. For a detailed record of the blank folios, see ibid., p. 32

55. Gursharan Kaur Jaggi, *Babe Mohan valian Pothian*, p. 44, and Bhai Jodh Singh, *Sri Kartarpuri Biṛ de Darshan*, p. *kaka*.

56. Bhai Jodh Singh, "Sri Kartarpur vali Pavitar 'Adi' Biṛ," in Piar Singh, ed., *Bhai Jodh Singh Gadd Saurabh*, p. 491. Whether Bhai Jodh Singh's view was based on examination of the Kartarpur Pothi itself, or was offered as an impressive explanation that fit well into the traditional belief about the slow collection of the hymns of the gurus and their editing by Guru Arjan, cannot now be discerned. One problem, however, becomes immediately evident. Bhai Jodh Singh argued that each gathering consisted of eight folios. Why, then, did the actual text of the Kartarpur Pothi begin on folio 45? According to Bhai Jodh Singh's own argument, if five gatherings were set aside for a table of contents, then the text should have begun on folio 41; if six, then it should have begun on folio 49; see *Sri Kartarpuri Biṛ de Darshan*, p. 46. It is clear that Bhai Jodh Singh's neat scheme does not conform to the basic structure of the Kartarpur Pothi.

57. The following data show the precise placement of the beginning of each *rag* section in the Goindval Pothis:

rag	First folio	Gathering no.	Folios in gathering
POTHI AT JALANDHAR			
Prabhati	folio 63	gathering 8	folios 57–65
Dhanasri	folio 120	gathering 15	folios 113–121
Basant	folio 169	gathering 21	folios 163–171
Bhairo	folio 228	gathering 29	folios 227–235
Maru	folio 277	gathering 35	folios 275–283
POTHI AT PINJORE			
Soraṭhi	folio 122	gathering 16	folios 119–127
Malar	folio 183	gathering 23	folios 175–183
Sarang	folio 216	gathering 27	folios 209–217

This leaves no doubt that Bhai Jodh Singh's explanation of keeping separate gatherings for each *rag* section does not work here.

58. In the pothi at Jalandhar, this numbering begins with 1 and continues successively to 29, notation and number being written on the following folios: 9, 18, 27, 38, 45, 54, 70, 79, 92, 99, 110, 124, 133, 145, 156, 174, 189, 197, 206, 211, 227, 234, 241, 250, 259, 264, 270, 283, 289. An additional example of the notation numbered 29 was entered on folio 183 but was later struck out. This has to do with the initial placement of folio 183 toward the end of the pothi, but when the pothi was rebound, it was somehow moved forward. An implied notation number 30 is to be assumed at the end of the pothi. In the pothi at Pinjore, this sign is found on folios 9, 15, 22, (?), 33, 53, 74, 92, 117, 125, 133, 144, 154, 163, 170, 186, 191, 201, 208, 215, and 224.

In the pothi at Jalandhar, the first time this notation appears, it is at the end of Guru Nanak's *chaupadas*. On the basis of this particular placement, Bawa Prem Singh was misled into believing that the sign had been meant to mark the end of the groups of hymns of Guru Nanak. See Gursharan Kaur Jaggi, *Babe Mohan valian Pothian*, p. 15, and Piar Singh, *Gatha Sri Adi Granth*, pp. 99–100. Such an interpretation is not, however, applicable elsewhere in the text.

59. Under the title of *rag* Maru in the pothi at Jalandhar, there are only ten hymns by Guru Nanak and Guru Amardas, but in the corresponding *rag* section in the Kartarpur Pothi, seventy-six hymns are recorded. In the original writing of the pothi, *rag* Maru is combined with *rag* Kedara. The principle of combining these two *rags* appears to have been revised later and in all likelihood some hymns were recorded under *rag* Kedara, but since the text of *rag* Kedara is not available in the extant pothis, we cannot say anything about what was recorded in it. Therefore, reference to hymns in *rag* Maru in the Goindval Pothis is omitted from the following discussion.

60. Three hymns in the Goindval Pothis, which are absent from the Kartarpur Pothi, include two hymns attributed to Guru Nanak, one each in *rag* Suhi (folios 31–32) and *rag* Tilang (folio 184), and one attributed to Guru Amardas in *rag* Dhanasri (folio 128). For a detailed discussion, see my *Goindval Pothis: The Earliest Extant Source of the Sikh Canon*, pp. 33–34, 100–102, and notes, chapter 2, *rag* Suhi, n. 18, *rag* Dhanasri, n. 56, and *rag* Tilang, n. 131.

61. Five hymns in the Kartarpur Pothi are not present in the corresponding sections in the Goindval Pothis. These include two hymns of Guru Nanak in *rag* Tilang (*Ihu tanu maia pahia piare litṛa labhi rangae* and *Ianaṛie manaṛa kai karehi*, M3, AG, 721–722), and three hymns of Guru Amardas: one hymn in *rag* Sarang (*Man mere hari kai nami ki vadai*, M3, AG, 1233), one in *rag* Malar (*Gurmukhi koi virla bujhai jis no nadari karai*, M3, AG, 1258), and one in *rag* Prabhati (*Mere man guru apaṇa salahe*, M3, AG, 1334–1335). For details of changes in *rags*, see my *Goindval Pothis: The Earliest Extant Source of the Sikh Canon*, Notes, chapter 2, *rag* Prabhati, nn. 41, 46, 47; *rag* Bhairo, n. 108; *rag* Ramkali, n. 149; *rag* Soraṭhi, n. 161, and *rag* Malar, n. 177.

62. See n. 33.

63. In literature related to Sikh *rahit*, familial or social relationships with the followers of Prithi Chand, Dhirmal, or Ramrai are prohibited. Written reference to this proscription goes back to the first decade of the eighteenth century; see Sainapati, *Sri Gur Sobha*, p. 81. For the precise identification of these groups, see W. H. McLeod, *Historical Dictionary of Sikhism*, p. 159. This sentiment still exists within the Sikh community, according to *Sikh Rahit Maryada*, p. 33.

Instead, a recently surfaced *hukamnama* of Guru Gobind Singh issued in 1699 suggests that the Sikh congregation at Goindval maintained close contact with Anandpur, the center of Sikh activities during the last quarter of the seventeenth century. This *hukamnama*, recorded under the signature of Guru Gobind Singh and dated 1699 (Katak 4, Samat 1756), is addressed to the Sikh congregation at Goindval. This rare document is in the custody of Bibi Inderjit Kaur, the wife of Harbhajan Singh Yogi, at their residence in Albuquerque, New Mexico. I found this document during my examination of their archival collection in Albuquerque and Española in April 1996.

64. Kesar Singh Chhibbar, *Bansavlinama Dasan Patishahian ka*, pp. 42–46.

Chapter 4

1. These stages are well marked in early sources discussed in chapter 2.

2. Piar Singh, *Gatha Sri Adi Granth*, pp. 135–173; Pashaura Singh, "An Early Sikh Scriptural Tradition: The Guru Nanak Dev University Manuscript 1245," *International Journal of Punjab Studies* 1:2 (1994), pp. 197–222. For a response to their research results, see Balwant Singh Dhillon, "Myth of Early Draft of Adi Granth (MS 1245)," in Bachittar Singh Giani, ed., *Planned Attack on Aad Sri Guru Granth Sahib*, pp. 85–107. I was extremely grateful to

Vice Chancellor Gurdip Singh Randhawa, Guru Nanak Dev University, Amritsar, for providing me with a microfilm of this manuscript.

3. During the controversy that surrounded Pashaura Singh's doctoral research in 1992–1993, the Chawla brothers were subjected to severe pressure to reveal the source of their purchase of MS 1245 by people associated with the International Centre of Sikh Studies, Chandigarh. The Chawlas succeeded in evading the question, however, by claiming that they bought it along with "a few other Miharban manuscripts from Rajasthan"; see Gurnam Kaur and Kharak Singh, "Blasphemous Attacks," in Bachittar Singh Giani, *Planned Attack on Aad Sri Guru Granth Sahib*, p. 51.

4. A few instances of different handwritings are also available. One unusually curly hand inscribed Guru Arjan's *chaupadas* 27 to 54 and the opening *ashṭpadi* of Guru Nanak in *rag* Bhairo (folios 1057–1068); the change of hand in the middle of the hymn's text indicates that this writing is part of the original inscription of the manuscript. Elsewhere, the opening verses of some of Guru Arjan's hymns are recorded in the hand of the primary scribe but the text is later completed in a different hand; see folios 577, 578, 583, 773, 782, and 789.

5. The sequence of *rag* sections in MS 1245 runs as follows: Sri (folios 39–104), Majh (folios 105–155), Gauṛi (folios 157–328), Asa (folios 340–453), Gujri (folios 456–490), Devgandhari (493–500), Bihagṛa (folios 502–519), Vaḍhans (folios 522–599), Dhanasri (folios 561–589), Jaitsri (folios 590–603), Soraṭhi (folios 604–651), Kaliaṇ (folios 652–659), Natnaraiaṇ (folio 661–669), Toḍi (folios 670–676), Beraṛi (folios 676–677), Tilang (folios 679–684), Gonḍ (folios 685–694), Suhi (folios 697–755), Bilaval (folios 758–815), Ramkali (folios 817–906), Maligauṛa (folios 910–914), Maru (916–1020), Kedara (folios 1025–1029), Tukhari (folios 1030–1039), Bhairo (folios 1040–1071), Basant (folios 1072–1094), Sarang (folios 1096–1148), Malar (folios 1149–1182), Kanṛa (folios 1183–1207), and Prabhati (folios 1209–1228).

6. The following hymns of Guru Arjan, which appear in the Kartarpur Pothi and the Adi Granth, are not present in MS 1245:

Gobind Gobind Gobind sangi Namdau manu liṇa (Asa, AG, 487)

Tu samrathu sarni ko data . . . sukhrai (Gujri, AG, 502)

Ṭhakur hoe api daial (Devgandhari, AG, 532)

Apune satigur pahi binau kahia (Devgandhari, AG, 533)

Anath nath prabh hamare (Devgandhari, AG, 533)

Prabhu ihai manorathu mera (Devgandhari, AG, 533)

Darsan kau lochai sabhu koi (Suhi, AG, 744–745)

Mu lalan siau priti bani (Bilaval, AG, 827)

Raṇ jhunjhnaṛa gau sakhi hari eku dhiavahu (Ramkali, AG, 927)

Hari ka namu dhiai kai hohu haria bhai (Basant, AG, 1193)

Hari ke sangu base hari lok (Sarang, AG, 1253)

Prabh ko bhagati vachhalu birdaiau (Malar, AG, 1270).

7. There is some ambivalence regarding the presence of the *var* of Satta and Balvand in MS 1245. The *var* is mentioned in the table of contents, folio 819 but is not present in the main text. Piar Singh explains this anomaly by arguing that the table of contents and the main text came to the scribe from separate sources; see his *Gatha Sri Adi Granth*, p. 162. Balwant Singh Dhillon interprets the absence of the *var* as a conscious deletion from the text of MS 1245 in his "Myth of Early Draft of Adi Granth (MS 1245)," pp. 88–89. But there is a much simpler explanation. According to the table of contents, the *var* of Satta and Balvand should have fol-

lowed Guru Arjan's *var*, which finishes on folio 906. But the next four folios (907–910) are currently missing from the manuscript, with a new *rag* section duly beginning on folio 911. There is no doubt that the *var* of Satta and Balvand was originally present on the folios now lost. For other examples of missing folios, see n. 22.

The panegyrics by the Bhaṭs, however, are not available in their entirety. The last section of MS 1245 is in extremely preliminary shape, and only an incomplete set of the panegyrics appears on folios 1264–1267. For details, see Piar Singh, *Gatha Sri Adi Granth*, pp. 167–168.

8. Pashaura Singh, "An Early Sikh Scriptural Tradition: The Guru Nanak Dev University Manuscript 1245," p. 202, Piar Singh, *Gatha Sri Adi Granth*, p. 135, and Balwant Singh Dhillon, "Myth of Early Draft of Adi Granth (MS 1245)," pp. 95 and 98. Dhillon argues that the death dates of the first five gurus are recorded in the hand of the primary scribe in MS 1245 (folio 1255), and hence its date of origin has to be later. In my view this entry does not necessarily prove that the manuscript was compiled after Guru Arjan's death. I believe that this entry was recorded later and cannot be used in determining the date of this manuscript.

9. I have slightly modified the translation of the invocation found in John Stratton Hawley and Mark Juergensmeyer, *Songs of the Saints of India* (New York: Oxford University Press, 1988), p. 78.

10. The present structure of the *Japji* is a string of thirty-eight stanzas with one couplet each placed at the beginning and the end. The evolution of this structure is not entirely clear. Early Sikh literature refers to the tradition according to which Guru Angad "culled" the thirty-eight stanzas of the *Japji* from the corpus of Guru Nanak's hymns and then placed them in the present sequence; see *Janam-Sakhi Sri Guru Nanak Dev Ji*, vol. 2, pp. 249–250. The attribution of the two couplets and the time of their connection with the text of the *Japji* is not entirely clear. For debate on this issue, see Piar Singh, *Gatha Sri Adi Granth*, pp. 137–138; Pashaura Singh, "The Text and Meaning of the Adi Granth," pp. 100–103; and Joginder Singh, *Japji de Ṭike* (Jalandhar: Hindi Press, 1981), pp. 48–52.

11. With the exception of two undated manuscripts, the Bahoval Pothi presently at Bhai Vir Singh Sahitya Sadan, New Delhi, and a manuscript associated with Bhai Painda, which is no longer extant, the *rag* sequence of the Kartarpur Pothi is reproduced in all the later manuscripts I have examined. For basic information on these two manuscripts, see Piar Singh, *Gatha Sri Adi Granth*, pp. 120–134, and Giani Mahan Singh, "Bahoval vali Pothi Sahib" *Kheṛa* (March, 1980). I am grateful to Dr. Mohinder Singh, Director, Bhai Vir Singh Sahitya Sadan, for permitting me to photograph the Bahoval Pothi.

12. Sarupdas Bhalla, *Mahima Prakash*, p. 204.

13. For Hariji's writing, see Raijasbir Singh, *Guru Amardas: Srot Pustak*, pp. 196–201.

14. With the exception of S5, the stanzas 32–37 open with the following address: "O my tongue, O my body, S5: O my body, O my eyes, O my ears," respectively. The reasons for the introduction of S5 at this particular position are not at all clear. The peculiar placement of this stanza has not been addressed in the literature on the *Anand*.

15. The arrangement of the couplets in the text of the *vars* has not been addressed in any detail in Sikh literature, although it surfaces briefly in Sahib Singh, *Sri Guru Granth Sahib Darpaṇ*, vol. 1, pp. 534–535, and Piara Singh Padam, *Punjabi Sahitt di Ruprekha* (Patiala: Kalam Mandir, 1971), p. 170. Both scholars attribute the introduction of the couplets into the text of the *vars* of the gurus to Guru Arjan.

That this new version of the *vars* was preliminary explains the repetition of couplets at places in MS 1245; see Balwant Singh Dhillon, "Myth of Early Draft of Adi Granth (MS 1245)", pp. 102–104. This structure further evolved in the Kartarpur Pothi, as discussed in chapter 6.

16. Teja Singh, ed., *Shabadarth Sri Guru Granth Sahib Ji*, pp. vol. 1, 200, vol. 2, 396, 500, 618–625, vol. 3, 806, 807, 818, 819, 821, and vol. 4, 1137. See also Surjit Hans, *A Reconstruction of Sikh History from Sikh Literature*, pp. 140, 148, 158, and 170.

17. In addition to finishing the hymns (with the exception of numbers 1 and 20) mentioned in chapter 6, Guru Arjan composed only a dozen or so more hymns that are present in the Kartarpur Pothi. This small size of his poetic creation clearly suggests that the date of MS 1245 was fairly close to that of the Kartarpur Pothi itself.

18. Piar Singh, *Gatha Sri Adi Granth*, pp. 169 and 437–438.

19. For the two manuscripts that do not conform to Kartarpur Pothi, see n. 11. These manuscripts, which include the hymns of Guru Arjan, were certainly compiled after the Kartarpur Pothi. An explanation for the structural differences between them and the Kartarpur Pothi should be found, but the use of these manuscripts by Piar Singh to argue for a loose method of compilation of the early Sikh texts is not very convincing.

20. Balwant Singh Dhillon, "Myth of Early Draft of Adi Granth (MS 1245)," pp. 88 and 96–97.

21. Pashaura Singh, "An Early Sikh Scriptural Tradition: The Guru Nanak Dev University Manuscript 1245," pp. 206–207.

22. The text of MS 1245 contains fewer blank folios than those in the Kartarpur Pothi. These folios, however, as in the Goindval Pothis, appear toward the end of *rag* sections and also surface at the end of subsections within the large *rag* sections. A tentative list of the blank folios is as follows: 37, 118–120, 183–188, 223–225, 238, 246–253, 322, 329–339, 344, 356, 366–367, 454–455, 473–475, 491–492, 501, 520–521, 525–527, 560, 651, 653, 660, 669, 678, 695–696, 756–757, 763–764, 816, 841–843, 853, 864–866, 887–888, 909–910, 915, 920, 937, 946–948, 967, 1005, 1006, 1021–1024, 1095, 1133–1135, 1148, 1170, 1202, 1208, 1229–1231, and 1256, totaling 101.

A set of nine folios—156 (*rag* Majh), 255 (*rag* Gujri), 651 (*rag* Soraṭhi), 669 (*rag* Natnarain), 683 (*rag* Tilang), 907–910 (*rag* Ramkali)—are missing from the text. Folio 522 is bound at the very opening, and folio 670 appears in place of 666.

23. Guru Arjan's hymn in *rag* Basant—*Suṇi sakhi man japi piar. Ajamalu udharia ek bar*—appears as explicitly in MS 1245 (folio 1094) as in the Kartarpur Pothi (folio 853) and the Adi Granth, p. 1192.

24. The tension regarding these writings may be related to the growing Sikh awareness of their distinct communal identity. After all, the guru himself declared emphatically that he would not follow the traditions of the Turks and the Hindus: *Varat na rahau na maha ramdana* (M5, AG, 1136). This hymn by Guru Arjan elaborates on the verse of Kabir, *Pandit mulan chhaḍe dou* (AG, 1158).

25. For a discussion of this issue, see Pashaura Singh, "An Early Sikh Scriptural Tradition: The Guru Nanak Dev University Manuscript 1245," pp. 199–200.

26. Giani Gurdit Singh claims that he has never seen an early manuscript that lacks the hymns of the Bhagats; see his *Itihas Sri Guru Granth Sahib*, p. 467.

27. The Sodhi lineage is as follows: Dhirmal, Ram Chand, Paharmal, Bhopaji, Dhanpat, Gulab Singh (d. 1806), Sadhu Singh (d. 1861), Jawahar Singh (d. 1882), Naunihal Singh (d. 1929?), Amarjit Singh (d. 1998), and Karamjit Singh. Amarjit Singh died on November 4, 1998, and the *dastarbandi* of Karamjit Singh was performed on November 15, 1998. The information regarding the death of Amarjit Singh and the ascension of Karmjit Singh was given to my Bibi Kanwaljit Kaur Sodhi, the mother of the present guru. The custodian of the Sodhi *gaddi* is popularly addressed as Guru Sahib in the Kartarpur area.

28. Originally the fairs at the seat of this family took place on Vaisakhi and Divali, but at some later time the Divali fair was apparently moved to the birth anniversary of Guru Nanak (both come in the late fall). The earliest reference to the gatherings of the Sodhi followers appears in Sarup Singh Kaushish, *Guru Kian Sakhian*, p. 80.

29. Piar Singh, *Bhai Jodh Singh Gadd Saurabh*, pp. 424–425.

30. Cited in G. B. Singh, *Sri Guru Granth Sahib dian Prachin Biṛan*, pp. 106–107.

31. Giani Avtar Singh, the caretaker of the Kartarpur Pothi, explained to me that the minor damage to some folios of the text occurred when the pothi was placed in the waters of the river Beas. For other references to the same story, see John Clark Archer, "The Bible of the Sikhs," *Panjab Past and Present* 11: 1 (1977), pp. 22–31, and C. H. Loehlin, "Textual Criticism of Kartarpur Granth," in Juergensmeyer and Barrier, *Sikh Studies: Comparative Perspectives on a Changing Tradition*, p. 113.

32. G. B. Singh, *Sri Guru Granth Sahib dian Prachin Biṛan*, pp. 99–100. This view is supported by two other scholars, Gopal Singh, "Adi Granth te usda Prabhav Punjabi Boli te Sahitt te," in Surinder Singh Kohli, ed., *Punjabi Sahitt da Itihas, Bhag Pahila*, p. 292, and Pashaura Singh, "The Text and Meaning of the Adi Granth," p. 40.

33. G. B. Singh, *Sri Guru Granth Sahib dian Prachin Biṛan*, pp. 167–177. The earliest reference to this manuscript appears in Sarup Singh Kaushish, *Guru kian Sakhian*, p. 41. The manuscript has historically been kept at the Darbar Sahib Sri Guru Ramrai, Dehra Dun.

34. Piar Singh, *Bhai Jodh Singh Gadd Saurabh*, p. 428.

35. Chaupa Singh, *Rahit-nama*, p. 82; Kesar Singh Chhibbar, *Bansavlinama Dasan Patishahian ka*, p. 126; and Sarup Singh Kaushish, *Guru Kian Sakhian*, pp. 82–83.

36. See Ram Sukh Rao, *Sri Fateh Singh Partap Prabhakar*, p. 204. It seems Jassa Singh was instrumental in bringing the Sodhis closer to the mainstream Sikh community.

37. On the basis of a note in the Kartarpur Pothi itself, Bhai Kahn Singh Nabha reports that the original tax-free land granted to the Kartarpur *gaddi* in 1598 by the Mughal administration under Akbar included 8,946 acres; see his *Mahan Kosh*, p. 302. Given the time, this grant must have come to Guru Arjan. It is not clear to me whether the land granted to Dhirmal in 1643 exceeded this figure, or whether it was some sort of affirmation of the original grant. For Maharaja Ranjit Singh's association with the Sodhis, see Sohan Lal Suri, *Umda-ut-Tvarikh*, daftar II, trans. Amarvant Singh, ed. J. S. Grewal and Indu Banga (Amritsar: Guru Nanak Dev University, 1985), p. 70; *Umda-ut-Tvarikh*, daftar III, trans. V. S. Suri, pp. 105, 179, 183, 259, 315, 347, and 614; *Umda-ut-Tvarikh*, daftar IV, trans. V. S. Suri (Chandigarh: Punjab Itihas Prakashan, 1972), pp. 9–10.

In these references Suri reports the maharaja's visits to Kartarpur. In 1806 the maharaja bestowed official recognition on Sadhu Singh as the heir of Gulab Singh by declaring him to be "the rightful occupant of the temporal and spiritual seat (*piri te amiri di gaddi*) at Kartarpur." We have testimony that Maharaja sent expensive gifts to the Sodhis upon the birth of Sadhu Singh's son, Jawahar Singh, in 1835, and on a number of other occasions. At the time of Maharaja Ranjit Singh's death, Sadhu Singh was given the honor of tying the turban of authority onto the head of prince Kharak Singh. All this indicates the respect and honor with which the Sodhis of Kartarpur were regarded in the Sikh court at Lahore.

38. Pashaura Singh, "The Text and Meaning of the Adi Granth," pp. 82–83; Daljeet Singh, *Essay on the Authenticity of Kartarpuri Biṛ*, pp. 8–9; G. B. Singh, *Sri Guru Granth Sahib dian Prachin Biṛan*, pp. 250–251. G. B. Singh cites Santokh Singh to support his view that the pothi was brought to Lahore but does not read Santokh Singh carefully—in Santokh Singh's view, the pothi remained with the Sodhis as the maharaja did not take it away from them (*Kari kripa nahi lin su chhin*). For the Bauli Sahib *gurdwara*, see Iqbal Qaiser, *Historical Sikh Shrines in Pakistan* (Lahore: Punjabi History Board, 1998), p. 218.

39. *District and States Gazetteers of the Undivided Punjab*, vol. 3, p. 512; and Griffin and Massey, *Chiefs and Families of Note in the Punjab*, p. 167.

40. Nahar Singh, "Some Documents Regarding Sacred Sikh Relics in England," *Panjab Past and Present* 8: 2 (1974), pp. 304–315.

41. Christopher Shackle, *Catalogue of the Panjabi and Sindhi Manuscripts in the India Office Library* (London: India Office Library and Records, 1977), p. 8. A photocopy of this manuscript

is now available at the library of Bhai Vir Singh Sahitya Sadan, New Delhi. I am grateful to Dr. Mohinder Singh for arranging to make a photocopy of this document for my use.

42. Griffin and Massey, *Chiefs and Families of Note in the Punjab*, p. 167.

43. Gopal Singh, "Adi Granth te usda Prabhav Punjabi Boli te Sahitt te," p. 295. I examined this manuscript during my work at Moti Bagh in 1992. The colophon reads, "*Samat 1919 Chet sudi puran 15, sapuran granth ji likh pahunche*," which places the date of the manuscript at 1862.

44. Bhai Kahn Singh Nabha, *Mahan Kosh*, pp. 304 and 436–437.

45. The signed note dated May 16, 1957, reads: "The respected *biṛ* of Sri Guru Adi Granth Sahib Ji is preserved by Shri Basant Singh Rekhi, between October 10, 1956 to October 31, 1956, and from April 21, 1957 to May 16, 1957." Two copies of this signed note, one in Punjabi and the other in English, are pasted at the beginning and the end of the manuscript, respectively.

46. Only two scholars were permitted to view the pothi between 1960 and 1990. Daljeet Singh examined the Kartarpur Pothi briefly with the help of Kuldip Singh Virk of Jalandhar in the mid 1980s. As Virk told me, it was a very brief event, and they spent less than twenty minutes with the manuscript. In his *Essay on the Authenticity of Kartarpuri Bir*, Daljeet Singh essentially reproduces Bhai Jodh Singh's work. Pashaura Singh was the second scholar to examine the manuscript in 1990, for four hours. In his "Text and Meaning of the Adi Granth," he has registered some disagreement with Bhai Jodh Singh, particularly on the entry of the *chhant* in *rag* Ramkali. However, Pashaura Singh takes for granted the originality of the manuscript and did not see the need to address the issue of its dating or contents in any detail.

47. These eleven hymns are as follows:

1. *Tun samrathu sarni ko data . . . sukhrai* (*rag* Gujri, folio 392)
2. *Ṭhakur hoi api daial* (*rag* Devgandhari, folio 415)
3. *Apune satigur pahi binau kahia* (*rag* Devgandhari, folio 415)
4. *Anath nath prabh hamare* (*rag* Devgandhari, folio 415)
5. *Prabh ihai manorathu mera* (*rag* Devgandhari, folio 415)
6. *Tisu binu duja avaru na koi* (*rag* Suhi, folio 551)
7. *Darsan kau lochai sabhi koi* (*rag* Suhi, folio 551)
8. *Mu lalan siau priti bani* (*rag* Bilaval, folio 617)
9. *Prabh ko bhagati vachhalu birdiau* (*rag* Malar, folio 891)
10. *Hari ka namu dhiai kai hohu haria bhai* (*rag* Basant, folio 854)
11. *Raṇjhunjhaṛa gau sakhi hari ek dhiavahu* (*rag* Ramkali, folio 703)

With the exception of the opening verse of hymn 6, which appears in MS 1245 (folio 715), none of the other hymns are present there.

Between the writings of MS 1245 and the original inscription of the Kartarpur Pothi in 1604, Guru Arjan seems to have completed thirty-five hymns (discussed in the text) and composed two new ones in note 6 (1 and 11). Between 1604 and his death in 1606, he composed these eleven hymns.

48. For scholars who do not accept the Kartarpur Pothi as the document prepared during Guru Arjan's time, see Piar Singh, *Gatha Sri Adi Granth*, pp. 174–209, and *Gatha Sri Adi Granth and the Controversy*, pp. 75–115; Piara Singh Padam, *Sri Guru Granth Prakash*, p. 100; Sant Inder Singh Chakarvarti, "Sri Guru Granth Sahib dian Biṛan de Bhed," in Jeet Singh Sital, ed., *Gurmat Sahitt* (Patiala: Punjab Language Department, 1989), p. 212, Pritam Singh, "Bhai Banno Copy of the Sikh Scripture," *Journal of Sikh Studies* 11: 2 (1984), p. 99; Giani Gurdit Singh, "Adi Biṛ da Rachna Kal," *Prakash*, June 30, 1952; and G. B. Singh, *Sri Guru Granth Sahib dian Prachin Biṛan*, pp. 247–273.

49. Bhai Jodh Singh, *Sri Kartarpuri Biṛ de Darshan*, p. 45. For a facsimile of this folio, see Piar Singh, *Gatha Sri Adi Granth and the Controversy*, p. 90.

50. Cited in Piar Singh, *Gatha Sri Adi Granth*, p. 208.

51. Bhai Jodh Singh, *Sri Kartarpuri Biṛ de Darshan*, p. 4.

52. G. B. Singh, *Sri Guru Granth Sahib dian Prachin Biṛan*, p. 146; Randhir Singh, ed., *Guru Praṇalian* (Amritsar: Sikh Itihas Research Board, 1977), pp. 146-147.

53. Giani Gurdit Singh and Randhir Singh in *Punjabi Dunia* (Patiala: Punjab Language Department, May 1952).

54. Giani Mahan Singh, *Param Pavitar Adi Biṛ da Sankalna Kal*, pp. 5–35.

55. For details of blank folios, see the relevant entries in Bhai Jodh Singh, *Sri Kartarpuri Biṛ de Darshan*.

56. Bhai Jodh Singh, *Sri Kartarpuri Biṛ de Darshan*, p. haha.

57. This information appears in a letter written by Bhai Kahn Singh Nabha published in *Panth Sevak*, December 12, 1918. For the text of the letter, see Bhai Jodh Singh, *Sri Kartarpuri Biṛ de Darshan*, pp. uṛa–eṛa.

58. Bhai Jodh Singh, *Sri Kartarpuri Biṛ de Darshan*, p. iṛi.

59. Piar Singh, *Gatha Sri Adi Granth*, p. 452.

60. Bhai Jodh Singh, *Sri Kartarpuri Biṛ de Darshan*, p. 122.

61. Ibid., p. 4.

62. Pashaura Singh, "The Text and Meaning of the Adi Granth," pp. 36–37. It is not possible to accept Pashaura Singh's argument that this particular entry was inserted into the pothi after its original inscription, nor his view that someone tried to add the *Singhladip ki Shivnabh Raje ki Bidhi* to the pothi by entering it first in the table of contents.

63. See nn. 41 and 43.

64. In one of our conversations, Giani Gurdit Singh told me that Pandit Kartar Singh Dakha spoke to him about the rebinding of the pothi and removing some folios from it.

65. Bhai Jodh Singh, *Sri Kartarpur Biṛ de Darshan*, pp. 121–122.

66. See n. 48.

67. Piar Singh, ed., *Bhai Jodh Singh Gadd Saurabh*, pp. 412–496.

68. The SGPC has resolved in 1936 that the ceremonial reading of the Adi Granth should be deemed complete at the *Mundavaṇi* couplet of Guru Arjan; see Shamsher Singh Ashok, *Shiromani Gurdwara Prabandhak da Punjah Sala Itihas* (Amritsar: Sikh Itihas Research Board, 1982), p. 228. Later this position was revised and a provision was added to include the recitation of the *Ragmala*; see *Sikh Rahit Maryada*, p. 18.

69. The twenty-one compositions attributed to the gurus (three to Guru Nanak; four to Guru Amardas, and fourteen to Guru Arjan) which appear in the Goindval Pothis and MS 1245 but are absent from the Kartarpur Pothi and the later manuscripts are as follows:

THE GOINDVAL POTHIS

Kari lalach manu lobhaṇa kiau kari chhutiai ji (*rag* Suhi, *Mahala* 1, folios 31–33).

Alah ek qarimu qudrati sachu qadaru paqu (*rag* Tilang, *Mahala* 1, folio 184)

Kamu karodh maia madu miṭhe dal badal jiau uni virahe (*rag* Suhi, *Mahala* 3, folio 128)

MS 1245

Jina hari hirdai hari namu na bhaia (*rag* Asa, *Mahala* 1, folio 408)

Bharmi bhuli mere babola tu me sachu bujhai (*rag* Sri, *Mahala* 3, folios 102–104)

Khare khoṭe api kitianu gurmukhi sojhi pai (*rag* Asa, *Mahala* 3, folio 414)

Utamu jogu girahu hai jogi gurmati vicharai (*rag* Ramkali, *Mahala* 3, folio 852)

Sagale rogu miṭae merai satiguri oukhadu hari ka nam laia (*rag* Asa, *Mahala* 5, folio 398)

Satiguri purai kaḍhi mari (*rag* Asa, *Mahala* 5, folio 398)

Oni mili bhupati jai chaṛaia (*rag* Asa, *Mahala* 5, folios 398–399).

Ramdaspuri jab ae ta anand mangal sukh pae (*rag* Soraṭhi, *Mahala* 5, folio 635)

Santan ka sahibu sabh upari onu ko na pahuchanhara (*rag* Soraṭhi, *Mahala* 5, folio 635)

Nirmala sukh riti suami nirmala sukh riti (*rag* Tilang, *Mahala* 5, folio 684)

Karan kravanharu bidhata (*rag* Ramkali, *Mahala* 5, folio 839)

Ape dinau apiau (*rag* Ramkali, *Mahala* 5, folio 839)

Agam agochar gurmukhi dhiaia (*rag* Maru, *Mahala* 5, folio 1002

Hari ke charanu niti namaskaru (*rag* Kedara, *Mahala* 5, folio 1029)

Hari ke log sada guṇ gavahi (*rag* Bhairo, *Mahala* 5, folio 1065)

Saraṇi pare prabhu karaṇhar (*rag* Basant, *Mahala* 5, folios 1087–1088)

Prabh mere bedhe darasi tumari (*rag* Malar, *Mahala* 5, folio 1165)

Ram bina jete ras kite (*rag* Malar, *Mahala* 5, folio 1165)

For a complete text of these compositions, see my *Goindval Pothis: The Earliest Extant Source of the Sikh Canon*, pp. 100–102, and " The Making of Sikh Scripture" (Ph.D. diss., Columbia University, 1993), pp. 280–313.

70. This distinction between the Kartarpur Pothi and the Adi Granth is absent from Bhai Jodh Singh's angry critique of G. B. Singh's evaluation of the Kartarpur Pothi; see Piar Singh, ed., *Bhai Jodh Singh Gadd Saurabh*, pp. 415 and 486. The same situation is at the basis of Daljeet Singh's *Essay on the Authenticity of Kartarpuri Bir*. As the argument unfolds, Daljeet Singh's strong perception that scholars who question the authenticity of the pothi have ulterior motives of attacking the Sikh faith becomes amply clear.

Chapter 5

1. Sarupdas Bhalla, *Mahima Prakash*, pp. 372–373, and Kesar Singh Chhibbar, *Bansavlinama Dasan Patishahian ka*, pp. 126–127.

2. *Dekh prasan satigur bhaai sahi sahi likh din* (Sarupdas Bhalla, *Mahima Prakash*, p. 373).

3. *Sri Gurbilas Patishahi* 6, p. 89–90, and Santokh Singh, *Sri Gurpratap Suraj Granth*, vol. 6, pp. 2136–2140.

4. Tara Singh Narotam, *Gurmat Nirṇai Sagar* (Rawalpindi: Rai Bahadur Buta Singh, 1877), p. 355.

5. Giani Gian Singh, *Tvarikh Guru Khalsa*, vol. 1, p. 420.

6. Charan Singh, *Sri Guru Granth Baṇi Biaura*, pp. 3–4.

7. In the opening decades of the twentieth century, the debate around the Adi Granth was dominated by scholars who supported the *Ragmala* as part of the original text, and since the *Ragmala* was absent from this branch of manuscripts, no effort was made to incorporate them into the discussion. For a description of early manuscripts of this branch, see G. B. Singh, *Sri Guru Granth Sahib dian Prachin Biṛan*, pp. 108–121, and Piar Singh, *Gatha Sri Adi Granth*, pp. 442–445.

8. Sahib Singh, *Adi Biṛ bare*, pp. 127–147 and 155–159.

9. Pashaura Singh, "The Text and Meaning of the Adi Granth," pp. 68–78.

10. Piar Singh, *Gatha Sri Adi Granth*, pp. 439–447.

11. Ibid., pp. 475–489.

12. The manuscript prepared in 1610 was present in the Sikh Reference Library, Amritsar, until 1984. It was used extensively by Randhir Singh and others in their study of the variants in the seventeenth-century manuscripts; see Randhir Singh, et al., eds., *Sri Guru Granth Sahib dian Santha-Sainchian ate Puratan Haṭh Likhit Pavan Biṛan de Praspar Paṭh-Bhedan di Suchi*, p. 820. Reference to manuscripts prepared in 1605, 1637, 1640, and 1641 appear in colophons copied in later seventeenth-century manuscripts; see also Piar Singh, *Gatha Sri Adi Granth*, pp. 224, 227, and 256.

13. MS 21 is a rare manuscript that I stumbled on in Gurdwara Bal Lila, Maiṇi Sangat, Patna, which is under the control of Nirmala Akhaṛa, Kankhal. Structurally, this manuscript conforms to MS 1245, since the table of contents appears alongside each *rag* section. The hymns of the Bhagats are recorded separately and appended at the end. I was grateful to Mahant Giandev Singh for permitting me to photograph this important document.

For a discussion of manuscript number 14, see G. B. Singh, *Sri Guru Granth Sahib dian Prachin Biṛan*, pp. 304–305. This is an interesting manuscript with table of contents attached to some *rag* sections. The sequence of compositions in the final section is enigmatic and does not conform to either of the other two branches. I plan to write a separate essay describing these two documents in detail.

14. Pashaura Singh is the only scholar who claims to have found two undated copies of the Kartarpur Pothi; see his "The Text and Meaning of the Adi Granth," pp. 23 and 35–40. While registering the substantive differences between the Kartarpur Pothi and its supposed copies, he argues that these two documents were originally true copies of the Kartarpur Pothi but their contents were later expanded to conform them to the Kanpur Pothi.

15. Sahib Singh, *Adi Biṛ bare*, p. 155.

16. Harbhajan Singh, *Gurbaṇi Sampadan Nirṇai*, pp. 219–220.

17. Giani Gurdit Singh, *Itihas Sri Guru Granth Sahib*, p. 456, and Piar Singh, *Gatha Sri Adi Granth*, p. 1.

18. Sant Inder Singh Chakarvarti, "Sri Guru Granth Sahib dian Biṛan de Bhed," p. 212, and Pritam Singh, "Bhai Banno Copy of the Sikh Scripture," p. 99.

19. For the tradition of the maharaja's visit, see G. B. Singh, *Sri Guru Granth Sahib dian Prachin Biṛan*, pp. 108–109. The maharaja was in the area in 1813 and 1818, though it is not clear to me when he visited the Bhallas and bestowed upon the manuscript this large grant. See Sohan Lal Suri, *Umdat-ut-Tvarikh*, daftar II, pp. 173 and 286.

20. Charan Singh, *Sri Guru Granth Baṇi Biaura*, pp. 3–4, and Piar Singh, *Gatha Sri Adi Granth*, pp. 442–443.

21. The original text of the Amritsar Pothi ends with the colophon. The compositions that appear in the closing section of the Kartarpur Pothi were inscribed later in a different hand, and there is no reference to their presence in the table of contents.

22. As mentioned, above Guru Arjan's *var* in *rag* Basant is appended at the end of the Amritsar Pothi.

23. Piar Singh takes this as evidence for his contention that the Kartarpur Pothi and the Amritsar Pothis represented only two distinct lines among many others created at that time; see his *Gatha Sri Adi Granth*, pp. 442–43.

24. Bhai Jodh Singh, *Sri Kartarpuri Biṛ de Darshan*, pp. 97, 110, and 106.

25. Ibid., pp. 73, 82, and 83.

26. Pashaura Singh suggests that the absence of the reference to the tunes of the *vars* resulted from the Mughal pressure on the Sikhs; see his "The Text and Meaning of the Adi Granth," pp. 63–67. In his view the tunes were introduced by the gurus to infuse the Sikh community with the spirit of heroism, a feature not considered welcome by the Mughal ad-

ministration. In the Amritsar Pothi, references to the tunes do appear in the titles of five *vars*, and the argument that they were removed from the remaining four under external pressure is difficult to accept.

27. The differences in the structure of the table of contents in the two texts is clear. First, while in the Kartarpur Pothi the table of *rags* is in two sections, the Amritsar Pothi does not have the second section. Second, in the Kartarpur Pothi we see only the sporadic use of the invocation at the opening of a new segment; the Amritsar Pothi follows this format more consistently.

28. For example, the opening couplet of Guru Nanak's *Japji* later appears under Guru Arjan's name in his *Sukhmani*; the concluding couplet of Guru Nanak's *Japji* appears under Guru Angad's name in *Majh ki Var Mahala 1*; another couplet that appears under Guru Angad's name in *Majh ki Var Mahala 1* is attributed to Guru Nanak in *Shalok Sahaskriti*. For the continuation of these discrepancies in the manuscripts of branch 1, see MS 1084, folios 1 and 106; 18 and 65; and 66 and 431, respectively

29. G. B. Singh, *Sri Guru Granth Sahib dian Prachin Biṛan*, p. 111.

30. Piar Singh, *Gatha Sri Adi Granth*, p. 257.

31. The sequence of the compositions toward the end of MS 1229 corresponds completely with the Kartarpur Pothi.

32. I have come across only one later manuscript of this branch, dated 1705 and currently in the custody of Anurag Singh, E-462 Bhai Randhir Singh Nagar, Ludhiana; see Piar Singh, *Gatha Sri Adi Granth*, pp. 367–372. Pashaura Singh, however, claims that this tradition continued to enjoy popularity in some sections of the Panth right up to the beginning of the nineteenth century but refers only to a single manuscript of this branch "prepared in early nineteenth century:" see his "Text and Meaning of the Adi Granth," p. 67.

33. Giani Rajinder Singh Bal, *Bhai Banno Darpaṇ ate Khare vali Biṛ* (Jalandhar: Central Town, 1989), p. 27.

34. Sardar Nahar Singh, "Some Documents regarding Sacred Sikh Relics in England," p. 306.

35. Pritam Singh, "Bhai Banno's Copy of the Sikh Scripture," p. 100.

36. Bhai Gurdas, *Varan*, pp. 136–142, and Fauja Singh, *Guru Amardas: Life and Teaching*, pp. 125–126.

37. Bhai Jodh Singh, *Sri Kartarpuri Biṛ de Darshan*, pp. 45 and 86; Pritam Singh, "Bhai Banno's Copy of the Sikh Scripture," p. 102. There may even be a tradition of a two-volume Sikh text. The Central Sikh Museum, Amritsar, holds a manuscript that begins with *rag* Suhi and includes the second half of the Kartarpur Pothi; see *Album Central Sikh Museum, rev. ed.* (Amritsar: Shiromani Gurdwara Prabandhak Committee, 1996), p. 100.

38. Sahib Singh, *Adi Biṛ bare*, pp. 153–159. See also Davinder Singh Vidayarthi, "Guru Nanak Dev te Kacchi baṇi di Samasaya," in Pritam Singh, ed., *Pahili Patishahi, Sri Guru Nanak Dev* (Ludhiana: Punjabi Sahitt Academy, 1969), pp. 315–326.

39. Bhai Jodh Singh, *Sri Kartarpuri Biṛ de Darshan*, pp. 83, 97, and 113.

40. Pashaura Singh, "The Text and Meaning of the Adi Granth," p. 74, 137–38. See also Giani Badan Singh, *Adi Sri Guru Granth Sahib Ji Saṭik*, vol 3, p. 1906, and Teja Singh, ed., *Shabadarth Sri Guru Granth Sahib Ji*, vol. 3, p. 927.

41. G. B. Singh refers to a manuscript extant until the time of the partition in village Vasu, in the vicinity of Khara Mangat, which included the hymns of Surdas; see his *Sri Guru Granth Sahib dian Prachin Biṛan*, pp. 154–160. Prepared in the same geographical area, in all likelihood it was a copy of the Kanpur Pothi.

42. Sarup Singh Koushish, *Guru kian Sakhian*, p. 41; see G. B. Singh, *Sri Guru Granth Sahib dian Prachin Biṛan*, pp. 167–177. I am very grateful to Mahant Indreshcharandas for his warm hospitality during my visits to the dehra in 1997 and 1999.

43. A note in MS 1192 reads, *Ih darshan naven patashah ji di hazuri vich hazar ho ke prapat kite gae Samat 1731 bikrami punia Jeṭhe di samet sangat de.* Both the Amritsar Pothi and MS 115338, two early manuscripts of branch 1, contain the invocations recorded in the hand of the gurus.

44. Chaupa Singh, *Rahit-nama*, p. 82. See also Sarup Singh Kaushish, *Guru kian Sakhian*, pp. 82–83.

45. Kesar Singh Chhibbar, *Bansavlinama Dasan Patishahian ka*, pp. 126–127.

46. Giani Gian Singh, *Tvarikh Guru Khalsa*, vol. 1, pp. 1084–1085. During his stay at Damdama, Bhatinda, Guru Gobind Singh seems to have initiated the compilation of manuscripts of Sikh literature, including that of the Adi Granth. In later sources, the activity of refurbishing the lost literature in the battle at Anandpur seems to have become confused with the original making of the Adi Granth at this time.

47. For the earliest manuscripts of the Adi Granth, see Harbhajan Singh, *Gurbaṇi Sampadan Nirṇai*, pp. 95–96 and 219; and Swami Harnamdas Udasi, *Adi Shri Guru Granth Sahib dian Puratani Biṛan te Vichar*, vol. 2, p. 76. Piar Singh refers to two other manuscripts of the Adi Granth prepared in this period; see his "Giani Gurdit Singh Ji di Khuli Chiṭhi da Khula Javab," *Punjabi Tribune*, Feb. 14, 1993. See also Khushwant Singh, *A History of the Sikhs*, vol. 1 (Princeton: Princeton University Press, 1984), p. 93.

48. G. B. Singh, *Sri Guru Granth Sahib dian Prachin Biṛan*, pp. 76 and 215–234.

49. MS 1192 was acquired by the Panjab University from the Chawla brothers of Amritsar in the mid 1960s.

50. Piar Singh has completely missed the importance of this manuscript; see his *Gatha Sri Adi Granth*, pp. 305–308.

51. This situation is very different from Patna, where the seventeenth-century manuscripts continued to be copied and are available in large numbers in the local archives.

Chapter 6

1. Charan Singh, *Sri Guru Granth Baṇi Biaura.*

2. Mohinder Kaur Gill, *Guru Granth Sahib di Sampadan Kala* (Delhi: Rabi Prakashan, 1974), and Joginder Singh Talwaṛa, *Baṇi Biaura, Bhag 1* (Amritsar: Singh Brothers, 1992).

3. See W. H. McLeod, *The Evolution of the Sikh Community*, pp. 70–74; W. Owen Cole and Piara Singh Sambhi, *The Sikhs: Their Religious Beliefs and Practices*, pp. 212–217, Harbhajan Singh, *Gurbaṇi Sampadan Nirṇai*, pp. 40–80; Piara Singh Padam, *Sri Guru Granth Prakash*, pp. 266–322; and Sahib Singh, *Sri Guru Granth Sahib Darpaṇ*, vol. 1, pp. 7–19.

4. It seems very hard for scholars to come out of the traditional mindset of attributing the organization of Sikh scripture exclusively to Guru Arjan; see Surinder Singh Kohli, *Sikhism and Guru Granth Sahib* (Delhi: National Book Shop, 1990), pp. 101–112, and Pashaura Singh, "The Text and Meaning of the Adi Granth," pp. 17–18.

5. Pritam Singh, "Keertana and the Sikhs," *Journal of Sikh Studies* 3:2 (1976), pp. 182–183. Pritam Singh offers fifteen references to establish the importance of *kirtan* in the Adi Granth, but with the exception of one verse of Guru Amardas appearing in *rag* Basant, all others are from the hymns of Guru Arjan. These appear in the Adi Granth, pp. 178, 213, 289, 297, 624, 747, 818, 867, 926, 962, 979, 1000, and 1085. For more references, see pp. 827, 893, and 1357.

6. In the stories recorded in the janam-sakhi literature, Guru Nanak used *kirtan* as a medium to convey the divine message and make people change their worldly ways. Mardana plays on a rebec while Guru Nanak sings. For some typical stories, see Kirpal Singh, ed., *Janam-Sakhi Prampra*, pp. 27–28, 41, 43, and 63.

7. See W. H. McLeod, *Historical Dictionary of Sikhism*, p. 48 and 135.

8. Bhai Gurdas, *Varan*, 11: 16, p. 137, 11: 18, p. 138, and 1: 27, p. 70.

9. See Harold Coward, *Sacred Word and Sacred Text* (New York: Orbis Books, 1988), p. 134. Coward writes: "The written word fulfills the same function as that of the musical score in relation to the performed music. Just as the written music has no value until it is performed, the written text of the Adi Granth has spiritual power only as it is sung."

10. This understanding can be achieved by reflecting on the words of the guru (*Sikhi sikhia gur vichari*, M1, AG, 465), which in itself is a sign of divine grace (*Baṇi biralau bicharsi je ko gurmukhi hoe*, M1, AG, 935). In his *Japji*, Guru Nanak presents the realm of knowledge (*gian khanḍ*) as the foundation for any spiritual progress. He is emphatic that only a seeker of truth is saved (*Khoji upajai*, M1, AG, 1255), and his conception of this search is not purely mystical but includes a strong dimension of rational understanding (*akal*). Guru Nanak writes:

> *Akali eh na akhiai akali gavaiai badi.*
> *Akali sahibu seviai akali paiai manu.*
> *Akali paṛi kai bijhiai akali kichai danu.*
> *Nanaku akhai rahu ehu hori galan saitanu.* (M1, AG, 1245)

11. O. C. Gangoly, *Ragas and Raginis* (Bombay: Nalanda Publications, 1935), pp. 96–104.

12. For official *maryada* of the Darbar Sahib, see *World Sikh Meet–1995* (Amritsar: Shiromani Gurdwara Prabandhak Committee, 1995), pp. 23–24.

13. The following are the direct references to *rags* appearing in the hymns of Guru Amardas in the Adi Granth:

Raga vichi Sri ragu hai je sachi dhare piaru.

Sada hari sachu mani vasai nihchal mati aparu. (AG, 83)

Gauṛi ragi sulakhaṇi je khasmai chiti karae.

Bhaṇai chalai satiguru kai aisa sigaru karae. (AG, 311)

Gujri jati gavari ja sahu pae apaṇa.

Gur kai sabadi vichari andinu hari japu japaṇa. (AG, 516)

Sabad rate Vaḍhans hai sachu nami urdhari.

Sachu sangarhahe sad sachi rahahe sachai nami piari. (AG, 585)

Suhavie nimaṇie so sahu sada samali.

Nanak janamu savarahe apaṇa kulu bhi chhuti nali. (AG, 785)

Bilavalu taba hi kijiae jabu mukhi hove namu.

Rag nad sabadi sohaṇe ja lagai sahaji dhianu. (AG, 849)

Bilaval karihu tum piariho ekasu siu liva lae. . . .

Sada bilaval anandu hai je chalahi satiguru bhae. (AG, 849)

Ramkali ramu mani vasia ta bania sigara.

Gura kai sabadi kamalu bigasia ta saupia bhagati bhandaru. (AG, 950)

Kedara raga vichi jaṇiai bhai sabade kare piaru.

Sata sangati siau milado rahai sache dhare piaru. (AG, 1087)

Tina Basantu jo hari guṇ gae. Pure bhaga hari bhagati karae.

Isa mana kau Basant ki lagai na soi. Ihu manu jalia dujai doi. (AG, 1176)

Malaru sital ragu hai hari dhiaiai santi hohi. (AG, 1283)

Dhanasri dhanvanti janiai bhai jan satigur ki kar kamae. (AG, 1419)

14. Parashuram Chaturvedi, *Kabir Sahitya ki Parakh* (Allahabad: Bharati Bhandar, 1964), pp. 280–290, and John Stratton Hawley, "The Music in Faith and Morality," *Journal of American Academy of Religions* 52: 2 (1984), pp. 243–262.

15. Winand M. Callewaert and Mukund Lath, eds., *The Hindi Padavali of Namdev* (Delhi: Motilal Banarsidass, 1989), pp. 58–60.

16. O. C. Gangoly, *Ragas and Raginis*, p. 26, and Swami Prajnanananda, *A Historical Study of Indian Music* (Delhi: Munshiram Manoharlal, 1981), pp. 13–14.

17. Winand M. Callewaert and Mukund Lath, eds., *The Hindi Padavali of Namdev*, p. 55.

18. Gopal Narayan Bahura, ed., *The Padas of Surdas* (Jaipur: Maharaja Sawai Man Singh II Museum Trust, 1982). The latter part of the manuscript contains the following *rag* sections: Bilaval (folios 111–122), Asavari (folios 122–127), Dhanasri (folios 127–140), Gujri (folios 140–144), Gauṛi (folios 144– 152), Kalayan (folios 152–154), Kanaṛa (folios 154–158), and Kedara with one hymn in *rag* Malar at the beginning and two at the end (folios 158–163). For reference to the *Panchavaṇi* manuscripts, see Karine Schomer, "Kabir in Guru Granth Sahib," in Mark Juergensmeyer and N. Gerald Barrier, eds., *Sikh Studies: Comparative Perspectives on a Changing Tradition*, p. 76. Schomer traces the origin of these manuscripts to the last quarter of the sixteenth century. See also W. M. Callewaert and Mukund Lath, eds., *The Hindi Padavali of Namdev*, pp. 99–101; W. M. Callewaert and Bart Op de Beeck, eds., *Devotional Hindi Literature* (New Delhi: Manohar, 1991), vol. 1, pp. 201–270 (with the exception of pages 481–487 and 547–584, the *rag* assignments are not mentioned in this text).

19. This distinction appeared for the first time in Narada's *Sangita-makaranda* (eleventh century) and became popular during medieval times; see O. C. Gangoly, *Ragas and Raginis*, pp. 21–23.

20. Narada's *Sangit-makaranda* is the first written source that refers to an elaborate system of associating *rags* with seasons and times of day. This system achieved a great degree of popularity in north India. There were alternative schemes of relations between different *rags* and times; see O. C. Gangoly, *Ragas and Raginis*, pp. 80–87. Gangoly refers to several sources dealing with this issue: *Sangit-makaranda*, *Sangit-ratnakara*, *Raga-tarangani* (fourteenth century), and Pundarika Vitthal's *Ragmala* and *Sad-raga-chandrodaya* (sixteenth century).

21. Other titles in the Goindval Pothis that indicate this distinction are the following: *Suhi Guru Babe di*, *Prabhati Babe di*, *Dhanasri Babe di*, *Ramkali Kabire ki*, and *Soraṭhi Babe Patishahu ki* (feminine forms); and *Basant Babe Patishahu da*, *Bhairo Guru Babe da*, *Maru Babe Patishahu ka*, *Tilang Guru Babe da bolaṇa*, *Malar Babe Patishahu da* (masculine forms). The word *ragini* is not used by the gurus and appears only once in the main body of the Adi Granth, 654, in a verse of Kabir in *rag* Soraṭhi: *Rag ragini ḍimbh hoe beṭha uni hari pahi kia lina.*

22. In the interest of separating *rags* from *raginis*, I have altered the sequence of *rags* of this pothi from that given in the *Tvarikh Guru Khalsa*: Sri, Asa, Gauṛi, Vaḍhans. It is difficult to say whether the pothi seen by Giani Gian Singh actually had the arrangement outlined in his account or whether his editors conformed the sequence to that available in the Adi Granth. The original manuscript of Giani Gian Singh's text might shed light on this point. I examined one such manuscript in Moti Bagh, Patiala, in January 1990, but because I did not yet know of this complication, I could not clarify it.

23. There are two exceptions to this layout of the *rags* in the Goindval Pothis. Guru Nanak also composed hymns in *rag* Tilang, which does not fit into this pairing of the *rags* and *raginis*. It includes a small set of hymns originally written on the last folios of the Goindval Pothi at Jalandhar and seems not to have been a part of the larger design of the Goindval Pothis. In my view, *rag* Tilang was also a favorite *rag* of Sufi poets, and hymns in this *rag* were appended in

the pothi beginning with *rag* Suhi. In addition, the pothi that Giani Gian Singh examined contained the section on *rag* Kanṛa which does not fit into our neat scheme. Like the brief section on *rag* Tilang, the section on *rag* Kanṛa included a single hymn of Namdev. Neither Guru Nanak nor Guru Amardas composed in this *rag*.

24. For a summary of his observations, see O. C. Gangoly, *Ragas and Raginis*, pp. 86–87.

25. With the exception of *rag* Soraṭhi, *rag* Vaḍhans, and *rag* Majh, which should have been in the Goindval Pothis and do not appear in Vitthal's scheme (see O. C. Gangoly, *Ragas and Raginis*, pp. 86–87), *rag* time relationship accounts for the groupings of other *rags* in these pothis.

26. O. C. Gangoly, *Ragas and Raginis*, p. 91.

27. Taran Singh, *Sri Guru Granth Sahib ji da Sahitak Itihas* (Amritsar: Fakir Singh and Sons, 1963?), pp. 76–77. See also his "Sri Guru Granth Sahib vich Kavita te Rag da Sambandh," in M. S. *Randhawa Abhinandan Granth*, pp. 68–71. Taran Singh believes that the metaphor of the bride dressed in red preparing to meet her lord, which is a common Sufi image, resulted in the Sufi affection for *rag* Suhi.

28. Teja Singh, ed., *Shabadarth Sri Guru Granth Sahib Ji*, vol. 3, p. 876.

29. Ibid., vol. 1, p. 14; Charan Singh, *Sri Guru Granth Baṇi Biaura*, pp. 21–22.

30. Surinder Singh Kohli, *A Critical Study of Adi Granth*, p. 112.

31. Pritam Singh, "Keertana and the Sikhs," pp. 182–183.

32. Pashaura Singh, "The Text and Meaning of the Adi Granth," pp. 197–198.

33. Jasbir Singh Sabar, "Gurbaṇi Sangit Sanketan te Sirlekhan da Gurmat Sangit vich Mahattav" (unpublished paper presented at Patiala: Punjabi University, summer 1991).

34. I have examined these folios in the Kartarpur Pothi myself; see also Bhai Jodh Singh, *Sri Kartarpuri Biṛ de Darshan*, pp. 45 and 87. Pritam Singh does not give the precise location of the decorated folio but mentions its presence "in the center;" see his "Bhai Banno Copy of the Sikh Scripture," p. 102.

35. Bhai Jodh Singh reproduces this entry without any comment on its significance; see his *Sri Kartarpuri Biṛ de Darshan*, p. 4. It needs to be pointed out that in this entry *rag* Natnarain is recorded as Nat, and *rag* Prabhati is noted as Bibhas-Prabhati. For a facsimile of this folio, see Piar Singh, *Gatha Sri Adi Granth and the Controversy*, p. 95.

36. Pritam Singh, "Keertana and the Sikhs," p. 182.

37. Having failed to work out the relationship of *rags* in these eight groups with seasons or times of the day, I attempted to analyze them on the basis of the *sur guru* (the primary tone), taking the technical information from Charan Singh's *Sri Guru Granth Baṇi Biaura*, pp. 51–81. The eight groups mentioned in the entry translate in terms of the primary tone as follows: (1) kharaj, (2) dhevat, (3) nikhadh, (4) kharaj, (5) pancham, (6) kharaj, (7) dhevat, (8) kharaj/nikhadh. Raja Mrigendra Singh, a prominent scholar and musician, was not convinced that the *sur guru* was the rationale behind the grouping of these *rags*, but he himself could not come up with a more appropriate explanation for this eightfold division of *rags* of the Kartarpur Pothi.

38. Frederic Pincott, "The Arrangement of the Hymns of the Adi Granth," *Journal of Royal Asiatic Society* 18 (1878), p. 440.

39. A few late-seventeenth-century manuscripts have come to my notice in which *rag* Jaijavanti appears between *rag* Jaitsri and *rag* Toḍi in some cases, and between *rag* Soraṭhi and *rag* Dhanasri in others.

40. Mohinder Kaur Gill *Guru Granth Sahib di Sampadan Kala* contains the most comprehensive analysis of this issue.

41. See relevant entries in Bhai Jodh Singh, *Sri Kartarpuri Biṛ de Darshan*, pp. 7–42.

42. The problems remain and at points all the hymns by one author still do not constitute a single group. For example, in the section on *rag* Maru in the Kartarpur Pothi (folios 809–810), sixteen hymns of the Bhagats appear as follows: Kabir (1–10), Namdev (11), Kabir (12), Jaidev (13), Kabir (14), and Ravidas (15–16). This sequence continues in the Adi Granth, folios 1105–1106.

43. To my knowledge, MS 1084 is the earliest manuscript containing a table of contents with the opening verse of each hymn of the Bhagats duly recorded in it.

44. For the workings of this system, see my *Goindval Pothis: The Earliest Extant Source of the Sikh Canon*, pp. 54–57.

45. This double refrain appears in *rag* Ramkali in the hymn that begins *Jit dari vasahi kavanu daru kahie* (folio 3). There is no authoritative answer as to how to deal with hymns with more than one refrain; each individual singer seems to choose one of these to begin his singing.

46. Mohinder Kaur Gill, *Guru Granth Sahib di Sampadan Kala*, pp. 96–102.

47. This usage is common among the Rajasthani manuscripts; see Gopal Narayan Bahurda, ed., *The Padas of Surdas*, pp. 176–177.

48. In the Kartarpur Pothi, there are more elaborate titles for some hymns. For example, the titles *Kuchaji* and *Suchaji* assigned to two hymns by Guru Nanak in *rag* Suhi (AG, 762) do not appear in the text of the Goindval Pothis.

49. For an earlier version of Guru Nanak's *var* in *rag* Malar, and *rag* Majh, see *Janam-Sakhi Sri Guru Nanak Dev Ji*, vol. 2, pp. 486–507. For other contemporary examples in this genre, see the *var* of Satta and Balvand (AG, pp. 966–968), Bhai Gurdas, *Varan*, and Piara Singh Padam, ed., *Punjabi Varan* (Patiala: Kalam Mandir, 1980). Why Guru Arjan decided to do this is not clear. For a discussion of this issue in relation to MS 1245, see chapter 4.

50. See Bhai Jodh Singh's *Sri Kartarpuri Biṛ de Darshan*, pp. 62, 73, 76, 78, 80, 83, 105, and 115.

51. For a brief discussion, see Piara Singh Padam, *Sri Guru Granth Prakash*, pp. 210–212.

52. Nirmala scholars immersed in Sanskrit learning regarded the Adi Granth as the fifth Veda but never took any interest in analyzing its structural affinity with that of the Veda.

53. Frederic Pincott, "The Arrangement of the Hymns of the Adi Granth," p. 439.

54. For the text of the Veda, see Barend A. van Nooten and Gary B. Holland, eds., *Rig Veda*, Harvard Oriental Series (Cambridge: Harvard University Press, 1994).

55. For Islamic bookmaking, see Gulnar K. Bosch, John Carswell, and Guy Petherbridge, *Islamic Bindings and Book Making* (Chicago: Oriental Institute, University of Chicago, 1981), pp. 45–47, and Jeremiah P. Losty, *The Art of the Book in India* (London: British Library, 1982).

56. An examination of *The Padas of Surdas* does not indicate any inclination on the part of the scribe to embellish the text or decorate the margins. Among the Hindus, folios tended to be collected and pressed together between two pieces of cardboard or wood. This type of binding can be seen even today in the making of account books (*vahis*).

57. I have borrowed this interpretation from Teja Singh. See Pritam Singh, ed., *Sikh Concept of the Divine*, p. 21. See also chapter 3, n. 20.

58. Bhai Gurdas, *Varan*, 23: 19, p. 209.

Chapter 7

1. For some of the studies on these saints, see Charlotte Vaudeville, *A Weaver Named Kabir* (Delhi: Oxford University Press, 1993); Nirmal Dass, *Songs of Kabir from the Adi Granth* (Albany: State University of New York Press, 1992); and Parashuram Chaturvedi, *Kabir Sahitya ki Parakh*, p. 315; Winand M. Callewaert and Mukund Lath, eds., *The Hindi Padavali of Namdev* pp. 315–316; Nirbhai Singh, *Bhagat Namadeva in the Guru Grantha* (Patiala: Punjabi University, 1981); Bhagirath Mishra, ed., *Sant Namdev ki Hindi Padavali* (Pune: Pune University, 1964); Winand M. Callewaert and Peter G. Friedlander, *The Life and Works of Raidas* (New Delhi: Manohar, 1992); and Darshan Singh, *A Study of Bhakta Ravidasa* (Patiala: Punjabi University, 1981).

2. See Giani Gurdit Singh, *Itihas Sri Guru Granth Sahib*, Pashaura Singh, "Sikh Self-Definition and the Bhagat Baṇi" (M. A. diss., University of Calgary, 1987); Sahib Singh, *Bhagat Baṇi Saṭik*

(Amritsar: Singh Brothers, 1974); Bhai Jodh Singh, *Bhagat Baṇi Saṭik* (Ludhiana: Lahore Book Shop, 1957); and Tara Singh Narotam, *Bhagat Baṇi Saṭik* (Lahore: Munshi Gulab Singh, 1907).

3. The relevant verses read:

Iha sabh sant mo pe the ae. Ham sabhan suna tum granth banae.
Hamari baṇi taha likhije. Nikat asan ham ko bhi dije. . . .
Sabh santan baṇi granth likhai. Jese khat par pare gavahi. (Sarupdas Bhalla, *Mahima Prakash*, p. 371)

4. *Sikhan di Bhagatmala*, pp. 122–123.

5. See *Sri Gurbilas Patishahi* 6, ed. Inder Singh Gill, p. 76; Santokh Singh, *Sri Gurpratap Suraj Granth*, vol. 6, pp. 2085–2095, and Giani Gian Singh, *Tvarikh Guru Khalsa*, vol. 1, p. 419.

6. Tara Singh Narotam, *Bhagat Baṇi Saṭik*, pp. 1–3.

7. *Namdev sang Sadhna Seṇ avar Trilochaṇ sant.*
Pipa Jaidev Dhanna bhagat Beṇi sant anant.
Parmanand aur Mirabai. Bhikhan Surdas sukhdai.
Kamal Araf Shaikh Farid. Tum dekhe sabh did-b-did. (Sarupdas Bhalla, *Mahima Prakash*, p. 371)

There is some justification for including the name of Mirabai in this list, since one of her hymns was originally inscribed in the Kartarpur Pothi. The identity of Araf and Kamal is not available.

8. *Saman Musan aur Jamal. Maskan charo bhae nihal. . . .*
Sabhi bhagat dekhe Gurdas. Tabh maya man bhai udas. (*Sri Gurbilas Patishahi* 6, p. 76)

The impression given in this narrative is that the hymns of these four were also included in Sikh scripture. For reference to Saman, Musan, Jamal, and Patang (not Maskan), see a note in the *Chaubole* of Guru Arjan in Teja Singh, ed., *Shabadarth Sri Guru Granth Sahib Ji*, vol. 4, p. 1363. These individuals were apparently members of the early Sikh community.

9. Teja Singh, ed., *Shabadarth Sri Guru Granth Sahib Ji*, vol. 1, pp. 83; vol. 2, 729; vol. 3, 1088; vol. 4, 1379, 1384, and 1411; and Sahib Singh, *Adi Biṛ bare*, pp. 93–108. Although published in 1970, the articles in *Adi Biṛ bare* appeared in the late 1940s and had been part of the debate since then.

10. Sahib Singh, *Adi Biṛ bare*, pp. 93–108.

11. Sahib Singh, *Sri Guru Granth Sahib Darpaṇ*, vol. 3, pp. 841–916.

12. For the recognition assigned to their argument, see Harbhajan Singh, *Gurbaṇi Sampadan Nirṇai*, pp. 22–40, Piara Singh Padam, *Sri Guru Granth Prakash*, pp. 41–53, and Pashaura Singh, "Sikh Self-Definition and the Bhagat Baṇi."

13. Mohan Singh Dewana, *A History of Punjabi Literature* (Jalandhar: Bharat Prakashan, 1971), pp. 37 and 46, and G. B. Singh, *Sri Guru Granth Sahib dian Prachin Biṛan*, p. 24.

14. Giani Gurdit Singh, *Itihas Sri Guru Granth Sahib*, pp. 481–482; Balbir Singh Dil, *Amar Kavi Guru Amardas* (Patiala: Punjab Language Department, 1975), p. 53.

15. For the Guru Harsahai Pothi, see chapter 3.

16. See chapter 6. There is further textual complexity related to couplet numbered 113 at the heart of this discussion. It reads as follows:

Dati sahib sandia kia chalai tisu nali.
Iki jagande na lahani ikna sutia dae uthal.

This couplet is attributed to Guru Nanak on the basis of its appearance in *Sri Rag ki Var Mahala* (AG, 83). In the Kartarpur Pothi (folio 116), however, this couplet does not appear in the original text of the *var* but is later added in the margin. The text originally recorded is covered with yellow paste but is readable. It is not clear whether the authorship of Guru Nanak refers to the original couplet or to the one recorded in the margin. The text of the original couplet reads as follows:

Gur binu gianu dharam binu dhianu.
Sach binu sakhi na mulo na baki. (folio 94)

In another early manuscript of the *vars* presently in the custody of Piara Singh Padam, the following appears in place of this couplet:

Akhar Nanak akhio api. Lahe bharati hovai jise dati. (folio 79)

17. Ernest Trumpp, *The Adi Granth or the Holy Scripture of the Sikhs*, p. cxxv.

18. W. H. McLeod, "Guru Nanak and Kabir," *Proceedings of Punjab History Conference* (Patiala: Punjabi University, 1966), pp. 90–92.

19. Some Sikh scholars have been extremely uncomfortable with Sahib Singh's view that Guru Nanak borrowed his words and ideas from other Bhagats. For a denunciation of this position, see Gurdit Singh, *Itihas Sri Guru Granth Sahib*, pp. 479–481.

20. For instance, over one hundred couplets of Farid which do not appear in the Adi Granth are available in early manuscripts; see Piara Singh Padam, *Sufi Kavidhara* (Patiala: Kalam Mandir, 1993), pp. 73–84. Did Guru Nanak have access to these but reject them for entry into the Sikh sacred text or did he not know them? Such issues are not addressed at all.

The link, if any, between Teja Singh Bhasoṛ's efforts to delete the bhagat baṇi from the Adi Granth and Sahib Singh and Teja Singh's efforts to locate its arrival at the very origin of Sikh tradition is not clear to me. For the Bhasoṛ's debate, see N. Gerald Barrier, "Sikh Politics and Religion: The Bhasaur Singh Sabha," in Indu Banga, ed., *Five Punjabi Centuries* (New Delhi: Manohar, 1997), pp. 140–156, and Shamsher Singh Ashok, *Shiromani Gurdwara Prabandhak Committee da Punjah Sala Itihas*, pp. 53–54 and 58.

21. The following are some instances of this engagement:

Farida kali jini na ravia dhauli ravai koe.
Kari sain siau pirhari rangu navela hoe. (AG, 1378)

To this couplet Guru Amardas responded:

Farida kali dhauli sahibu sada hai je ko chiti kare.
Apaṇa laia piramu na lagai je lochai sabhu koe. (AG, 1378)

This response is quite pointed and addressed directly to Farid. Two other instances of the same type of response by Guru Amardas to the couplets of Farid may also be noted (AG, 1380 and 1383).

In the hymns of Guru Amardas, we also find responses to Kabir's ideas. A characteristic example appears in connection with two couplets of Kabir which are included in the *Ramkali ki Var Mahala 3*:

Kabir mahidi kari kai ghalia apu pisae pisae.
Tai sah bat na puchhiai kabahu na lai pae. (AG, 947)

Guru Amardas's reply reads:

Nanak maidi kari kai rakhia so sahu nadari karae.
Ape pisai ape ghasai ape hi lai lae.
Ihu piram piala khasam ka jai bhave tai dae. (AG, 947)

22. Guru Amardas's response to the hymns of earlier writings is not restricted to those of the saints only but includes the hymns of Guru Nanak as well. One of Guru Nanak's hymns in *rag* Dhanasri begins:

Kiau simri sivria nahi jae. Tapai hiau jiara bilalae.
Siraji savare sacha soe. Tisu visriai changa kiau hoe. (AG, 661)

Guru Amardas composed a reply and recorded it next to Guru Nanak's hymn in the Goindval Pothis (folios 122–123), breaking the rule of subsectioning based on authorship:

Nadari kare ta simria jae. Atama dravai rahai liv lae.
Atama partama eko karai. Antr ki dubidha antri mare. (AG, 661)

The hymn is assigned to Guru Nanak in the printed edition (AG, 661), but the early manuscripts leave no doubt that it belongs to Guru Amardas.

For later gurus' responses to the hymns of the Bhagats, see Guru Ramdas's hymn in *rag* Suhi—*Nich jati hari japatia utam padavi pae* (M4, AG, 733)—and Guru Arjan's in *rag* Asa: *Gobind Gobind Gobind sangi Namdeu manu liṇa* (M5, AG, 487). One example, in fact, involves a couplet by Kabir with a comment by Guru Amardas, to which another comment by Guru Arjan is appended:

Kabir jo mai chitavau na karai kia mere chitave hoe.
Apana chitvia hari karai jo mere chiti na hoe. (AG, 1376)

Guru Amardas's response is as follows:

Chinta bhi api karaisi achintu bhi ape dae.
Nanak so salahiai ji sabhana sar karae. (AG, 1376)

To this Guru Arjan added the following:

Kabir ramu na chetio firia lalach mahe.
Pap karanta mari gaia audh puni khin mahe. (AG, 1376)

23. See the following repetition of phrases in the hymns of Namdev and Guru Amardas in *rag* Bhairo, AG, 1133 and 1165:

Namdev	Guru Amardas
Sandamarka jai pukare	*Sandamarka sabhi jae pukare*
Chatia sabhai bigare	*Sabhi chatṛe vigaṛe*
Dusat sabha mili mantar upaia	*Dusat sabha mahi mantr pakia*
Haṇakhasu jini nakhah bidariao	*Haṇakhasu nakhi bidaria*

The corresponding phraseology also appears in Kabir's hymn in *rag* Basant (AG, 1194).

24. For the tradition of Guru Amardas's love for devotional poetry, see Kesar Singh Chhibbar, *Bansavlinama Dasan Patishahian ka*, pp. 20–21.

25. We have contemporary evidence that Guru Amardas traveled to Hindu pilgrimage centers. Guru Ramdas writes:

Pratham ae Kulkheti gur satigur purab hoa.
Khabari bhai sansari ae trai loa. . . .
Dutia Jamun gae guri hari hari japanu kia. . . .
Tritia ae Sursari tah kautaku chalatu bhaia. (AG, 1116–1117).

26. See n. 3.

27. See chapter 1, n. 36, and chapter 2, n. 28.

28. Bhai Vir Singh, *Shri Ashṭ Guru Chamatkar* (Amritsar: Khalsa Samachar, 1990 [1952]), vol. 2, pp. 54–55.

29. Teja Singh and Ganda Singh, *A Short History of the Sikhs*, p. 29. See also Piara Singh Padam, *Sri Guru Granth Prakash*, p. 40; Surjit Hans, "The Secular Heritage of the Sikhs," in Joseph T. O'Connell et al., eds., *Sikh History and Religion in the Twentieth Century*, p. 79; and Mohinder Kaur Gill, *Guru Granth Sahib di Sampadan-Kala*, pp. 13–16. Gill interprets the incorporation of the writings of the Bhagats in Sikh scripture as an early attempt at national integration.

30. Harnamdas Udasi, *Adi Shri Guru Granth Sahib dian Puratini Biṛan te Vichar*, vol. 1, pp. 64–66.

31. Dharmpal Maini, "Adi Granth te Puratan Adhiatmak Granth," in Jeet Singh Sital, ed., *Gurmat Sahitt*, pp. 5 and 8. For a discussion of the early anthologies of devotional literature, see John Stratton Hawley, "The *Nirguṇ/Saguṇ* Distinction in Early Manuscript Anthologies of Hindi

Devotional Poetry," in David N. Lorenzen, ed., *Bhakti Religion in North India: Community Identity, and Political Action* (Albany: State University of New York Press, 1995).

32. Denis Matringe, "The Future Has Come Near, The Past Is Far Behind: A Study of Saix Farid's Verses and Their Sikh Commentaries in the Adi Granth," in Anna Libera Dallapiccola and Stephanie Zingel-Ave Lallemnat, eds., *Islam and Indian Regions* (Stuttgart: Franz Steiner Verlag, 1993), pp. 417–443. I am grateful to Matringe for sending this paper to me.

33. Bhai Kahn Singh Nabha, *Mahan Kosh*, p. 901.

34. W. Owen Cole, *Sikhism and Its Indian Context, 1469–1708*, p. 157. The period of Guru Amardas witnessed a considerable expansion of the community. By incorporating these hymns into the scriptural text, Guru Amardas opened the Sikh community to the followers of Hindu saints of all castes, as well as to the devotees of Punjabi Sufis. All who were willing to join the Sikhs were welcome within the fold irrespective of their previous religious affiliations or social status.

35. There seems to be no possibility that the hymns of these three saints were not available to the gurus. Kahna seems to be popular enough that his hymns were incorporated in *The Padas of Surdas* compiled far away from his hometown Lahore.

36. Karine Schomer, "Kabir in the Guru Granth Sahib: An Exploratory Essay," in Juergensmeyer and Barrier, *Sikh Studies: Comparative Perspectives on a Changing Tradition*, p. 77.

37. Linda Hess, "Three Kabir Collections: A Comparative Study," in Karine Schomer and W. H. McLeod, eds., *The Sants: Studies in a Devotional Tradition of India* (Delhi: Motilal Banarsidass, 1987), pp. 121–123

38. See ch. 3, n. 59.

39. Seven hymns appearing in the Goindval Pothis are recorded in different *rag* sections in the Kartarpur Pothi:

Author	Goindval Pothis	Kartarpur Pothi
Kabir	Prabahti (folio 105)	Suhi (folio 588, AG p. 793)
Kabir	Prabhati (folio 112)	Suhi (folio 588, AG, p. 793)
Dhanna	Dhanasri (folio 160)	Asa (folio 380, AG, p. 488)
Ravidas	Bhairo (folio 270)	Gauṛi (folio 278, AG, p. 345)
Kabir	Ramkali (folio 104)	Asa (folio 374, AG, p. 484)
Kabir	Soraṭhi (folio 161)	Gauṛi (folio 265, AG, p. 330)
Namdev	Malar (folio 215)	Gonḍ (folio 663, AG, p. 874)

40. Hymn number twenty-three is recorded in a different hand in *rag* Gauṛi in the Kartarpur Pothi; see Bhai Jodh Singh, *Sri Kartarpuri Biṛ de Darshan*, p. 64.

41. Ibid., p. 73.

42. For a discussion of this issue, see Pashaura Singh, "Scriptural Adaptation in the Adi Granth," *Journal of American Academy of Religion* 64: 2 (1996), pp. 347–348.

43. Sahib Singh, *Adi Biṛ bare*, pp. 197–198.

44. Pashaura Singh, "Scriptural Adaptation in the Adi Granth," p. 349.

45. John Stratton Hawley, "The *Nirguṇ/Saguṇ* Distinction in Early Manuscript Anthologies of Hindi Devotional Poetry," p. 176.

46. *Pothi Prem Ambodh*, ed. Davinder Singh Osahan (Patiala: Punjabi University, 1989), pp. 108–119. The colophon of the original text reads: *Samat satra sai panchasa. Sukala pakh ikadas maghar masa*, giving the year of the composition of the text as 1693. The passage on Mirabai opens with a claim that she was initiated into devotion by Ravidas:

Puni Ravidas ki sangat pai. Ta charan kamal siau prit lagai.

47. A similar situation occurs in the case of Guru Arjan's hymns addressed to Dhanna (*rag* Asa, AG, 487) and to Kabir (*rag* Bhairo, AG, 1160), in which he uses their signatures.

48. The text of Surdas's hymn in the Kanpur Pothi is as follows:

Chhadi mani hari bemukhan ko sangu.
Kaha bhae pipai piai bikh na taje bhuiang, rahau.
Kaga kaha kapur chugai suan navae Gang.
Khar kau kaha agar ko lepanu markat bhudan ang.
Pahan patit ban na bedhe rite hohi nikhang.
Surdas oi kari kamri charat na duje rang.

49. Bhai Gurdas, *Varan*, 12: 15 p. 146; the text reads as follows:

Bhagat Kabiru vakhaṇiai bandikhane te uṭh jai. . . .
Benu hoa adhiatami Sainu nich kul andari nai.
Peri pai pakhak hoe gursikha vichi vaḍi samai.
Alakhu lakhae na alakhu lakhai.

See also pp. 128–130 and 133–142.

50. Kesar Singh Chhibbar, *Bansavlinama Dasan Patishahian ka*, pp. 135–136.

51. For a brief description of this manuscript, see Piara Singh Padam, *Dasam Granth Darshan*, p. 30.

52. Sevadas, *Parchi Patishahi Dasvin ki*, pp. 31–33.

53. Guru Arjan is reported to have told Bhai Gurdas: *Ona di rasana thi notan baṇian uchar karvai ke charavaṇia, Sikhan di Bhagatmala*, pp. 122–123. See also Bhai Santokh Singh, *Sri Gurpratap Suraj Granth*, vol. 6, p. 2088:

Sabhihini ko shri guru farmayo. Pratham jo tum ne kuchhu banayo.
So na chaḍvahi granth majhari. Rachahu abhi iske anusari. . . .
Lage banavani gira navin. Beṭhi samipi guru prabin.

54. Tara Singh Narotam, *Bhagat Baṇi Saṭik*, pp. 1–3.

55. *Sri Guru Granth Sahib ji Adi* (Amritsar: Gurmat Press, 1915).

56. Giani Gurdit Singh was honored by the SGPC for having written this book; see *Giani Gurdit Singh Ji* (Amritsar: Shiromani Gurdwara Prabandhak Committee, 1991).

Chapter 8

1. During the past ten years of my research, I examined a large number of manuscripts and printed editions of the Adi Granth presently available at the following places: Sri Takhat Harmandirji, Patna; the Takhat at Damdama, Bhatinda; Dehra Baba Miṭha Singh, Damdama, Bhatinda; Motibagh Palace, Patiala; Guru Nanak Dev University, Amritsar; Panjab University, Chandigarh; Punjabi University, Patiala; Punjab Language Department, Patiala; Bhai Vir Singh Sahitya Sadan, New Delhi; Balbir Singh Sahitya Kendar, Dehradun; and the archives of Harbhajan Singh Yogi at Albuquerque and Española, New Mexico.

2. Pashaura Singh, "The Text and Meaning of the Adi Granth," pp. 74–78 and 81–91.

3. For instance, Piar Singh in his book records ten eighteenth-century manuscripts all of which belong to branch 2. His very selection of these manuscripts implies that they are authentic manuscripts of the Adi Granth; see Piar Singh, *Gatha Sri Adi Granth*, pp. 356–407.

4. G. B. Singh. *Sri Guru Granth Sahib dian Prachin Biṛan*, pp. 215–234, and Harbhajan Singh, *Gurbaṇi Sampadan Nirṇai*, p. 235.

5. For more details and traditions about this manuscript, see Piara Singh Padam, *Dasam Granth Darshan*, p. 30, and Kesar Singh Chhibbar, *Bansavlinama Dasan Patishahian ka*, pp. 135–136.

6. Giani Gurdit Singh writes that he saw several copies of this manuscript; see his *Itihas Sri Adi Granth*, pp. 458–460. He reports that a copy of this manuscript was at Dehra Baba Ajaipal Singh, Nabha. I visited this *gurdwara* in January 1995 but was told that all old manuscripts were sent to Goindval for "cremation" in the late 1980s.

7. A manuscript of this type recorded in 1754 is presently in my possession; I am grateful to Piara Singh Padam for this invaluable gift. For other manuscripts of this type, see Piar Singh, *Gatha Sri Adi Granth*, pp. 356–360 and 367–372.

8. The family was closely associated with the Phulkian States, and their ancestors were held in great respect among Sikh royalty of the region. I visited their home in early 1994 and was given a warm welcome. Another manuscript of this type is available in the Darbar Sahib, Amritsar.

9. See Harveen Kaur Randhawa, "Early Printing History of Guru Granth Sahib" (M. Phil. term paper, GNDU, 1985). I am grateful to Dr. Harsharan Singh of Guru Nanak Dev University for making this very important piece of research available to me.

10. For various discussions of this issue, see Shamsher Singh Ashok, *Shiromani Gurdwara Prabandhak Committee da Punjah Sala Itihas*, pp. 58, 110, 163, 223, 249, 290, and 303.

11. Sardar Rawel Singh of Chandigarh (1357 Sector 15-B) very kindly gave me a copy of this historic edition of the Adi Granth. For details of the publication of this edition, see Rawel Singh, *Shiromani Gurdwara Prabandhak Committee valon Chhapi Gai Biṛ bare Zaruri Vakfiat* (Amritsar: Shiromani Gurdwara Prabandhak Committee, n. d. [1959]). Sardar Rawel Singh and Giani Mohinder Singh of Amritsar (61 Katṛa Jaimal Singh), both of whom had worked for the SGPC during this period, were extremely helpful to explain the details of this event. According to them, this edition was originally published during the presidency of Udam Singh Nagoke, and it continued to be published throughout the 1950s. In order to win the support of the Sant Samaj and the Chief Khalsa Diwan for his SGPC presidential candidate, Sant Chanan Singh, in 1962, Sant Fateh Singh promised to discontinue the publication. Having won the election with their support, he kept his word.

12. Ganga Singh, Sahib Singh, and Teja Singh were instrumental in the creation of the SGPC edition of the Adi Granth. The undated manuscript of the Adi Granth that they used along with the Kartarpur Pothi is presently available at Damdama. I examined this manuscript during my visits to Damdama. It is important to mention that Bhai Jodh Singh was not part of this project and he did not support the publication of this text.

13. Piar Singh, *Gatha Sri Adi Granth and the Controversy*, pp. 75–115.

14. I met Jathedar Joginder Singh Vedanti, Giani Joginder Singh Talwaṛa, and other members of the committee in July 1999. They told me that the collation of the text has reached page 1100. With the change in leadership in early 1999, however, it seems that the SGPC will withdraw its support from the committee, making its existing work redundant.

15. Pashaura Singh mentions this publication of a non-Adi Granth version printed at Gian Press, Gujranwala, 1881; see his "The Text and Meaning of the Adi Granth," pp. 88–89.

16. Shamsher Singh Ashok, *Shiromani Gurdwara Prabandhak Committee da Punjah Sala Itihas*, pp. 48, 53, and 57. For this edition, see chapter 7, note 55.

17. Ibid., p. 261. See also Manmohan Singh, *Sri Guru Granth Sahib*, vol. 1, 54, and Pritam Singh, "The Translation of the Guru Granth Sahib into Devanagari Script," *Journal of Sikh Studies* 4: 1 (1977), pp. 5–8. I came across a number of the Adi Granth texts printed in Persian script at various places during my fieldwork.

18. Pritam Singh Chahil, *Sri Guru Granth Sahib*.

19. These people can be reached at the following addresses:

Balwant Singh Uppal, 94 Mars Street, Carlysle, Western Australia 6181

Preet Mohan Singh Kapoor, 108 Destry Court, San Jose, Ca. 95136
email:*preet@amsinf.com*

Kulbir Singh Thind, 3724 Hacienda St., San Mateo, Ca. 94403

Joginder Singh Ahluwalia, 1930 Francisco Way, Richmond, Ca. 94805

Raghbir Singh Bains, email:*rbains@direct.ca*

Joginder Singh Ahluwalia is now working on the digitization of the text of the Dasam Granth and other early Sikh literature. I am grateful to him for alerting me to the progress in this area, and help me compile this information.

20. For contemporary sources, see Sainapati, *Sri Gur Sobha*, p. 170, and Koer Singh Kalal, *Gurbilas Patishahi 10*, p. 284.

21. W. H. McLeod, "The Sikh Scripture: Some Issues," pp. 103–104.

22. Bhai Gurdas, *Varan*, p. 160, and Piara Singh Padam, ed., *Punjabi Varan*, p. 24.

23. Fauja Singh, *Guru Amardas: Life and Teachings*, pp. 121–124.

24. Sainapati, *Sri Guru Sobha*, p. 81.

25. Chaupa Singh, *Rahit-nama*, pp. 82–83; Sarupdas Bhalla, *Mahima Prakash*, pp. 825–826; and Sarup Singh Kaushish, *Guru kian Sakhian*, pp. 113–115.

26. Hariji, *Gosaṭi Guru Miharvanu*, pp. 175–177.

27. Given the overall lowly status of the profession of scribes in seventeenth-and eighteenth-century India, the honor assigned to the scribes in the Sikh tradition stands out. Baba Dip Singh, another eighteenth-century figure belongs to this list.

28. The earlier term Gursikh (the Sikh of the Guru) is replaced by the "Vahiguru Ji ka Khalsa (the Khalsa of God) by the beginning of the eighteenth century. This change was rooted in the belief that the Khalsa does not recognize any temporal authority and was answerable only to God.

29. Chaupa Singh, *Rahit-nama*, pp. 63, 65, 66, 74–76, 78, 100, 107, and 111.

30. The practice of distributing the *kaṛah prashad* as part of Sikh religious service can be traced back to the early seventeenth century; see Bhai Gurdas, *Varan*, 20: 10, p. 191.

31. Chaupa Singh, *Rahit-nama*, pp. 63, 65, 74, and 110.

32. Sarup Singh Kaushish, *Guru kian Sakhian*, pp. 62, 79, 82, 85, 85, 88, 89–92, 118, 177, 187, and 190–191.

33. A document prepared in 1856 and entitled "Hukamnama Akal Purakh Ji ka sabh Sikhan prati" states the use of the Adi Granth in Sikh ritual ceremonies; see Surinder Singh Nirankari, ed., *Nirankari Gurmati Prarambhata* (Amritsar: Young Men's Association, 1951), pp. 157–170.

34. The case in point is that of the Sant Nirankari leader Gurbachan Singh. In his public appearances, he sat at the same elevation as the Adi Granth. He also revered a text, *The Avtarbaṇi*, which he expected his followers to read alongside the Adi Granth. This was disconcerting to many Sikhs. The acrimonious environment that culminated in his assassination in 1980 resulted from the discomfiture of the orthodox segment of the Sikh community.

35. Kesar Singh Chhibbar, *Bansavlinama Dasan Patishahian ka*, p. 215. The tradition of the small *guṭkas* goes back to the early seventeenth century; one *guṭka* associated with Guru Arjan is in the custody of the Sodhi family at Kartarpur, and another one present at Gurdwara Chola Sahib, Ghuraṇi Kalan (Ludhiana) is believed to have belonged to Guru Hargobind.

36. Chaupa Singh, *Rahit-nama*, p. 136.

37. For a discussion of this, see chapter 6, n. 10.

38. Chaupa Singh, *Rahit-nama*, p. 136.

39. The verses from the Adi Granth were inscribed on Sikh weapons. The Metropolitan Museum of Art, New York, in a recent exhibition of arms and armor, displayed a Sikh *chakar* (round metal disk with sharp extensions); see Donald J. LaRocca, *The Gods of War: Sacred Imagery and the Decoration of Arms and Armor* (New York: Metropolitan Museum of Art, 1996), p. 37. The *chakar* has the following inscription:

Sir mastak rakhah parbrahamang hast kaya rakhah parmesvrah.
Atam rakhah gopal suami dhan charaṇ rakhah jagdisvrah.
Sarab rakhah gur dayalah bhai dukh binasnah.
Bhagati vachhal anath nathe saraṇi Nanak purakh achutah. (AG, 1358–1359)
Guru Nanak Gobind Singh puran gur avatar
Jagmag jot biraj rahi sri Abchal nagar apar. Sri vahiguru ji ki fateh hai.

The translation of this follows:

Lord is protector of our forehead, our hands, and body.
Lord protects our soul and body.
Lord is the savior of all and remover of fear and suffering.
Nanak seeks the Lord, who loves his devotees and protects the helpless
Guru Nanak and Guru Gobind Singh were the perfect Gurus
Their boundless light is situated in the city of Abachal Nagar. The victory belongs to God.

See also Kerry Brown, ed., *Sikh Art and Literature* (New York: Routledge, 1999), p. 41.

40. S. S. Shanti Kaur Khalsa, ed., *The History of Sikh Dharma of the Western Hemisphere* (Española, N.M.: Sikh Dharma Publications, 1995). For local press coverage of Harbhajan Singh Yogi in the World Sikh Sammelan-1995, Amritsar, see the front page of *Ajit* (September 22, 24, 26, and October 1, 1995), and *The Tribune* (September 22, 1995).

41. Chaupa Singh, *Rahit-nama*, p. 78, and Piara Singh Padam, *Rahitname* (Amritsar: Singh Brothers, 1989), pp. 74 and 138

42. Sarup Singh Kaushish, *Guru kian Sakhian*, p. 115, and *Prem Sumarag Granth*, ed. Randhir Singh (Jalandhar: New Book Co., 2000 [1953]), p. 21. This association continued to be strengthened in the nineteenth century and emerged as a major item on the Sikh agenda during the Singh Sabha period. For a brief history of this period, see J. S. Grewal, *The Sikhs of the Punjab*, pp. 144–150.

43. I take this distinction from Frederick M. Denny and Rodney L. Taylor, eds., *The Holy Book in Comparative Perspective* (Columbia: University of South Carolina Press, 1993), pp. 7–9.

44. The Hindus are a special case: while still living in their ancient habitat, they have lost touch with Sanskrit, their sacred language, and are presently involved in devising ways to revive this link.

45. In December 1996, Pritam Singh Chahil's text of *Sri Guru Granth Sahib* was at the center of a ceremony performed at the residence of Raṇi and Dalbir Singh Chaudhary of Manhattan.

46. Satkiran Kaur Khalsa of Brooklyn, New York, gave this interesting information to me.

Glossary of Punjabi Terms

Adi Granth (*ādi granth*) "original book" the Sikh scripture.

Akal Takhat (*akāl takhat/akāl takht*) "Throne of the timeless" historically came into being as seat of the temporal authority of the guru located on the premises of the Darbar Sahib, Amritsar, and developed into the central place where communal decisions are announced.

Akhaṇḍ paṭh (*akhaṇḍ pāṭh*) "unbroken reading" an uninterrupted recitation of the entire Adi Granth by a group of readers (*paṭhis*).

ardas (*ardās*) "supplication" the daily Sikh congregational prayer.

arti (*ārtī*) "praise" a song of praise.

Baba (*bābā*) "father/grandfather" a term of affection and respect often used for religious figures, including the Adi Granth.

Baṇi (*bāṇī*) "utterances," "compositions" the compositions recorded in the Adi Granth. The hymns of the gurus are called *gurbaṇi*; those of the saints are *bhagat baṇi.*

bauli (*baulī*) "well" a large well with steps going down to the water.

Bhagat (*bhagat*) "devotee": a believer in ardent worship based on an attitude of loving devotion (cf. Sanskrit *bhakti*).

Bhai (*bhāī*) "brother" a title applied to Sikhs of acknowledged learning and piety, or any Sikh congregational leader.

bhog (*bhog*) "completion" the completion of a reading of the Adi Granth.

Biṛ (*bīṛ*) "volume," "recension" term used for scriptural manuscripts as well as the printed text of the Adi Granth.

chhant (*chhant*) "song."

Darbar Sahib (*darbār sāhib*) "the honorable court": the central *gurdwara* in Amritsar, the holy city of the Sikhs.

Dasam Granth (*dasam granth*) "book of the tenth master" the text includes the sacred writings traditionally attributed to Guru Gobind Singh.

Giani (*giānī*) "a learned man" a scholar well versed in Sikh scriptures.

granth (*granth*) "book" scripture.

granthi (*granthī*) "keeper of the Adi Granth" the official who is in charge of the *gurdwara*, leads the daily worship, and performs ceremonies such as weddings and the naming of new born children. These ceremonies may or may not be held in the *gurdwara.*

gurdwara (*gurdvārā/gurduārā*) "guru's place" the Sikh place of worship. The key area of a Sikh *gurdwara* is a spacious room housing the Adi Granth, where people sit and listen to scriptural recitation. This room is also used as center for social activity and has a community kitchen attached to it, in which meals are served.

gurmata (*gurmatā*) "the resolution of the guru" the will of the guru, as expressed in a formal decision made by an assembly of Sikhs.

Gurmukhi (*gurmukhī*) "from the mouth of the guru," "the script of the Gurmukhs/Sikhs" the script in which the compositions of the gurus were first written. It has become the script in which Punjabi is written by all Sikhs.

guru (*gurū*) "preceptor" the mode of God as teacher and guide which in the past was revealed to Sikhs in ten human Gurus, and persists in the form of the Adi Granth.

Guru Granth Sahib (*gurū granth sāhib*) "the honorable guru in book form" honorific title of the Adi Granth.

guru panth (*gurū panth*) "community as the guru" the doctrine of the authoritative presence of the eternal guru in a Sikh assembly.

hukamnama (*hukamnāmā*) "decree" announced from the Akal Takhat, considered to be binding on the entire Sikh community.

Janam-Sakhi (*janam-sākhī*) "birth story" traditional hagiographic narratives of Guru Nanak.

Japji (*japjī*): a composition of Guru Nanak that is recited by Sikhs every morning. This is the most commonly known Sikh liturgical prayer.

Jathedar (*jathedār*) "commander" the title of a leader of a Sikh band. The title is applied to custodians of the five historic *gurdwaras*, singled out from the others and known as *takhats*.

Kaṛth prashad (*kaṛah prashād*) "sacramental food" Made of flour, sugar, and clarified butter, it is distributed after each *gurdwara* service.

Khalsa (*khālsā*) "God's own" the title assigned to the Sikh community by Guru Gobind Singh. The implication is that the Sikhs do not recognize any personal authority, and were expected to take nectar prepared with the double-edged sword and respond to the call of dedicating themselves to God and working for His victory on earth (Khalsa Raj).

kirtan (*kīrtan*) "devotional singing" a significant part of Sikh piety.

Laṇgar (*laṇgar*) "community kitchen" attached to every *gurdwara*, from which food is served to all, regardless of caste or creed.

Mahala (*mahalā*): "palace, section" designates the attribution of the compositions of the gurus in the Adi Granth: Mahala 1 (Guru Nanak), Mahala 2 (Guru Angad), Mahala 3 (Guru Amardas), and so forth.

mahant (*mahant*) "abbot" title traditionally used for Nirmala and Udasi custodians of the Sikh *gurdwaras*. The position tended to be hereditary before the Gurdwaras Act of 1925.

masand (*masand*) "guru's deputy" authorized leader of a local congregation in the early Sikh community.

mulmantar (*mūlmantar*) "the root formula" the invocation placed at the head of the text of the Adi Granth.

Nanak Panth (*nānak panth*) "the way of Nanak" term often used for the early Sikh community.

Nath Yogi (*nāth yogī*) a member of a Shaivite sect of ascetics which was very influential in medieval Punjab. The writings of the Sikh gurus indicate their engagement with these ascetics, whose seats were known as *tillas* (mounds).

Nirankari (*nirankārī*) "a follower of Nirankar" a revivalist Sikh movement started by Baba Dayal in the middle of the nineteenth century. At present the movement has bases in Chandigarh and Delhi.

Nirmala (*nirmalā*) "a pure one" a line of Sikh scholars said to have originated during the time of Guru Gobind Singh. Because of their emphasis on Sanskrit learning, their interpretation of Sikh scriptures has a strong Vedantic coloring.

pada (*padā*) "stanza" hymns in the Adi Granth are organized according to number of *padas*. For example we have *dopadas* (two stanzas), *tipadas* (three stanzas), *chaupadas* (four stanzas), . . . *ashṭpadis* (eight stanzas).

pothi (*pothī*) "volume" term used for scriptural manuscripts in the early Sikh community.

puranmashi (*pūranmāshī*) "full month" night of the full moon.

rag (*rāg*) "melody" the main body of the text of the Adi Granth is classified under thirty-one *rag* sections.

Ragmala (*rāgmālā*) "rosary of *rags*" a composition that refers to eighty-four *rags* and *raginis* and appears at the closing of the Adi Granth.

rahau (*rahāo*) "refrain" the verse assigned this status is repeated simultaneously with the singing of the hymns recorded in the Adi Granth.

rahit (*raihat/raiht*) the Khalsa/Sikh code of conduct.

rahit maryada (*raihit maryādā/raihat maryādā*): the code of discipline of the Khalsa/Sikh; also a specific text on this subject.

rahitnama (*raihatnāmā*) one of several manuals of Sikh conduct.

sangat (*sangat*) "congregation": With its emphasis on community, Sikhism gives great importance to congregational worship.

sangrand (*sangrānd*): the first day of the month in the local calendar in India.

sant (*sant*) "saint" a title for a Sikh holy person; also used to describe a devotional tradition of North India in which God is worshiped as formless and transcendental reality.

seva (*sevā*) "service" holding the remembrance of God in one's heart, personal purity, and serving the community are the three pillars of Sikh faith.

shabad (*shabad*) "word," "hymn" term used to refer to both to the Word received from God and a hymn contained within the Adi Granth.

shalok (*shalok*) "couplet," "type of stanza."

Sikh (*sikh*) "disciple," "learner" any person who believes in God, in the ten gurus, in the Adi Granth and other teachings of the gurus, and in the ceremony of the nectar of the double-edged sword. This definition, systematized in the middle of the twentieth century, is considered authoritative in the mainstream Sikh community.

Sufi (*sūfī*) "a Muslim mystic" As a group, Sufis had a major religious impact in medieval Punjab. From centers known as *khanqahs*, these saints taught their disciples, fed travelers, and gave medicine to the sick.

takhat (*takhat/takht*) "throne" one of the five major seats of authority among Sikhs. The *takhats* are located at Amritsar, Anandpur, Damdama (all in the Punjab), Patna (in Bihar), and Nandeṛ (in Maharashtra).

taksal (*taksāl*) "mint" Sikh seminaries where religious education is offered.

Udasi (*udāsī*) "melancholic" an order of ascetics begun by Baba Sri Chand, the eldest son of Guru Nanak.

var (*vār*): a long composition comprising both *shaloks* and a type of stanza called *pauṛi*.

Bibliography

In Punjabi

Abnash Kaur. *Professor Sahib Singh: Jivan te Rachna.* Patiala: Punjabi University, 1983.

Akali Kaur Singh. *Guru Shabad Ratan Prakash.* Patiala: Punjab Language Department, 1986 [1963].

Amol, S. S. *Professor Teja Singh.* Patiala: Punjabi University, 1977.

Ashok, Shamsher Singh. *Punjabi Haṭhlikhatan di Suchi.* 2 vols. Patiala: Punjab Language Department, 1961-1963.

——. *Shiromani Gurdwara Prabandhak Committee da Punjah Sala Itihas 1926 ton 1976.* Amritsar: Sikh Itihas Research Board [Shiromani Gurdwara Prabandhak Committee], 1982.

Badan Singh, Giani, ed. *Adi Sri Guru Granth Sahib Ji Saṭik (Faridkot vala Ṭika).* 4 vols. Patiala: Punjab Language Department, 1970 [1905].

Bal, Giani Rajinder Singh. *Bhai Banno Darpaṇ ate Khare vali Biṛ.* Jalandhar: Central Town, 1989.

Balbir Singh. *Ragmala da Saval te Jodh Kavi ate Alam.* Amritsar: Khalsa Samachar, 1969 [1945].

Bhalla, Sarupdas. *Mahima Prakash, Bhag Duja.* Ed. Gobind Singh Lamba and Khazan Singh. Patiala: Punjab Language Department, 1971.

Bhandari, Sujan Rai. *Khulastut Tvarikh.* Trans. Ranjit Singh Gill, ed. Fauja Singh. Patiala: Punjabi University, 1972.

Charan Singh. *Sri Guru Granth Baṇi Biaura.* Amritsar: Khalsa Tract Society, 1945 [1902].

Chaupa Singh. *The Chaupa Singh Rahit-nama.* Ed. W. H. McLeod. Otago: University of Otago Press, 1987.

Chhibbar, Kesar Singh. *Bansavlinama Dasan Patishahian ka.* Ed. Rattan Singh Jaggi. Chandigarh: Panjab University, 1972.

Dil, Balbir Singh. *Amar Kavi Guru Amardas.* Patiala: Punjab Language Department, 1975.

Ganda Singh, ed. *Punjab, 1849-1960 (Bhai Jodh Singh Abhinandan Granth).* Ludhiana: Punjabi Sahitt Academy, 1962.

——, ed. *Hukamname.* Patiala: Punjabi University, 1985 [1967].

G. B. Singh. *Sri Guru Granth Sahib dian Prachin Biṛan.* Lahore: Modern Publications, 1944.

——. *Gurmukhi Lippi da Janam te Vikas.* Chandigarh: Panjab University, 1981 [1950].

Gian Ratanavali: Janam-Sakhi Sri Guru Nanak Dev Ji. Ed. Jasbir Singh Sabar. Amritsar: Guru Nanak Dev University, 1993.

Gian Singh, Giani. *Tvarikh Guru Khalsa.* Ed. K. S. Raju. Patiala: Punjab Language Department, 1993 [1970].

Giani Gurdit Singh Ji. Amritsar: Dharam Prachar Committee [Shiromani Gurdwara Prabandhak Committee], 1991.

Gill, Mohinder Kaur. *Guru Granth Sahib di Sampadan-Kala*. Delhi: Rabbi Prakashan, 1974.

Grewal, Amarjit Singh, "Ikkivin Sadi de Manav ate Samaj di Sirjiṇa lai Guru Granth Sahib di Prasangikta." In *Vismad Nad* 3. 1. Ludhiana: International Institute of Gurmat Studies, 1994, pp. 1–100.

Gurdas, Bhai. *Varan*. Ed. Gursharan Kaur Jaggi. Patiala: Punjabi University, 1987.

——. *Kabbitt Savaiye*. Ed. Onkar Singh. Patiala: Punjabi University, 1993.

Gurdit Singh, Giani. "Adi Biṛ da Rachna Kal," *Prakash*, June 30, 1952,

——. *Bhaṭ ate unahan di Rachna*. Ludhiana: Punjabi Sahitt Academy, 1961.

——. *Itihas Sri Guru Granth Sahib, Bhagat Baṇi Bhag*. Chandigarh: Sikh Sahitt Sansathan, 1990.

Harbhajan Singh. *Gurbaṇi Sampadan Nirṇai*. Chandigarh: Satnam Prakashan, 1989 [1981].

Historian, Karam Singh. *Sardar Karam Singh Historian di Itihasak Khoj*. Ed. Hira Singh Dard. Amritsar: Sikh Itihas Research Board [Shiromani Gurdwara Prabandhak Committee], 1960.

Jaggi, Gursharan Kaur. *Babe Mohan valian Pothian*. Delhi: Arsi, 1987.

——. *Guru Arjan Dev: Jivan ate Rachna*. Patiala: Punjabi University, 1988.

Jaggi, Rattan Singh. *Varan Bhai Gurdas: Shabad-Anukramaṇika ate Kosh*. Patiala: Punjabi University, 1966.

——. "Praṇ Sangali da Karatritava." In M. S. *Randhawa, Abhinandan Granth*. Delhi: Navyug, 1969, pp. 131–147.

Janam-Sakhi Sri Guru Nanak Dev Ji. Vol 1 and 2. Ed. Kirpal Singh. Amritsar: Sikh History Research Department, Khalsa College, 1969.

Jodh Singh, Bhai. *Bhagat Baṇi Saṭik*. Ludhiana: Lahore Book Shop, 1957.

——. *Sri Kartarpuri Biṛ de Darshan*. Patiala: Punjabi University, 1968.

——. *Bhai Jodh Singh Gadd Saurabh*. Ed. Piar Singh. Patiala: Punjabi University, 1986.

Joginder Singh, *Japji de Ṭike*. Jalandhar: Hindi Press, 1981.

Kalal, Koer Singh. *Gurbilas Patishahi 10*. Ed. Shamsher Singh Ashok. Patiala: Punjabi University, 1986 [1969].

Kang, Kulbir Singh, ed. *Shabad Shalok*. Patiala: Punjab Language Department, 1990.

Kaushish, Sarup Singh. *Guru Kian Sakhian*. Ed. Piara Singh Padam and Giani Garja Singh. Patiala: Kalam Mandir, 1986.

Khalsa, Giani Gurbachan Singh Ji. *Gurbaṇi Paṭh Darshan, Bhag Duja*. Bhindar Kalan: Gurdwara Sri Akhanḍ Prakash, 1990.

Kirpal Singh, ed. *Janam-Sakhi Prampra: Itihasak Drishtikoṇ ton*. Patiala: Punjabi University, 1969.

Kohli, Surinder Singh, ed. *Punjabi Sahitt da Itihas*. 3 vols. Chandigarh: Panjab University, 1973.

Lal Singh, Giani, ed. *Guru Arjan Dev: Jivan te Rachna*. Patiala: Punjab Language Department, 1988 [1985]

Mahan Singh, Giani. *Param Pavitar Adi Biṛ da Sankalna Kal*. Amritsar: Khalsa Samachar, 1952.

——. "Bahoval vali Pothi Sahib." *Kheṛa*. New Delhi: Bhai Vir Singh Sahitya Sadan, March 1980. pp. 13–16.

Mohinderjit Singh, *Arthan di Rajniti*. Ludhiana: Simran Publications, n. d. [1997?].

Nabha, Bhai Kahn Singh. *Ham Hindu Nahin*. Amritsar: Singh Brothers, 1995 [1898].

——. *Gurushabad Ratanakar Mahan Kosh*. Patiala: Punjab Language Department, 1981 [1930].

——. *Gurmat Sudhakar*. Patiala: Punjab Language Department, 1970.

Narotam, Tara Singh. *Gurmat Nirṇai Sagar*. Rawalpindi: Rai Bahadur Buta Singh, 1877.

——. *Bhagat Baṇi Saṭik*. Lahore: Munshi Gulab Singh, 1907.

Neki, Jaswant Singh. *Ardas: Darshan, Rup, Abhias*. Amritsar: Singh Brothers, 1989.

Padam, Piara Singh. *Gurmukhi Lippi da Itihas*. Patiala: Kalam Mandir, 1988 [1953].

——. *Dasam Granth Darshan*. Patiala: Kalam Mandir, 1990 [1968].

——. *Punjabi Sahitt di Rup Rekha*. Patiala: Kalam Mandir, 1971.

——. *Sri Guru Granth Prakash*. Patiala: Kalam Mandir, 1990 [1977].

——, ed. *Prachin Punjabi Gadd*. Patiala: Kalam Mandir, 1978.

——. *Sri Guru Amardas Ji di Baṇi*. Patiala: Punjabi University, 1979.

——, ed. *Sufi Kavidhara*. Patiala: Kalam Mandir, 1993.

Piar Singh. *Gatha Sri Adi Granth*. Amritsar: Guru Nanak Dev University, 1992.

Pothi Prem Ambodh. Ed. Davinder Singh Oshan. Patiala: Punjabi University, 1989.

Prem Sumarag Granth. Ed. Randhir Singh. Jalandhar: New Book Company, 2000 [1953].

Punjabi Dunia. Patiala: Punjab Language Department, May 1952.

Puratan Janam-Sakhi Sri Guru Nanak Dev Ji ki. Ed. Shamsher Singh Ashok. Amsritsar: Dharam Prachar Committee [Shiromani Gurdwara Prabandhak Committee], 1969.

Pritam Singh, ed. *Pahili Patishahi, Sri Guru Nanak Dev*. Ludhiana: Punjabi Sahitt Academy, 1969.

——, ed. *Nirmal Sampradae*. Amritsar: Guru Nanak Dev University, 1981.

——. *Bhai Kahn Singh Nabha*. Amritsar: Guru Nanak Dev University, 1989

——, ed. *Ahiapur vali Pothi*. Amritsar: Guru Nanak Dev University, 1998.

Ragmala bare Vichar. Amritsar: Sura Masak Patar, 1986.

Rahitname. Ed. Piara Singh Padam. Amritsar: Singh Brothers, 1989 [1974].

Raijasbir Singh, ed. *Guru Amardas: Srot Pustak*. Amritsar: Guru Nanak Dev University, 1986.

——. *Punjab de Samajik Itihas te Ik Nazar*. Amritsar: Navin Prakashan, 1999.

Ram Singh, *Japji de Panj Khanḍ*. Patiala: Punjabi University, 1989.

Randhawa, Mohinder Singh, ed. *Punjab*. Patiala: Punjab Language Department, 1960.

Randhir Singh. "Adi Granth da Kal." *Punjabi Dunia* . Patiala: Punjab Language Department, May 1952.

——. *Sri Guru Gobind Singh Ji di Shabad-Murati*. Amritsar: Shiromani Gurdwara Prabandhak Committee, 1962.

——, ed. *Guru-Praṇalian*. Amritsar: Sikh Itihas Research Board [Shiromani Gurdwara Prabandhak Committee], 1977.

Randhir Singh, et al., eds. *Sri Guru Granth Sahib Ji dian Santha-Sanchian ate Puratan Haṭhlikhit Pavan Biṛan de Praspar Paṭh-Bhedan di Suchi*. Amritsar: Shiromani Gurdwara Prabandhak Committee, 1977.

Rao, Ram Sukh. *Sri Fateh Singh Partap Prabhakar*. Ed. Joginder Kaur. Patiala: Editor, 1980.

Rawel Singh. *Shiromani Gurdwara Prabandhak Committee valon Niyat Vidvanan da Sarab-Samat Faisala*. Amritsar: Shiromani Gurdwara Prabandhak Committee, n. d. [1958?].

——. *Shiromani Gurdwara Prabandhak Committee valon Chhapi Gai Biṛ bare Zaruri Vakfiat*. Amritsar: Shiromani Gurdwara Prabandhak Committee, n. d. [1959?].

Sabar, Jasbir Singh. "Gurbaṇi Sangit Sanketa te Sirlekha da Gurmat Sangit vich Mahattav." Unpublished paper presented at a conference on "Gurmat Sangit." Patiala: Punjabi University, Summer 1991.

Sadhu Singh. "Utri Amrika vich Sikh Adhiain da Sarvekhaṇ." *Watan* (Vancouver), 5. 3 (1994), pp. 29–33.

Sahib Singh. *Gurbaṇi Viakaraṇ*. Amritsar: Rabbi Pustakavali, 1939.

——. *Gurbaṇi te Itihas bare*. Amritsar: Singh Brothers, 1986 [1946].

——. *Sri Guru Granth Sahib Darpaṇ*. 10 vols. Jalandhar: Raj Publishers, 1962–1964.

——. *Adi Biṛ bare*. Amritsar: Singh Brothers, 1987 [1970].

——. *Bhagat Baṇi Saṭik*. Amritsar: Singh Brothers, 1974.

Sainapati. *Sri Gur Sobha*. Ed. Ganda Singh. Patiala: Punjabi University, 1988 [1967].

Santokh Singh, Bhai. *Sri Gurpratap Suraj Granth*. Vol. 6. Ed. Bhai Vir Singh. Amritsar: Khalsa Samachar, 1963 [1929].

Sevadas. *Parchi Patishahi Dasvin ki*. Ed. Piara Singh Padam. Patiala: Kalam Mandir, 1988.

Seva Singh. *Shahid Bilas*. Ed. Giani Garja Singh. Ludhiana: Punjabi Sahitt Academy, 1961.

Shan, Harnam Singh. *Guru Granth Sahib di Koshkari*. Patiala: Punjab Language Department, 1994.

Sharma, Krishaṇ Lal, ed. *Guru Amar Das: Jivan ate Chintan*. Amritsar: Guru Nanak Dev University, 1986.

Sikh Rahit Maryada. Amritsar: Shiromani Gurdwara Prabandhak Committee, 1978 [1950].

Sikhan di Bhagatmala. Ed. Tarlochan Singh Bedi. Patiala: Punjabi University, 1994.

Sital, Jeet Singh. *Punjabi Siharfian*. Patiala: Punjab Language Department, 1972.

——, ed. *Gurmat Sahitt*. Patiala: Punjab Language Department, 1989 [1970].

Sri Gurbilas Patishahi 6. Ed. Giani Inder Singh Gill. Amritsar: Vazir Hind Press, 1977.

Sukha Singh. *Gurbilas Dasvin Patishahi*. Ed. Gursharan Kaur Jaggi. Patiala: Punjab Language Department, 1989.

Suri, Sohan Lal. *Umda-ut-Tvarikh*, daftar II. Trans. Amarvant Singh, ed. J. S. Grewal and Indu Banga. Amritsar: Guru Nanak Dev University, 1985.

Talwaṛa, Joginder Singh. *Baṇi Biaura, Bhag 1*. Amritsar: Singh Brothers, 1992.

Taran Singh. *Sri Guru Granth Sahib ji da Sahitak Itihas*. Amritsar: Faqir Singh and Sons, n. d. [1963?].

——. "Sri Guru Granth Sahib vich Kavita te Rag da Sambandh." In M. S. *Randhawa Abhinandan Granth*. Delhi: Navyug, 1969, pp. 68–71.

——. *Gurbaṇi dian Viakhia Praṇalian*. Patiala: Punjabi University, 1980.

Teja Singh, ed. *Shabadarth Sri Guru Granth Sahib Ji*. 4 vols. Amritsar: Shiromani Gurdwara Prabandhak Committee, 1969 [1936–41].

Udasi, Swami Harnamdas. *Adi Shri Guru Granth Sahib dian Puratani Biṛan te Vichar*. 2 vols. Kapurthala: Kantesh Pharmacy, n. d. [1969?].

Vir Singh, Bhai. *Sri Ashṭ Guru Chamatkar, Bhag I te II*. Amritsar: Khalsa Samachar, 1990 [1952].

——. *Santhaya Sri Guru Granth Sahib*. 7 vols. Amritsar: Khalsa Samachar, 1972 [1958].

In Hindi

"Anant," L. B. Ram. *Kabir Granthavali*. Delhi: Regal Book Depot, 1968.

Bahura, Gopal Narayan, ed. *The Padas of Surdas*. Jaipur: Maharaja Savai Man Singh II Museum, 1982.

Callewaert, Winand M., and Mukund Lath, eds. *The Hindi Padavali of Namdev*. Delhi: Motilal Banarsidass, 1989.

Callewaert, Winand M, and Bart Op de Beeck, eds. *Devotional Hindi Literature*. Vol. 1. New Delhi: Manohar, 1991.

Chaturvedi, Parashuram. *Kabir Sahitya ki Parakh*. Alahabad: Bharati Bhandar, 1964

Gupta, Mataprasad, ed. *Kabir Granthavali*. Alahabad: Lokbharati, 1969.

Hariji. *Goshaṭi Guru Mihirvanu*. Ed. Govindnath Rajguru. Chandigarh: Panjab University, 1974.

Mishra, Bhagavatsvarup, ed. *Kabir Granthavali*. Agra: Vinod Pustak, 1969.

Mishra, Bhagirath, and Rajnarayan Maurya, eds. *Sant Namdev ki Hindi Padavali*. Pune: Pune University, 1964.

Pantal, Gita. *Punjab ki Sangit Prampra*. Delhi: Radha Publications, 1988.

In English

Album Central Sikh Museum. Amritsar: Sri Darbar Sahib, 1996 [1991].

Archer, John Calrk, "The Bible of the Sikhs." *Panjab Past and Present* 11. 1 (1977), pp. 22–31.

Attar Singh, ed. *Socio-Cultural Impact of Islam on India*. Chandigarh: Panjab University, 1976.

Avtar Singh, *Ethics of the Sikhs*. Patiala: Punjabi University, 1983.

Bachittar Singh, Giani, ed. *Planned Attack on Aad Sri Guru Granth Sahib*. Chandigarh: International Centre of Sikh Studies, 1994.

Banga, Indu, ed. *Five Punjabi Centuries*. New Delhi: Manohar, 1997.

Barque, A. M. *Eminent Sikhs of Today*. Lahore: Barque and Company, 1942.

Barrier, N. G., and V. A. Dusenbery, eds. *The Sikh Diaspora: Migration and Experience beyond Punjab*. Columbia, Mo.: South Asia Books, 1989.

Bhagat Singh. *Maharaja Ranjit Singh and His Times*. New Delhi: Sehgal Publishers Service, 1990.

Bhatkhande, V. N. A. *Comparative Study of Some of the Leading Musical Systems of the 15th, 16th, 17th, and 18th Centuries*. Baroda: Indian Musicological Society, 1972.

Bosch, Gulnar K., John Carswell, and Guy Petherbridge. *Islamic Bindings and Book Making*. Chicago: Oriental Institute, University of Chicago, 1981.

Brown, Kerry, ed. *Sikh Art and Literature*. New York: Routledge, 1999.

Callewaert, Winand M., and Pater G. Friedlander. *The Life and Works of Raidas*. New Delhi: Manohar, 1992.

Chandar, Satish. "Jizayah and the State in India during the 17th Century." *Journal of the Economic and Social History of the Orient* 12. 3 (1969), pp. 322–340.

Cole, W. Owen. *Sikhism and Its Indian Context 1469–1708*. New Delhi: D. K. Agencies, 1984.

Cole, W. Owen, and Piara Singh Sambhi. *The Sikhs: Their Religious Beliefs and Practices*. Brighton: Sussex Academic Press, 1995 [1978].

Coward, Harold. *Sacred Word and Sacred Text: Scripture in World Religion*. New York: Orbis Books, 1988.

Coward, Harold, and David Goa. *Mantra: Hearing the Divine in India* Chambersburg, Pa.: Anima Books, 1991.

Cunningham, Joseph Davey. *A History of the Sikhs*. Delhi: S. Chand and Company, 1985 [1849].

Daljeet Singh. *Essay on the Authenticity of Kartarpuri Biṛ and the Integrated Logic and Unity of Sikhism*. Patiala: Punjabi University, 1987.

Darshan Singh, *A Study of Bhakta Ravidasa*. Patiala: Punjabi University, 1981.

Dass, Nirmal. *Songs of Kabir from the Adi Granth*. Albany: State University of New York Press, 1992.

Denny, Frederick M., and R. L. Taylor, eds. *The Holy Book in Comparative Perspective*. Columbia: University of South Carolina Press, 1993.

Dewana, Mohan Singh. *A History of Punjabi Literature*. Jalandhar: Bharat Prakashan, 1971.

Districts and States Gazetteers of Undivided Punjab. Vol. 3. Delhi: B. R. Publishing, 1985 [1914].

Fauja Singh. *Guru Amardas: Life and Teachings*. Delhi: Sterling, 1979.

Fauja Singh and Gurbachan Singh Talib. *Guru Tegh Bahadur: Martyr and Teacher*. Patiala: Punjabi University, 1975.

Ganda Singh, trans. "Nanak Panthis from the Dabistan-i-Mazahib." *Panjab Past and Present* 1. 1 (1967), pp. 47–71.

Gandhi, Surjit Singh. *Perspectives on Sikh Gurdwara Legislation*. New Delhi: Atlantic Publishers, 1993.

Gangoly, O. C. *Rags and Raginis*. Bombay: Nalanda Publications, 1935.

Gonda, J. *Mantra Interpretation in the Satpatha-Brahmana*. Leiden: E. J. Brill, 1988.

Grewal, J. S. *Guru Nanak in History*. Chandigarh: Panjab University, 1979 [1969].

——. *The Sikhs of the Punjab*. New York: Cambridge University Press, 1990.

——. *Sikh Ideology Polity and Social Order*. New Delhi: Manohar, 1996.

——. *Contesting Interpretations of the Sikh Tradition*. New Delhi: Manohar, 1998.

Grewal, J. S., and S. S. Bal. *Guru Gobind Singh*. Chandigarh: Panjab University, 1987 [1966].

Griffin, Lepel H., and Charles Francis Massy. *Chiefs and Families of Note in the Punjab*. Lahore: Punjab Government Press, 1939.

Hans, Surjit. *A Reconstruction of Sikh History from Sikh Literature*. Jalandhar: ABS Publications, 1988.

Harbans Singh. *The Heritage of the Sikhs*. New Delhi: Manohar, 1983.

Harvey, Alper. *Understanding Mantras*. Albany: State University of New York Press, 1989.

Hawley, John Stratton. "The Music in Faith and Morality." *Journal of the American Academy of Religion* 52. 2 (1984), pp. 243–262.

——. "Author and Authority in the *Bhakti* Poetry of North India." *Journal of Asian Studies* 47. 2 (1988), pp. 269–290.

——. "The Nirgun/Sagun Distinction in Early Manuscript Anthologies of Hindi Devotional Poetry." In David N. Lorenzen, ed. *Bhakti Religion in North India: Community Identity, and Political Action*. Albany: State University of New York Press, 1995, pp. 160–180.

Hawley, John Stratton, and Mark Juergensmeyer. *Songs of the Saints of India*. New York: Oxford University Press, 1988.

Hawley, John Stratton, and Gurinder Singh Mann, eds. *Studying the Sikhs: Issues for North America*. Albany: State University of New York Press, 1993.

Hunter, Dard. *Paper Making: The History and Technique of an Ancient Craft*. New York: Dover Publications, 1974 [1943].

Juergensmeyer, Mark, and N. G. Barrier, eds. *Sikh Studies: Comparative Perspectives on a Changing Tradition*. Berkeley Religious Studies Series. Berkeley: University of California Press, 1979.

Khalsa, S. S. Shanti Kaur, ed. *The History of Sikh Dharma of the Western Hemisphere*. Española, NM: Sikh Dharma Publications, 1995.

Khushwant Singh. *A History of the Sikhs*. 2 vols. Princeton: Princeton University Press, 1984 [1963].

Kohli, Surinder Singh. *A Critical Study of Adi Granth*. Delhi: Motilal Banarsidass, 1976 [1961].

——. *Sikhism and Guru Granth Sahib*. Delhi: National Book Shop, 1990.

LaRocca, Donald J. *The Gods of War: Sacred Imagery and the Decoration of Arms and Armor*. New York: Metropolitan Museum of Art, 1996.

Leitner, G. W. *Indigenous Education in the Punjab Since Annexation*. Patiala: Punjab Language Department, 1970 [1882].

Levering, Miriam, ed. *Rethinking Scripture: Essays from a Comparative Perspective*. Albany: State University of New York Press, 1989.

Losty, Jeremiah P. *The Art of the Book in India*. London: The British Library, 1982.

Mann, Gurinder Singh. "The Making of Sikh Scripture." Ph. D. diss., Columbia University, 1993.

——. *The Goindval Pothis: The Earliest Extant Source of the Sikh Canon*. Harvard Oriental Series 51. Cambridge: Harvard University Press, 1996.

Matringe, Denis. "A study of Saix Farid's verses and Their Sikh Commentaries in the Adi Granth." In Anna Libera Dallapiccola and Stephanie Zingel-Ave Lallemnat, eds. *Islam and Indian Regions*. Stuttgart: Franz Steiner Verlag, 1993, pp. 417–443.

McLeod, W. H. "Guru Nanak and Kabir." *Proceedings of the Punjab History Conference*. Patiala: Punjabi University, 1965, pp. 87–92.

——. *Guru Nanak and the Sikh Religion*. Oxford: Clarendon Press, 1968.

——. "Hakikat Rah Mukam Raje Sivanabh ki." *Proceedings of the Punjab History Conference*. Patiala: Punjabi University, 1969, pp. 96–105.

——. *The Evolution of the Sikh Community: Five Essays*. Oxford: Clarendon Press, 1996 [1976].

——. *Early Sikh Tradition: A Study of the Janam-sakhis*. Oxford: Clarendon Press, 1980.

——. *Textual Sources for the Study of Sikhism*. Chicago: Chicago University Press, 1990 [1984].

——. *The Sikhs: History, Religion and Society*. New York: Columbia University Press, 1989.

——. *Historical Dictionary of Sikhism*. Lanham, Md.: The Scarecrow Press, 1995.

——. *Sikhism*. New York: Penguin, 1997.

Nahar Singh. "Some Documents regarding Sacred Sikh Relics in England." *Panjab Past and Present* 8. 2 (1974), pp. 287–315.

Nikki-Guninder Kaur Singh. *The Name of My Beloved*. San Francisco: Harper SanFrancisco, 1995.

Nirankari, Surinder Singh, ed. *Nirankari Gurmati Prarambhata*. Amritsar: Young Men's Association, 1951.

Nirbhai Singh. *Bhagata Namadeva in the Guru Grantha*. Patiala: Punjabi University, 1981.

Nizami, Khaliq Ahmad. "Some Aspects of Khanqah Life in Medieval India." *Studia Islamica* 8 (1957), pp. 51–69.

——. *Some Aspects of Religion and Politics in India during the Thirteenth Century*. Delhi: Idarah-i Adabiyat-i Delli, 1974.

Nripinder Singh, *The Sikh Moral Tradition*. Columbia, Mo.: South Asia Publications, 1990.

O'Connell, Joseph T., et al., eds. *Sikh History and Religion in the Twentieth Century*. Toronto: University of Toronto, 1988.

Pashaura Singh. "Sikh Self-Defintion and the Bhagat Baṇi." M. A. diss., University of Calgary, 1987.

——. "The Text and Meaning of the Adi Granth." Ph. D. diss., University of Toronto, 1991.

——. "An Early Sikh Scriptural Tradition: The Guru Nanak Dev University Manuscript 1245." *International Journal of Punjab Studies* 1. 2 (1994), pp. 197–222.

——. "Scriptural Adaptation in the Adi Granth." *Journal of American Academy of Religion* 64. 2 (1996), pp. 337–357.

Piar Singh. *Gatha Sri Adi Granth and the Controversy*. Grandledge, Mich.: Anant Education and Rural Development Foundation, 1996.

Pincott, Frederic. "The Arrangement of the Hymns of the Adi Granth." *Journal of Royal Asiatic Society* 18 (1878), pp. 437–461.

Prajnanananda, Swami. *A Historical Study of Indian Music*. Delhi: Munshiram Manoharlal, 1981.

Pritam Singh. "Keertana and the Sikhs." *Journal of Sikh Studies* 3. 2 (1976), pp. 5–8, 182–185.

——. "The Translation of the Guru Granth Sahib into Devanagari Script." *Journal of Sikh Studies* 4. 1 (1977), pp. 5–8, 183–187.

——. "Bhai Banno Copy of the Sikh Scripture." *Journal of Sikh Studies* 11. 2 (1984), pp. 98–115.

——, ed. *Sikh Concept of the Divine*. Amritsar: Guru Nanak Dev University, 1985.

Qaiser, Iqbal. *Historical Sikh Shrines in Pakistan*. Lahore: Punjabi History Board, 1998.

Randhawa, Harveen Kaur. "Early Printing History of *Guru Granth Sahib*." M. Phil. term paper, Guru Nanak Dev University, 1985.

Schomer, Karine, and W. H. McLeod, eds. *The Sants: Studies in a Devotional Tradition of India*. Delhi: Motilal Banarasidass, 1987.

Shackle, Christopher. *Catalogue of the Punjabi and Sindhi Manuscripts in the India Office Library*. London: India Office Library and Records, 1977.

——. *A Guru Nanak Glossary*. London: School of Oriental and African Studies, 1981.

——. *An Introduction to the Sacred Language of the Sikhs*. London: School of Oriental and African Studies, 1983.

Smith, Wilfred Cantwell. *What Is Scripture: A Comparative Approach*. Minneapolis: Fortress Press, 1993.

Suri, Sohan Lal, *Umdat-ut-Tvarikh*, daftar III. Trans. V. S. Suri. Delhi: S. Chand and Company, 1961.

——. *Umda-ut-Tvarikh*, daftar IV. Trans. V. S. Suri. Chandigarh: Punjab Itihas Prakashan, 1972.

Talib, Gurbachan Singh. *Bani of Sri Guru Amar Das*. New Delhi: Sterling Publishers, 1979.

Tatla, Darshan Singh.*The Sikh Diaspora: The Search for Statehood*. London: University College London Press, 1999.

Teja Singh, and Ganda Singh. *A Short History of the Sikhs*. Patiala: Punjabi University, 1989 [1950].

Van Nooten, Barend A., and Gary B. Holland, eds. *Rig Veda*. Cambridge: Harvard Oriental Series 50. Cambridge: Harvard University Press, 1994.

Vaudeville, Charlotte. *A Weaver Named Kabir*. Delhi: Oxford University Press, 1993.

World Sikh Meet–1995. Amritsar: Shiromani Gurdwara Prabandhak Committee, September 1995.

Translations of the Adi Granth

Chahil, Pritam Singh. *Sri Guru Granth Sahib*. New Delhi: Crescent Printing, n. d. [1995?].

Gopal Singh, *Sri Guru Granth Sahib*. 4 vols. Delhi: Gurdas Kapur and Sons, 1960–1962.

Khalsa, Sant Singh. *Sri Guru Granth Sahib* (digitized version).

Macauliffe, Max Arthur. *The Sikh Religion: Its Gurus, Sacred Writings and Authors*. New Delhi: S. Chand and Company, 1985 [1909].

Manmohan Singh, *Sri Guru Granth Sahib*. 8 vols. Amritsar: Shiromani Gurdwara Prabandhak Committee, 1962.

Talib, Gurbachan Singh. *Sri Guru Granth Sahib*. 4 vols. Patiala: Punjabi University, 1985.

Trumpp, Ernest. *The Adi Granth or the Holy Scripture of the Sikhs*. Delhi: Munshiram Manoharlal, 1978 [1877].

Jarnail Singh, *Sri Gourou Granth Sahib*. 4 vols. Providenciales, West Indies: Intellectual Services International, 1998. (in French).

Index

Adi Granth
  authority of, 4, 10, 12, 15, 16, 18, 21, 22, 30, 31, 69, 118–119, 122, 123, 129, 131, 133–134, 136
  compilation, 16, 17, 71, 73, 82–85
  contents, 4, 52
  digitized texts, 128
  interpretation, 16, 18, 134
  language, 5, 107, 136
  organization, 5, 87–94
  printing, 125–128, 136
  structure, 5, 54, 86, 89, 94–101
Akal Takhat, 28, 29
Amritsar, 13, 14, 15, 16, 19, 33, 35, 40, 57, 60, 103, 125, 131, 135, 136
Amritsar Pothi, 75–79, 84, 131
Anand, Ramkali, 39, 40, 54–55, 56, 95, 132
Anandpur, 15, 16, 19, 23, 24, 25, 28, 83, 85, 122, 123
ardas (supplication), 132, 133

Badan Singh, Giani, 11, 25, 81
Banno, Bhai, 22, 25, 69, 70, 75, 79, 81
bards at the Sikh court, 5, 18, 21, 22, 52, 87, 94, 124
Beṇi, Bhagat, 102, 105, 107, 108, 118
Bhagat baṇi (hymns of the non-Sikh saints), 38, 39, 45, 46, 51, 52, 58, 59, 63, 94, 99, 102, 124
  criterion of selection, 111–112
  date of inclusion, 103–109
  purpose of inclusion, 109–111
  status, 117–118
Bhalla, Kanwarjit Singh, 41
Bhalla, Sarupdas, 19, 20, 22, 69, 70
Bhalla, Vinod, 41
Bhasoṛ, Teja Singh, 120, 127, 129
Bhikhaṇ, Bhagat, 102
Bhindranwale, Sant Jarnail Singh, 4
Buḍḍha, Baba, 59
Buṛa Sandhu, 78, 131

Charan Singh, 25, 70, 75, 86, 91
Chaupa Singh, 19, 20, 31, 36, 83, 131, 132, 133, 134, 135
Chhibbar, Kesar Singh, 19, 20, 21, 22, 28, 30, 36, 49, 64, 65, 83, 119, 124
Chief Khalsa Diwan, 125, 126

Daljit Singh, 146 n. 48, 161 n. 46
Damdama, Bhatinda, 16, 24, 25, 28, 31, 83, 85, 123, 125
Darbar Sahib, Amritsar, 14, 33, 34, 73, 88, 129, 130
Dasam Granth, 21, 22, 124
Dehra Dun Pothi, 77, 82, 131
Dewana, Mohan Singh, 104, 108
Dhanna, Bhagat, 102, 119
Dhillon, Balwant Singh, 53, 57–58
Dhirmal, 19, 22, 24, 49, 59, 60, 61, 73, 131
Divali, 13, 15

Farid, Shaikh, 5, 102, 105–106, 107, 108, 112, 113, 119
Faridkot vala Ṭika. See Badan Singh, Giani

G. B. Singh, 26–27, 28, 31, 61, 64, 67, 70, 78, 83, 84, 104, 108
Gian Singh, Giani, 24, 25, 31, 43, 44, 83, 90
Gill, Mohinder-Kaur, 86
Goindval, 12, 13, 14, 22, 41, 42, 57
Goindval Pothis, 13, 15, 17, 20, 23, 26, 29–30, 32, 33, 39, 53, 57, 58, 65, 68, 86, 96, 104, 112, 113, 114
  date of inscription, 42–43
  history, 40–42
  number, 43–45
  structure, 45–47, 94–95
Grewal, Amarjit Singh, 29
Grewal, J. S., 6, 31
Griffen, Lepel H., 35
Gulam Sadasevak, 30, 42–43
Gurdas, Bhai, 7, 14, 19, 20, 21, 22, 36, 41, 51, 64, 79, 103, 118, 119, 130
Gurdit Singh, Giani, 27, 37, 38, 39, 40, 43, 44, 64, 67, 104, 120
Gurdita, Baba, 61, 64
gurdwara, 5, 22, 31, 79, 126, 127, 131, 135
Gurmukhi, 5, 39, 52, 127, 135, 136
Guru Amardas, 12, 13, 15, 21, 23, 26, 39, 40, 41, 42, 43, 46, 55, 77, 84, 87, 92, 104, 106, 108, 109, 110–111, 114, 117, 120, 134
Guru Angad, 7, 10, 12, 26, 37, 38, 39
Guru Arjan, 3, 5, 14, 15, 16, 19, 20, 23, 24, 26, 28, 30, 32, 33, 34, 35, 36, 37, 38, 40, 41, 49, 50, 51, 54, 55, 57, 58, 59, 62, 63, 64, 65, 67, 70, 73, 78, 80, 81, 84, 87, 92, 93, 103, 104, 106, 109, 116, 119, 130
Guru Gobind Singh, 3, 15, 16, 19, 21, 24, 25, 28, 31, 61, 69, 83, 84, 118, 121–122, 123, 124, 126, 129, 130, 132
Guru Granth Sahib, see Adi Granth
Guru Hargobind, 15, 24, 33, 34, 57, 60, 61, 63, 64, 65, 73
Guru Harirai, 15, 23, 61
Guru Harkishan, 15
Guru Harsahai Pothi, 12, 13, 17, 32, 44, 49, 50, 51, 54, 57, 68, 86
  date of inscription, 36–38
  history, 33–36
  structure, 39–40
Guru Nanak, 3, 5, 6, 7, 10, 11, 12, 15, 16, 24, 26, 34, 35, 37, 38, 39, 46, 49, 50, 54, 85, 87, 88, 96, 104, 105, 106, 108, 117, 129, 130
Guru Ramdas, 5, 7, 13, 14, 26, 34, 35, 37, 39, 40, 41, 42, 43, 49, 50, 54, 59, 79, 80, 88, 96, 118, 130
Guru Tegh Bahadur, 5, 15, 24, 26, 27, 28, 60, 61, 67, 68, 69, 71, 73, 79, 83, 84, 94, 118, 122, 123, 124, 130

Harbhajan Singh, 28
Hariji, 33, 35, 36, 56
Hawley, John Stratton, 115
Hehar, 33, 34
Hess, Linda, 112
Historian, Karam Singh, 25
Holi, 15

invocation (*mulmantar*), 37, 53–54, 63, 68, 83, 126, 149 n. 20

Jaidev, Bhagat, 89, 102
Janam-Sakhi literature, 7, 18, 36, 37, 130
Japji, 5, 9, 39, 52, 79–80, 88, 132
Jodh Singh, Bhai, 11, 27, 46, 62, 64, 65, 66, 67, 68
Jiziyah, 12, 14

Kabir, Bhagat, 5, 52, 76, 80, 85, 94, 102, 103, 107, 108, 111–112, 113, 114, 116, 119
kachi baṇi, 36, 111
Kahna, Bhagat, 111
Kanpur Pothi, 22–23, 24, 25, 30, 70, 71, 73, 79–82, 93, 106, 116, 122
Kartarpur (Guru Nanak's town), 6, 7, 9, 10, 12, 14, 32, 57
Kartarpur Pothi, 15, 16, 17, 22, 26, 27, 29, 30, 32, 37, 38, 40, 44, 46, 47, 48, 49, 51, 53, 54, 56, 57, 58, 69, 73, 74, 75, 76, 77, 78, 79, 80, 82, 83, 84, 85, 86, 89, 93, 106, 112, 114, 122, 126, 129, 131
  date of inscription, 63–65
  history, 60–62
  structure, 65–67, 95–97
Kateb (Semitic scriptures), 11–12, 24, 44, 99–100, 101, 136
Kaushish, Sarup Singh, 21–22, 132
Khadur, 12
Khalsa Panth, 15, 19, 130
Kiratpur, 19, 61, 73
kirtan (devotional singing), 41, 87–88, 135

Koer Singh, 19
Kohli, Surinder Singh, 91-92, 93

Lahore, 3, 15, 16, 60, 62, 70, 71, 74, 79, 111, 122, 125, 127
Lala, a female saint of Kashmir, 111
laṇgar (community kitchen), 9, 12, 41, 111

Macauliffe, Max Arthur, 145 n. 39
Mahan Singh, Giani, 28, 64-65
Maini, Dharmpal, 110
Mani Singh, Bhai, 19, 21, 23, 25, 31, 83, 119, 120, 124, 127, 129, 130
manji (system of authority), 13, 129
Masand, 129, 130
McLeod, W. H., 6, 30, 107-108
Miharban, 20, 22, 33, 36, 38, 39, 57, 58, 130
Mirabai, a female saint of Rajasthan, 76, 80, 85, 103, 111, 114, 115-116, 117
Mohan, Baba, 13, 20, 22, 23, 26, 30, 32, 39, 40, 41, 42, 43, 49, 61
MS 1192, 15, 83-85, 123, 125
MS 1245, 17, 28, 51-59, 63, 68, 115, 118, 120
mulmantar. *See* invocation

Nabha, Bhai Kahn Singh, 10, 11, 35, 62, 65, 66, 67
Namdev, Bhagat, 43, 95, 102, 108, 113, 118
Narotam, Tara Singh, 70, 119
Nirankari, Man Singh, 44
Nirmalas, a school of Sikh scholarship, 10, 23, 109

Padam, Piara Singh, 28, 44, 67
Pashaura Singh, 28, 29, 51, 52, 58, 66, 71, 81, 92, 122-123
Parmanand, Bhagat, 102
Piar Singh, 28-29, 51, 52-53, 57, 67, 71, 75, 76, 78, 84
Pincott, Frederic, 94, 100
Pipa, Bhagat, 102
Praṇ Sangali, 20, 23, 24
Prem Singh, Bawa, 27, 42
Pritam Singh, 30, 67, 92
Prithi Chand, 19, 20, 32, 33, 34, 36, 40, 49, 58, 61, 130, 131

Quran. *See* Kateb

Ragmala, 5, 66, 68, 75-76,77, 80, 127
Rahiras/Sodar 5, 9, 52, 54
rahit (Sikh code of conduct), 4, 7, 15, 31
Ramanand, Bhagat, 102
Ramrai, 23, 61, 82, 130, 131, 132
Ramdaspur. *See* Amritsar
Randhir Singh, 27, 64, 67
Ranjit Singh, Maharaja, 3, 42, 62, 65, 75, 79, 122, 124, 132
Ratanmala, 65, 80
Ravidas, Bhagat, 76, 102, 113, 115, 118

Sabar, Jasbir Singh, 92
Sadhana, Bhagat, 102
Sahib Singh, 25, 26, 27, 31, 71, 73, 81, 104, 105-106, 107, 108
Sainapati, 19
Saiṇ, Bhagat, 102, 118
Santokh Singh, Bhai, 23, 24, 60, 61
Schomer, Karine, 111-112
Sevadas, 119, 120
Shiromani Gurdwara Prabandhak Committe (SGPC), 16, 28, 29, 32, 33, 35, 41, 42, 62, 125-127, 128, 135
Sikhan di Bhagatmala, 19, 20, 22, 103, 119, 120
Sodhi, Amarjit Singh, 62
Sodhi, Karamjit Singh, 15, 59, 67
Sodhi, Haresh Singh, 33, 39
Sri Chand, Baba, 12, 26
Sri Gurbilas Patshahi 6, 23, 70
Surdas, Bhagat, 80, 81, 89, 102, 111, 114, 116-117, 119
Suri, Sohan Lal, 35

Talvaṛa, Giani Joginder Singh, 86
Teja Singh, 25, 26, 27, 31, 81, 91, 104, 105, 108, 110
tirath (pilgrimage center), 7, 14
Trilochan, Bhagat, 102
Trumpp, Ernest, 25, 107

Udasi, Harnamdas, 27, 110

Vaisakhi, 13, 15, 60
vars in the Adi Granth, 38, 52, 54, 55, 56-57, 75, 76, 97, 106
Veda, 10, 11, 24, 44, 99-101
Vir Singh, Bhai, 109

Yogi, Harbhajan Singh, 135